Hard Target

Hard Target

*The United States War
Against International
Drug Trafficking, 1982–1997*

by
RON CHEPESIUK

McFarland & Company, Inc., Publishers
Jefferson, North Carolina, and London

British Library Cataloguing-in-Publication data are available

Library of Congress Cataloguing-in-Publication Data

Chepesiuk, Ronald.
    Hard target : the United States war against international drug
trafficking, 1982–1997 / by Ron Chepesiuk.
       p.   cm.
    Includes bibliographical references and index.
    ISBN 0-7864-0507-4 (library binding : 50# alkaline paper) ∞
    1. Drug traffic — Government policy — United States.
2. Narcotics, Control of — United States.   3. Narcotics and crime.
4. Organized crime. 5. International offenses. 6. United
States — Politics and government. 7. United states — Foreign
relations. I. Title.
HV5825.C442   1999
363.45'0973 — dc21   98-46221
                                                  CIP

Manufactured in the United States of America

McFarland & Company, Inc., Publishers
 Box 611, Jefferson, North Carolina 28640

For the Family Aranda:
Gracias for your support and love

Acknowledgments

Many relatives, friends, colleagues, experts, and sources have made this book possible, and I am deeply grateful. First I would like to thank my wife, Magdalena, for her invaluable help in arranging interviews, transcribing tapes, sharing her insights on Colombian history and society, and, above all, for her patience and understanding as I completed this project.

Several relatives in Bogotá saved me enormous amounts of time and helped to keep the project moving toward its completion. They include Rosa Aranda, Oscar Anulfo Aranda, Francisco Aranda, and Ramiro Aranda. Special thanks to Gonzalo Aranda and Sadia Aranda for their time and help with arranging and coordinating many of the key interviews, and to Sonia Aranda for her time and effort in helping to locate photos.

My friend Edward Lee at Winthrop University and colleagues German Velasquez and Ernesto Salazar in Bogotá, Colombia, read the manuscript and offered valuable suggestions on how to improve it. German also played a big role in the research of this book by helping to arrange interviews with key Colombian officials. Several colleagues at the Winthrop University Library gave generously of their time. Gina Price White, Greg Ellis, and Alicia Cook helped invaluably with research and photocopying and kept the Archives Department functioning smoothly while I was away on sabbatical working on the book. Sara McIntyre was patient and helpful with the numerous interlibrary loan requests I made. Lois Walker and Nancy White helped open up the riches of the Documents Department at Winthrop University Library. The staff of the Library of Congress; the York County Library in Rock Hill, South Carolina; the Mecklenburg County Library in Charlotte, North Carolina; and the Colombo American Library in Bogotá, Colombia, were extremely helpful in locating important research materials.

Over the past decade, several individuals have offered insights on the complex topic of international drug trafficking or helped to locate those experts who could. They include but are not limited to German Baquero, Luis Alberto Becerra, Tommy Burns, Jorge Cardona, P. Sante Cervellin, Merrill Collette, Jan Crijiins, Clara Teresa de Arlaez, J.R. De-Groot, Myriam Mejia de Godoy, Maria Jimena Duzan, Juan Ferro, Myles Frechette, Leonardo Gallego, Larry Gallina, Ely Rubio Gomez, Julio Orlando Gomez, Gustavo Gorriti, Jorge Graitman, Gary P. Keith, Terry Kneebone, Charles Intriago, Carlos Landeros, Rennselaer Lee, Victor T. Le Vine, Arturo Madrigal, Maria Luisa Mejia, Mike Marcial, Elsa Martínez, Alfredo Molano, Clara López Obregon, Andres Pastrana, Charles Rangel, Alexandro Reyes, Fernando Brito Ruiz, Gustavo Ramírez Salgado, Obido Salinas, Ernesto Samper, Alexandro Saenz de Santamaria, Enrique Santos, Fernando Santos, Rafael Santos, Rosso Jose Serrano, Carlos Lemos Simmons, Jim Sutton, Juan Tokatlian, Alfonso Valdivieso, Giel Van Brussel, John Vance, Bert Van Hecke, Rob Van Velsen, Francisco José Sintura Varela, Alfredo Vasquez, Bruce Wyrick, and Fernando Zarate.

Thank you all for your advice, information, consideration, and much more.

Contents

Preface

T his book focuses on U.S. efforts to combat the $400 billion a year international drug trade in the period from 1982, the year U.S. president Ronald Reagan declared war on drugs and intensified a century-old battle against the distribution and importation of illegal drugs, through three successive presidential administrations, and up to 1997. It chronicles and analyzes the background and development of U.S. antidrug policy during this period and shows how Presidents Ronald Reagan, George Bush, and Bill Clinton steadily militarized the War on Drugs and made it a central component of U.S. foreign policy.

The book is divided into five sections. Section one provides the context in which the modern War on Drugs began and offers a glimpse at the nature of the problem. It also launches the discussion of one of the book's central themes; namely, that U.S. antidrug policy has often been responsible for the growth of the problem it has tried to stop.

To understand how the modern war of the United States against drugs began, section two looks at U.S. history and the antecedents of the country's antidrug policy, as well as the steady growth of international drug trafficking into what is today the world's fastest-growing criminal enterprise.

Section three profiles the "hard targets" or major criminal organizations that are involved in international drug trafficking and responsible for supplying the U.S. population with heroin, cocaine, marijuana, and a variety of synthetic drugs. How did the hard targets get started? How are they organized? How do they operate? In what aspect or aspects of the international drug trade are they involved? What has been the response of law enforcement in the United States and worldwide? What are their futures? The profiles address these questions.

Section four examines the worldwide social, political, and economic impact of the international drug trade. It investigates the collaboration between the powerful criminal syndicates, which today resemble the legitimate multinationals in organization and method, and exposes the menacing threat that the "globalization" of international drug trafficking poses for the United States and its allies in the War on Drugs. It describes and analyzes the impact of money laundering, the "life blood" of international drug trafficking, and shows how the international drug trade is corrupting countries, disrupting their economies and political systems, fueling drug abuse, breeding violence and terrorism, creating human rights violations, threatening democracies, and ensnaring more and more countries in one way or another. One chapter in this section looks at the impact of international drug trafficking on the United States and reveals how the U.S. response to the onslaught is changing the country.

The last section assesses the impact and puts forth the lessons to be drawn from U.S. antidrug efforts in the 15-year period. The book concludes with the presentation of some practical options the United States should exercise if it is to regain control of the drug war.

The author hopes this book will help readers better understand why U.S. antidrug policy has failed and why genuine debate about that policy is necessary to turn the tide of war around. Otherwise, the United States may continue to win some of the battles some of the time, but also continue to lose the war.

— Ron Chepesiuk
October 1998

Chronology

1840 — Opium imports to United States begin to increase significantly
 — Opium Wars begin
1875 — San Francisco passes first significant U.S. antidrug law
1880 — United States bans smoking of opium by Asians
1898 — Bayer Laboratories introduces heroin
 — American Medical Association endorses heroin as safe for respiratory ailments
 — United States acquires Philippines
1905 — United States bans opium use in Philippines
1906 — U.S. Congress passes Pure Food and Drug Act
1909 — Shanghai Congress meets to examine opium trade
 — U.S. Congress passes ban on importation of opium for other than medical purposes
1912 — International opium convention
1914 — U.S. Congress passes Harrison Act
1917 — U.S. Congress passes Eighteenth Amendment, which will impose prohibition of alcohol
1920 — Eighteenth Amendment goes into effect
 — League of Nations creates Advisory Committee on Traffic in Opium and Other Dangerous Drugs
1922 — U.S. Congress passes National Drug and Export Act
1930 — Harry Anslinger appointed head of Federal Bureau of Narcotics (FBN)
1931 — Under Italian mobster Lucky Luciano's leadership, La Cosa Nostra establishes a "National Commission"
 — International convention for limiting the manufacture and distribution of narcotic drugs
1933 — Repeal of Eighteenth Amendment
1937 — U.S. Congress passes Marijuana Tax Law

3

1942 — U.S. Congress passes Opium Control Act
1945 — Lucky Luciano deported to Italy
1948 — Chinese Revolution gives boost to international drug trade
1951 — U.S. Congress passes Boggs Act
    — The U.S. Kefauver Senate Committee begins investigation of the Italian Mafia
1956 — U.S. Congress passes Narcotics Control Act of 1956
1957 — La Cosa Nostra meets in Appalachian Mountains in New York State
    — Italian Mafia summit in Palermo, Italy
1958 — Great Sicilian Mafia War begins
1959 — Cuban Revolution
1960 — U.S. Congress passes Narcotics Control Act
1961 — Bay of Pigs invasion
    — United Nations Single Convention on Narcotic Drugs
1962 — First White House Conference on Narcotics and Drug Abuse
1963 — Joseph Valachi testifies against Italian Mafia
1964 — Coup in South Vietnam topples Ngo Dinh Diem
1965 — U.S. Immigration Act
    — U.S. Congress passes Drug Abuse Control Amendments
1966 — U.S. President Lyndon Johnson establishes President's Commission on Law Enforcement and Administration of Justice
1968 — U.S. President Richard Nixon creates Bureau of Narcotics and Dangerous Drugs
1970 — U.S. Congress passes Organized Crime Control Act
    — U.S. Congress passes Drug Abuse Prevention and Control Act
    — U.S. Congress passes Bank Security Act
1971 — United Nations Convention on Psychotropic Substances
1972 — U.S. Congress passes Drug Abuse and Treatment Act
    — *The New York Times* notes South Florida's increasing importance for smuggling of heroin and cocaine
1973 — The Drug Enforcement Administration (DEA) is established
    — Oregon becomes the first state to legalize marijuana
    — Centac is established
    — U.S. immigration laws favor Russian political refugees
1975 — Fall of Saigon, Vietnam
    — Drug lord Gilberto Rodríguez Orejuela sends Hernando Giraldo Soto to New York City
1978 — Medellín cartel founded
1979 — Soviet Union invades Afghanistan

1980 — U.S. Customs Office and IRS launches Operation Greenback
   — Mariel boatlift
1981 — Delegation of prominent Miamians go to see President Reagan in White House
   — DEA establishes Centac 26
1982 — Drug trafficker Pablo Escobar elected alternative to the Colombian Congress
   — Ronald Reagan launches U.S. War on Drugs
   — South Florida Task Force made operational
   — U.S. Congress passes Department of Defense Authorization Act
1984 — Colombian Justice Minister Rodrigo Lara Bonilla is assassinated
   — U.S. Congress passes Comprehensive Crime Control Act
   — Raid on Tranquilandia, Colombia
   — Medellín cartel bombs U.S. Embassy
   — United States pushes Colombia to start a marijuana eradication campaign
   — U.S. Army and Transportation Department initiates a drug testing program
1985 — DEA agent Enrique Camarena Salazar murdered in Mexico
   — U.S. Department of Justice creates the National Assets Seizure and Forfeiture Fund
   — U.S. Senate approves a bill requiring random drug testing of airline pilots
1986 — Operation Blast Furnace launched in Bolivia
   — Maxi trial in Italy
   — Ronald Reagan signs National Security Directive Number 221
   — U.S. Congress passes Money Laundry Control Act
   — U.S. Congress passes Anti–Drug Abuse Act
   — Organization of American States ratifies hemisphere antidrug plan
   — United States launches Operation Caribbean Cruise
   — Jaime Ramírez Gomez, head of Narcotics Unit of the Colombian National Police, is assassinated
   — Ronald Reagan calls for "Zero Tolerance"
1987 — Carlos Lehder captured in Colombia
1988 — United States launches Operation Rum Punch
   — Soviet government relaxes restrictions on travel
   — U.S. Congress passes Anti-Drug Abuse Amendment Act
   — *Fortune* magazine names Pablo Escobar one of the world's richest men

1988 — War breaks out between Medellín and Cali cartels
    — Colombian attorney general Carlos Hoyos is assassinated
    — Drug trial of Colombian drug kingpin Carlos Lehder begins in
        the United States
    — U.S. Congress passes Chemical Diversion and Trafficking Act
    — United Nations passes UN Convention Against Illicit Traffic in
        Narcotic Drugs and Psychotropic Substances
    — Vietnamese gang Born to Kill founded
    — Congressional hearings on Asian organized crime
1989 — Colombia presidential candidate Luis Carlos Galan is assassi-
        nated
    — U.S. Congress establishes Finance Crimes Enforcement Network
        (FINCEN)
    — U.S. Supreme Court upholds the U.S. government's right to de-
        mand urine tests of workers in "sensitive" positions
    — U.S. Kerry Commission report
    — George Bush announces national drug control strategy
    — G-7 establishes Financial Action Task Force
    — United States invades Panama and arrests Manuel Noriega
    — Medellín cartel bombs a Bogotá-to-Medellín flight, killing all
        aboard
    — U.S. Andean strategy unveiled
1990 — Cartagena Summit
    — President Bush signs Andean Trade Preference Act into law
1991 — Collapse of the Soviet Union
1992 — Italian government launches Operation Clean Hand
    — NAFTA formed
1993 — Pablo Escobar killed
    — Sammy Gravano testifies against Italian-American Mafia leader
        John Gotti
    — European Union established
1994 — United States decertifies Nigeria
    — Number of U.S. prisoners held in state and federal jails tops one
        million for the first time
    — The presidential campaign of Colombian president Ernesto Sam-
        per is accused of accepting money from the Cali cartel
1995 — Colombia is decertified by the United States
    — Colombian authorities capture Gilberto Rodríguez Orejuela
    — U.S. Supreme Court upholds legality of drug testing of student
        athletes in public schools

1996 — Khu Sa, a Burmese warlord and drug trafficker, surrenders to Burmese authorities
  — Colombia is decertified by the United States for second straight year
  — Colombia passes assets forfeiture law
  — Gilberto Rodríguez Orejuela agrees to pay $105 million fine and confesses to involvement in narcotics trade
  — Colombian drug trafficker Efrain Hernandez Ramírez is killed
  — University of Michigan survey shows marijuana use among young people is rising
  — Arizona and California vote to ease restrictions on medical use of marijuana
1997 — Great Britain returns Hong Kong to People's Republic of China
  — Two U.S. congressional panels conduct hearings on drug-related corruption along U.S. border
  — United States and Colombia sign antidrug maritime agreement
  — Colombian drug kingpin Pastor Parafan is captured in Venezuela and extradited to the United States
  — Group of Rio denounces U.S. certification program
  — Connecticut considers the revision of its state antidrug laws

Section 1
Prologue

Chapter 1

The Nature of the Beast

"Escobar was to cocaine what Ford was to automobiles."
— Thomas V. Cash, DEA Agent

"The Cali cartel will kill you if they have to, but they would rather use a lawyer."
— Robert Bryden, DEA Agent

December 2, 1993 — For more than six months, the world's most wanted gangster had somehow managed to elude Search Block, the elite 1,500-man Colombian police force that had been specially trained to hunt him down. The previous May, Pablo Escobar Gaviria, the "King of Cocaine," had discovered what should have been a state secret: the authorities planned to move him to less accommodating quarters.[1]

The prisoner had the laser-sharp instincts of a drug trafficker who had survived two decades in the brutal criminal underworld. He sensed danger. The new prison would not only be less accommodating, it would also make him more vulnerable to an assassin's bullet.

The head of the powerful Medellín cartel knew he had become an embarrassment to the Colombian government. On June 19, 1991, Escobar had turned himself in to the Colombian authorities under a special plea-bargain program designed by the administration of President Cesar Gaviria Trujillo to end the violent war between the government and the Medellín cartel. The previous decade, this fierce conflict had taken its toll on Colombia; thousands had died — judges, journalists, lawyers, leftist leaders, police officers, and even presidential candidates.

Escobar had been responsible for most of those deaths, but he had turned himself in only hours after Colombia's Constitutional Assembly voted to ban the extradition of Colombians, and so he ensured that he would never have to stand trial in the United States, where he faced ten indictments for drug trafficking and murder.[2]

But soon after Escobar's imprisonment, Colombians began wondering who was the jailer and who was the jailee despite the government's official assurances. "It is a prison that is no better than any for a similar criminal in the United States," President Gaviria told the nation. "I do not think any of us would like to spend any time there."

Unofficially, the media began painting a sharply different picture of life at La Catedral, the name cynical Colombians gave to Escobar's new home. La Catedral stood high on hill, a part of a ten-acre spread that included a soccer field, a recreation center, a gymnasium, a discotheque, a bar and game room, and a sweeping view of the Medellín Valley below. Escobar, in fact, had supervised the prison's construction. His 1,000-square-foot cell was bigger than the warden's accommodations, and it had a king-size bed and a private bath with jacuzzi, as well as other furnishings handpicked by the "prisoner."[3]

As one writer described the situation, "The Cathedral was built and organized by Escobar himself with the government's complicity, not to keep in prisoners so much as to keep assassins out. Instead of seeking to protect society from a murderous villain, jail existed to protect the villain himself."[4]

For company, the 41-year-old Escobar had six of his top lieutenants, including his brother Roberto. No police were allowed inside the prison, but the press reported comings and goings from La Catedral at all hours of the day. It soon became evident that within the walls of the prison Escobar continued to run and direct his criminal empire.

In light of these revelations, President Gaviria's popularity in the opinion polls plummeted, and the government's policy for combating drug trafficking became a national joke. So on May 16, 1993, shortly after midnight, the president ordered five hundred policemen to surround La Catedral and secure the drug lord's transfer. Escobar had other plans, however. He snuck out under the cover of darkness, thanks to the helping hands of the prison warden and two guards.

The truce had ended; once again Pablo Escobar was the world's Public Enemy Number One — at large and at war with Colombia. Colombians knew no one in the country was safe from the Medellín-induced terror that was sure to follow.

The cartel could find anyone, no matter where in the world they fled. In 1986, for instance, the Colombian government gave one of its ministers, Enrique Parejo Gonzalez, who had offended the cartel, a diplomatic posting to Hungary. The government thought the cartel wouldn't dare try to kill their man while he was behind the Iron Curtain. It thought wrong. In January 1987, cartel gunmen shot the diplomat as he was leaving his residence in Budapest and then vanished. Miraculously, the diplomat survived; but the Medellín cartel had made its point.

No crime was unthinkable. Cross the cartel and be prepared to face your worst nightmare. Rafael Santos, an editor with the Bogotá-based *El Tiempo* newspaper, described the impact of the Medellín cartel on Colombia: "They have bribed, intimidated and murdered officials, particularly judges, to create a climate of fear and, until quite recently, they have been able to move freely around the country. Their influence is paralyzing the judiciary. A democracy without an independent judiciary cannot work."[5]

Like a raging bull, the cartel unleashed its wild fury against Colombia. No such thing as a "civilian" in this war of terror. In 1989 Escobar and the cartel badly wanted to kill two of its associates who they believed had betrayed them, so they planted a bomb on an Avianca airplane flying between Medellín and Bogotá. The death toll: 107 passengers, including the two suspected stool pigeons.

Colombian authorities linked all these atrocities — and many more — to Pablo Escobar, the billionaire drug baron. The gang leader from Medellín made Al Capone seem like a kinder, gentler gangster. While on the run, Escobar faced 12 arrest warrants for killing at least 100 people with 40 car bombs and for murdering at least 215 police officers.

The thought of Pablo Escobar chilled the spines of many Colombians, but those who saw him in the flesh were startled to see how unremarkable he looked. Pudgy, soft-spoken, and badly in need of a tailor, Escobar's ten-dollar haircut gave him the look of a greaser. His most distinctive feature was a black bristled mustache worn in the manner of his hero, Pancho Villa, the Mexican outlaw and hero of the 1919–20 Mexican revolution. He was polite and formal in the company he kept and in the numerous letters he wrote to the Colombian authorities, sternly warning them to get off his back or face unspecified consequences. Not the style of a hoodlum who would blow up a plane, or explode bombs in downtown Bogotá without warning, or put a $5,000 price tag on the head of every cop in Medellín.

Escobar relished his fame, but he always looked painfully uncomfortable in the glare of a television camera. To friend and foe alike, though, Escobar was a man to be feared, and even respected, according to which side of the law one was on. In reality, he was a quick learner, brilliant and ambitious — a natural leader with an enterprising mind for business and an unforgiving memory.

"It's his eyes," one DEA agent explained. "He looks totally nonde-script, but his eyes reveal the soul of a cunning, cold-blooded killer."[6]

From the beginning of his criminal career, Escobar craved respectability. In the early eighties, while still largely unknown to the general public, he altered his criminal past to hide one uncomfortable detail: in the late sixties, he got his start in crime as a teenage entrepreneur stealing and reselling gravestones. Police also arrested him for stealing a car in 1974, but he intimidated judges into dropping the case. This initial brush with the law set the pattern for Escobar's criminal career. Until his luck ran out two decades later, Escobar would somehow manage to stay one step ahead of the authorities.

In 1976 two policemen stopped his pickup truck and caught him red-handed with 30 pounds of cocaine, a serious crime that should have led to a long prison term; instead, the drug dealer was out of jail three months later, his arrest warrant mysteriously revoked. Soon after, the corpses of both arresting officers in the case were found stuffed in the back of their patrol car. At the morgue, relatives couldn't recognize the corpses. A decade later, Escobar murdered the judge who had issued the arrest warrant.

By 1979, the year he turned 30, Escobar was helping to pioneer the use of air transport to move illegal drugs. Four years later, he had clawed his way to the top rung in the leadership of the Medellín cartel, a loose association of drug dealers based in the Colombian city of Medellín, who, in their drug dealings, formed associations of convenience with each other. Escobar forged alliances with soon-to-be famous kingpins such as José Rodríguez Gacha, Carlos Lehder, and the Ochoa brothers (Fabio, Jorge Luis, Juan David) to build a pipeline that transported tons of cocaine from the Andean highlands to the streets of Uncle Sam.

"Escobar was to cocaine what Ford was to automobiles," explained Thomas V. Cash, a special agent in charge of the DEA's Miami office.[7]

By 1988, the year that marked the peak of Escobar's power, *Forbes* magazine had named the powerful drug lord one of the world's richest men, calculating his personal fortune at $2.5 billion, or perhaps more, thanks to the roughly 80 percent share of the cocaine trade the DEA said he and associates controlled.

Escobar loved the good life and took pleasure in flaunting his wealth. He fancied Chinese porcelain and exotic animals, even stocking Hacienda Napoles, his 7,000-acre ranch in his native Antioquia province, with camels, giraffes, bison, and llamas. He fitted his bathrooms with gold-plated fixtures; his wife, Victoria, had more shoes than Imelda Marcos, according to Medellín lore. Among his vast holdings were a $1 million condominium in Plantation, Florida, and a $750,000 house in Miami Beach.

Escobar shrewdly began to cultivate a romantic image of a Robin Hood who stole from the establishment and gave to the poor. He built a housing project for 1,000 poor families in his powerbase, Medellín, naming it "Medellín Without Slums." Soccer was his passion; he paid for lights so that children could play on their soccer fields at night. In respect for the gangster-benefactor, Colombians from all walks of life started deferring to him as Don Pablo. By 1982 the people elected Don Pablo an alternate to the Colombian Congress.

Escobar revelled in the legend he was becoming. Asked by a group of journalists, "Are you violent and arrogant?" he replied, "Those who know me know I have a good sense of humor and that I keep a smile on my face. And I'll say one thing: I always sing in the shower."[8]

U.S. and Colombian authorities grew increasingly frustrated trying to put the powerful drug lord behind bars. There were indictments, plenty of them, going back to 1977 and stretching from Miami to Los Angeles. The drug lord had transported more than 12 tons of cocaine into the United States, the indictments charged. A federal grand jury in Miami named him codefendant in a 1988 indictment of deposed Panamanian dictator Manuel Noriega that led to the general's conviction and imprisonment. The U.S. government vainly tried to extradite the drug dealer from Colombia to stand trial, but through murder and intimidation, Don Pablo and his associates cowed the Colombian judicial system and broke the government's will to act.

But as the eighties progressed, the King of Cocaine had more than the U.S. and Colombian governments to worry about. In his ruthless dog-eat-dog climb to the top of the criminal drug world, he had made many enemies among the drug traffickers who worked with and competed against him. Escobar's desire to be a public figure would be his downfall.

Escobar's most serious rival was the cartel from Cali, a city known for its music, fair weather, and beautiful women. During 1988, a vicious struggle broke out between the two gangs after a car bomb detonated in front of Monaco, an apartment building in Medellín, owned and occupied by Escobar and his family. The blast killed no one, but Escobar retaliated in characteristic form — murdering 60 people from Cali in the following two months. On behalf of the Medellín cartel, fellow drug lord Rodríguez Gacha journeyed to New York City to see if the cartel could muscle in on the Cali organization's longstanding distribution network. The result — New York City's version of the War of the Cartels.

Escobar seethed and Medellín's war with Cali intensified. These were the usual assassinations of rival gang members. "The police are not pursuing those bastards as vigorously as they are going after me," he complained to underlings. He suspected Miguel Masa, the head of DAS (the Administrative Department of Security), Colombia's equivalent of the FBI, to be on the Cali cartel's payroll, and so Escobar flooded the streets of Colombia with leaflets, offering $1.3 million for Masa's head.

While Escobar seethed, Colombia shivered. A 400-pound bomb exploded outside DAS headquarters in Bogotá. Masa lived, but 104 innocent Colombian citizens in the vicinity didn't.

The drug lord had a point. It wasn't publicly acknowledged as government policy, but it was becoming increasingly evident to many observers that the authorities were more intent on wiping out narcoterrorism than they were on pursuing those drug traffickers who had stuck to "business" and not declared war against the state.

This strategy certainly opened the doors of opportunity for the Medellín cartel's ambitious rivals. While Escobar was killing such prominent government officials and political leaders as Justice Minister Rodrigo Lara Bonilla (1984), Attorney General Carlos Hoyos (1988), and presidential candidate Luis Carlos Galan (1989), the Cali cartel was subtlely cultivating its political influence through bribes and diplomacy. They took to establishing legitimate business ventures as a means of forging contacts with key people in business, politics, the law, and the press. They invested plenty of narco-dollars to establish an intelligence network that rivaled those of many South American governments, which kept them informed of the government's every move in the war on drugs.

The low-key businesslike style worked. Even the police began to speak of the los caballeros (gentlemen) of Cali in contrast to the los hampones (hoodlums) of Medellín. "The Cali Cartel will kill you if they have to, but they would rather use a lawyer," observed Robert Bryden, head of the DEA's New York City office.[9]

"They [the Cali cartel] are much more astute than the leaders of the Medellín Cartel," explained Fernando Brito Ruiz, former director of DAS. "They have economic power and they know how to use it."[10]

Los Hampones craved respectability; los Caballeros enjoyed it. Many Colombians looked upon the drug lords from Cali as Horatio Alger success stories, who by brains, enterprise, and hard work had worked their way out of the slums of Cali and the backwater of the Cauca

Valley. The chief executive officers of the Cali cartel included José Santacruz Londono, who had studied engineering and had transformed himself into the cabellero Don Chepe, the billionaire construction magnate; his close associate Gilberto Rodríguez Orejuela, who started out as a kidnapper but ended up owning a vast network of business enterprises — La Rebaja, the biggest drugstore chain in Colombia, as well as banks, car dealerships, apartment buildings, and Cali's talented America soccer team; Miguel Rodríguez Orejuela, Gilberto's handsome brother, who oversaw the business side of the criminal empire; cousin Jamie and his three brothers, prominent impresarios of concerts and sporting events, who travel frequently to New York City and have business offices in Los Angeles; Helmer Pacho Herrera, believed to be the son of Benjamin Herrera Zuleta, a legendary Afro-Colombian smuggler known as the Black Pope, who played a big role in the Cali cartel's early development, and a wealthy Cauca Valley rancher with business ties to New York.[11]

Unlike the Medellín cartel, the Cali drug lords run their criminal enterprise conservatively, much like other big corporate heads. It's a cerebral approach that depends more on planning, shrewd calculation, and the use of a boardroom than on the gun to do business.

Play by the company rules, don't mess up, and one would have a good life as a Cali corporate man or women. It could be difficult, though, if one screwed up or tried to sever ties. Instead of being fired, many are discretely executed. As distasteful as violence is to the cartel, it keeps a gun in the desk drawer, just in case.

But while the organization is authoritarian — one that demands absolute discipline and loyalty — it still allows for creativity. Under the chief executive officers and serving as the senior vice presidents of acquisitions, transportation, sales, finance, and enforcement are some of Colombia's best and brightest. They supervise and coordinate the logistics of importing, storing, and delivering the product and they oversee, through daily and often, hourly phone calls, ambitious underlings in dozens of overseas branch offices, who move the drugs to wholesalers.

Employees of the Cali cartel, whether executive officer or underling, are expected to be conservative in their lifestyle: no flashy clothing or cars, no drinking or drug problems, and no loud parties or activities that could attract attention.

The flamboyant and undisciplined Escobar could have learned from the slick Cali style. It might have prevented him from making his biggest mistake. The drug lord's confrontational style cost lots of money. As a narco-terrorist on the rampage with scores of enemies to worry about, he needed huge wads of cash to keep his drug empire afloat. Moreover, he was using the white powder himself with increasing frequency, a habit that fueled his megalomania.

The drug lord began calling his war with Colombia "my struggle" and demanded that his associates in the Medellín cartel not only pay him a fee for each drug shipment they made, but also cash for "taxes" to help finance his violent terror campaign. "The problem with Escobar is that he began to kidnap all of the people closest to him," Gabriel Toboada, a federal prisoner who had worked for the Medellín cartel, told the Senate Subcommittee on Terrorism, Narcotics and International Operations in 1994. "He became a person who wanted to do evil to everybody.... From his computers he knew how much each politician had earned, how much each member of the Medellín cartel had earned, so he began to demand money from them, because he said that he was the one that had put his name forward in the fight against extradition, and this thing went out of control."[12]

Some associates dug deep into their pockets and shelled out a hard-earned million or two; others like Gerardo and William Julio Moncada and Fernando and Mario Galeano refused. In July 1992, their mutilated corpses were found on the roadside a few miles from La Catedral.

The relatives of the four dead gangsters had no intention of taking the murders of their loved ones meekly. They organized a vigilante group called Los Pepes (short for "the persecuted by Pablo Escobar") and, in classic Medellín cartel style, made plans to seek revenge.

In March 1993 they struck, killing Escobar's most trusted front man. Next they shot one of his lawyers, but not actually killing him (the shock of being shot triggered a fatal heart attack before he took a bullet). The next to die was Don Pablo's smartest lawyer, followed by his closest brother-in-law. A rocket attack on the Bogotá hotel where Escobar's wife Victoria and their two children — 17-year-old Juan Pablo and 5-year-old Manuela — were hiding failed in its bad intentions, but the frightened mother took the two children and fled to Germany. The German government, however, already had plenty of headaches from dealing with the country's violent skinheads and saw no need to set the stage for a possible narco-terrorism campaign. So Victoria and family were whisked onto a plane and shipped back to Bogotá.

By now, Escobar was the central character in the nightmare he had created. Worried about his family, his drug empire in ruins, Los Pepes in hot pursuit, Escobar got careless.

On December 2, 1993, his 44th birthday, the drug lord made his

The body of Pablo Escobar on the roof of his home, where he was killed by the Colombian Antinarcotics Police in 1993 (courtesy Colombian Antinarcotics Police).

most serious mistake. He dialed a cellular phone, as he always did for security reasons, and called his Victoria. She was holed up with the two children under government protection in a luxury Bogotá hotel. The time — 11:39 A.M.[13]

Escobar asked Victoria how she was being treated and told her that he missed her. He gently instructed Juan Pablo to be strong — the man of the house — in his absence. Escobar sounded like a doting father rather than the cold-blooded killer who had bombed a passenger plane out of the sky.

Mindful of his fugitive status, Don Pablo hung up. He had talked a mere ten minutes.

Too much time: an eternity. Despite his extensive intelligence network, Escobar didn't know that the U.S. Drug Enforcement Agency (DEA) had supplied the Colombian government with new sophisticated electronic monitoring equipment programmed to recognize his voice and locate him within two minutes of a phone call.

At 2:51 P.M. of the same day, two heavily armed members of Search Block kicked in the front door of the beige three-story brick house in the upper-middle-class neighborhood in western Medellín. Escobar was still in the third-floor bedroom next to the phone, perhaps mulling the tender words that he had shared with his wife, or perhaps thinking about his next move against the government. In any case, the startled drug lord was caught completely off guard.

Two hundred police and soldiers had swooped in and blocked off the streets around the house, cut the neighborhood telephone lines, and cordoned the area. Some residents didn't even know the security forces had flooded the barrio until two bursts of gunfire made the day suddenly sound like a Fourth of July celebration.

The safe house was like so many of the others Escobar had used to escape 15,000 house searches and keep on the run. It had exits on two streets and a secret getaway under the parquet floor. Normally he could have escaped. In fact, in the past, his security precautions had allowed him to flee in the nick of time, often in his underwear, with cigarettes still burning in the ashtray.

This time the fugitive was cut off from his underground hiding place. The only chance he had was to head for the roof. Don Pablo and his loyal bodyguard, Alvaro de Jesus Aguela, "The Lemon," scrambled up the stairs and climbed out a window to the rooftop. Bad move; no place to go.

Dressed in a red shirt, black jeans, and tennis shoes, the bearded, overweight Don Pablo was an odd sight as he scurried over the rooftop of his safe house desperately searching for a way to escape. "I was working when I heard some shouting in the street, and I realized that this fat man was wandering on the roof opposite," a witness recalled the next day, "At that moment a man jumped toward another roof of the house, and you could hear an amazing shootout."

Escobar had always said that he would go down fighting, if cornered. He was a man of his word. But first the Lemon tried to give his boss a chance to escape by jumping off the roof. Twenty-five bullets riddled his body as he crashed to the hard pavement below.

His boss followed, opening up with a pair of 9 mm pistols. They were no match for Search Block's firepower. Twelve bullets hit the fugitive, including one to the right temple. The billionaire gangster who had cowed a nation lay sprawled on the rooftop, a bloody heap, his two guns at his side.

The shooting stopped, and soldiers cautiously approached the body of the legendary outlaw, not yet sure if they had finally got their target. One soldier tapped Escobar's body with his combat boots and then shouted excitedly, "We got Pablo! We got Pablo!" The soldier's figure and the corpse of Escobar would fill the cover of next week's *La Semana*, Colombia's most widely read magazine. Fortunately for the soldier,

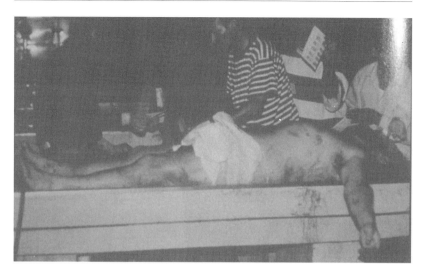

The corpse of Pablo Escobar in a makeshift field morgue (courtesy Colombian Antinarcotics Police).

his family, and his pets, *La Semana* thought it wise to blacken out his eyes.

Meanwhile, other soldiers hugged each other and yelled, "We won! We won!" Some smiled broadly and flashed the "V for Victory" sign to their comrades. The security forces allowed news photographers on the scene to photograph the historic occasion, and during the following days, graphic images of Escobar's blood-soaked corpse filled the media.

Within the hour, Colombians began hearing the news. Many felt as if they had awoken from a bad dream. A Bogotá radio station in mantra-like fashion continually repeated the news of Escobar's death, as carolers sang "Joy to the World" in the background. Colombian newspapers, once bludgeoned into timidity by Escobar's power, printed bold headlines: "Escobar has fallen!" "The king is dead!"

During a nationally televised speech honoring the police and soldiers who had successfully hunted Colombia's most wanted criminal, a beaming President Gaviria, whose popularity now jumped dramatically skyward in the public opinion polls, told his country that the dead drug lord was "a delinquent who received the punishment that criminals deserve." He added, "No one should remember Medellín as the city of the cartel. There is no more Medellín Cartel. That name died with Escobar."

But in Medellín there was much wailing and gnashing of teeth. Residents were not yet willing to forget Don Pablo, whose generosity had made him a folk hero. "There was a lot of tears, a lot of desperation, because for us it was like losing a father," recalled Marcela Jaramillo, a 26-year-old homemaker who lived in "Medellín Without Slums."

The outpouring of grief was so overwhelming, in fact, that Don Pablo's funeral had to be canceled when an emotional crowd of 5,000 pushed so hard to get into the mortuary to see his body that they shattered its windows. While police discreetly withdrew, the frenzied mob seized the silver-metal coffin and carried it in the pouring rain to the gravesight. In the chaos, a phalanx of twenty heavily armed bodyguards hustled Escobar's widow and children to a bulletproof Mercedes-Benz and away to safety.

In the weeks that followed Escobar's death, U.S. and Colombian officials savored their victory. They lauded their close cooperation, and in several public statements, issued a stern warning to other drug traffickers. The message — you will suffer the same fate as Escobar unless you choose another line of work. There was even cautious talk about how the forces for good might have finally turned a corner in the War on Drugs.

But many experts, who for more than a decade had followed law-and-order's longest-running melodrama, the War on Drugs, scoffed, emphasizing that Pablo Escobar's death was merely symbolic and any talk about winning the drug war was premature. Some observers were openly cynical. "The associations, the killings, the violence, and the corruption will continue because the business of drug trafficking will continue," wrote Antonio Caballero in his influential column in *La Semana*. "The only novelty is that with Pablo Escobar's death there will be no one to blame for everything that happens."[14]

That was not exactly true, and government and law enforcement officials worldwide knew it. Somebody was definitely to blame for the continued scourge of cocaine, and even before Escobar's body was cold in the ground, they had begun to cast a wary eye toward Cali. After years of mayhem and bloodshed, the authorities had succeeded in disrupting one center of drug trafficking only to have a more powerful group emerge.

In the previous decade, while security forces had concentrated on getting Escobar and shutting down the Medellín drug pipeline, the dozen or so gangs comprising the Cali cartel had quietly expanded cocaine production and grabbed the lion's share of the market, about 80 percent according to DEA sources. Now disturbing signs suggested that the cartel was gliding smoothly into new markets and concentrating on making the drug-trafficking business a truly multinational enterprise. The cartel had succeeded in making cocaine a global poison that was undermining and corrupting governments and destroying lives almost everywhere.

Not content to rest on their laurels, they were looking to the future, hoping to hook the world with another habit-forming drug that would keep enslaved users paying forever. "Heroin will be to the nineties what cocaine was to the eighties," the U.S. State Department predicted in a 1994 report. "Latin American trafficking organizations are poised to cash in on the coming heroin epidemic."[15]

Not only is the Cali cartel cooking what experts say promises to be the best heroin on the planet, they are also now growing the drug's raw material — the poppies — themselves. "It has taken Burma the better part of a century to get where it is: a supplier of the best heroin available," marveled one DEA official. "The Colombians have been at it for five years, and already they are number two."[16]

One morning the United States and its allies woke up to find that the gang from Cali had quietly developed the most sophisticated drug network ever organized. The criminal entrepreneurs, who brilliantly introduced the business concept of vertical integration into the international traffic in cocaine, were about to do the same to the heroin trade. It would just be a matter of time before the number of junkies skyrocketed. "It's easy to see why the Cali cartel is moving into heroin," explained one U.S. official knowledgeable in the ways of the Cali cartel. "As a stimulant, cocaine will burn out a user in maybe a few months to a few years, whereas heroin is a depressant and will be used by a junkie over a period of decades."[17]

No wonder then that organized crime syndicates all over the world are lusting to marry operations with the marketing geniuses from Cali. Even the powerful warlords from the Golden Triangle, eager to learn the ways of Cali, began loaning their heroin cooks to the Colombians so that they could teach the newcomers the chemistry of junk.

Business success has no bounds for the ambitious and enterprising CEOs of the fastest growth industry on earth, criminal or otherwise. Every country was a potential market for its dope, a conduit for the product, or a potential recruiting ground for foot soldiers or useful allies.

In May 1993, Russian police stopped a container truck headed toward Finland. Inside, packed into cans of "meat and potatoes" were 2,400 pounds of white powder. It was Russia's biggest cocaine bust ever, but the authorities feared it was an ominous sign of something bigger: a Cali cartel–Russian mob alliance. "The cocaine was being brought in from Colombia and they were going to take it from Russia to Europe," Alexander S. Sergeyev, antidrug chief of the Russian Interior Ministry, explained in a news conference.[18]

The looming Russian-Colombian connection doesn't surprise U.S. officials. Greg Passic, chief of the DEA's money-laundering section, revealed that Franklin Jurado, a top financial operator in the Cali cartel, was about to fly to Moscow in 1993 when the authorities arrested him. "He was researching Russia," Passic explained. "It's an area they're interested in."[19]

Russia is not the only country of interest to the Colombians. Disturbing signs suggested that the Japanese mob, known as the Yakuza, are about to flood Japan with cocaine, thanks to the Cali cartel. A white paper by Japan's National Police Agency warned that "If nothing is done to reverse the trend, Japan's drug problem would soon match that of the U.S."[20]

The booming illegal drug market means huge profits, a potential problem for the typical mob on the fast track. But the Cali cartel isn't typical, and its criminal genius isn't limited to marketing. Beginning in the early 1990s, Cali went high-tech and revolutionized the way organized crime could hide its filthy lucre. The sophisticated money-laundering scheme it put in place relies on a system of computerized bookkeeping, wire transfers, and cellular phones to monitor and keep the money flowing.

U.S. officials were the first to admit that they were having little success at disrupting Cali's criminal enterprise. As one official explained to the *Washington Post*, "If we get one in four shipments, it's okay with the traffickers and we are getting one in a hundred. It's going to take more manpower, resources, and intestinal fortitude to get serious about this, and I haven't seen that by any country."[21]

Money seizures from the Cali cartel average about $200 million a year, reveal DEA officials, but that's pocket change for the brothers Rodrígues Orejuela and their associates. Each year, the Cali syndicate nets an estimated $3 to $5 billion from its criminal activities.

In the War on Drugs, the forces for good now had a much more formidable adversary, worried officials worldwide readily acknowledged. Adios hampones; the caballeros had arrived. There would be no narco-terrorism, no Avianca airliners blown out of the sky, no fears of being on the wrong Colombian street at the wrong time, no raging bulls unleashing their fury on a quivering nation, no flaunting of wealth, no exotic animals on ranches in Antioquia province. Still, it would be business as usual — the flow of drugs continuing unabated into the United States and other countries.

One era in the War on Drugs had ended, and another was about to begin. Bright, efficient, and imaginative, with a style as smooth as fine French cognac, the low-keyed Mafia from Cali posed one of the biggest challenges in the history of law enforcement.

"I would think the discos and bars will be full in Cali tonight," Thomas V. Cash said the day after Escobar became history. "I think you see the changing of the guard here from Medellín to Cali. Medellín is a falling star with the death of Escobar."[22]

Added Bryden, "The Cali Cartel gets stronger by virtue [of the fact] that it doesn't have any competition. Now they can go into any corner of this country [Colombia], and nobody in the drug business can oppose them."[23]

Enter the new dons of drug trafficking.

Chapter 2

Reagan Declares War

"We need to break the grower to user chains which stretch across five continents. To do it we must have a comprehensive program of international control."
— Walter J. Stoessel, U.S. Deputy Secretary of State

"It just frightens me that we can't find other ways of combating this [drug traffic] in our country without now going to the military and bringing them into our civilian lives."
— Shirley Chisolm (D–N.Y.)

The modern era of the U.S. war against international drug trafficking began eleven years before the changing of the drug kingpins, early in the first term of President Ronald Reagan's administration, when Reagan told the American public that drug abuse was "one of the gravest problems facing us as a nation" and vowed to establish a foreign policy that "vigorously seeks to interdict and eradicate illegal drugs, wherever cultivated, processed and transported."[1] Nineteen days before the 1982 congressional elections, with Republicans in need of votes, Reagan made a radio address in which he announced that he had "a bold confident plan to stop international drug trafficking." Reagan said he intended to hire 900 new agents and 200 federal prosecutors, establish special task forces in twelve major cities, and build new prisons at a cost of $150 million.[2]

A number of developments precipitated Reagan's tough talk on drugs. The U.S. government was concerned about reports of the large quantities of drugs that were pouring into the United States from Asia and South America. Drug analysts estimated that four metric tons of heroin and perhaps as much as 15,000 metric tons of cocaine were being smuggled into the United States each year by drug traffickers.[3] The U.S. Drug Enforcement Administration (DEA) estimated that illegal drug sales in the United States exceeded $80 billion a year.[4]

The statistics on international drug trafficking were indeed staggering and suggested that, if something was not done soon, the drug problem would get out of control. Afghanistan's opium production had skyrocketed from 100 tons in 1971 to 300 tons in 1982, while a bumper opium crop in 1981 had created — in the words of U.S. Attorney General William French Smith — "enough heroin to glut the world market."[5] U.S. officials, moreover, predicted that the figures would rise further. Another disturbing statistic came to light as well — the U.S. heroin population had jumped to 450,000, an increase of 25 percent over the previous year.[6]

In the spring of 1980, the U.S. Senate's Permanent Committee on Investigations noted that organized crime, particularly its involvement in drug trafficking, had become a national security issue. Six years later, the President's Commission on Organized Crime released its report, reviewing the history of the U.S. war on drugs, and noted in its report that "the violence and corruption that are integral parts of organized crime drug trafficking takes the lives of American and foreign officials and private citizens, undermines drug control efforts, and threatens entire governments. To the extent that the stability of friendly nations is threatened, particularly in this hemisphere, our national security is jeopardized."[7]

Meanwhile, the American public was becoming increasingly concerned about what it perceived as a dramatic increase in drug abuse. A large number of parents believed that illegal drugs such as marijuana and cocaine threatened their children and wanted to see the government do something about it. About three thousand parent groups had organized nationally under the umbrella of the National Federation of Parents for Drug Free Youth. The politicians sensed the mood of the country. The House Select Committee and the Attorney General's Task Force on Violent Crime advised President Reagan to get tough on drugs.[8] Researchers fueled the alarm by publishing statistics that purportedly showed a dramatic increase in the American public's acceptance of drug use. The National Institute on Drug Abuse, for example, estimated that each month about 20 million Americans smoked marijuana, another 5 to 10 million used cocaine, and more than 4.5 million used depressants and stimulants.[9] The press heightened the public's anxiety, as it had done in early engagements of the war on drugs, by reporting that every sector of American society was involved with heavy drug use. In rhetoric that was common for the time, one magazine quoted a former DEA agent as saying "Drug use at the workplace is as common as the coffee break."[10]

In November 1981 a delegation of prominent leaders from Miami, which included former astronaut Frank Borman, chairman of Eastern Airlines, and Alvah Chapman, chairman of the Knight-Ridder newspaper chain, the corporate owner of the *Miami Herald*, came to see Ronald Reagan at the White House. The delegation, which called itself Citizens Against Crime, wanted federal help to deal with an epidemic of violent crime and a flood of illegal drugs that was wreaking havoc on South Florida, the prosperous and lush center of the Sunshine State.[11] The problem was not new. As early as May 1972, the *New York Times*, citing information provided by federal law enforcement officials, reported that "enterprising Frenchmen, South Americans, Puerto Ricans and Cuban refugees are turning South Florida into a premier entry point for smuggled heroine and cocaine."[12]

During the course of the 1970s, the drug problem in South Florida worsened. By 1980 James Smith, Florida's attorney general, told U.S. senators in the nation's capital, "Through an accident of nature and geography, Florida has become an international port of entry for illicit drugs entering the United States. We now accept the fact that the drug industry is, indeed, the biggest retail industry in Florida."[13] A year later, authorities were estimating that drug smuggling in Florida was worth $7 billion to $12 billion a year, with about 70 percent of the marijuana and cocaine smuggled into the United States passing through South Florida. In 1981 authorities seized 3.5 million pounds of marijuana and 2,508 pounds of cocaine, two-thirds of all national seizures.[14] Further, drug money had created a currency surplus of $5 billion at Miami's Federal Reserve Bank, more than the combined holdings of the nation's twelve federal reserve banks.[15]

Drug trafficking made homicide a common event in South Florida. The number of murders in Miami had skyrocketed, going from 349 in 1979 to 569 in 1980 to 621 in 1981, with about 40 percent of the murders related to drugs.[16] So many people were being murdered in Miami that the mortuaries could not handle all the corpses, forcing the Dade County Medical Examiner's Office to use refrigerated trucks to accommodate the overflow.[17] In September 1980 Miami (population 347,000) attained the dubious distinction of heading the FBI's annual list of the nation's ten most crime-ridden cities with the nation's highest murder rate (70 per 100,000 residents).[18]

Drug money had corrupted all aspects of the South Florida economy, banking as well as real estate and law enforcement. Economist Charles Kimball said that the state of Florida was so dependent upon drug money that, if it wasn't cut off soon, the state would experience a gigantic crisis in the real estate sector. Kimball said his research revealed that about 40 percent of all Florida real estate worth $300,000 or more was bought through off-shore, drug-supported corporations.[19]

Before the Miami delegation arrived at the White House, the federal government had been involved in the drug crisis in South Florida. In 1980, U.S. Customs and the Internal Revenue Service had launched Operation Greenback, an investigation of narcotics money and money laundering in South Florida that was designed to take the profits out of drug trafficking by using bank records to trace the flow of drug-related funds. "Hitting the traffickers where it hurts — in their wallets — is an effective weapon," Peter Bessinger, an administrator of the DEA from 1976 to 1981, explained in testimony before the Subcommittee on Security and Terrorism of the Committee of the Judiciary of the U.S. Senate. "Removing the organization's assets removes its lifeblood."[20]

Through Operation Greenback the federal government, for the first time, began to make use of computers and to treat drug syndicates as if they were illicit multinationals with an audit trail. "People thought I was crazy when I proposed pursuing narcotics traffickers through an audit trail," explained William Rosenblatt, the Area Special Agent in Charge of the U.S. Customs Service in Florida's Southeast Region, who is credited with being the architect of Operation Greenback. "Nobody thinks I'm crazy anymore. It's a very arduous long-range investigation, but the payoff is big. We have now a computer system that can tell us a lot of things about people who are moving money or why they are moving money and who they are moving money for."[21]

Before the Greenback investigation, it was not uncommon for drug traffickers to come up to a teller's window at a bank and count out deposits of just under $10,000 from bags overstuffed with currency bills, while corrupt tellers and bank officials, who were on the payroll of the drug traffickers, would look the other way. This practice would keep the deposits of the drug traffickers within the requirements of the law known as the Bank Secrecy Act, which requires banks to file currency transaction reports for deposits of $10,000 or more. Some South Florida banks would ignore the law altogether and allow customers to deposit over-the-limit amounts without complying with the law.[22] Customs officials estimated that in 1981 alone, banks failed to report more than $3.2 million in cash deposits.[23]

To launder their money, all the drug traffickers had to do was to use the same planes that flew drugs into the country to fly money out to safe offshore banks in, say, the Bahamas or the Cayman Islands, which had strict laws governing the secrecy of financial transactions. Offshore banks would disguise the source of the money and convert it into "clean money" before being returned to the United States. As time went by, the drug traffickers, in order to stay one step ahead of the authorities, became increasingly ingenious in how they laundered their illicit drug profits, foreshadowing how formidable an enemy they would become in the war on drugs. A favorite ploy was to set up a phony account in a bank in South Florida under a bogus name and then quickly transfer the money out of the country before federal agents could pick up the audit trail. The money is sent back to drug traffickers as a "loan" or as payment for services rendered to a phony corporation, which allows them to disguise the money and use it as clean money.[24]

Greenback agents raided several banks in Miami and Fort Lauderdale and arrested and charged several Colombians with laundering millions of dollars. Operation Greenback, for example, brought an indictment against the Great American Bank, charging that the bank laundered more than $94 million from January 1980 through February 1981 and deliberately failed to file the appropriate forms with the government during that period. In return for receiving a fee for processing the large currency deposits, the indictment revealed that bank personnel allowed drug traffickers to maintain large balances in their accounts. Using an account named Interfil, one narcotics trafficking organization made cash deposits of more than $71 million during that period, the average deposit being in excess of $250,000 daily. All the defendants, who were not fugitives, including the bank's vice president of the installment loan department, a loan officer, and the head teller, pleaded guilty to various charges.[25]

By November 1981 *Time* magazine could report that the Greenback operation had traced $2 billion in suspicious funds to their original source, made fifty-one indictments, and confiscated $20 billion in assets and cash.[26] While noting that Operation Greenback had made it difficult for drug traffickers to launder money secretly, the magazine added that money was still getting out of the country. "Every week a Colombian airforce C-130 transport plane flies to Fort Lauderdale with wooden crates containing up to $10 million from Colombia's central bank. The surplus greenbacks are being legally returned from Bogota to the federal reserve system in exchange for credit."[27]

In December 1981 the DEA began to make its presence felt in South Florida, establishing an elite secret force known as CENTAC 26, which consisted of DEA agents, New York City police officers and Metro Dade County detectives who could be trusted not to have succumbed to the corrupt temptations of the narcotics trade. Established in 1973, CENTAC, which stood for Central Tactical Unit, had conducted a number of special investigations of drug trafficking organizations. For example, CENTAC 12, which was initiated in August 1977 and ended in December 1978, was able to obtain the first seizure of Swiss bank accounts related to drug traffickers' assets.[28] CENTAC 26 set its sights on some of the biggest cocaine traffickers in South Florida, and during the next few years it began to pursue its prey.

Hoping to sustain the momentum built by Operation Greenback and CENTAC 26, Reagan responded to the reports of a growing crisis in Florida and the visit of the Miami delegation by creating the South Florida Task Force to coordinate efforts against drug trafficking in South Florida. He named Vice President George Bush to head the task force and made it operational on March 15, 1982. In explaining the rationale for the initiative, Reagan told the press, "The nearly two million people in South Florida are unfairly burdened financially in addition to being denied their constitutional right to live in peace without fear and intimidation."[29]

True to his words, Reagan sent a veritable army of federal law enforcement officials to South Florida to bolster the front lines of defense in the war on drugs: from the DEA, 73 agents and support staff to its Miami office; from the FBI, 43 new agents; and from Customs, which was given the added responsibility of investigating drug-related crimes, 145 more agents. The Bureau of Alcohol, Tobacco and Firearms added 45 more agents and declared it would concentrate on stopping the proliferation of automatic weapons, while the IRS pledged to crack down on money laundering. In addition, the Coast Guard, the U.S. Marshals, and the U.S. Border Patrol were all recruited to fight civilian crime in South Florida. To handle the anticipated increase in the federal prosecutions of drug-related cases, Bush said that the federal government would provide as many federal prosecutors as were needed.[30]

In a major policy shift, the Reagan administration reorganized the chain of command in the war on drugs, putting the FBI, for the first time in its history, in charge of drug enforcement and investigation. The DEA had to report to the director of the FBI, who now had the added responsibility of supervising drug law enforcement officials and policies. To further coordinate federal drug-enforcement efforts, Reagan also issued two executive orders. The one on June 24, 1982, strengthened the

Office of Policy Development to help the president perform his duties under the Drug Abuse, Prevention, Treatment and Rehabilitation Act, and the second, issued on December 9, 1981, authorized agencies of the U.S intelligence community to "participate in law enforcement activities to investigate or prevent international narcotics activities and to render assistance and cooperation to law enforcement authorities not otherwise precluded by law."[31]

Meanwhile, the U.S. Congress lent its support to the war on drugs, amending a law known as Posse Comitatus, which had been on the books since the U.S. Civil War and prohibited military involvement in civilian affairs. Congress, in its zeal to pursue the war on drugs, authorized the U.S. Department of Defense to provide military training intelligence and equipment to civil law enforcement agencies and allowed members of the army, navy, air force, and marines to operate military equipment for civil agencies responsible for enforcing the nation's laws. For the first time in American history, U.S. naval vessels began directly to interdict drug smuggling ships in international waters. The move sparked a fierce debate in Congress, as some members of Congress questioned the wisdom of using the military as posse comitatus. "It just frightens me that we can't find other ways of combating this in our country without now going to the military and bringing them into our civilian lives," said Shirley Chisholm (D–N.Y.).[32] Reagan signed the new antidrug law in December 1981, allowing civilian authorities to use in the war on drugs an impressive array of military technology, intelligence resources, and a sophisticated network of Navy E-2C's, so called "Mini Awacs" radar planes operating out of Jacksonville, Cape Canaveral, and Homestead Air Force Base in Florida and Guantánamo in Cuba. Many drug smugglers liked to fly their planes at night, so the U.S. Army loaned U.S. Customs two helicopter gunships to track them down and a balloon-shaped NORAD radar, nicknamed "Fat Albert," was set up 10,000 feet above Key West.[33] While the South Florida Task Force was intended to be a multifaceted anticrime agency, it was clear that its focus was going to be interdiction and the arrest and prosecution of drug dealers.

Within weeks of its formation, the South Florida Task Force began to score some stunning successes. On March 9 the U.S. Customs at the Miami International Airport seized 3,906 pounds of cocaine valued at $1.3 million aboard a cargo plane arriving from Bogotá, Colombia. It was the most cocaine ever impounded by the federal agency. Then in April authorities intercepted a Cessna 402B aircraft and seized another 115 pounds of cocaine worth $166 million.[34]

The seizures of marijuana were equally impressive. Customs intercepted a 65-foot trawler called the *Misfit*, which was bound for Florida, and found 70,000 pounds of marijuana aboard valued at $54,400,000. Another interception of a 110-foot coastal freighter heading toward Florida with about 103,000 pounds of marijuana worth $76,656 hidden inside a secret compartment of the boat. Then in November 1982, still another interdiction uncovered 67,500 pounds of marijuana aboard a 130-foot vessel, the *Shooting Star*.[35] Between February and September 30, 1982, the Task Force reported the seizure of 1,700,000 pounds of marijuana and 6,565 pounds of cocaine, a significant increase over a corresponding figure the first year.[36]

Meanwhile, during the first year of the Task Force's operation, drug traffickers were being hauled into court. At the federal level, the U.S. Attorney General's Office prosecuted a total of 664 drug-related cases, up 64 percent from the previous year. Ronald Reagan was quick to gain political capital from what appeared to be the government's winning war against international drug trafficking. He journeyed to Miami, and in press conferences stood before the seizures of his war on drugs and called the South Florida Task Force "a brilliant example of working federalism."[37] Critics charged that the president's well-orchestrated visits to South Florida were giving away the task force's operational plans to the enemy. "Every move was telegraphed to the smuggling community," one task force official told Newsweek magazine. "The only doper who doesn't know about it has been away somewhere."[38]

Even before the first year ended, though, it appeared that the ever-resourceful drug traffickers were shifting the battlefield of the war on drugs, bringing to other parts of the country the violence, the drug addiction, the corruption, and the dirty money that had plagued South Florida. In response to Operation Greenback, the drug traffickers began to shift their money to Southern California, where the cash surplus in Los Angeles soon topped $3 billion.[39] As the South Florida Task Force began to cut off the traffic from Colombia to Florida, drug smugglers were opening up different routes along both coasts of the country. To their dismay, authorities in such states as Maine, Georgia, Tennessee, New Mexico, and Louisiana were having to interdict cocaine and marijuana shipments. They worried about how many drug shipments were getting through to be sold in the towns and cities of their states.

In New England, 100 tons of marijuana was seized in the first nine months of 1982, compared to only nine tons the same period the previous year. In Georgia authorities reported that law enforcement officials in ten Georgia counties had been prosecuted during the past two years for receiving payoffs.[40] On March 22, 1982, radar tracked a DC-4 crammed with 8.5 tons of marijuana to a pasture in Hurtsboro, Alabama. The following month, authorities intercepted ten tons of marijuana in a Louisiana swamp. In July a search of a shrimp trawler at Morehead City, North Carolina, uncovered $20 million worth of marijuana.[41] Representative Leo Jeferetti (D–N.Y.), chairman of the House Narcotics Committee, summed up the obvious: "A concentrated drug-interdiction effort in one area will only force traffickers to channel their efforts elsewhere."[42]

In response to the shifting crime scene, the federal government set up South Florida–style task forces wherever a new drug smuggling route seemed to be developing. The so called "El Dorado" units soon began operation in Chicago, Houston, Philadelphia, New York, and Los Angeles.[43]

Many observers, however, were wondering how the authorities could sustain the intensity of the Task Force operation. How would they find the money for personnel and equipment when the trend in Washington was to shrink, not increase, the federal budget? "We just can't sustain this level of operation if we don't get additional help," warned Deese Thompson, a Coast Guard admiral. "Every [federal] agency is going to need more money to get through this year."[44]

During the 1980s and 1990s, however, the federal government would insist that the strategy of stopping the supply of drugs from entering the country was the key to victory in the war on drugs. Federal authorities maintained that no nation could cope with drug abuse by relying solely on treatment and domestic law enforcement. They argued that the supply of cocaine, heroin, and marijuana was so big that their production had to be made the number one priority. "We need to break the grower to user chains which stretch across five continents," explained Ambassador Stoessel. "To do it, we must have a comprehensive program of international control."[45]

During the next decade and a half, the United States would never waver from this resolve. It would pay lip service to the idea of curbing demand and pursue a policy that emphasized finding a military solution to the war on drugs. Law enforcement would hunt down and either capture or kill drug lords such as Pablo Escobar, Carlos Lehder, José Rodríguez Gacha, and Gilberto and Miguel Rodríguez Orejuella, but ambitious drug lords would surface to take their place and keep the supply of drugs moving. The United States would even kidnap one head of state, General Manuel Noriega, dictator of Panama, but his country would remain a major center of money laundering. The United States would send arms, equipment, and state-of-the-art military technology to Colombia, Peru, Bolivia, and other countries battling drug trafficking, but the cartels would maintain their power and ability to corrupt their governments and destabilize their societies. The United States and its allies would eradicate the poppy and coca crops, the sources of heroin and cocaine, but the peasants who depended on those crops for their livelihood would keep finding ways to grow them.

And in 1997, 15 years after President Reagan's declaration of war against international drug trafficking, the United States and its allies would be no closer to claiming victory in the war on drugs. The battle against the hard target, it seemed, would never end.

Section 2

Background

Chapter 3

The Birth of the Underground Empire, 1840–1960

"Every generation assumes that it discovers or endures problems for the first time, but the fact is the United States has always had a drug problem."
— H. Wayne Morgan, historian

"Drug trafficking is almost certainly the largest source of illegally-earned income in the United States."
— President's 1984 Commission on Organized Crime

International drug trafficking is the world's second most profitable illicit business after arms trafficking, taking in earnings estimated to be as high as $400 million annually. Heroin is believed to account for $200 million of the total, cocaine for $100 million, and the rest of the amount is divided up between marijuana, hashish, and several psychotropic drugs. Researchers say that at least 104 countries are involved in some way — production, distribution, or laundering of illicit profits — in the criminal enterprise, and thousands of entrepreneurial criminals from all over the world are willing to risk death and jail to get a piece of the lucrative action. The profits are so huge that drug traffickers find it difficult to hide, let alone spend. The drug lords who control the traffic regularly appear on *Forbes* magazine's annual list of the world's richest individuals, while the power and wealth of the trafficking networks they have created threaten the stability and social fabric of countries all over the world. Each year, thousands of unfortunate people of all colors, ages, and classes die or have their lives wrecked or derailed because of international drug trafficking. Illegal drug use claims an estimated 40,000 lives in the United States each year, while in Europe between 500,000 and a million people are addicted to heroin, and the problem, together with the criminality associated with the illegal trade in cocaine, makes drug trafficking Europe's number one problem.[1]

Much of the criminal attention is directed to the huge market in the United States (population 260 million), where experts say drug trafficking has become the country's largest source of illegally earned income. The illegal drug traffic has made drug abuse a problem of national concern, particularly, as we have read, since the early 1980s, when President Ronald Reagan declared a war on drugs. Since Reagan left the Oval Office in 1988, his two successors, George Bush and Bill Clinton, have renewed the pledge to fight the war and have spent more billions combating international drug trafficking.

As serious as the U.S. considers today's drug abuse and international drug trafficking, they are not new problems, for throughout its history the United States has been a drug-consuming nation, often to the point of attracting the concern of its media, political establishment, religious leaders, and medical community, who feared that drug use and abuse was getting out of control and undermining American values.

In order to understand the current war on drugs, it is necessary to look at the roots and development of international drug trafficking and its impact on U.S. history. Doing so can lead to a better understanding of why the trade has become a huge and alarming problem.

It is not an exaggeration to say that, during the nineteenth century, the United States was one of the most drug-abusing nations in history; in fact, of the four major drugs in illegal use today — opium, heroin, cocaine, and marijuana — were widely prevalent in American society, and it was all legal. Chinese immigrants got the drug wagon rolling in the early nineteenth century when they brought opium with them to the United States. The Chinese had been smoking opium for at least 1,000 years by the time the British opium trade with China began in the early nineteenth century.

Beginning about 1840, opium imports increased significantly, the result of the U.S. opium trade with China, which the British dominated but with significant U.S. participation. In addition to being imported, opium was grown legally in many parts of the United States during the nineteenth century, especially in the southern states of Georgia, Florida, Louisiana, Virginia, Tennessee, and South Carolina. Doctors used opium regularly — without a second thought — as part of their regular practice to control and treat a variety of ailments and diseases, including fevers, dysentery, rheumatism, swellings, and broken limbs and to ease the pain of dying patients.[2] In 1860, no less eminent an American than Oliver Wendel Holmes enthused that "the Creator himself seems to prescribe [opium] for we see the scarlet poppy growing in the cornfields … as if it were foreseen that wherever there is hunger to be fed, there is pain to be soothed."[3] By the 1870s, opium dens were flourishing in Chicago, Washington, St. Louis, New Orleans, and New York City, attracting non–Chinese in search of a high.[4]

Also about 1840, cannabis became popular in the treatment of certain ailments: insomnia, tetanus, migraine, and venereal disease, and even as an antidote for strychnine poisoning.

In the 1870s, cocaine derived from the coca leaf grown in South America began arriving in the United States and Europe, and within a decade, a number of famous personalities had hailed the wonder drug. For example, Sigmund Freud, the "Father of Psychiatry," and his wife experimented with the drug, praising it as a cure for migraine and alcohol addiction and claiming that the "user (has) absolutely no craving for further use of cocaine."[5] The American general and president U.S. Grant used cocaine to keep himself alive while he finished his memoirs, and U.S. President William McKinley, Pope Leo XIII, inventor Thomas Edison, and the king and queen of Norway enjoyed a popular drink called Vin Mariani that consisted of wine mixed with a new drink called Coca-Cola that was sold all over the world.[6] Ordinary Americans enjoyed cocaine as well; in fact, many enjoyed a shot of whiskey laced with a pinch of cocaine.[7]

In 1898 Bayer Laboratories — the same Bayer that makes aspirin today — introduced heroin as a non-addictive substitute for morphine, and doctors began to prescribe the drug to patients, using it as a cure for the worst coughs and chest pains. Made from opium, heroin was viewed as a powerful painkiller that didn't have the addictive qualities of morphine, which had come into general use in the 1820s and was popular in medical treatment. Heroin, like other drugs, could be bought by mail order or in any drugstore. In 1898 the American Medical Association endorsed the new drug as safe for respiratory ailments.[8]

In the late nineteenth century, however, the prevailing permissive attitude, easy access to narcotics, and the rising number of drug abuse cases caused public concern. No one could be sure of the accuracy of the statistics, but surveys conducted by doctors and pharmacists during this period suggested that the number of drug addicts was in the range of 100,000 to 200,000. As Morgan explains, "The statistics can never be exact, but the divining (the number of addicts) lent credence to the general fear that opium addiction and drug use was spreading and undermining American values."[9] When the physically and psychologically addictive qualities of the many thought-to-be wonder drugs became apparent, politicians, religious leaders, pharmacists, doctors, and journalists spoke out for tighter controls on the use of drugs.

The medical establishment warned that heroin, while itself not physically addictive, could become habit forming for people with "susceptible" minds. Sigmund Freud began to have second doubts about the miracle nature of cocaine after one of his close friends died of an overdose, and, in his lectures and scientific writings, he began warning the public about dependency on the drug. By the early 1900s, many doctors had abandoned heroin in the treatment of their patients, concerned that patients were needing stronger and stronger doses of the drug. Many of the addicted fit the image of the stereotypical addicts, but they also included middle-aged women from rural America. "We have an army of women in America dying from the poison habit — larger than our standing army," a doctor concluded in 1894. "The profession is wholly responsible for the loose and indiscriminate use of the drug."[10]

Despite the changing public mood, the United States was slow to adopt antidrug legislation. The city of San Francisco passed the first significant law in 1875, banning opium dens and other commercial establishments where opium was smoked, and in 1880, the United States banned the smoking of opium by Asians when it signed a commercial treaty with the Chinese.[11] Congress did not pass the first important piece of domestic antidrug legislation until 34 years later.

The U.S. move toward the regulation and ultimate prohibition of drugs was largely guided by its foreign policy, especially its desire to open up the Chinese market, which Japan and the major European powers had cornered, as well as its acquisition of the Philippines in 1898 after winning a four-month war with Spain. The Spanish had allowed Chinese residents in the Philippines to purchase opium and taxed its sale, but drug addiction had spread to the native population, which began to use the drug as a way to stave off cholera. Under pressure from clergy and others in the growing and increasingly active U.S. anti-opium movement, President William Taft formed the Philippines Commission to investigate the opium trade and report back to him. The Commission's conclusion that the opium trade was one of the most serious problems in the Orient led Congress to ban opium use in the Philippines in 1905.[12] This was the beginning of an international anti-opium crusade that lobbied successfully for a series of treaties restricting the opium trade.

Meanwhile in the United States, the popular press began to shape the public's attitudes about drugs by publishing articles that revealed the horrors of drug abuse and asserted that the addicted population was growing to alarming proportions. One report claimed that an Atlanta sanitarium had treated 100,000 addicted patients and that many others were receiving as many 50,000.[13] Many of the stories were wild exaggerations, claiming, among other things, that drug abusers had superhuman strength and the police could do nothing — not even use bullets — to stop them.[14] It would not be the last time that news reporters fueled the country's imagination and apprehension about drugs.

Another important feature in the history of the U.S. antinarcotics movement — racism — began to take shape in the early twentieth century. As one writer explained,[15]

> the most passionate support for legal prohibition has been associated with fear of a given drug's effect on a special community. Certain drugs were dreaded because they seemed to undermine essential social restrictions that kept those groups under control. Thus an important factor in the move to ban opium was the fear that smoking opium would lead to sexual contacts between Chinese and whites. As early as 1902 cocaine abuse became linked with African Americans and had a definite sexual connotation.

In 1902, the American Pharmaceutical Association reported that "the use of cocaine by unfortunate women generally, and by the negro in certain parts of the country, is simply appalling. The police of these districts tell us that the habitants ... have no difficulty at all in buying (cocaine)."[16] During the 1920s, heroin became associated with youth gangs and rebellious youth, and in the following decade, smoking marijuana was linked to violence by Mexicans and other minorities.[17]

Many critics of U.S. drug policy would agree with the conclusion of one scholar who wrote, "customary use of a certain drug came to symbolize the differences between that group and the rest of society" and so would-be social architects hoped that "eliminating the drug might alleviate disharmony and preserve the old order."[18]

The growing fear of drug abuse created strong public support in the early twentieth century for passage of national legislation that would lead to the control of the domestic traffic in opium and cocaine. It was the Progressive Era, a time of reform and political ferment.[19] In 1906

Congress passed the Pure Food and Drug Act, which made it illegal to sell food or medicine if the ingredients, including heroin and cocaine, were not stated on the label. Two years later, shipping cocaine and heroin from one state to another became illegal, although the sale of the drugs was still legal, as was the trafficking of drugs within states. In 1909 Congress passed another act that prohibited the importation and use of opium for other than medical purposes. Opium could still be imported for medical purposes, but only to 12 ports.[20] Meanwhile, states with big urban populations like New York caught the Progressive Era spirit and began to regulate and apply laws that controlled the sale of drugs.[21]

After the Shanghai Conference of 1909, the United States continued to attend and support other international anti-opium conferences. In December 1911 a conference at the Hague convened to sanction the resolutions adapted at Shanghai and led to the signing of the International Opium Convention of January 23, 1912. Signatories committed themselves to the enactment of laws that would suppress "the abuse of opium, morphine, cocaine, as well as drugs prepared or derived from these substances."[22]

The strong U.S. support for international opium control, as well as the popular consensus against drug use and addiction that had been building since the late nineteenth century, led to the passage in 1914 of the Harrison Act, one of the most famous and important drug laws in U.S. history. Named after Representative Francis B. Harrison of New York State, who introduced the measure in U.S. Congress, the act was signed by Woodrow Wilson on December 17, 1914, and went into effect on March 1, 1915. It had the long-winded title of "an Act to provide for the registration of, with collectors of internal revenue, and to impose a special tax upon all persons who produce, import, manufacture, compound, deal in, disperse, sell, distribute, or give away opium or coca leaves, their salts, derivatives, or properties and for other purposes."

With the act's passage, anyone selling, importing, or dispensing drugs had to be registered with the U.S government. Heroin and cocaine, moreover, could now be obtained legally only with a doctor's prescription. Marijuana was excluded from the law, and not until 1937 did lawmakers bring it under control. While intense lobbying by the U.S. drug industry stopped the total regulation of drugs, the Harrison Act became the cornerstone for U.S. domestic drug policy for the next 65 years.[23] More laws would follow in the belief that legislation at both the national and the state levels could, if not eliminate, at least control the country's drug use. In the coming decades, however, drug abuse, as a perceived social problem, would not go away.

The enforcement of the Harrison Act became the responsibility of a special narcotics unit under the direction of the deputy commissioner of prohibition in the Department of the Treasury, and, during the eight years after the Harrison Act's passage, the unit arrested about 50,000 individuals for violations, including many doctors who had continued to provide their patients, many of whom were addicts, with opium and heroin. The arrests created much controversy. *American Medicine* magazine noted that the addict "was deprived of the medical care he urgently needs; open, above-board sources for which he formerly obtained his drug supply are closed to him, and he is driven to the underworld where he can get his drug."[24]

By then, the crusade to regulate drugs had culminated in the ratification of the Eighteenth Amendment in 1919, which totally prohibited the sale, manufacture, or drinking of alcoholic beverages of any kind after 1920. Little did the amendment's proponents and supporters realize that their moralistic intentions would lead to the beginning of widespread drug trafficking, the emergence of organized crime on a prodigious scale, and the accumulation of huge illegal profits that would spur the growth of criminal activity.

It is true that organized crime existed in the United States before Prohibition. Sicilian secret societies, which would spawn the Sicilian Mafia, were operating in most Italian American communities in the 1890s, while other ethnic gangs — including Jews, Japanese, Chinese, and Irish — were also involved in organized criminal activity. But as one scholar explained, "all of the living pre-prohibition mobsters, extortionists, racketeers, criminals would have remained in the lower depths without the passage of the Eighteenth Amendment. Prohibition not only gave them opportunity, it gave them respectability and legitimacy. Prohibition not only provided a means of making vast sums of money, it created a need for organization, cooperation and syndication."[25] And with their big bank accounts, the gangsters of the Prohibition era were able to corrupt public officials such as police, attorneys, politicians, and prosecutors with unprecedented and depressing regularity.

During Prohibition, the United States continued to pass laws that put tighter restrictions on drug sales. The National Drug Import and Export Act of 1922, for example, prohibited the importation of heroin. Meanwhile, the United States attended several international forums and conferences at which it made known its views on narcotic drugs. They should be used only for medical and scientific purposes, the United States argued, and the only way to limit their distribution was to curb the production of raw materials, such as opium and the coca leaf, at the source. These principles, however, were never ratified into law by any international organization.

Governments were no longer actively promoting drugs, but that didn't stop the emergence of new criminal syndicates in major cities of Asia and the West to organize the underground traffic in illegal drugs. By 1924 many source countries began to make a complaint that would become a major issue in the 1980s: the need for development assistance from the source countries to help them control drug production materials. In 1923, Turkey, one of the major source countries, rejected a request by the United States to implement a crop substitution program, and within a decade, the country had become one of the world's largest centers for heroin traffic.[26]

In the 1920s, heroin trafficking, under the direction of Jewish gangs in New York City, became big business in the United States. Historians credit Jewish Prohibition-era gangster Arnold Rothstein with turning narcotics trafficking into a big-time operation. In describing Rothstein's role, one historian wrote, "He dispatched a number of employees with experience purchasing liquor in Europe to locate major sources of supply. They found that buying narcotics on the continent was ridiculously easy. Legitimate pharmaceutical firms in France, Germany, and Holland were happy to see big orders of heroin, morphine, and cocaine, no questions asked. Rothstein used his own people to arrange giant orders and overseas shipments to be sent back to the U.S. as innocuous sea freight. Once in the U.S., the drugs were distributed by Rothstein's people to the wide network of big-city Prohibition gangsters."[27]

Federal statistics show that illegal drugs entering the United States increased significantly in the late 1920s, no doubt, thanks to the Rothstein network. In the fiscal year ending June 20, 1926, U.S. Customs confiscated 449 pounds of opium, 3.5 pounds of heroin, 10 pounds of cocaine, and 42 pounds of morphine. By mid–1928, those figures had jumped to 27 pounds for heroin, 30 of cocaine, 91 for morphine, and a staggering 2,354 pounds of opium.[28] By the mid 1930s, the Italian Cosa Nostra had joined the Jewish Mafia in the international narcotics trade and was importing opium and heroin from Asia, France, and the Middle East.

When the repeal of the Eighteenth Amendment in 1933 ended Prohibition, many leading gangsters who had made huge profits in bootlegging — such as Meyer Lansky, Frank Costello, Bugsy Siegel, and Lucky Luciano — stayed in the liquor business legally, buying and establishing companies that sold wine, whiskey, and other spirits. Some of them moved into narcotics trafficking and other lucrative criminal activities.

During the Great Depression of the 1930s, drug use was low because people had little money to spend on nonessentials, but the federal government continued to tighten the country's drug laws. By 1931 it was illegal in 36 countries to possess cocaine or opiates as well in eight others, and every state in the Union had outlawed marijuana use by 1937, the year Congress passed the Marijuana Tax Law and added marijuana to the list of drugs the federal government would try to control.

The antidrug campaign in the U.S. was led by the Federal Bureau of Narcotics (FBN) director Harry J. Anslinger, who served as the bureau's director from 1930 to 1966. As the first United States drug czar, Anslinger worked tirelessly for tough law enforcement, believing that drug trafficking posed one of the most serious threats to the country's well being. Anslinger focused on stopping the supply of illegal drugs as the way to decrease the number of addicts.

During the 1920s and 1930s the international control of opiates and other narcotics became one of the most successful activities of the League of Nations. The League sponsored several opium treaties that were ratified by 67 nations, and its Permanent Central Control Opium Board supervised the legal international trade in opium and other drugs it considered dangerous and applied effective sanctions against countries that exceeded estimates.[29]

With the outbreak of World War II, the problem of international drug trafficking was put on hold as the United States and its allies concentrated their energy and resources on defeating the Axis powers. It was a difficult time for addicts in the United States to find illegal drugs, but with the country's war machine in full throttle, an increasing number of Americans began to try so-called goof balls (a mixture of amphetamines and barbiturates) for relaxation and diversion. The major piece of U.S. antidrug legislation passed during World War II was the Opium Control Act of 1942, which prohibited the domestic production of poppy without FBN permission. For propaganda purposes, the United States made an effort to tie the enemy to international drug trafficking. In 1946 the *New York Times* wrote, "Of all the indictments against Japan, that of the use of opium and its derivative heroin, as deliberate government policy to control the minds of conquered people, or all of Japan's enemies, is perhaps the most damning."[30]

During World War II, some important developments in international drug trafficking occurred. Several countries met with the United States in Washington in 1942 to discuss the question of the discontinuance of government monopolies for opium smoking after the war when territories held by Japan would be returned to the European allies that formerly controlled them. In 1943 the allies announced that the system of opium smoking under government license would end with the return of the liberated territories. In June 1944 the U.S. Senate and House passed a joint resolution sponsored by Walter Judd, a congressman from Minnesota and former missionary to China, authorizing the president to urge opium-producing countries to restrict their production of opium to the purpose of meeting the world's scientific and medical needs.[31]

With the defeat of the Axis powers in 1945, international drug trafficking once again became the focus of international attention. The United Nations assumed the drug control functions of the defunct League of Nations and gave high priority to working for greater cooperation among the drug enforcement agencies around the world. The FBN expanded its operation overseas into Europe and the Middle East. It looked like the problem of international drug trafficking was well under control. To the casual observer, "the hope of finally stopping supplies and cutting production [sic] of new addicts seemed about to come true."[32] International drug trafficking, however, would continue to grow and expand, thanks to two major developments in the late 1940s.

After the War, La Cosa Nostra, under the leadership of Charles "Lucky" Luciano, took control of the U.S. heroin market. Luciano had been convicted of 91 counts of extortion and prostitution in the 1930s and began serving a long prison sentence in New York State, but the U.S government deported him to his native Italy in 1945, reportedly for "services" he had performed for the United States during the war, the nature of which has never really been explained. Luciano quickly took advantage of his freedom, taking control of the local Mafia soon after arriving in Italy and developing a plan of action to ship heroin to the U.S.

During the war, drug traffickers had had a difficult time importing heroin into the United States, and so without access to the drug, many addicts had cured themselves. The FBN estimated that there were no more than 20,000 addicts in the entire country at the time, a figure that represented about a 0.13 percent addict rate for the U.S. population.[33] But with a helping hand from Uncle Sam, Luciano's arrival in Italy changed that statistic dramatically. The federal authorities had underestimated the mafia don, thinking that he was nothing more than a hood and a thug, but Luciano had much experience in the heroin trade, for in the 1930s he had led his fellow Italian mobsters into the illegal business in the course of controlling his prostitutes. After moving to Italy in the late 1940s and imposing his control over the Sicilian mafia, Luciano began buying raw opium from the poppy fields in Turkey, Lebanon, and other producing countries, setting up heroin processing labs in Sicily, and developing a sophisticated drug-smuggling network that transported heroin to markets in the United States and Europe. By 1952 the FBN had revised its estimate of the number of addicts in the country, putting the figure at three times what it was before World War II.

The Italian government finally banned the manufacture of heroin in the early 1950s, when an investigation showed that heroin had been smuggled into the United States from Italy since 1948. That didn't deter the enterprising Italian mob, which devised a new system by which supplies of morphine base were refined to heroin in Marseilles, shipped to Montreal or Sicily, and then sent directly to the United States. This new arrangement became known as the "French Connection," and it allowed the Italian mafia to dominate the heroin trade from the 1950s to the early 1970s. At its peak, the French Connection supplied an estimated 95 percent of the heroin distributed to the United States.

The Chinese Revolution of 1948, which deposed Chiang Kai-Shek and brought the Communists to power under Mao Tse-Tung, also gave international drug trafficking a boost. Chiang's Fifth Kuomintang Army (KMT) fled China, going south across the border into Burma. To get money for arms and materials, the KMT got involved in the local opium trade, helping to turn the Golden Triangle into one of the world's biggest producers of opium. Besides, as James Traub explained, "The KMT established a pattern: as the politics of Southeast Asia became more chaotic, more gangs sprang up to challenge government's turning to opium for money and finally became very little different from bands of smugglers. The difference, in Southeast Asia, is that the drug trade is controlled by entire armies with thousands of troops and modern weapons."[34] Some of these armies also get a boost from the U.S. Central Intelligence Agency (CIA), which, in the interest of fighting communism in the region, would ignore, or tacitly approve, the shady activities of these huge rogue armies.

During the 1950s, international drug trafficking continued to grow, keeping the crime syndicates on the move between the United States, Canada, and Europe. Early in the decade, U.S. newspapers began to write about drugs again, heightening public fears about drug abuse. In 1948

Newsweek magazine had reported the drug issue dead, but three years later it was publishing stories about increasing heroin use among young people in urban areas, warning that the youngsters are "turning their arms and legs into pincushions."[35] The media also reported on the strange life-styles of the so-called Beatniks of San Francisco and Greenwich Village in New York City, who used cocaine and marijuana as a way of rebelling against convention and society. By the late 1950s, Harlem and other predominantly black inner-city areas began experiencing an upswing in heroin use.

Combating drug abuse and international drug trafficking, though, was not a high priority in the 1950s. In the spring of 1956, a congressional investigation found that the FBN is "one of the few federal agencies whose personnel and funds have not been increased to reflect population growth and greater responsibility. Over a period of 25 years, federal narcotics laws have been enforced with a force of approximately 227 agents and a budget of less than $2 million. This restriction on manpower and operating funds has seriously curtailed investigations of the addict traffic in the United States and of sources of supply in foreign countries."[36]

During the 1950s, however, the U.S. government did pass two important pieces of antidrug legislation. Statistics showed that between 1946 and 1950 the number of narcotics-related arrests had doubled and that the average age of the people being committed to hospitals because of drug abuse had decreased during the same period. Concerned about these statistics, Congress passed the 1951 Boggs Act, which increased the penalties for violating narcotics laws.[37]

Statistics showed an apparent decline in drug abuse by 1956, and Congress attributed this trend to the Bogg Act. Believing that tougher laws were the best way to continue the deterrence of narcotics addiction and international drug trafficking, Congress passed the Narcotics Control Act of 1956, which increased mandatory minimum sentences, eliminated probation, allowed narcotics agents to carry firearms for the first time, and made the sale of heroin to individuals under 18 years of age a capital offense, although the death penalty was not made mandatory.[38] As the 1950s came to a close, the federal government seemed smug in its belief that tough laws and regulations could curb the drug problem. That attitude would change in the 1960s when the amount of drug use exploded in the United States.

Chapter 4

America Rediscovers the Drug Habit, 1960–1980

"Drugs became socially acceptable in the 1960s as a whole generation defied the law."
— Barry Melton, musician and cofounder,
Country Joe and the Fish

"The nation's drug problem at the end of 1980 was as great, if not greater, than the problem in 1970."
— The President's 1984
Commission on Organized Crime

O piates more than any other narcotic substance had dominated the attention of the U.S. antidrug movement in the first half of the twentieth century, but that focus changed in the 1960s, as heroin, marijuana, and cocaine became a part of the international trade in illegal drugs and Americans from all walks of life began experimenting with a variety of drugs. Cheap and easy to find, marijuana was especially popular among white middle-class college students. Cocaine, which had declined in use after World War I, made a big comeback beginning in the late 1960s. U.S. Customs impounded a mere 3 kilograms of cocaine in 1961, but that figure jumped to 29 kilos in 1968 and to 197 in 1971.[1] LSD, a hallucinogenic and extremely powerful drug, became an integral part of the life-style of the young people who joined the counterculture that emerged in the mid-sixties. Rejecting the value of mainstream America, members of the counterculture did such things as wear their hair long, eschew materialism, practice "free" love, live in communes, flock to rock concerts, practice eastern mysticism, perform street theater, and, of course, take drugs.[2]

"LSD had a phenomenal impact on San Francisco in the 1960s," recalled Barry Melton, a founding member of the popular 1960s rock group Country Joe and the Fish. "When our band was founded in 1965, LSD was still legal and you ran no risk if you carried and used it. LSD is a powerful drug. Being free and plentiful, acid had an enormous impact on the counterculture. It was less than cheap. Ask someone for a hit of acid and they would give it to you. Drugs became socially acceptable in the 1960s as a whole generation defied the law."[3]

Hippies, as members of the counterculture became known, were highly visible examples, reflecting the changing pattern of drug use in the United States, for illegal drug consumption was no longer confined to the fringes of society. "Many substances, especially marijuana, were clearly popular with a wide range of people who did not fit the inherited ideas about drug users," wrote historian H. Wayne Morgan. "Affluent professionals and business people were as likely to use marijuana, cocaine, and even LSD as were the thrill-seeker, ignorant youngsters or petty thieves of legend.... Factory workers and truck drivers employed marijuana, amphetamines and barbiturates to help tolerate boring and repetitive labor."[4]

The huge demand for illegal drugs arising in the 1960s created the conditions that allowed international drug trafficking to expand and flourish. Until the 1960s, the cost of cocaine was such that it was known as the "champagne of drugs," but in the late 1960s, drug traffickers responded to the strong demand for new drugs with which to experiment by persuading coca growers to plant more coca leaves. This, in turn, spawned the growth of the powerful Latin American cartels, which produced increasing amounts of cocaine to meet demand. But as the cocaine supply increased, the price decreased, making it possible for more people to buy cocaine. So by the late 1960s, cocaine had become the drug choice for many Americans, and the United States had another kind of drug epidemic on its hands.

In the early 1960s, the U.S. government implemented a number of antidrug initiatives that almost seemed to anticipate the coming drug explosion. The Narcotics Control Act in 1960 was designed to help meet the country's international obligations under the 1931 Convention for Limiting the Manufacture and Regulating the Distribution of Narcotic Drugs and a 1948 protocol that sought to make the obligations imposed by the 1931 Convention applicable to synthetic drugs, which had first been developed in 1940. In 1961, the United States participated in the Single Convention on Narcotic Drugs, which simplified and streamlined the international narcotics control machinery that had grown haphazardly since the first international treaty in 1912.[5]

The convention was hailed as a major international agreement, but in retrospect, many of its articles proved to be impractical. The convention, for example, declared that "the use of cannabis for other than medical or scientific purposes must be discontinued as soon as possible, but, in any case, within twenty-five years." This proclamation, of course, was made just a few years before marijuana use exploded on the world scene. The convention also agreed to try to cut off heroin trafficking at the source, by paying the growers not to plant poppy crops, but despite several initiatives during the past three decades, this strategy has proved to be a dismal failure.[6]

U.S. President John F. Kennedy, aware of the growing national concern about drug abuse, convened the First White House Conference on Narcotics and Drug Abuse in 1962. This, in turn, led to the establishment of the President's Advisory Commission on Narcotics and Drug Abuse, the so-called Pettyman Commission, which recommended tougher measures against international drug trafficking. The commission, for example, proposed that the U.S. government assign more federal agents to investigate the illicit importation and trafficking in narcotics, marijuana, and other dangerous drugs, and to control, by federal statute, all non-narcotic drugs "capable of producing serious psychotropic effects when abused." The wide net of control was extended three years later with the passage of the Drug Abuse Control Amendments of 1965, which sought to control the diversion of depressant and stimulant drugs such as barbiturates and amphetamines from legal channels. To enforce the amendments, the federal government expanded the drug-fighting bureaucracy by creating the Bureau of Drug Abuse Control.[7]

These federal initiatives did not relieve the public's worry about crime and drug abuse, and so in 1966 President Lyndon B. Johnson established the President's Commission on Law Enforcement and Administration of Justice (the Katzenbach Commission) in order to undertake "a comprehensive study of the nation's crime problem and to provide recommendations to coordinate its eradication on all fronts." The commission's recommendations sought to deal with both the supply and demand of drugs on the one hand by increasing the enforcement staffs of the Federal Bureau of Narcotics (FBN) and the Bureau of Customs and on the other by recommending that the National Institute of Mental Health develop and distribute educational materials about drugs. In response to the commission's recommendations, President Johnson restructured the federal government's drug law-enforcement machinery, among other changes, abolishing the FBN and shifting its responsibilities to the newly created Bureau of Narcotics and Dangerous Drugs and giving the Department of Justice major responsibility for enforcing federal drug laws for the first time in its history.[8]

The federal government's efforts to structure and coordinate its forces in the emerging war on drugs culminated during Richard Nixon's presidency in the Comprehensive Drug Abuse Prevention and Control Act of 1970, which was designed to put "diverse laws in one piece of legislation based upon new scientific information, the restructured federal law enforcement efforts under Reorganization Plan No. 1 of 1968, and greater information concerning the scope of the problem."[9]

By 1970 the United States was experiencing serious social problems on many fronts, and the country had become far different from what it was in 1960. The civil rights movement had started peacefully in the early 1960s with sit-ins and peaceful nonviolent demonstrations, but by the late 1960s many African Americans and their white supporters were disillusioned with the progress made with civil rights, and the movement turned violent, culminating in race riots in several cities, including New York City, Detroit, Chicago, and Newark, New Jersey. Three widely respected public figures — John F. Kennedy, Martin Luther King, Jr., and Robert Kennedy — were assassinated, crushing the idealism of many Americans. Students began occupying buildings at their universities to protest university policy and the military draft, and, as the Vietnam War escalated, hundreds of thousands of frustrated Americans took to the streets to protest U.S. policy in Southeast Asia.

At the end of the 1960s "change was happening so fast that everything seemed compressed," recalled Jane Adams, a political activist in the late 1960s. The Vietnam War "wouldn't stop. It was like a juggernaut that kept going. We had masses of young people uprooted and traveling around, rootless and living hand to mouth. It was a pretty incredible time. What was happening, I believe, was that the people had become unmoored, and drugs were a way to escape from existential anxiety. We did not know where we were going, and it looked like we didn't have a future."[10]

By the early 1970s, marijuana had become the most popular high in America. Marijuana's ardent proponents considered the drug to be harmless and even beneficial, and, for an increasing number of Americans, "a stand of marijuana in the countryside, or in a pot in the window, was as comforting as homemade wine was to many older people."[11] Marijuana became so popular that public support for harsh sentences for marijuana users weakened. The federal government under presidents Kennedy, Johnson, and Nixon reacted reflexively to the surge in marijuana use, increasing law enforcement efforts and passing tougher sentences. At the federal level, there were a mere 169 arrests relating to marijuana in 1960, but that figure climbed to 7,000 in 1965, and a year later the figure had jumped to 50,000. Several states followed the federal government's lead and increased the penalties for possessing and selling marijuana. Louisiana, for example, increased the mandatory sentence for first offense possession of marijuana from five to fifteen years at hard labor, while in politically liberal Massachusetts, a person arrested in the company of someone possessing marijuana, or in a place where it is kept, could receive a five-year prison sentence.[12]

Despite the crackdown, widespread marijuana use had made drug trafficking a booming multibillion dollar business by the 1970s, and many criminal syndicates were eager to get a piece of the action. The Italian American mafia gave other ethnic criminal organizations an opening when its leadership decided in the 1950s to prohibit its members from trafficking in the lucrative narcotics. They feared a new federal conspiracy law that allowed the federal government to prosecute the mafia leadership for narcotics trafficking, even when they had not handled drugs personally.[13]

Cuban criminals were the first to take advantage of the Italian American mafia's decision. In Cuba during the corrupt regime of dictator Fulgencio Baptista, the American mafia was given a free hand to run the casinos, brothels, loan-sharking operations, and other criminal activities and to protect its thriving businesses, they put numerous government officials, policemen, businessmen, members of the military, and local criminals on their payroll. The mob and many of their Cuban associates fled the island for the safety of the United States in 1959, when Fidel Castro overthrew Baptista and established a communist dictatorship, but during the early 1960s, they conspired to overthrow the new Cuban dictator. The Italian American mafia was involved in several plots to kill Castro, while many of their former Cuban associates joined the CIA's failed Bay of Pigs Invasion of Cuba in 1961. In the wake of that disaster, Cuban criminals set up base in South Florida and organized La Companía, whose primary criminal activity was importing heroin and cocaine to the United States. Establishing its headquarters in Miami, with branch operations in California, Nevada, Texas, Arizona, and New

Colombian paramilitaries (courtesy Colombian Antinarcotics Police).

Jersey, la Companía dominated the drug trafficking trade from South America during the 1960s and early 1970s.[14]

The ranks of the Cuban mafia in the United States were bolstered by two more waves of Cuban immigration: the Camarioca boatlift, or "freedom flotilla," which brought 250,000 Cubans to the United States between 1965 and 1972, and the so-called Mariel boatlift of 1980, in which U.S. officials estimated about 2 percent of the immigrants were criminals, prostitutes, drug addicts, and vagrants. While most Cubans who have fled to the United States came in search of political freedom and the opportunity to build better lives, Cuban immigrant communities did become bases of operation for Cuban-organized crime networks.[15]

The powerful Colombian cartels also got their start in the drug trade in the 1960s as the middlemen who bought raw coca from farmers in the Andean region of South America, turned the coca into cocaine, and then sold the finished product to the Cubans. The large number of Colombians who emigrated to the United States in the 1960s and settled in major cites like Miami, Chicago, New York, and Los Angeles gave the Colombian trafficking networks a solid, sympathetic, and helpful base for its operation. By 1965 the Colombians were supplying nearly all of the cocaine moving through Cuban trafficking networks. By the early 1970s, the Colombians had gained control over the cocaine producers in Peru and Bolivia and the refineries in Chile and were challenging the dominance of the Cubans in the U.S. drug trade.[16] The Colombians bought cocaine paste from Bolivian and Peruvian suppliers and used chemicals manufactured and supplied by U.S. and European companies to refine the paste in clandestine laboratories hidden in remote areas of Colombia before shipping the finished product to Florida and the U.S. market.

The Colombians started small, paying individuals to carry cocaine on regular commercial flights in shoe heels or sewn into linings of coats or suitcases. By the 1970s, they would revolutionize the way drugs were smuggled into the United States from Latin America. So successful did the Colombians become in drug trafficking that by the early 1980s cocaine had supplanted coffee as Colombia's number-one foreign exchange earner.[17]

While marijuana had became the most popular illegal drug in the 1970s, and an increasing number of Americans had begun experimenting freely with cocaine, LSD, and other so-called "psychedelic" drugs, heroin use was once again on the rise, spreading from the poor inner cities to the middle class, predominantly neighborhoods of suburbia and threatening to reach epidemic proportions. Between 1960 and 1970 the number of heroin users in the United States rose from 40,000 to 500,000. Among the users were many GIs who had become addicted to heroin while serving in Vietnam.[18] By 1971, an estimated 25,000 to 37,000 American soldiers in Vietnam were using heroin, with about 14 percent of them addicted to the drug.[19]

Fred Hickey, a helicopter pilot in Vietnam in the early 1970s told Staney Karnow, a journalist and historian of the Vietnam War, that almost entire American units, including officers, were using heroin and other drugs. "The majority of people were high all the time," Hickey recalled. "For ten dollars you could get a vial of pure heroin the size of a cigarette butt, and you could get liquid opium, speed, acid, anything you wanted. You could trade a box of Tide for a carton of prepackaged, pre-rolled marijuana cigarettes soaked in opium."[20]

Top Vietnamese government officials, including Prime Minister Nguyen Kao Ky and his successor General Tran Thien Khiem, were reportedly involved in the heroin trade. "Periodic attempts by American agents to smash the elaborate smuggling network were thwarted by their superiors in the U.S. mission, since a crackdown would have exposed nearly every prominent member of the Saigon regime," Karnow revealed.[21]

Investigations have shown that the U.S. government, through its

Central Intelligence Agency (CIA), shared responsibility in getting American soldiers in Vietnam addicted to heroin. Not only was the CIA involved in covering up for its drug-trafficking allies in Southeast Asia, the agency was also actively engaged in the transportation and distribution of heroin.[22]

The heroin traffic in Southeast Asia centered in the Golden Triangle, an area of rugged terrain occupying parts of Laos, Thailand, and Burma, which today, says the DEA, supplies 70 percent of the world's heroin and opium. First the French during their colonial rule of Southeast Asia and then the CIA during the Vietnam War supported the warlords in the area as allies and a buffer against communist expansion in the region and turned a blind eye to their involvement in the cultivation and trafficking of the local opium crop.[23]

The 1964 coup that toppled South Vietnam president Ngo Dinh Diem gave a big boost to the narcotics trade in the Golden Triangle, because corrupt South Vietnam government officials and generals were given a free hand to use Vietnamese and Laotian planes, paid for by the U.S. government, to ship heroin from the Golden Triangle. Once the loads arrived in South Vietnam, the traffickers bribed corrupt customs officials not to inspect the bags and bundles carrying the heroin.[24] Later, after the United States invaded Cambodia in 1970, the heroin was carried from the Golden Triangle to Cambodia by mule and then flown or shipped to South Vietnam.[25]

Around 1968, Hong Kong chemists, under the protection of the CIA's local allies, including the commander in chief of the Royal Laotian Army, opened heroin laboratories in the Golden Triangle that produced large quantities of a new kind of 90 percent pure heroin called Number Four. This heroin was ideal for injecting and was superior in quality to the type of heroin being sold at the time in the United States, which was only 25 to 50 percent pure. By the early 1970s, GIs were spending an estimated $88 million a year on heroin and bringing their habit home with them once they had finished their tour of duty.[26] A 1973 survey revealed that the U.S. heroin trade was worth $4 billion, making it the country's "largest single consumer import."[27]

As late as 1971 the official U.S. response was to blame the Communists for the drug trade in Southeast Asia, and as of this writing, the CIA was still denying any involvement. Given the covert nature of the CIA, and the fact that there has been little government oversight of the agency, it has been difficult to prove the CIA connection with international drug trafficking. But as Alfred J. McCoy, author of the classic *Politics of Heroin:*

CIA Complicity in the Global Drug Trade, explained, "those who look for the CIA officers to actually dirty their hands with drugs during the line of duty are missing the point. In most covert actions, the CIA avoids direct involvement in combat or espionage and instead works through local clients whose success often determines the outcome of an ongoing operation. Thus the CIA's involvement in the drug trade revolves around the indirect complicity in the drug dealing of its assets, not in any direct complicity in the actual traffic."[28]

It would not be the last time there would be "indirect complicity" on the part of the CIA in the international narcotics trade. Later, the agency would be accused of involvement in the narcotics traffic in Afghanistan and Central America and of fueling the demand for crack in the United States, and critics would continue to charge that the CIA, in the name of anticommunism, had become part of the problem, not the solution in America's vaunted War on Drugs.

The country's growing heroin epidemic did catch the attention of President Richard Nixon, who on June 17, 1971, made a major television speech in which he said, "America has now the largest number of heroin addicts of any nation in the world... If we cannot destroy the drug menace in America, then it will surely destroy us."[29] Nixon's speech marked a major turning point for the U.S. government's attitude toward illegal drugs and international drug trafficking. As Catherine Lamour and Michael R. Lamberti explained, "Thereafter, the battle against narcotics was regarded by Washington as one of the most urgent items in the American political program, and concrete measures were put in hand so as to convince the country that the Republican administration was not simply making a promise."[30]

Among the several measures implemented, Nixon established the Cabinet Committee on International Narcotics Control (CCINC) and a narcotics policy and narcotics trafficking program within the International Revenue Service (IRS). Chaired by the secretary of state, the CCINC had responsibility for "developing a strategy to check the illegal flow of narcotics in the U.S. and coordinating the efforts undertaken abroad by involving federal departments and agencies to implement that strategy."[31]

In 1972, Nixon established the Office for Drug Abuse Law Enforcement (ODALE) within the Department of Justice under a director who was to advise the president on how to improve the effectiveness of federal antidrug enforcement and help state and local governments improve their antidrug efforts. Several months later, the president established the

Office of National Narcotic Intelligence (ONNI) within the Department of Justice to collect and disseminate narcotics intelligence to federal, state, and local officials who had a "legitimate official use" for it.[32] In 1968 Nixon had created the Bureau of Narcotics and Dangerous Drugs with only 60 agents and a budget of $14 million. By the end of 1972, the number of agents had tripled and the budget had increased fourfold.[33] The following year, Nixon reorganized the federal law enforcement machinery and established the Drug Enforcement Administration (DEA), which was to become the point agency on the U.S. War on Drugs.

At the international level, Nixon summoned his ambassadors from France, Turkey, and Mexico and told them to help their foreign counterparts move more aggressively against international drug trafficking. He also signed the 1971 Convention on Psychotropic Substances, which extended control measures over hallucinogens, amphetamines, barbiturates, and tranquilizers not previously covered by international treaties.[34]

Congress reacted to Nixon's call for a war on drugs by passing the Drug Abuse and Treatment Act of 1972, which its supporters touted as an important milestone in the history of drug abuse legislation because it "called for a balanced response to the problem of drug abuse by adding a vigorous prevention and treatment program to the existing law enforcement effort." But as the 1984 President's Commission on Organized Crime later pointed out, "although commitments to the 'balanced' response were enshrined in the 1972 Drug Abuse Office Act ... they have not generally been translated into action, as measured by budget authorizations and expenditures."[35] In other words, Nixon and future U.S. presidents would focus on the interdiction of illegal drugs, not treatment and prevention, as their prime strategy against international drug trafficking

Initially, the Nixon administration did have some success, particularly against heroin. In 1971 the United States began pressuring Turkey, Mexico, and Southeast Asia's Golden Triangle to eradicate their opium crops. The famous French Connection, which was dominated by Sicilian and Corsican drug trafficking organizations, supplied about 80 percent of the heroin entering the U.S. via a smuggling route stretching from Turkey to Marseilles and southern France, where chemists, working in hidden laboratories, converted the raw opium to a type of heroin called "China White" before traffickers shipped the finished product to the United States. By 1973 the French government had shut down the laboratories in southern France, and Turkey, supported by $20 million in U.S. aid, had convinced its farmers to switch from poppies to alternative crops. The heroin sold in the United States dropped in purity to half what it was, while the price of heroin in New York City, the drug's principal market, tripled, an indication that heroin was in short supply. In September 1973, Nixon told the American people: "We have turned the corner on drug addiction."[36]

Nixon's declaration proved to be premature, for the basic principle of supply and demand once again went to work. Trafficking syndicates in southeast Asia filled the gap left by the dismantling of the French Connection's laboratories, while opium production quickly shifted to new centers. As Alfred J. McCoy and Alan A. Block noted, "During the next ten years, drug trafficking syndicates simply shifted their resources — from Turkey to Southeast Asia to Mexico, and then to Southeast Asia (again) — remaining one step ahead of U.S. diplomats and drug agents."[37] Amsterdam replaced Marseilles as the center of the European heroin trade and new trafficking syndicates — the Triads, Colombians, and African Americans, among others — arose to plug the heroin distribution pipeline. The heroin trade subsequently expanded in the U.S. from New York City as the sole major distribution point to Miami, Chicago, and Los Angeles. Ironically, the French Connection may have revived during the late 1970s, when law enforcement noted that the heroin processing labs had reappeared in southern France, staffed by the same employees who worked in the original French Connection's labs a decade earlier.[38] Nixon's get-tough strategy had misfired. Demand increased and international drug trafficking continued to expand the supply network.

While Nixon got tough on illegal drugs, public support grew for decriminalization of marijuana. In 1972 the Consumer Union declared, "Marijuana is here to stay. No conceivable law enforcement program can curb its availability."[39] The same year, a presidential commission, the National Commission on Marijuana and Drug Abuse and chaired by former Republican governor of Pennsylvania Raymond P. Shafer, called for federal decriminalization of marijuana. The commission's report concluded that "society should seek to discourage use, while concentrating its attention on the prevention and treatment on heavy and very heavy use. The commission feels that the criminalization of possession of marijuana for personal use is socially self-defeating as a means of achieving this objective."[40]

In 1973 Oregon became the first state in the Union to decriminalize marijuana, making the use of the drug a "violation," comparable to a parking ticket. In all, eleven states eventually followed Oregon's lead, decriminalizing the possession and use of marijuana in private by adults.[41] Two years later, a task force organized by President Gerald Ford published a white paper that concluded that not all drugs were equally dangerous and that law enforcement should concentrate on suppressing the traffic in heroin, amphetamines, and mixed barbiturates.[42] The drive to decriminalize marijuana continued during Jimmy Carter's presidential administration when Senator Jacob Javits and representative Edward Koch introduced a bill in Congress that was based on the rationale that it was undesirable and impractical to try to imprison more than 13 million marijuana users, which the United States was estimated to have.[43]

Although the white paper did not mention cocaine, many in the federal government felt it was a dangerous drug that should be suppressed. In 1973 the National Commission on Marijuana and Drug Abuse recommended that the federal government try to "reduce the legitimate cocaine production in this country (including the import of coca leaves for purposes of extracting cocaine) to the minimum quantities needed for domestic research and medical uses. If not required, the government should eliminate the manufacture all together. In addition, the U.S should work through diplomatic channels to persuade other countries not to manufacture cocaine for export."[44]

The Ford administration continued the interdiction strategy begun by Richard Nixon. From the 1930s to 1975, Mexico supplied nearly all the marijuana used in the United States, but in a joint effort, U.S. and Mexican authorities began using the potent herbicide paraquat to eradicate the Mexican crop. The program created an uproar in the United States because paraquat poisoned but did not destroy the marijuana crop and many Americans who used Mexican marijuana got sick. The program did prove successful, though, in that many American marijuana users became reluctant to smoke Mexican marijuana and its overall use declined. By 1979 Mexico supplied only about 11 percent of the marijuana for the U.S market and that figure declined to just 4 percent by 1981. The United States launched a similar eradication program in Jamaica, the supplier of about 9 percent of the American marijuana supply. This effort was successful as well, eliminating the country from the American marijuana trade for a number of years.[45]

American drug consumers, though, would not have to worry about a shortage of marijuana. Colombian criminal syndicates, which had been minor players in the marijuana trade since the 1960s, moved in to fill the vacuum. A government report described what happened: "Once the Colombians established a position as major marijuana traffickers, their role in the trade expanded rapidly. By 1975, airstrips capable of handling heavy 4-engine planes with the capacity to hold one ton of marijuana were common along the Guajara Peninsula (the area in Colombia where marijuana was grown). Load facilities for "mother ships," large vessels capable of transporting tons of marijuana dotted the coast. By the early 1980s, a congressional committee estimated that between 50,000 and 60,000 tons of marijuana were exported from that country to the United States each year."[46]

Jorge Luis Ochoa Vasquez, druglord and founding member of the Medellín drug cartel forces.

Later, in the early 1980s, as Reagan intensified the War on Drugs, U.S. authorities persuaded Colombia to eradicate its crop, but the country's reduced production was offset by increased cultivation and trafficking in Mexico and Jamaica. By 1984 the President's Commission on Organized Crime was cautioning that "Mexico, now ranked third in the world marijuana production, could be the leading producer in 1986, given a Mexican bumper crop and continuing eradication in Colombia."[47] In the ten-year period, the U.S. marijuana interdiction effort had come full circle.

Early in the Carter administration, the federal government's antidrug policy changed. At the March 1977 House of Representatives hearings on decriminalization, the chief of the Department of Justice testified that the federal government could no longer effectively prosecute marijuana and admitted, "nor do we, in any conceivable way, in the Federal Government, have the resources to do so."[48] The Carter administration also was softening its position on cocaine. Dr. Peter Bourne, the president's director of the Office of Drug Abuse Policy (ODAP), described cocaine as "probably the most benign of illicit drugs currently in widespread use. At least as strong a case could be made for legalizing it as for legalizing marijuana. Short acting — not physically addicting — cocaine has found increasing favor at all socioeconomic levels."[49]

Bourne's analysis was at least partly true. Cocaine, like heroin and marijuana before it, was beginning to hit the American mainstream in a big way. Many musicians, intellectuals, artists, politicians, and government bureaucrats saw nothing wrong with snorting the drug. In 1978 the White House was embarrassed by a story in the *Washington Post* that alleged that Peter Bourne himself used cocaine at a party.[50] The good doctor resigned, but before leaving his post, he had set the tone for the Carter administration's drug policy. "Deciding that imprisonment was worse than narcotics use and that international intervention would not slow the drug flow, the Carter White House adopted a more cautious policy," Alfred McCoy and Alan Block explained. "With the exception of comparatively modest suppression operations against opium in Mexico, Carter de-emphasized the CIA and restrained its covert operations during its first three years in office."[51]

By December 1979, however, the Carter administration was worrying about the Soviet invasion of Afghanistan and began shipping arms to the Mujahideen guerrillas. Not all Carter officials agreed with the administration's Afghanistan policy. Dr. David Musto and Joyce Lowinson, members of the White House Strategy Council on Drug Abuse, wrote an op-ed article for the *New York Times* expressing their concern about the growing of opium poppies in Pakistan and Afghanistan by rebel tribesmen. "Are we erring in befriending these tribes as we did in Laos which Air America (chartered by the Central Intelligence Agency) helped transport crude opium from certain tribal areas?" asked Musto and Lowinson.[52]

The answer is yes, said Alfred McCoy. He believed that the evidence shows that Afghan heroin had begun flooding the U.S. market in 1979, substantially increasing the number of hardcore addicts, as well as overdose deaths, in the early 1980s. "Although the drug epidemic of the 1980s had complex causes, the growth in the global heroin supply could be traced in large part to two key aspects of U.S. policy: the failure of the DEA interdiction efforts and the CIA's covert operations," McCoy concluded. "[J]ust as the CIA support of nationalist Chinese troops in Shan States had increased Burma's opium crop in the 1950s, so the agency's aid to the Mujahideen guerrillas in the 1980s expanded opium production in Afghanistan and linked Pakistan's nearby heroin laboratories to the world market. After a decade as the sites of major CIA covert operations, Burma and Afghanistan ranked respectively as the world's largest and second largest suppliers for illicit heroin in 1989."[53]

By 1980 the United States had little to show for its get-tough antidrug policy. During the Nixon administration, budget for the U.S. antidrug program had increased significantly and drug enforcement infrastructure underwent a major reorganization to provide the leadership in the War on Drugs and to reduce interagency rivalries, but one of the federal agencies, the CIA, had helped fuel drug use in the United States by helping allies in Southeast Asia and possibly Afghanistan who were heavily involved in international drug trafficking. The federal government had tried eradication programs in Turkey and Mexico, but sources for heroin and marijuana had sprung up in other countries and drugs continued to flow freely into the United States. During the 1970s, the U.S. government put antidrug policies in place in cocaine source countries, such as Peru and Colombia, and in the transit countries of the Caribbean and Central America, but they were small and ineffective, since the United States concentrated most of its attention and resources on heroin during the decade. Meanwhile, the ambitious criminal cartels based in the Colombian cities of Cali and Medellín were poised for their big entrance on the international drug trafficking scene in which they would make cocaine the drug of the 1980s. This abysmal record led the 1984 President's Commission on Organized Crime to conclude that "the nation's drug problem at the end of 1980 was as great, if not greater, than the problem in 1970."[54]

Chapter 5

Full of Sound and Fury, 1980–1990

"We are serious about your active role in the war on drugs, even if it means we have to drag you screaming every step of the way."

— Rep. Larry Hopkins (R–Ky.)

"The only law that the narco terrorists don't break is the law of supply and demand."

— Virgilio Barco, former president of Colombia

Despite the failures of the 1970s, the Reagan administration pushed ahead in the early 1980s with a hard-line agenda for the War on Drugs that emphasized military action. In launching his war on drugs in 1982, the president reorganized the chain of command and sent an impressive array of military hardware, intelligence, and other resources to South Florida and the front line in the drug battle. It was not a unilateral decision, for Congress strongly supported the Reagan administration's actions, and calls for a tougher stance on the War on Drugs came from a variety of legislative sources, including the powerful House Foreign Affairs Committee and the House Select Committee on Narcotics Control.

After its initial response and outlay of resources, the Reagan administration pushed further antidrug measures through Congress. The 1982 Department of Defense Authorization Act contained a provision titled "Military Cooperation with Civilian Law Enforcement Officials," which was designed to codify the cooperative practices that had developed between the military and civil law enforcement authorities. Specifically, the provision clarified precisely the kind of assistance the military could give civilian drug enforcement agencies and the type of military equipment the civilian agencies could use. The rationale for the provision, which substantially increased the interdiction capability of federal drug law enforcement agencies, was to foster cooperation between the military and civilian law enforcement because "only through the additional work of all federal, state and local law enforcement agencies can we begin to stem this tide."[1] Although the legislation's sponsors cautioned that "we must recognize the need to maintain the traditional balance of authority between civilian and the military,"[2] the focus of the U.S. antidrug policy had changed significantly, and, as Professor Bruce Bagley explained, U.S. policy "was no longer based purely on health concerns but on criminal factors where significant profits were being 'earned' by criminal organizations."[3]

In 1984 Congress passed the Comprehensive Crime Control Act, an important piece of legislation containing several provisions designed to strengthen interdiction efforts of U.S. drug law enforcement. The Aviation Drug Trafficking Control Act, for example, amended the Federal Aviation Act of 1958 and allowed the Federal Aviation Administration (FAA) to revoke the pilot's license of anyone violating federal and state law relating to controlled substances, except for offenses involving possession of drugs.[4] The Controlled Substances Registration Protection Act of 1984, among other measures, strengthened the penalties for those who steal controlled substances from pharmacists. "The effective regulation of the commerce in controlled substances has resulted in very high prices for drugs on the black market," the 1984 President's Commission on Organized Crime wrote, in explaining the act's rationale. "As a consequence theft of controlled substances from registrants has become a common yet serious problem. The frequency of these crimes has terrorized the community of dispensing pharmacists. Some pharmacists have ceased to carry drugs that are highly desired on the black market, although this interferes with their patients' ability to obtain necessary medicine. This has a serious potential to impede the delivery of health care around the nation."[5]

Other provisions of the comprehensive crime legislation package included the Bail Reform Act of 1984, which made it more difficult for accused drug offenders to stay out on bail; the Comprehensive Forfeiture Act of 1984, designed to "eliminate limitations and ambiguities" that "have significantly impaired the full realization of forfeiture's potential as a powerful law enforcement tool"; the Controlled Substances Amendment Act; the Dangerous Drug Division Control Act; and the Currency and Foreign Transactions Reporting Act Amendments.[6]

While Congress was passing the Comprehensive Crime Control Act of 1984, U.S. authorities were seizing more illegal drugs than ever before, according to DEA statistics. In 1984 law enforcement confiscated 27,525 pounds of cocaine and 664 pounds of heroin, as compared to 1,438 pounds of cocaine and 123 pounds of heroin in 1979, respectively twentyfold and fivefold increases in five years. The amount of marijuana seized actually decreased from the 1979 figure, but that trend appeared to end the following year.[7] The stats looked impressive, but U.S. Customs officials admitted they were confiscating only about 15 percent of the drugs pouring into the United States. "More drugs are being confiscated because more drugs are crossing the U.S. border," explained John Cusak, chief of the House Narcotics Committee staff, who put the War on Drugs in perspective: "We are doing good work, but it doesn't mean we are winning the war."[8]

With the emphasis on interdiction of drugs in Latin America, the focus of the War on Drugs shifted from heroin to cocaine and marijuana, drugs the Reagan administration believed Americans were using the most. But by the mid 1980s, the United States was having to deal with another dangerous drug. Crack, the most potent and addictive — and certainly the cheapest — form of cocaine, had begun appearing in the inner cities of Miami, Los Angeles, and New York City and was spreading across America to other cities. Crime rates were beginning to soar to record levels in the inner city, as gang warfare raged between drug dealers determined to protect their turf in the lucrative drug trade. This new development heightened the public's concern about the impact of illegal drugs and led President Reagan to react in predictable fashion. He increased the funding for the drug war from $1.5 billion in 1981 to $2.75 billion in 1986 and pushed for the passage of the 1986 Anti-Drug Abuse Act, which not only authorized $1.7 billion in additional money to fight drug abuse, but also provided for prison sentences for drug dealers who either sold drugs near schools or recruited young people to peddle them.[9]

While the United States intensified its antidrug effort at home, the War on Drugs heated up overseas. During the 1970s, Colombian drug traffickers had operated throughout Colombia without much interference from the authorities, but by 1984 Colombia was under pressure from the United States to change its laissez-faire ways and begin to get tough on the traffickers. Rodrigo Lara Bonilla, Colombia's Minister of Justice, reopened the case that involved Pablo Escobar's arrest in 1976 on drug possession charges. The investigation had been terminated because the case file had "mysteriously been misplaced." Later, the two police officers who had arrested Escobar were murdered. The press reported on the case, and Escobar, who was then serving as an alternate congressman and had higher political aspirations, suddenly found himself in the harsh uncomfortable glare of public scrutiny. Escobar sued Lara for libel, claiming, "I'm a victim of a persecution campaign," but he eventually dropped out of politics.[10] Lara began to receive death threats, but experiencing some success against the powerful cartels, he was determined to go after Escobar and his associates.

Lara authorized the spectacular raid on the major cocaine-processing plant known as Tranquilandia, located in Colombia's desolate southeast Llanos region in the Amazon. Learning of a major shipment to Colombia of ether (the most important chemical in the production of cocaine), the DEA secretly attached radio transmitters to two of the drums in the shipment and followed the signal by satellite from Chicago to the Amazon and Tranquilandia. The raid caught the plant by surprise. Forty workers were arrested, 10,000 barrels of chemicals were seized, and more than $1 billion in cocaine was confiscated, although Medellín drug lord Carlos Lehder, one of the plant's managers, escaped. The confiscated cocaine was half the amount that had been seized by authorities the entire previous year. Johnny Phelps, DEA chief in Colombia, jubilantly described the plant as the "silicon valley" of cocaine. It was history's most spectacular drug raid, and soon afterward the wholesale price of cocaine per kilo began to rise, an indication that the raid had hurt the Medellín cartel's cocaine supplies.

The raid angered the Medellín cartel, which was determined to get even with those responsible. Colombian police warned Lara that there was a plot to kill him, but the minister didn't take it seriously enough. In an August news release, he boasted, "I'm a dangerous minister for those who act outside the law," but added, "I only hope they don't take me by surprise."[11] Unfortunately for Lara, the traffickers did so a few weeks later, machine-gunning him to death on a residential Bogotá street. Earlier, Colombian president Belisario Betancur Cuertas had refused to sign papers presented to him by Lara, which would have initiated extradition proceedings against Escobar, Lehder, and some of the other Medellín cartel leaders wanted in the U.S. on drug-trafficking charges. Six days after Lara was murdered, however, Betancur signed the order for Carlos Lehder's extradition and declared a war "without quarter" on all Colombian drug traffickers.

Lehder and his cartel associates went into hiding and moved their processing operations to neighboring countries and the United States.

The Colombian authorities continued the pressure and more plants were found and destroyed. In 1984 21 processing plants were discovered and destroyed in South Florida alone, compared to just 11 in 1983.[12] The Medellín cartel retaliated, bombing the U.S. embassy eight months after Lara's death, and on November 17, 1986, they killed another important figure in Colombia's antidrug effort, Jaime Ramírez Gomez, head of the narcotics unit of the Colombian National Police. There was even a rumor that the Medellín cartel had sent a hit squad to the United States to kill top U.S. drug-enforcement officials.[13]

Betancur engaged the resources of the Colombian armed forces and declared a State of Siege, under whose rules civilians charged with a narcotics offense could be tried by

Luis Carlos Galan, a Colombian presidential candidate who was murdered by drug traffickers in 1989 (courtesy Colombian Antinarcotics Police).

court-martial. Like their counterparts in the United States, the Colombian military, at least at this stage of the War on Drugs, were reluctant warriors. As General Paul Gorman explained at the time, "Colombian military leaders view the propensity of their President to throw them into the anti-narcotics campaign with deep misgivings. The last time they responded to a government mandate to roundup narcotraficantes, the criminals responded by buying officers, and in some instances, whole units. The resultant corruption almost destroyed professional cohesion."[14]

In a show of solidarity, Reagan and Betancur met in April 1985 and agreed to "fight against drug trafficking at all levels." Reagan said the United States would continue to interdict drug trafficking but at the same time would fight drugs on all fronts, "taking away drugs from the consumers through increased efforts to diminish the use and demand of drugs and by destroying crops abroad."[15]

More impressive raids followed. From July to November 1986, Bolivia, with the help of the U.S. military, launched a major assault against drug trafficking that became known as Operation Blast Furnace.

Several cocaine-producing facilities were destroyed and the supply of cocaine was disrupted for several months. Between 1984 and 1986, the amount of cocaine seized in raids rose, from just 2 tons of cocaine in 1981 to 27 tons in 1986, and if statistics were the sole measure of success, it appeared that the forces for good were winning the drug war.

The death of college basketball star Len Bias in 1986 from a cocaine overdose shocked the country, riveted public attention on drug abuse, and sent Congress in the months leading up to the 1986 elections on a drug-bashing frenzy, as legislators competed to see who could be the toughest warrior in the War on Drugs. The increase in attention on drug abuse also spurred the Reagan administration to step up its antidrug offensive. In a major television address on September 14, 1986, the president called for "zero tolerance" toward everybody involved with drugs, including casual users of any illegal drug. Casual users shared responsibility for the violence and crime resulting from the international drug trade, Reagan told the American public. In October 1986, Congress passed and Reagan signed the 1986 Anti-Drug Abuse Act, which authorized $1.7 billion in additional money to fight drug abuse and international drug trafficking and increased once again the prison sentences for dealers, providing for mandatory sentences for drug dealing. In assessing the impact of the legislation, Professor Bagley wrote, "Without question, this new law represents the most comprehensive effort in modern history to reduce the flow of narcotics from the Third World into the United States."[16]

While calling for resolve in the War on Drugs, Reagan was still much concerned about the Cold War and communist expansion. By 1986 his administration was heavily involved in covert operations to topple the Marxist Sandinista regime in Nicaragua, which had taken power in 1979, through training and financing the Nicaraguan rebels known as Contra forces. To justify his Central American policy, the president tried to link the two wars. "The link between the governments of such Soviet allies as Cuba and Nicaragua and international narcotics trafficking and terrorism is becoming increasingly clear," Reagan told the American people. "These twin ends — narcotics trafficking and terrorism — represents the most insidious and dangerous threats to the hemisphere today."[17]

By the mid 1980s there appeared to be no quick end to the fighting in Nicaragua, and increasing U.S. involvement had raised fears about a Vietnam style war. Certain that Congress would cut military aid to the Contras, the Reagan administration began earnestly developing covert sources of money and arms for the Contras. Oliver North, a staff mem-

An agent of the Colombian Antinarcotics Police carry a boy wounded by a drug traffickers' bomb to safety in Bogotá in 1993 (courtesy Colombian Antinarcotics Police).

ber of the National Security Council, created an operation called "The Enterprise," which used various U.S. and Latin American connections to funnel arms and equipment to the Contras.[18]

Rumors circulated about weapon shipments being flown to the Contras and how, on return flights from Nicaragua, drugs were being sent to the United States, no questions asked. Southern Air Transport, a Miami-based cargo airline that had ties to the CIA, was suspected of involvement in the Contra arms-for-drugs network. In press interviews, drug smugglers claimed they had worked with the Contras. Smuggler

Jorge Morales, who had been indicted in March 1989, said that the CIA had approached him with a deal in which they would take care of his legal problems and allow him to fly drugs into the United States if he would fly arms to the Contras.[19]

Public pressure for an investigation of the allegations mounted, and the Senate Subcommittee on Terrorism, Narcotics and International Operations of the Foreign Relations Committee initiated hearings under the leadership of Senator John F. Kerry (D–Mass.). In the so-called Kerry Commission hearings evidence once again came to light that the U.S. government had turned a blind eye to the involvement of their anti-communist allies in the drug trade and that CIA-sponsored covert operations were "entangled" with criminal activities such as drug smuggling. The subcommittee found that "substantial evidence of drug smuggling through the war zones on the part of individual countries, Latin suppliers, Contra pilots and mercenaries who worked with the Contras and Contra supporters throughout the region" and concluded that "U.S. officials involved in Latin America failed to address the drug issue for fear of jeopardizing the war efforts against Nicaragua." Once again, the objectives of War on Drugs had been subordinated to other foreign policy interests.[20]

By 1988, Reagan's last year in office, the United States had little to show for its much-hyped War on Drugs. On the contrary, events and statistics showed that the war effort had been marked by inconsistent leadership, conflicting priorities, bureaucratic infighting, and inadequate resources.

First Lady Nancy Reagan had launched a much-publicized "Just Say No" campaign but, despite the propaganda, many Americans were willing to risk jail and public opprobrium in the pursuit of illegal drugs. The United States still had an estimated 5.8 million regular users of cocaine and 20 to 25 million marijuana smokers, another half a million heroin users, all together spending about $150 billion a year on illegal drugs.[21] The U.S prison population rose from 329,821 in 1980 to 627,402 in 1988, making the United States the country with the largest proportion of its population kept behind bars.[22] The authorities were confiscating more cocaine than ever, but between 1981 and 1988, the price of a kilogram of pure cocaine had actually fallen, a development that showed that supply was still strong. Government reports in 1987 by the General Accounting Office and the House Committee on Government Operations found the U.S. drug policy to be "diffuse and overlapping."[23] Reagan's fiscal 1988 budget request called for the elimination of nearly $1 billion from the budgeted drug war allocations, and as a result U.S. allies in the War on Drugs were not receiving adequate financial support from Uncle Sam.[24] "We're being left to fight the war alone," complained Francisco Bernal, head of Colombia's narcotics bureau in the office of the attorney general. "We're supplying the dead, the country is being destabilized, and what help are we getting?"[25]

Critics of the War on Drugs noted the huge gap between action and result and concluded that it had failed badly to attain its objectives. "No president has spent more against drugs than President Reagan," wrote one of the critics. "No president has signed more anti-drug treaties or spent more money to stem the flow of drugs into this country. But as the Reagan years drew to a close, American law enforcement officials acknowledge that they are losing ground in the fight against a new generation of drug smugglers who have the business skill—and capital—to threaten not only the streets of America but even the stability of countries long friendly to the United States."[26]

By 1988 a small but influential group of distinguished Americans began to criticize the objectives of the War on Drugs. The dissenters came from across the political spectrum and a variety of backgrounds and included economist Milton Friedman, writer and arch-conservative William Buckley, Baltimore mayor Kurt Schmoke, and the editors of the influential *Economist* magazine, among others. "By 1988 it had long been decided by numerous observers that the seventy-four years of federal prohibition since the passage of the Harrison Act of 1914 was not only costly ... but a totally doomed effort as well," wrote James Inciardi. "It was argued that drug laws and drug enforcement had served mainly to create enormous profits for drug dealers and traffickers, overcrowded jails, police and other government corruption, a distorted foreign policy, predatory street crime carried on by users in search of the necessary funds to purchase black market drugs, and urban areas harassed by street-level drug dealers and terrorized by violent groups."[27]

These critics, however, did not sway the leaders of the War on Drugs, who continued to pursue a military solution and optimistically predicted that victory was just around the corner, if only American resolve remained firm and enough resources were applied to the problem. They pointed to the statistics that showed increased arrests, overflowing prisons, massive cocaine seizures, the killing or kidnapping of drug kingpins, and declining drug use and insisted, in the words of drug czar William Bennett, that "the scourge is beginning to end."[28]

The United States did not win a single lasting victory against international drug trafficking during the Reagan administration, but this did not deter the next U.S. president, George Bush, from publicly renewing the U.S. pledge to wage the War on Drugs and continuing the same policy. Public opinion polls showed that Americans wanted their political leaders to get even tougher on illegal drugs and combat the increasing drug-related violence in many American cities, and George Bush was certainly not going to disappoint the voters. Congress responded by adopting measures that further militarized the country's antidrug effort. The U.S. military was given a much broader role, despite continuing opposition from many military leaders, who felt that the new policy would divert the armed forces from its primary role of defending U.S. interests abroad against such forces as Communism and terrorism. Congress approved and Bush appointed a "drug czar" as a kind of top commander in the War on Drugs who would have direct access to the president. The first czar, William Bennett, a conservative former philosophy professor, revealed his antidrug plan in the summer of 1989. Bennett called for an even tougher stance against the enemy: more federal agents, more prosecutors, more judges to hear more cases, and more federal prisons to hold more drug offenders. Instead of interdicting drugs at the border, Bennett proposed interdicting drugs in the countries where they were grown and on the streets of America where they were consumed. The Bennett plan called for $7 billion a year in funds, but the czar projected that, if given the money, the United States would reduce drug use in the country by 10 percent within 25 months and by 50 percent within a decade.[29] How exactly that would happen was not spelled out.

In unveiling his National Drug Control Strategy in September 1989, Bush endorsed Bennett's plan of action and proposed that 70 percent of the $2.2 billion additional money allocated to the drug issue over the next several years be spent on law enforcement. Bush also urged Congress to give more military and economic assistance to Andean countries to help stem the flow of cocaine to the United States. "In the past, programs have been hampered by the lack of importance given by this country to the drug issue as a foreign policy concern," Bush declared. "We must develop ... a broad, meaningful public diplomacy program in a manner that would increase the level of international support programs for illicit drugs."[30]

The militarization of the War on Drugs, begun by Reagan in 1982, reached a climax in the 1989 invasion of Panama and the capture of the country's dictator General Manuel Antonio Noriega, who had been indicted in U.S. court for alleged involvement in international drug trafficking. The United States knew about the general's drug-smuggling activities for nearly two decades but had tolerated them because, as a paid employee of the CIA since at least 1967, he had been a useful intelligence source. Norman Bailey, former National Security Council official, testified at the Contra hearings that "clear and incontrovertible evidence was, at best ignored, and at worst, hidden and denied by many different agencies and departments of government of the United States in such a way as to provide cover and protection for Noriega's activities."[31]

José Blandon, a former Noriega aide, testified before Congress that "When they [the Medellín cartel] have a problem with someone who hadn't paid, then they turn the matter over to the DEA. So their work is to keep the DEA happy [giving] up those people they do not want." The DEA response?—"Panama authorities have always provided their full cooperation in every request made by the DEA."[32] While maintaining close ties to the CIA, Noriega also had a long, friendly, and profitable relationship with the Medellín cartel. At his trial in the United States in 1988, drug kingpin Carlos Lehder testified that the cartel paid Noriega $1,000 per kilogram of cocaine to allow the drug to be shipped through Panama and on to Costa Rica and Florida, or to Mexico and then to Los Angeles.[33]

The United States nevertheless pulled out the Monroe Doctrine and did what it had done countless other times in its history when facing a problem in its backyard. With a force of 24,000 troops, the United States launched Operation Just Cause — an invasion of Panama that led to the arrest of their former ally and his trial in the United States on drug-trafficking charges.

U.S. officials defended their action arguing that kidnapping was a legitimate strategy that the United States could use to improve its role in the War on Drugs. "Some foreign governments have unfortunately failed to take steps to protect the United States from drug traffickers," said William P. Barr, a deputy attorney general in the U.S. Justice Department's Office of Legal Counsel.[34]

Critics of Operation Just Cause said the United States had actually kidnapped Noriega — a move that violated international law. The United States shouldn't be breaking its own laws abroad, they admonished. "That the DEA and FBI take off the Constitution like an overcoat when they cross the border is unacceptable," said Andreas Lowenfeld, a New York University law school professor.[35]

Professor Lowenfeld was alluding to the fact that the United States

Rodríguez Gacha, a Colombian drug trafficker who died in 1989 (courtesy Colombian Antinarcotics Police).

had kidnapped individuals suspected of drug trafficking and other crimes many times before. In April 1988, for example, drug lord Juan Ramón Matta Ballesteros was kidnapped in Tegucigalpa, Honduras, and hauled back to the United States, where he was convicted of drug trafficking and sentenced to life in prison. Ballesteros was wanted for suspected involvement in the death of DEA agent Enrique Camarena Salazar, whose tortured body was found at a ranch in the state of Michoacan, Mexico, in 1985. Earlier, Mexican authorities has pushed Rene Verdugo-Urquidez, another suspect in the Camerena murder, through a broken fence on the U.S.– Mexican border to waiting DEA agents in Calexico, California. In April 1990 Dr. Humberto Alvarez Machain was abducted from his medical office in Guadalajara, Mexico, by U.S. federal agents and taken across the border to stand trial in the United States for suspected involvement in Camarena's murder. "If Mexico came into [the United States] and kidnapped a U.S. citizen, I can guarantee you two divisions of American troops would be occupying Mexico City today," Alvarez's lawyer told the press.[36]

One reason for the kidnapping policy was the U.S. frustration over the refusal of many countries to extradite suspected drug traffickers to the United States. The United States insisted that extradition was an essential weapon in the War on Drugs, but Colombia, Mexico, Burma, and other source countries considered extradition to be a form of imperialism and an affront to their sovereignty. The legal strategy, moreover, was highly unpopular among the citizens of those countries.

In Colombia, the government of President Virgilio Barco Vargas was seriously considering unilaterally repudiating its 1979 extradition treaty with the United States, when Senator Luis Carlos Galan, presidential candidate for the 1990 Colombian presidential elections and strong opponent of drug trafficking, was killed at a Bogotá rally on August 18, 1989. Minutes after Galan's killing, Barco made a major television address in which he declared all-out war against the drug traffickers and said he would begin extradition proceedings of Colombian drug traffickers wanted abroad.[37] Six days later, Colombia changed its extradition policy. The Medellín cartel's members started calling themselves "the extraditables" and launched a vicious terrorist bombing campaign to force the Colombian government to change its policy. In the week following Barco's declaration, the cartel exploded 20 small bombs in Bogotá, Colombia's capital, and it began targeting prominent Colombians, including their families, for assassination. By the end of October, there had been 200 bombing attacks that left 10 people killed and 160 wounded or injured.[38]

On September 6, 1989, Eduardo Martínez Romero, suspected to be the cartel's chief financial officer, was extradited to the United States under Colombia's new extradition policy. Two more members were to be extradited to the United States, but the courts freed them instead in September. Meanwhile, the terrorist attacks continued, culminating on November 21 with the bombing of a Bogotá-to-Medellín Avianca airlines jet, which killed all 107 passengers and crew members aboard.[39] Under the relentless assault from the Medellín cartel, the Colombian government eventually wilted and changed its policy.

By the beginning of 1990, the United States had escalated the War on Drugs to an unprecedented level. In late 1988 the Bush administration asked the military to "play a major role in helping to interdict drug traffic in the United States, to create an integrated intelligence and communications network, and to train foreign military personnel and both U.S. and foreign police forces."[40] The United States had begun to use its elite special forces, such as the Green Berets, in preemptive strikes against the drug-trafficker enclaves in source countries like Peru and Colombia. The justification was an opinion issued by the Justice Department's Office of Legal Counsel that concluded that U.S. military forces could go overseas and arrest drug dealers and other criminals, even without the consent of the host country.[41]

In September 1989 Secretary of Defense Dick Cheney issued a directive to all military commanders ordering them to develop policies and to play a major role against international drug trafficking. "Detecting and countering the production and trafficking of illegal drugs is a high priority national security mission," Cheney told the military.[42] Under the new policy, the Department of Defense began to assume a new and bigger responsibility in the interdiction of legal drugs at the southern U.S. borders. Congress — not just the presidency — wanted the military to play a more active role in the drug battle. The mood of the legislature was expressed by Representative Larry Hopkins (R–Ky.), who told the Pentagon in early 1989, "We are serious about your active role in this war on drugs, even if it means we have to drag you screaming every step of the way."[43] Times had changed, though, and the military would no longer have to be dragged screaming into a more active participation in the latest U.S. crusade. The Pentagon had changed its position, not just because of pressure from the president and Congress, but also for economic reasons. With the Soviet Union collapsing and becoming less of a threat to U.S. security, Secretary Cheney announced in November 1989 that the administration would be cutting the Department of Defense budget by $180 million over five years.[44] The announcement sent shock waves through the military, which could not but conclude that Congress would continue to reduce military expenditures, manpower, and operational commitments worldwide.

As David Isenberg explained, "Pentagon leadership began arguing that military manpower should not be reduced because Congress is mandating increased military involvement in drug interdiction efforts."[45] General Paul C. Gorman, former head of the U.S. Southern Command in Panama, who earlier had had reservations about the military getting deeply involved in the War on Drugs, now said that "The American people must understand much better than they ever have in the past [that our] safety and that of our children is threatened by Latin drug conspiracies which are dramatically more successful at subversion in the United States than any created in Moscow." The War on Drugs was about to replace the Evil Empire as the bogeyman of U.S. foreign policy.[46]

In December 1989 General Gorman's allegations of conspiracy were extended to include the drug lords of Southeast Asia as well, when a U.S. prosecutor in Brooklyn indicted Khun Sa, Burma's so-called "heroin king," who was the most powerful drug trafficker in Southeast Asia. President Bush was about to open up another front in the 1990s, one that would focus on heroin trafficking.[47]

Drug trafficker Carlos Lehder (left) being extradited to the United States from Colombia in 1987 (courtesy Colombian Antinarcotics Police).

While unable to reduce the supply of cocaine, Bush still claimed that the United States was winning the War on Drugs because statistics purportedly showed cocaine use to be declining dramatically. While many experts on the drug war questioned the validity of the surveys upon which the statistics were based, the drug traffickers took note and changed their marketing plan. "When Bush's campaign reduced the cachet and quantity of illicit cocaine in 1989–90, the drug market filled the void with expanded heroin supplies marketed in a way that appealed to both lower class crack addicts and middle class cocaine users," wrote McCoy and Block.[48] In the 1990s the United States would continue to exercise all the military options it could muster, just as it had done earlier, but supply and demand would be the pivotal mechanism in the War on Drugs. In the words of Colombian president Virgilio Barco Vargas, "The only law that the narco terrorists do not break is the law of supply and demand."[49]

Chapter 6

The Longest War, 1990–1997

"People say the '80s are over, but they must be talking about lifestyles, not narcotics trafficking. Business is booming. Cocaine, heroin and marijuana are dropping out of the sky, being unloaded at sea and being moved up and down rivers and highways."

— Lee Stapleton, chief of narcotics,
U.S. Attorney's Office, Miami

"We are not saying that all drugs be summarily legalized, but every option — including decriminalization — should be considered in dealing with this complex problem that combines crime, public health and social disintegration."

—*San Francisco Chronicle* op-ed article

Both the Reagan and the Bush administrations had often called for a reduction in demand for drugs at home, but in reality the U.S. antidrug strategy during the 1980s and early 1990s had focused heavily on reducing the supply of illegal drugs from abroad through border and offshore interdiction efforts. By 1991 nearly 70 percent of the U.S. antidrug budget went toward reducing supply, particularly cocaine from South America.[1]

Bush's search for a military solution to the War on Drugs was evident in 1989 when he unveiled the so-called "Andean Strategy," a program in which the U.S. would provide some modest military assistance to the source countries of Peru, Colombia, and Bolivia while encouraging them to involve their militaries more in the War on Drugs. Annual U.S assistance to the Andean countries had been about $40 to $50 million, a minuscule amount compared to the billions generated by the region's drug-trafficking industry, but with the Andean strategy in place,

the U.S. antidrug expenditures for South American source countries
increased sevenfold from FY 1989 to 1991.[3]

"The Andean strategy amounted to a broad, triadic program com-
posed of military support, law enforcement advice, and economic assistance for the coca-growing and cocaine-producing countries of Bolivia,
Colombia and Peru," explained Raphael F. Pearl, drug policy analyst. "As
first designed, the strategy represented the culmination of more than a
decade of U.S. anticoca efforts in the region. These various programs had
been systematically impaired, however, by political instability — evident
on occasion in each of the source countries by economic and social
inequities, by a lack of will, by corruption, and also by dubious planning by policy makers in Washington D.C."[4]

To get the support of the Andean countries for his antidrug program and to show he was serious about his Andean initiative, Bush journeyed to Cartagena in February 1990 for a summit meeting with the
leaders of Peru, Colombia, and Bolivia, a move that led to the formation of what has been called "the world's first anti-drug cartel."[5] Participating nations at the summit vowed to attack international drug
trafficking from every angle — economic, political, and military. Bush
pledged to work hard to decrease the demand for drugs in the United
States, while the Andean leaders said they would work equally hard to
reduce drug-related corruption, strengthen the judiciary, and step up law
enforcement efforts against the drug traffickers operating in their countries. The Andean nations urged Bush to create new trade opportunities
that would provide more employment opportunities for workers displaced from the cocaine economy. This was sound advice, said many
drug policy analysts, for without such assistance, military interdiction
would be counterproductive. In a 1993 interview, Professor Bruce Bagley
said that he believed assistance for police and military programs in the
Andean countries needed to be complemented with at least another $200
to $300 million in annual economic assistance; otherwise "U.S. help
may be largely wasted."[6]

To meet his commitment at the Cartagena summit, Bush sent his
Andean trade preference bill to Congress for ratification in July 1990.
Signed into law on December 4, 1994, the Andean Trade Preference Act
(ATPA) was designed to "expand the economic alternatives for the source
countries that had been fighting to eliminate the protection, processing
and shipment of illegal drugs." Specifically, the act gave the president
the authority "to grant duty-free entry to imports of eligible articles
from countries designated as beneficiaries according to criteria set forth

in the act."[7] This economic incentive program was to remain in effect for ten years.

The announcement at the Cartagena summit that the participating countries would share information about the production and distribution of the chemicals used in cocaine production highlighted a problem that was — and still is — at the heart of the cocaine trade. Cocaine manufacturing requires a number of so-called precursor chemicals, such as methyl ethyl acetone and potassium permanganate, and without these key ingredients cocaine could not be made and the trafficking in the drug could not flourish. Or as one writer explained the irony: "Washington has been spending billions trying to keep drugs out of the country while doing little to keep drug-processing chemicals in."[8] From 1982 to 1988, roughly half the precursor chemicals shipped to Andean source countries came from the United States.[9] In 1988 the DEA estimated that as much 10,000 tons of precursor chemicals were shipped to Peru, Bolivia, Ecuador, and Colombia the previous year.[10]

The absence of universal, uniform regulations and the lack of adequate chemical control laws within many countries were two of the big reasons precursor chemicals were getting through to source countries. In 1988 the United States, Europe, and the United Nations moved to address the problem. The United States passed the Chemical Diversion and Trafficking Act of 1988 to monitor and halt the flow of legitimate chemicals into illegal uses by requiring chemical manufacturers, importers, and exporters to maintain records on all transactions involving chemicals considered necessary for cocaine manufacture.[11] In 1988 the UN also adopted the UN Convention Against Illicit Traffic in Narcotics, Drugs and Psychotropic Substances, which established procedures for controlling 12 of the most important chemicals in the manufacture of illegal drugs. Meanwhile, the European Community adopted communitywide chemical control regulations based on the UN convention.[13]

Despite these positive moves, reports still persisted that chemicals manufactured by U.S. chemical companies were getting through to drug source countries. In February 1990, about two weeks before the Cartagena summit, representatives of the U.S. chemical industry went before the U.S. Congress to defend its efforts to stop the diversion of chemicals. In their testimony, spokespersons for the Chemical Manufacturing Association and the Synthetic Manufacturers Association admitted that some U.S. manufactured chemicals were getting into the hands of drug traffickers, but they disagreed about the amount of the chemicals for which the U.S. chemical industry was responsible.[13]

"The U.S. chemical industry does not do business with criminals," Don Coticchia, a spokesman for the Chemical Manufacturers Association, told the Senate.[14] The DEA agreed with Coticchia — up to a point. "Although it is impossible to determine the exact percentage of U.S. chemicals used in the manufacture of cocaine, trade records and intelligence reports indicate that the United States is by far the largest exporter of chemicals to Latin America," said David L. Westrate, a DEA operations assistant administrator.[15]

In October 1991 federal agents raided a split-level house in upstate New York that had been turned into a cocaine-processing laboratory filled with chemicals. It was the first large-scale cocaine lab found in the area in six years, and the authorities took it as a sign that drug traffickers were having to rethink their strategy. Recent intelligence reports on Latin American drug trafficking seemed to indicate that the federal government's steps to limit exports of chemicals needed to make cocaine by American companies was working. The drug traffickers were having trouble getting precursor chemicals shipped to Colombia, and so they were moving their labs out of Colombia, Brazil, Venezuela, and Ecuador and even shipping semirefined cocaine to the United States for final processing.[16]

The move reflected a familiar pattern in the history of the War on Drugs. Every time the major Colombian cocaine cartels started to feel the pressure of interdiction, they would shift their operations to safer locations and develop new transportation routes to move their product. The crackdown by the Colombian government following the assassination of Luis Carlos Galan in 1989 was the major factor in accelerating this trend.[17] In December 1991 the DEA reported that as many as 300 Colombian drug traffickers had moved into the remote jungle areas of northern Bolivia and were taking over the local cocaine trade. In this region near Beni, the Bolivian antidrug police discovered and destroyed what he said was the biggest cocaine laboratory ever found in the country — one capable of producing five tons of cocaine a week.

The Cali cartel has moved into, bought, or rented farms, started corrupting officials and "the whole process of Colombianization has begun," explained DEA Robert Bonner. "These small countries are vulnerable and they know it."[18] The Colombian and Bolivian traffickers in the region got involved in a vicious battle for control of the drug-trafficking region in northern Bolivia, but as one DEA agent revealed, "The Bolivians were getting blown aside."[19]

By the late 1980s the Colombian cartels were no longer moving cocaine primarily through their home country to their U.S. and European markets. Instead, they were developing alternative routes through Brazil, Chile, Argentina, and Paraguay. By 1993 the Latin American distribution network was expanded to include Mexico and Central America.[20] In a short time, the amount of drugs the traffickers were able to move was as impressive as ever. In one antidrug operation in 1994, Nicaraguan authorities netted 606 pounds of cocaine in an initial raid and then uncovered another 386 pounds in a bakery on the outskirts of Managua, the country's capital.[21] One drug policy analyst described Nicaragua as a "black hole" because so many small planes carrying drugs landed there and the police couldn't trace them any farther.[22]

U.S. officials worried about the impact of the widening drug war on the Third World countries now caught in the web of international drug trafficking. They knew the lack of law-enforcement resources and the poverty and high unemployment rates in those countries would no doubt help create a ready labor market for the drug cartels and make it easy for them to ship drugs through the new distribution routes. In Nicaragua, where the unemployment rate was 54 percent, there were only about six full-time antidrug police in Managua (population 1.3 million) and no resources to patrol the country's Atlantic coast, which the Cali cartel was using as a transportation point.[23] "Latin America as a whole is sliding into the drug war," said Iban de Rementeria, a narcotics expert with the Andean Commission of Jurists. "Argentina and Brazil can see their future in Bolivia. Bolivia sees its own (future) in Peru. Peru in Colombia and Colombia in Lebanon. It's an endless cycle."[24]

The new drug-smuggling distribution network also took advantage of the flow of people across the U.S. border — illegal immigrants, some of whom were willing to make a little extra cash as drug couriers, and tourists, such as vacationing American citizens, who were tempted to smuggle larger shipments of drugs across the border in hidden compartments of their vehicles. With heroin, cocaine, and marijuana pouring into the United States from numerous directions and by every conceivable means of transportation, interdiction could not possibly make a significant dent in the traffic. "There are too many bad guys," explained one customs official at the Kennedy Airport in New York City. "I'm probably not aware of ninety percent of the drugs that come through my gate. These guys have a million tricks. I've seen plenty of them. But we can't search everybody — we don't have the staff or the time. Even if we could, these mules (drug carriers) can practically make the stuff invisible."[25]

By the early 1990s, international drug trafficking had become a far different illicit enterprise than it had been in the early 1980s when President Reagan first declared war on drugs. Traffickers had shown remarkable flexibility and imagination in responding to the challenge of law enforcement's increasingly sophisticated methods of interdiction. For much of the 1980s, aircraft and cargo ships were the main means and Miami and the surrounding region of South Florida was the prime center of cocaine smuggling.[26] The aircraft chosen for smuggling had the optimum balance between range and cargo capacity so that the largest amount of cocaine could be shipped to the largest range of destinations in the United States. The Aztec, Piper Navajo, and Cessna 400 Series, the most popular types of aircraft, could transport a ton of cocaine as far as 1,800 miles and stay in the air as much as 11 1/2 hours using the standard fuel systems.[27] The ships used for smuggling ranged in size from large commercial cargo carriers to small high-speed "cigarette" boats.

Only an estimated 4 percent of the 8 million cargo containers arriving at U.S. ports are searched, and, even if law enforcement officials know that drugs are aboard, they often cannot find them because they are so well hidden. In one incident described by the *Wall Street Journal*, customs officials used one of their trained dogs to search all the containers of one cargo ship arriving at the port of Miami, confident that thanks to hidden informants they would find illegal drugs. They searched for hours, carefully inspecting a container full of tires, and even smashed a box full of porcelain bowls in anticipation of finding the contraband. Nothing turned up.[28]

When law enforcement had some success with the interdiction in South Florida, the traffickers changed their strategy, using trucks, private vehicles, and tractor trailers to smuggle the cocaine across the southwest border of the U.S. The job of interdicting this movement of drugs involved guarding a 3,000-mile border that had thirty ports of entry through which daily passed 640,000 pedestrians and 240,000 cars, trucks, and other vehicles.[29] By 1996 the U.S government estimated that 70 percent of the cocaine smuggled into the United States came across the U.S.-Mexican border.[30] Meanwhile, traffickers were also using the longer more expensive eastern shipping routes through the Caribbean to the Mid-Atlantic and New England coast.[31] Given the billions of dollars at stake, the smugglers were more than willing to pay for the larger vessels and the sophisticated electronic equipment they needed.

The U.S. military and law enforcement have continued to develop a wide range of high-tech drug-busting devices — radar systems, surveillance aircraft and boats, computer networks, mobile x-ray vans, range finders, and night vision and other equipment — to combat international drug trafficking. In 1990 *Popular Mechanics* magazine described some of the impressive high-tech gadgetry employed in the drug interdiction network: Blue Thunder Camarans that can move up to seventy miles per hour in pursuit of smugglers in coastal waters, an Aerostat Radar Balloon that can sweep a 120-mile circle for boats and low-flying aircraft, and Sikorsky Black Hawk helicopters with a 192-knot top speed and a 900-mile range to chase smugglers. The interdiction network is coordinated through command centers that pull all the intelligence and land-based, airborne, and seaborne radar together.[32]

By 1992 fighting international drug trafficking with high tech had become a major U.S. growth industry. "The changing nature of the military threat facing the U.S. and the defense budgets have compelled traditional military systems manufacturers to look at the growing drug interdiction program as a new market for their high-tech systems," explained John Rhea, managing editor of the defense industry publisher, Washington Communications Service. According to Rhea, of the $10.6 billion spent by the Bush administration on the War on Drugs in 1992, the Defense Department is "spending an estimated $1.2 billion in various programs and procurement efforts in support of the military services and agencies with hands-on anti-smuggling duties, involving the U.S. Customs Service, Coast Guard, and the state National Guard units.[33] The latter are not DOD-funded." Some of the impressive high-tech equipment, networks, and systems used by the U.S. military in the 1992 Persian Gulf War, which annihilated the Iraqi invasion and liberated Kuwait, began to be employed in the War on Drugs.

As the antidrug forces further militarized the War on Drugs through the introduction of more sophisticated and expensive high-tech equipment and devices, the drug traffickers responded to the challenge, employing state-of-the-art equipment themselves — beepers, cellular phones, scramblers, encryption devices, and radar equipment — to further communication within their organizations and to monitor law-enforcement surveillance efforts. Digital encryption devices, for example, can send messages in code that are protected by security features, which allow only members of the drug-trafficking organization who have a special access code to send a message. Only through meticulous hard work and extensive investigations have the authorities been able to penetrate some of the high-tech security systems surrounding drug-trafficking operations.

In the early 1990s the Cali cartel believed its method of sending messages in code from randomly selected pay telephones and charging the calls to prepaid credit cards was free from police surveillance. The authorities, however, used high tech to figure out a way to track the movement of cartel members and to monitor cocaine shipments being smuggled into the U.S.[34] Realizing high tech could enhance their investigative powers, the authorities began developing a plan of action in the late 1980s that would use federal funds to further research and development (R and D). The Bush administration, however, allotted a mere half of 1 percent of the entire national drug budget to R and D. "There is a dynamic 'technology race' under way between the drug traffickers and the law enforcement community, [but] it is by no means clear which side is better funded or better equipped," warned one government report issued by a U.S Department of Defense advisory board.[35]

By the time the 1992 U.S. presidential elections got rolling, the consensus among drug analysts was that the Bush administration's War on Drugs strategy, which focused primarily on supply and looked for a military solution, had not worked. "U.S. drug policy in much of the hemisphere was viewed not merely as costly and ineffective, but as perversely counterproductive as well," explained Professor Bagley.[36] Despite the assurances made by the U.S. government since 1982 that "the scourge was about to end," the supplies of heroin, cocaine, and other illegal drugs were still plentiful, while their cost had remained low. The Bush administration's antidrug strategy, moreover, may have actually led to more drug abuse and drug-related violence.

The policy had also done little to alleviate drug-induced corruption, terrorism, and violence in the many countries that had been sucked into the War on Drugs. "The Peruvian-American anti-drug policy has failed," acknowledged Peruvian Alberto Fujimori. "For ten years, there has been a considerable sum invested by the Peruvian government, and this has not led to a reduction in the supply of coca leaf offered for sale. Rather, in the ten years from 1980 to 1990, it grew ten fold."[37]

Senator Patrick Leahy (D–N.H.), the chairman of the powerful Senate Appropriations Subcommittee that oversees foreign operations, concurred with President Fujimori's assessment, and in an interview appeared to agree with the opinion of many drug-policy analysts that the DEA should stop its support of raids on drug-trafficking operations in Peru. "We've spent over $1 billion down there so far and we've accomplished virtually nothing," Leahy explained. "We ought to realize it's not going to work."[38]

During the 1992 presidential elections, Bill Clinton saw the opening provided by the disillusionment with the War on Drugs and pledged to change U.S policy, promising the American people that he would combine tough law enforcement while expanding drug treatment and prevention programs. Clinton also announced that he would shift the emphasis away from the interdiction of drugs toward a policy that would help countries fight drug trafficking both economically and militarily.

In February 1993, the month after Clinton's inauguration as president, Lee Brown, the former police chief of New York City who was Clinton's choice for the new drug czar, said at his confirmation hearings that, if Congress approved his nomination, he would develop a "comprehensive and balanced" antidrug strategy, although he did not provide substantive details on how he would do that.[39] In February, Clinton also announced his plan to cut the support staff in the drug czar's office from 146 to 25, a number less than half that of the White House communications staff. Supporters of the move took this as a sign that the Clinton administration was serious about placing the emphasis of the drug policy on reducing demand. Critics, on the other hand, said Clinton's announcement reflected the typical lack of commitment that has been exhibited by the president's office all through the drug war.

The following month, the group called the U.S. Policy on International Counter Narcotics in the Western Hemisphere presented a strategy for combating cocaine production and trafficking, which, among other things, called for a "gradual" shift in focus away from transit countries of Mexico, the Caribbean, and Central America to the cocaine source countries of Peru, Colombia, and Bolivia.[40] At her confirmation hearings in May, attorney general nominee Janet Reno said that the U.S. antidrug policy should focus on prevention and treatment and not on combating drug trafficking abroad. In October 1993 the U.S. Defense Department announced that the military would cut spending on drug interdiction, which accounted for 71 percent of the $1.17 billion drug budget, by 11 percentage points, while increasing the amount spent on training and equipment for source countries to 16 percent, an increase of 5 percentage points.[41] The following month, the executive branch announced that, within 120 days, it would develop a separate strategy to combat the heroin trade because heroin use was reportedly increasing.[42]

The Clinton administration finally released its "new" drug control strategy on February 8, 1994, at a briefing for foreign ambassadors in Washington, D.C. The following day, Robert S. Gelbard, Assistant

Secretary for International Narcotics Matters, said the strategy "recognizes that America's first line of defense against drugs is to reduce the drug abuse here at home. We are the world's largest illegal drug market — nothing at all to be proud of — but definitely we should shoulder our share of the responsibility for combating the drug scourge." Gelbard went on to list the key elements of the Clinton administration's drug-control strategy: "We will help to build democratic institutions — the courts, law enforcement, community and political organizations — institutions strong enough to resist the reach of the drug trade. We will help drug-producing countries create economic alternatives to narcotics and advance applications for sustainable development. We will fight the multinational cartel ... with a multinational effort."[43]

As the Clinton administration made public the objectives of its antidrug policy, critics began questioning Clinton's commitment to the War on Drugs and his seriousness about changing U.S. drug policy. In a candid interview with the *New York Times*, outgoing DEA head Robert Bonner said that he had reservations about whether Clinton really wanted to "develop ... a drug strategy" or "has the will to move Congress and the American people."[44] Some observers looked at the Clinton administration's fiscal year 1994 budget, which it had submitted to Congress in March 1993, and noticed only a slight shift of priorities toward demand reduction programs. Both Democratic and Republican congressmen, as well as independent experts, criticized the Clinton administration for not giving any indication on how specifically the budget would be reapportioned. "The overall impression was that the new budget contained no fundamental changes in U.S. policy or priorities," concluded Bruce Bagley.[45]

The disenchantment grew during the year after Clinton's inauguration, and by early 1994 the Republican-controlled Congress was ready to abolish the office of the drug czar. "If at the end of this trial year (1994), we have not seen a ... substantial improvement, we will vote to eliminate the office," warned Rep. Jon Keyll (R–AZ). "Nobody is happy with the administration's lack of support."[46] Meanwhile, Congress rejected Clinton's proposal to cut the drug czar's office staff and budget and actually doubled the office's allocation from $5.8 million to $11.1 million, while increasing its office staff to forty from the twenty-five proposed by Clinton.[47]

Statistics showed that funding for drug interdiction did decline during Clinton's first term of office — from about $1 billion to $569 million — resulting in "fewer ships, flight hours, and ground-based radars devoted to drug interdiction and a drop in cocaine seizures in the transit zone from 70,336 kilograms in 1992 to 37,181 in 1995. The increased funding for source countries that was supposed to happen never did materialize."[48]

Before the mid 1980s, Italian organized crime generally dominated the heroin trade in the United States and Europe, using the famous French Connection to smuggle large quantities of heroin from Southeast Asia and the Golden Triangle into Europe and the United States. By 1986, however, Chinese criminals had begun to play a bigger role in heroin trafficking. In 1985 alone, law enforcement solved more than twenty major cases involving Chinese gangsters and seized about 200 kilograms of high-grade heroin. The following year, drug agents intercepted more than 100 kilos of heroin from Southeast Asia in cargo ships arriving at New Jersey ports.[49] By the early 1990s, the Colombians joined the Chinese as major players in the heroin trade, both as growers and suppliers, and within a few years, Colombia had become the world's second-biggest source of the poppy plant.[50] The face of international drug trafficking was changing rapidly.

In November 1993 the Clinton administration announced that within 120 days it would have a plan in place to combat the heroin trade, but as of June 1995 — nineteen months later — they still had not developed a heroin strategy. "Delays involving the strategy were due in large part to the difficulties in balancing U.S. objectives in Burma — the primary source of heroin," noted one government report.[51] As happened often in the War on Drugs, the administration had subordinated its antidrug strategy to other foreign policy objectives.

While heroin was making a strong comeback among American upper classes, a government study called the National Household Survey on Drug Use, released by the U.S. Department of Health and Human Services in August 1996, reported that between 1992 and 1995 teenage drug use of marijuana, cocaine, and LSD rose an average of 105 percent.[52] The report became political fodder for both the Republicans and Democrats during the 1995 election. The Republicans accused the Clinton administration of creating a "lost generation" of American youth by cutting the drug budget and failing to exercise strong leadership on the issue. The Democrats countered that the apparent surge in teenage drug use had begun well before Clinton came into office, and they tried to link the rise to the Republican leadership of the War on Drugs under Ronald Reagan and George Bush, who, they charged, had made things worse by cutting the antidrug budget.[53]

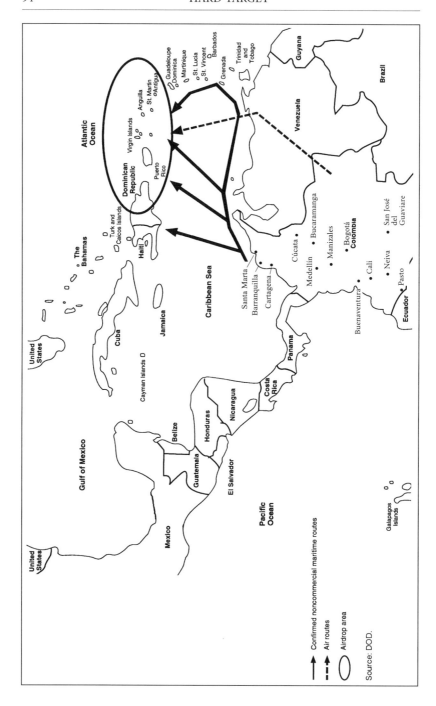

Confirmed noncommercial maritime routes

Air routes

Airdrop area

Source: DOD.

Dole unveiled his antidrug message, "Just Don't Do It," an obvious ripoff of Nancy Reagan's famous slogan of the 1980s, "Just Say No," and kept telling the American public how tough he would be in the War on Drugs. Not to be outflanked, Clinton promised that by September 30, 1996, he would give $75 million worth of helicopters, planes, arms, and other military equipment to the governments of Colombia, Peru, Bolivia, Venezuela, and the Caribbean countries, a strong indication that it was going to be drug war as usual if Clinton were reelected.[54] Dole called drug abuse "the most important news story of our time," but voters remained unimpressed. According to opinion polls, drugs ranked fifth among the issues that most concerned the voters.[55]

In the climate of heated rhetoric over the poll about teenage drug use, both presidential candidates weren't listening to the experts who had studied the big issue and said that reasons for teenage drug use were complex and advised the candidates not to make the drug issue so partisan. "Kids are not getting the strong messages they got in the 1980s," explained Diane Barry, communications director for Join Together, a Boston-based national resource center for communities fighting substance abuse. 'When you look at those messages, it's no wonder that these kids are willing to start with marijuana. There's got to be leadership for the entire industry and there's got to be leadership for parents."[56]

Many drug-policy analysts would have added that there had to be leadership in the White House and Congress as well. Rensselaer Lee, an analyst of the War on Drugs, called the Dole-Clinton debate on national drug policy "artificial" and said, "No good ideas have come out of this campaign, either from [the Clinton] administration or Dole."[57]

Clinton defeated Dole easily and, as he began his second term of office, it was obvious there would be no new direction in the War on Drugs. The United States would continue to seek a military solution to the drug problem in a stubborn effort to stop the supply, while paying lip service to decreasing the demand for drugs. As a result, international drug trafficking would expand to more and more countries and the drug abuse, violence, and corruption, fueled by the enormous profits generated by the trade, would continue. The United States would pour billions more into interdiction programs, trying to keep drugs out of the country, imprisoning thousands more, overtaxing the criminal justice system, chipping away at the rights of Americans in a vain attempt to stamp out drug use and reduce drug abuse. Still, cocaine, heroin, marijuana, and other popular illegal drugs would be as cheap and plentiful as ever.

"People say the '80s are over, but they must be talking about lifestyles, not narcotics trafficking," said Lee Stapleton, chief of narcotics for the U.S. Attorney's Office in Miami, Florida. "Business is booming. Cocaine, heroin and marijuana are dropping out of the sky, being unloaded at sea and being moved up and down our rivers and highways..."[58]

In what was turning out to be America's longest war, history continued to repeat itself. In the fall of 1993, the press reported that in 1990 a Venezuelan antidrug program sponsored by the CIA was responsible for shipping a ton of almost pure cocaine to the United States in several installments. The case involved the same program under which a CIA-created Haitian intelligence service had earlier been involved in drug trafficking, as well as acts of terror. In the wake of Venezuela-related drug trafficking revelations, one CIA officer resigned, a second was transferred, and a federal grand jury launched an investigation. In November 1996 the grand jury indicted Ramón Guillen Davila, the head of the Venezuelan national guard, on drug-trafficking charges. An embarrassed CIA admitted that it had shown "poor judgment and management on the part of several CIA officers," but the incident further eroded the already weakened credibility of the agency in the War on Drugs.[59]

Even more sensational were the charges made in a three-part series of articles published by the *San Jose Mercury News*, which alleged that the CIA had been involved in a scheme to sell crack cocaine to Los Angeles street gangs and shift millions in profits to the CIA-backed Contra guerrilla army in Nicaragua. The *Mercury News* investigation claimed that the nation's crack explosion of the 1980s could be traced to Danilo Blandon and Juan Norwin Meneses, two Nicaraguan crack cocaine dealers and leaders of separate CIA-backed Contra commando groups in the 1980s. The newspaper never reported a direct CIA link to the drug-smuggling operation, but it was easy for readers to conclude that there was one. Several leading newspapers, including the *New York Times* and the *Los Angeles Times*, were critical of the series, and in testimony before the U.S. Senate Intelligence Committee, Contra leaders Adolpho Calero and Eden Pastora denied that the *Mercury News* findings were true and insisted that no link existed between the CIA-backed Contras and international drug traffickers. That didn't reassure leaders in the African-American community who feared another coverup of CIA complicity in international drug trafficking.[60]

These revelations reinforced the prevailing cynicism about the strategy employed in the War on Drugs and some of the media began speaking out for new, more creative approaches to the drug problem. In a November 1996 editorial, the conservative *National Review* concluded that the War on Drugs was lost and called for the legalization of drugs, while in another editorial, the *San Francisco Chronicle* declared, "We are not saying that all drugs be summarily legalized, but every option — including decriminalization — should be considered in dealing with this complex problem that combines crime, public health and social disintegration."[61]

It was also becoming obvious to America's allies that war as usual was not working, and they started calling for a global effort to combat international drug trafficking, pointing out that the dynamics of the illegal trade cut across national boundaries and involved criminal organizations that were now operating like multinationals in the cut throat world of international trade. In December 1996 members of the Organization of American States reached an agreement in Montevideo, Uruguay, which ratified a hemispheric antidrug plan. "This is a strategy that can lead to the reduction of drug consumption and supply through international multilateral strategies," said Diego Cardona, foreign affairs adviser to Colombian president Ernesto Samper.[62]

The one-hundred-plus countries around the world that were connected in some way to international drug trafficking would need to cooperate more and rethink strategy, for the vast, complex world of international drug trafficking was now populated by many players, all after the fabulous riches and the power the illegal business had to offer. What one writer said about the drug trade in 1982, the year Reagan declared War on Drugs, was just as true in 1997. "American narcotics experts used to preach that the global heroin rackets were controlled by one or two grand conspiracies — the Chinese Tong-Corsican connection or the Mexican connection or whatever," wrote Rob Schultheis in *Mother Jones* magazine. "If we could just nail Fu Manchu (or the Godfather or the Big Boss) in some final Armageddon-like battle, they would say, the war on heroin would be won. Well, the big syndicates are gone in Hong Kong today but the business continues carried on by dozens, perhaps hundreds of amorphous little gangs, scamsters and fly-by-night plotters. And what is true of Hong Kong appears to true world wide. The narcotics infrastructure is not one big Evil with a capital E that can be beheaded with a single stroke or destroyed in one great set-piece battle."[63]

Section 3
Hard Targets

Chapter 7

The Changing Face
of International
Drug Trafficking

"Since drug trafficking has become widespread and worldwide in the last twenty-five years, traffickers have come from every part of the world. They represent numerous nationalities, ethnic groups and cultures."
— Dennis Rose, author, *International Drug Trafficking*

"True to the tradition bequeathed by Prohibition, many of the new arrivals — Chinese, Vietnamese, Jamaicans, Mexicans, Colombians, Dominicans, and even Sicilians — turn to crime not because the society is closed off to them, but because it is so wide open."
— Robert J. Kelly, criminologist

That the big Evil with a capital E cannot be beheaded with a single stroke is evident by looking at the recent history of the Italian American Mafia. During the 1980s, U.S. law enforcement had some stunning success against Italian-American organized crime, and, in many cases, prosecutors were able to win long sentences against such well-known mob leaders as John Gotti of New York City and Nicky Scarfo of Philadelphia and even put away entire government commissions of some of La Cosa Nostra's ruling families. Since the 1980s, more than 1,000 mob members and their associates have been convicted of various crimes, including drug trafficking.[1] The Italian mob had dominated crime in America for nearly half a century, and law enforcement initially viewed this success as a major turning point in its long battle against organized crime.

The weakening of the Mafia, however, has provided golden opportunities for other ambitious ethnic criminal organizations, and, today, hundreds of such organizations flourish in the United States, which has become the land of opportunity for ambitious and enterprising criminals. They are involved in a range of criminal activities, from extortion to gambling to loan sharking, but, while these activities generate millions of dollars, drug trafficking remains the largest source of criminal revenue.[2] The 1984 President's Commission on Organized Crime described drug trafficking as "the most sophisticated and lucrative organized-crime operation in the United States" and estimated at the time that it accounted for nearly 40 percent of U.S. organized crime activity, generating an annual take that could be as high as $110 billion.[3] Given the money involved, no wonder many of these gangs focus solely on drug trafficking and exhibit a "degree of violence and corruption unsurpassed by any other criminal activity."[4]

Like the barbarian hordes during the time of the Roman Empire, these ethnic gangs have invaded the United States from every part of the globe — Asia, Africa, Europe, the Caribbean, and Latin America — in pursuit of drug money. "Since drug trafficking has become widespread and worldwide in the last twenty-five years, traffickers have come from every part of the world," explained, Dennis Rowe, author of *International Drug Trafficking*. "They represent numerous nationalities, institutions, ethnic groups and cultures."[5] And as criminologist Robert J. Kelly pointed out, "True to the tradition bequeathed by Prohibition, many of the new arrivals — Chinese, Vietnamese, Jamaicans, Mexicans, Colombians, Dominicans, and even Sicilians — turn to crime not because the society is closed off to them, but because it is so wide open."[6]

While law enforcement crippled La Cosa Nostra in the 1980s, the Triads, from their base in Hong Kong, muscled their way into the heroin market and now operate in 19 major American cities.[7] From 1984 to 1988, the Triad control of the biggest U.S. heroin market, New York City, rose from 3 percent to about 40 percent. "It's a stunning change," marveled Robert Stutman, a special agent in charge of the DEA's New York office. "It means that the (Italian) mafia has been supplanted as the leader in the heroin trade."[8]

Like many other ethnic gangs, the Triads were helped by the changes in the immigration laws that allowed more people than ever to emigrate from non-Western-European countries. Between 1970 and 1980, the formative period for the Triads in the United States, the number of Chinese immigrants jumped 85 percent, from 435,062 to 806,027, and among that number came what one U.S. immigration official described

A Colombian national police officer treats a wounded comrade after a battle with drug traffickers (courtesy Colombian National Police).

as "a young, bold street-smart type of criminal from the major industrial centers"[9] of China. Given their ambition, ruthlessness, initial success, and numbers (police estimate that in Los Angeles County alone there are 100 Asian, predominantly Chinese, gangs with 10,000 members), some law enforcement officials have predicted that the Triads will soon dominate American organized crime.[10]

The Jamaican posses were another ethnic group to ride the wave of changing U.S. immigration laws. Starting out in marijuana smuggling in the early 1980s, the Posses quickly came to dominate the emerging crack cocaine market, and today they operate in at least thirty states, controlling half the crack peddled in the United States. Like the Jamaicans, the Colombians have taken advantage of the big consumer demand for cocaine. Crack cocaine was almost unheard of in Europe in 1990, but thanks to the Colombian cartels, by 1995 crack was being described as the continent's fastest-growing narcotics phenomenon.[11] Today, by most estimates, Colombian drug traffickers control 70 to 80 percent of the world's cocaine traffic.

Some of the ethnic criminal organizations have only recently made their presence felt in the international drug trade, but they are rapidly gaining ground on the competition. With the collapse of the Soviet Union in 1991, members of Russia's organized crime began migrating to

New York City, Miami, Seattle, Philadelphia, and Los Angeles and at least 16 other cities, where they established criminal beachheads.[12] Described by one FBI official as "the most brutal, remorseless and wholly frightening criminals that America has ever seen,"[13] the Russian mafia has an estimated 5,000 gangs, making it one of the world's largest and strongest organized crime syndicates.[14] With its ranks in the United States swelling from the influx of Russian immigrants from the former Soviet Union, the Russian mob is giving the Triads stiff competition as the most powerful new criminal organization in America, a development that has made it one of U.S. law enforcement's top priorities.[15]

While the authorities begin to have some success against one ethnic gang, another one crops up as a powerful new force in drug trafficking. The crackdown on the Colombian cartels in the early 1990s, for example, created a golden opportunity for the Mexican trafficking syndicates. As described earlier, law enforcement put pressure on the Caribbean–South Florida distribution network of the Colombian cartels in the late 1980s, and so they shifted their network to Mexico and began smuggling drugs across the country's porous border with the United States. Mexican drug traffickers became the middlemen for the Colombians, but, by the mid 1990s, they had taken over huge drug distribution areas in the United States from the beleaguered Colombian cartels. The *Mexican Journal*, a prominent financial publication, estimates that the Mexican narcotics industry is worth today about $20 billion annually — a figure that dwarfs the country's oil industry in profits.[15]

Many ethnic gangs have shrewdly developed niches in the illegal U.S. drug market. Why try to dominate when the market is so big and money can be made so quickly? For the Japanese Yakuza, which operates primarily in Hawaii and California, the niche is amphetamine trafficking between the United States and Japan, while the Nigerians have established their international drug trafficking reputation on the fact that they are willing to travel anywhere, and risk body and death to smuggle heroin into the United States and Europe. From the Bronx in New York City, the Albanians traffic in heroin, and, across the country in California, Koreans focus on ice, or smokable methamphetamine. The Dominicans help the Colombians as "junior" partners, while the Christian Iraqis, the Chaldeans, dominate the drug trade in Detroit — and the list goes on.[17]

While diverse in background and nature, these gangs do share certain characteristics:

• They are willing to collaborate with each other when the need arises. The Italian American Mafia collaborates with the Sicilian Mafia, the Triads with the Italian Mafia, the Mexicans and Jamaican posses with the Colombians, the Nigerians with the Triads, who work with street gangs.

• At the same time, in competing for turf in the lucrative world of international drug trafficking, the ethnic gangs have raised violence on U.S. streets to unprecedented levels, no longer playing by the unwritten rules that once governed organized crime behavior in the heyday of the Italian American Mafia. As one writer explained, "The new diffusion of organized crime has caused many of the subtle controls that once governed the underworld and kept a lid on violence to be lifted. When the Italian Cosa Nostra ruled the underworld, they had strict rules about killing, and it made sure — although the rule was occasionally broken — that the official establishment, including judges, police, lawyers, reporters, would not become murder victims. The heat and publicity generated by such acts were usually not worth the trouble."[18]

• Today's ethnic gangs are willing to kill anybody who gets in their way, even if it means innocent bystanders have to die. On their way to cornering the crack cocaine market, the Jamaican posses killed an estimated 1,400 people between 1985 and 1988, many of whom had nothing do with drug trafficking.[19] The Cali cartel was willing to kill a prominent Hispanic journalist in Queens, New York, because he had been prying too closely into their business.[20] One Triad group thought nothing of wiping out several innocent people in a San Francisco restaurant, mistaking them for members of the competition.

• The new ethnic gangs are highly mobile, making use of jet transportation, computer systems, and forged documentation to move themselves and their drugs, information, and money between the United States and other bases of operation around the world. As we will see in subsequent sections, this has caused big problems for the United States and other countries and poses big challenges for international antidrug efforts and programs.

This section presents background reports on the major ethnic gangs involved in smuggling drugs to the United States. How did they get started? How are they organized? What drugs do they deal in? What is their impact on international drug trafficking? What has been the

View from a machine gun nest of the Colombian National Police (courtesy Colombian National Police).

response of the antidrug forces? What is their future? These are questions the reports answer.

It should be noted that, while major players in international drug trafficking, these ethnic gangs constitute only some of the criminal organizations operating in the huge international drug trafficking network. Many domestic gangs, such as the Hell's Angels, the Mexican Mafia, the Bloods and the Crips also make and distribute drugs, and they are part of the problem that is begging a solution and making drug abuse and drug trafficking issues of vital U.S. and international concern.

Chapter 8

Octopus: The Powerful Reach of the Sicilian Mafia

"There are signs, indeed evidence, that the Cosa Nostra is slipping."
— Pierluigi Vigna, chief prosecutor, Florence, Italy

"Today, the Sicilian Mafia is the most formidable criminal organization in this country, in control of a worldwide heroin distribution network. Their relationship with the LCN (the Italian-American La Cosa Nostra) seems to be in excellent shape, and their contacts with other criminal groups, the Blacks, the Colombians, etc., are increasing."
— FBI Report, 1994

Organized crime, Italian style, has come primarily in two varieties: the Sicilian Mafia, the "Octopus," which is an alliance of semiautonomous crime organizations based in the Italian state of Sicily, and the Italian American Mafia, which is also an alliance of semiautonomous crime groups, but not a branch of the Sicilian Mafia.[1] U.S. law enforcement knew little about the existence of the Sicilian Mafia's drug-trafficking activity in the United States until the Justice Department launched one of its most important crime investigations ever in the 1980s. The Pizza Connection Investigation, which the DEA and FBI conducted jointly, ran for almost three years and targeted the Joseph Bonanno mob family in New York City and its laundering of millions of dollars in revenue from heroin sales through pizza parlors owned by the family and other Sicilian Mafia members. In the U.S., the investigation led to thirty-four indictments against the Sicilian Mafia members illicit money. U.S. authorities scored triumphant victories, gathering the first hard evidence that the Sicilian Mafia had a large and powerful presence on the U.S. drug-trafficking scene[2] and forcing the Sicilian Mafia to make its first appearance in U.S. court.

The Sicilians who ran the pizza parlors came to the United States in the 1970s as part of the great influx of Mafia members who fled the scene of the "Great Sicilian Mafia War" in which hundreds of people in Italy were murdered, the result of mob turf wars. This war primarily took place from 1958 to the early 1970s but flared up again in 1980, ending three years later. During these two periods, many mob members came to the United States illegally because they were wanted in Italy on bombing and murder charges.[3]

From the early 1970s to the early 1980s, the Sicilian Mafia built a huge pizza parlor empire that by 1980 included pizza shops in 34 cities and towns all over the American landscape, from Pennsylvania to Florida to Colorado. This extensive network of shops was used to ship huge amounts of heroin to the United States.[4] In 1982 and 1983, for example, the Sicilian Mafia scheduled one and a half tons of heroin, street value $33 million, for shipment to New York City, the biggest U.S. heroin market.[5] A U.S. Customs report revealed that supplies for the pizza empire — everything from the oil and ovens to the tomato sauce and the mozzarella cheese — were "totally controlled from the time they are contracted for in a foreign country, to the time they are delivered to the ultimate consumer."[6]

The pizza parlor network was a part of a criminal empire that was mind-boggling in scope, one that spanned the globe to include not just the United States but other countries as well, such as Brazil, Canada, Spain, Switzerland, and several countries in southern Asia, the major source of the poppy plant, used in heroin production. Claire Sterling, an investigative journalist who studied the Sicilian Mafia extensively, put the annual income of the Sicilian Mafia at $30 billion, a figure three times the total budget of the Sicilian regional government and one that made the Mafia the twentieth richest "nation" on earth.[7] In 1989 the Rome-based Census Research Institute put the annual income of the Sicilian Mafia at $95 billion or 12 percent of Italy's gross national product, and called the Octopus the most important private industry in Italy, even bigger than the Fiat or Olivetti companies.[8]

The huge U.S. market nourished La Cosa Nostra's criminal empire. By the time the Pizza Connection trial opened in 1985, the FBI had established that from 1982 to 1985 the New York branch of the Sicilian Mafia transferred $40 million in cash from New York to Sicily via Switzerland.

Three years later, the agency estimated that Octopus had transferred $20 billion in drug profits from the United States in the previous 15 years.[9]

How did the illicit system work? A 1984 U.S. Justice Department report explained: "Out of the total take of some $2.5 billion from heroin sales, U.S. mafia families will send up to $1 billion in payments to suppliers in Sicily. There is a considerable probability that a substantial share of the U.S. profits is reinvested directly within the [Mafia] economic empire or laundered domestically for legitimate investment purposes, although some U.S. family drug money finds its way into Swiss bank accounts."[10]

As a result of the Pizza Connection trial, the Sicilian Mafia became the target of U.S. law enforcement's attention, and the FBI began using informants, surveillances, electronic "overhears," and information from Italian law-enforcement agencies to investigate. The FBI estimated that there were at least 25 Sicilian Mafia members operating in the United States, although several more Sicilian Mafia members were suspected of being in the country.[11] That figure seemed to reveal more about the FBI's knowledge of the Sicilian Mafia than it did about the size of the Mafia itself. In her book on the Sicilian Mafia, which was published in 1990, Claire Sterling put the number of Sicilian Mafia members operating in the United States at about 1,700.[12] While strengthening their base of operation in the United States, the Sicilian Mafia, according to the FBI, obtained the approval of certain Italian American Mafia families before initiating a major heroin smuggling operation in the United States and paid monetary tribute for the sanction, which could be up to $5,000 for each smuggled kilo of heroin.[13]

In 1987, two years after the Pizza Connection trial, the FBI gave this assessment of the Sicilian Mafia: "Today, the Sicilian Mafia is the most formidable criminal organization in this country, in control of a worldwide heroin distribution network. Their relationship with the LCN the American La Cosa Nostra) seems to be in excellent shape, and their contacts with other criminal groups, the Blacks, the Colombians, etc., are increasing."[14]

The Sicilian Mafia may have been news to U.S. law enforcement, but the crime syndicate has played a seminal role in organized crime in the United States since the early twentieth century, dominating the international heroin trade since the 1950s. Mafia gangs were operating in Sicily early in the nineteenth century, and, by the turn of the twentieth century, they had become de facto rulers of Sicily, infiltrating all branches of government and eliminating anybody who got in their way. Sicilian

Mafia members began emigrating to the United States in the early 1890s, settling in greatest numbers in New Orleans, where they dominated and terrorized the city's Italian American population and corrupted the local government.[15] Within a few years, the growing crime syndicate had established bases in such cities as Chicago, Detroit, New York, Kansas City, and St. Louis.[16]

In the 1920s, almost 500 members fled to the United States, the result of a purge by Italian dictator Benito Mussolini, and among the arrivals were such future mob leaders as Carlos Gambino, Joseph Profaci, and Joseph Bonanno, who would make up the leadership of organized crime in the U.S. during the next 40 years.[17] When Charles "Lucky" Luciano took over in 1931, "Sicily acquired its exclusive heroin concession, and the drugging of America began."[18]

Luciano came to power as a result of the Castellammare War, in which a Sicilian Mafia faction led by Salvatore Maranzano battled an Italian American faction led by Joseph Masseria. Luciano struck a deal with Maranzano and the war ended in April 15, 1931, when Masseria was shot to death in a Coney Island restaurant. Soon after, Maranzano called a meeting of all Mafia members at which the codes and principles of La Cosa Nostra were set out and where the organization was divided into new families. Luciano was made a family member, but he thanked Maranzano, his patron, by having him murdered in September 1931.[19]

Luciano launched the modern era of the Sicilian Mafia, establishing the so-called French Connection, which by the 1970s was responsible for 80 percent of the heroin smuggled into the United States. The Sicilian Mafia, in alliance with the French Corsicans, smuggled heroin that was processed in the French port city of Marseilles, using morphine base that came from Turkey.[20]

Lucky Luciano became one of the most important figures in international drug trafficking history, making the illicit enterprise modern and efficient in nature and global in size. "Luciano was a clear-sighted corporate executive with a rare gift for rational organization, the Lee Iacocca of organized crime," Sterling wrote. "He understood the laws of supply and demand, the benefits of scale, the advantages of a transnational operation joining raw material procurement to manufacturing transport and marketing. He was the seminal force behind what became the biggest commercial enterprise in the world: the multi billion dollar heroin conglomerate."[21]

Luciano helped set up another meeting in 1957, a historic summit in Palermo, Italy, which brought together leaders of both Sicilian and

Italian American Mafias. The exact nature of what went on at that meeting has never been established, but it is known that every leader who attended was a drug dealer and the meeting focused on international narcotics trafficking. As Claire Sterling explained, "Although there is no firsthand evidence of what went on at the four-day summit itself, what followed over the next thirty years has made the substance clear. Authorities on both sides of the Atlantic are persuaded by now that the American delegation asked the Sicilians to take over the import and distribution of heroin in the United States, and the Sicilians agreed."[22] The Italian American Mafia would never entirely get out of heroin trafficking, but, in effect, it gave the Sicilian Mafia what amounted to a heroin franchise in the U.S.

Working together, U.S., Italian, and French law enforcement managed to break the French Connection in the early 1970s, a development that led to the shift of heroin laboratories from southern France to Sicily and northern Italy, and the purchase of morphine base from Jordan, Syria, Lebanon, and other eastern Mediterranean countries. According to the FBI, "Because of increased Italian police enforcement activity from 1980 to 1985, Sicilian Mafia control of heroin laboratory production activity had diminished considerably. However, the Sicilian Connection, the trafficking of processed heroin to Europe and North American markets, solidified during this period."[23] By 1987, the Sicilian Mafia controlled the trafficking of processed heroin from both southeast and southwest Asia to the United States. Couriers wore body bags of two- to three-kilogram quantities of heroin or stored the drug in a wide variety of items, including mail, furniture, film canisters, shoes, clothing, provolone cheese, and even cases of baby powder.[24]

To disguise the billions of dollars in profits from its worldwide drug-trafficking operation, the Sicilian Mafia has made huge investments in legitimate businesses, buying cafes, bakeries, restaurants, auto dealerships, and, of course, pizza parlors in both the United States and Italy. One investigation conducted by the government pointed out that "the Sicilians have used other methods of legitimizing their illegal profits: an investment system for transporting bulk currency out of the United States to banks in the Bahamas and Bermuda, which would then transfer the funds to commercial accounts overseas. Sicilian Mafia members in this country have also purchased large amounts of real estate. The property can be resold for its true market value, and the proceeds are considered legitimate."[25]

During the 1970s, U.S., French, and Italian law enforcement continued their investigation of the flourishing Sicilian Mafia, but there seemed to be no limit to the growth in power of La Cosa Nostra. In one 1980 raid, authorities discovered two labs in Palermo, Sicily, capable of making up to fifty kilograms of heroin a week.[26] Two years later the Italian government, alarmed by a wave of bombings and murders of judges, police officers, and investigating magistrates, enacted an anti-mafia law, whose main features included making "association" with known Mafia figures illegal, whether a crime had been committed or not; making the confiscation of property suspected to be owned by the Mafia illegal; and authorizing wiretaps on people suspected of belonging to "Mafia type" associations.[27]

By the 1980s, the power of the Sicilian Mafia had become such that many Italians believed the country was facing a national crisis. Pino Arlacchi described the Sicilian Mafia syndicate as unique in its legacy and impact and explained why: "True, there is a strong mafia in the United States, but its influence on the highest levels of the federal government cannot compare to the entrepreneurial Italian Mafia on the Italian political system. There are instances of careless management and illegal use of public resources in many western countries, but nothing approaching the recent developments in Sicily, where mafia or mafia-related enterprises have gained a monopoly over public enterprises from national and international sources."[28]

In response to the increased pressure of Italian law enforcement, the Sicilian Mafia went on a murder spree in the early 1980s, but the Italian authorities were beginning to find success against the hard target. In 1984, 460 members and associates of the Sicilian Mafia were arrested and put on trial in Palermo in 1986. The so-called Maxi Trial has been described as the "collage" of all the Mafia investigations from 1970 to 1984.[29] Totaling forty volumes and 8,632 pages, the indictment described murders, numerous kidnappings, and the use of torture chambers by the Sicilian Mafia and called the crime syndicate "a very dangerous criminal association [that through] violence and intimidation has sown terror and death."[30] Informants such as Tommaso Buscetta and Salvatore Contorno provided invaluable insights into the workings and activities of the Italian Cosa Nostra.

Italian investigators succeeded in convicting 338 of the defendants, including Michele Greco, who was suspected of being the head of the Sicilian Mafia, to a total of 2,700 years in prison.[31] In assessing the significance of the trial, Sterling said, "The verdict in October 1987, after nearly two years of hearings confirmed the cardinal points in the indictment:

the "oneness" of the mafia, the heroin net built under its auspices, the murders done to order, the collective guilt of its governing body."[32] Many of its leaders were in jail, but the powerful Cosa Nostra went to work. Most of the convicted eventually had their sentences reduced or overturned, and by 1992 only 50 were still in jail.[33]

The brave and tenacious chief prosecutor in the trial, Giovanni Falcone, resigned his judicial post at Palermo, complaining of political interference. A national hero because of his work in the Maxi Trial, Falcone became the object of professional jealousy and a character-assassination campaign and was passed over for the post of Palmero's chief prosecutor.[34] Falcone narrowly escaped an assassination attempt in 1989, and when many associates intimated that he had fabricated the incident, Falcone quit his Palermo post and moved to Rome, going to work for the Justice Department. He was planning another judicial attack on the Mafia when he was murdered on April 7, 1992.

Claudio Martelli, the Minister of Justice, said Falcone's murder would prove to be "the Mafia's worst mistake," and the government's quick and tough response followed through on his words.[35] The Italian parliament enacted a package of antimafia measures, which set up an American-style witness-protection program, gave police special powers to investigate Mafia suspects, and established new rules for taking evidence at Mafia trials. The government sent several thousand police to Sicily, where they set up roadblocks and searched for Mafia suspects. By November 1992 Italian law enforcement had arrested 241 suspected Mafia members and seized Mafia assets said to be worth $1.4 billion. Meanwhile, more than 250 gang members had become informants and were revealing some of the mob's biggest secrets. "There is some good news," the *Economist* magazine wrote in January 1993, "For the first time since Mussolini's days, an attempt on the mafia appears to be winning results."[36]

In 1992 the Italian government launched Operation Clean Hand, one of the biggest criminal investigations in the country's history. Scores of politicians, including thirty-four members of parliament and three cabinet ministers, were arrested on corruption charges.[37] "There are signs, indeed evidence, that the Cosa Nostra is slipping," declared Pierluigi Vigna, Florence's chief prosecutor.[38]

Italy had won some big battles against the Sicilian Mafia, but the war was far from over. Octopus was wounded, but it was still capable of spreading terror and mayhem. In July 1993 a bomb killed six people in Florence, wrecking the Uffizi Gallery, one of the world's great art museums, and Italy began to fear that it was about to relive the urban terror that had paralyzed the nation in the 1970s. Some viewed the attack as an effort by the Sicilian Mafia to punish Pope John Paul for his condemnation of the Mafia during a recent visit to Sicily, while many analysts predicted it was going to be a part of a Mafia terrorist campaign that would retaliate for the arrest of Salvatore (Toto) Riina, the suspected head of the Sicilian Mafia.[39] The Mafia, however, didn't follow up in any substantial way until two years later when it went on another killing rampage, murdering several people who were related to Mafia turncoats.

Given the war of attrition that has been going on in Italy since the early 1980s, does that mean the power and reach of the Sicilian Mafia in the United States has waned? The answer is a definite no. While facing tough competition from drug-trafficking syndicates run by the Colombians, Triads, and Jamaicans, the Sicilian Mafia is still sending its members to the United States in significant numbers, and the crime syndicate continues to develop its heroin network. It makes sense, given the huge U.S. market for drugs and the fact that heroin is the most lucrative commodity ever handled by criminals. The FBI puts the current number of Sicilian mob members in the United States at between 10,000 and 20,000 members.[40]

The Sicilian Mafia is also forming strategic alliances with the other major drug-trafficking groups, particularly the Colombians and the Russians. "The Sicilian Mafia, pronounced dead by certain American enthusiasts, was rated officially with its American offspring as the country's 'most serious crime problem,'" wrote Claire Sterling. "According to the FBI, it's bringing in thousands of fresh troops to rejuvenate, if not replace, the American Mafia's geriatric leadership."[41]

Chapter 9

The Italian American Mafia: On the Ropes, But Not Out

"Fueled by greed, treachery and by what appears to be an insatiable bloodlust, the organization is self-destructing."
— George Anastasia, *Playboy* Magazine

"There will always be someone to step forward and say, 'I'll provide the criminal services.'"
— Patrick Healy, member of the Chicago Crime Commission

The advanced age of the family heads of the Italian American Mafia is just one of many reasons given by experts to explain why the mob has seen its best days as the undisputed leader of the criminal underworld. The increasing ethnicity of organized crime, the intense pressure of law enforcement, which has developed improved crime-fighting techniques, the inability to attract young Italian American talent to assume leadership positions in the organizations, the decline of the Mafia tradition and the inability of the mob's leadership to adapt to change are some of the other major reasons that help explain why the Mafia is not what it once was.[1]

Founded in the 1930s by Italian immigrant families, La Cosa Nostra (Our Thing) dominated organized crime for nearly 60 years, functioning independently of the Sicilian Mafia, although the two crime syndicates have interacted and cooperated on a number of criminal enterprises of mutual interest, including drug trafficking. That a powerful Italian American Mafia existed did not become public knowledge until a Senate committee headed by Senator Estes Kefauver began investigating it in 1951. J. Edgar Hoover, the longtime head of the FBI, remained skeptical that such an organization existed until November 14, 1957, when law enforcement stumbled upon a meeting of 60 or so Italian-American mobsters in the Appalachian Mountains of New York State.[2] In 1963 congressional testimony by Joe Valachi, a former soldier in the mob, shed further light on what was the mysterious workings of the world's most powerful criminal organization.[3]

By the early 1980s, when the U.S. government under President Ronald Reagan decided to target La Cosa Nostra, much was known about the Mafia thanks to law-enforcement investigations and congressional hearings. In 1986 the President's Commission on Organized Crime revealed that there were 24 mob families nationwide, containing about 1,700 members. "These figures represent a reduction of more than fifty percent from the FBI's 1966 estimates; FBI director William Webster attributes the decline to death, age, inactivity and law enforcement pressure," the commission reported. "The number of formal members, however, represents only a small portion of the criminal network by which the organization survives and prospers."[4]

La Cosa Nostra is under the control of a "national commission," which Mafia head Lucky Luciano established in 1931. The exception is the oldest and most established family in New Orleans, which works independently of the commission in most matters. The commission includes the bosses of the five New York mob families, as well as the heads of La Cosa Nostra branches in several major cities, including Detroit, Philadelphia, Chicago, and Buffalo. The National Commission "represents joint ventures between families, intervenes in family disputes, governs the initiation of new members, and controls relations between the U.S. and Sicilian branches of the La Cosa Nostra."[5] Each mob family has a typical organizational structure that includes the boss or head of the family; underbosses, who serve as the boss's right-hand men; consiglieri or counselors; capos or captains, who advise the bosses and supervise the family's day-to-day criminal operations; soldiers, who comprise the basic rank of the family; and associates, such as politicians, police, lawyers, and accountants.

Unlike many of today's other organized crime groups, which tend to focus on drug trafficking, the Italian American Mafia is engaged in a wide range of criminal activities, which, in addition to drug trafficking, includes prostitution, extortion, loan sharking, money laundering, illegal gambling, auto theft, embezzling, and labor racketeering, among others. According to the 1986 President's Commission on Organized

Crime, the Cosa Nostra may be involved with one or many of those criminal activities. For example, the New York mob families tend to focus on labor racketeering and the infiltration of the construction trades, while firearms trafficking is a common activity among mob families in the north-central region, and forgery and arson are common criminal activities of families in the southern and western regions.[6]

Historically, the Italian American Mafia has never adapted well to the emergence of the international drug trade, which, as we have read, has become the most important criminal enterprise in the United States in terms of money and power. In 1993 Salvatore (Sammy the Bull) Gravano testified before a federal district court in New York City that, during the 1970s and 1980s, the Gambino crime family of New York City, for whom he had worked as an underboss, had strict rules against drug trafficking and anybody in the crime family who got involved with the trade risked death. "Our policy was against drugs," Gravano told the court in testifying against John and Joseph Gambino, who were accused of running a major heroin distribution operation.[7]

With such an attitude, it is easy to understand why the five crime families of New York City never got control of the lucrative local heroin market and why they were never big players in the emergence and growth of the cocaine trade. As scholar Peter Reuter explained the mob's missed opportunity in the heroin trade, "Mexican-source heroin became available when the heroin market first expanded in the early 1970s, and the Mafia was never able to prevent its distribution in New York City, the home of perhaps one-third of the nation's heroin addicts. Its early control of the market apparently rested on its domination of the New York docks, through the longshoremen's union, as well as its connections with southern European processors. By the late 1980s, the traditional circuitous route for Southeast heroin through Sicily, Southern Italy or France had primarily been replaced by direct importation, via the West Coast, by Chinese and Vietnamese entrepreneurs. The Mafia proved helpless to deal with any of these incursions on its traditional territories."[8]

La Cosa Nostra reportedly has made money indirectly off the international drug trade. In the last chapter, we read how the Sicilian Mafia paid their American cousins "monetary tribute" in return for the approval of certain Italian-American families before initiating a major heroin smuggling operation. As the 1986 Commission on Organized Crime explained, "Sicilian organizations supply LCN (Italian American Mafia) affiliates with heroin; LCN networks either distribute the drug themselves or sell it in large quantities to major distributors."[9]

Two years later, another commission on organized crime indicated that there were reports that the Russian Mafia was linked to the Genovese Cosa Nostra family in drug deals and insurance frauds. "Apparently Russians that sell cocaine in New York's after-hour clubs must pay tribute to La Cosa Nostra members," the commission revealed.[10]

According to Peter Reuter and other experts on the Cosa Nostra, the high legal risks involved with heroin and cocaine trafficking have encouraged the Italian-American Mafia to shy away from drug-related criminal activities. Furthermore, they have not been willing to engage in the kind of violence that is necessary to maintain the hegemony in the world of cocaine trafficking. In comparing La Cosa Nostra with the Colombians, the most successful participants in the cocaine trade, Reuter noted that "the Colombian drug-dealing organizations have developed their own general reputation for violence. Indeed, the Colombians are known for their unwillingness to follow even the moderately restrictive rules of mafia murders e.g. that wives and children are exempt."[11]

Writer Michael Massing, an expert on the international drug trade, noted that the Italian-American Mafia may be criminals — at times ruthless thugs — but traditionally their actions have been tempered by an Old World code of honor. "If for whatever reason, a Mafioso had to be eliminated, the deed was to be carried out professionally, without injury to innocent parties. The new syndicates by contrast, don't hesitate to gun down a rival's family along with the man himself."[12]

The Italian American Mafia may have little direct involvement in the international drug trade, but that didn't stop the U.S. government from targeting the mob in the early 1980s. The political momentum to do something about the mob had been building since 1970, when the U.S. Congress expanded federal powers against the underworld by passing the Organized Crime Control Act of 1970, which among other measures, set up federal task forces against organized crime, expanded a federal witness-protection program set up in the late 1960s, gave prosecutors more latitude with witnesses, and most important, initiated the RICO statute (Racketeer-Influenced and Corrupt Organizations) Act, which allowed prosecutors to go after entire criminal organizations, not just individuals who may have been associated with it.

As Stephen Fox explained, "Any two of several dozen defined crimes over a ten-year period could convict someone of taking part in ongoing rackets enterprise; anyone planning or anyone discussing a crime was as guilty as the actual perpetrator. Different crimes by different crooks could still point to a single underworld organization. Bosses were no longer insulated from subordinates acting on their orders. RICO also let lawmen seize any stolen loot through property forfeitures."[13]

During the 15 years after the passage of the Organized Crime Control Act of 1970, federal and state authorities adopted other tools that also proved useful against organized crime, for example, according to the 1986 President's Commission on Organized Crime, "The consolidation of the DEA into the FBI in 1982 drastically increased the manpower and available intelligence."[14] It also helped that U.S. law-enforcement agencies developed closer coordination with their Italian colleagues, with whom they exchanged intelligence on both the Sicilian and Italian American Mafias.[15]

By the early 1980s, federal prosecutors had become highly sophisticated in their use of RICO and it became a major weapon against organized crime. The 1986 President's Commission on Organized Crime reported that there were 600 approved RICO prosecutions from 1970 through 1985, but that two-thirds of them occurred after 1981.[16] During the 1980s, the leaders of some 25 major Mafia families were indicted on criminal charges, including such well-known New York bosses as Carmine Persico of the Colombo family, Fat Tony Salerno of the Genoveses, and Tony "Ducks" Corallo of the Luccheses.[17] Between 1981 and 1987, there were more than 1,000 convictions of mobsters not just in New York but also in Boston, Chicago, Philadelphia, New Orleans, Kansas City, and Los Angeles.[18]

The relentless pursuit of La Cosa Nostra continued into the 1990s and culminated in the biggest catch of modern era of the mob: John Gotti, reportedly the most powerful Mafia leader in New York City and the most famous mob leader since Al Capone. Gotti had taken over control of the Gambino family in 1985 after the murders of Paul Castellano and Thomas Bilotti, two of the family's underbosses.[19] With his expensive haircuts and tailor-made suits and his penchant for fine cuisine, Gotti liked to keep a high profile and became known as the "Dapper Don." "Gotti is both sociable and volatile, mixing freely with underlings but prone to homicidal frenzy at petty slights," wrote Edward Conlon. "Beloved by the press for his designer clothes, quotable comic asides, and trio of acquittals, he bears a greater resemblance to fellow eighties loudmouths Trump and Steinbrenner than to any of his criminal ancestors."[20] Relying on FBI tape recordings and the testimony of Sammy Gravano, the federal authorities finally got Gotti on the third try, and he was convicted in 1992 and sentenced to life plus five years.

By 1996 the heads of the Italian American Mafia families in

Chicago, Detroit, Boston, Newark, Cleveland, and Philadelphia had been indicted and convicted of racketeering under the RICO statute. In March 1996 several members of Detroit's most important Cosa Nostra family were indicted under RICO for multiple alleged racketeering offenses, including extortion, loan sharking, and bookmaking. U.S. Attorney General Janet Reno called the main defendant, Jack William Tocco, "one of the longest-tenured and most powerful LCN bosses in the country."[21]

By the mid 1990s, the Mafia in some cities, most notably Philadelphia, had become its own worst enemy. A mob war that broke out in the City of Brotherly Love in the 1990s left several Mafia members dead, some turning informant and many arrested and put in jail, developments that seriously weakened the local Cosa Nostra. Evidence of how the mob had changed was the fact that Sicilian-born mobster John Stanfa, the Philadelphia boss, couldn't control the young members of his gang from going on a killing rampage and triggering the brainless gang war. "Fueled by greed, treachery and by what appears to be an insatiable bloodlust, the organization is self-destructing," wrote George Anastasia in *Playboy* magazine.[22] In March 1994 Stanfa and twenty-three other mobsters were convicted of racketeering charges.[23] Ronald Goldstock, the director of the New York State Organized Crime Task Force, summed up the trend: "The fate of anyone who assumes a leadership position in a [Mafia] family is a life prison sentence or assassination by a rival."[24]

La Cosa Nostra has been seriously weakened, but U.S. law enforcement is not ready to write its epitaph just yet, given the organization's experience and tradition. The mob is still considered a force in at least a dozen American cities, and even though hundreds of Mafiosi have been put behind bars, the FBI reports the number represents only 10 percent of La Cosa Nostra's total membership.[25] It is doubtful, though, that the Italian American Mafia will ever again regain its preeminence in the world of organized crime, especially since it has left much of the trafficking in illegal drugs to the Chinese, Colombians, Russians, and other increasingly powerful ethnic groups. While many of these gangs now use modern business techniques to conduct their illegal activities, the Italian American Mafia "languishes in suspicion of such sophistication, with nary a computer in sight."[26]

The decline of La Cosa Nostra will not have an impact on the direction and future of international drug trafficking, or, for that matter, organized crime, the experts agree. Mafia-watcher Robert Kelly believes that "the Italian American mob and their "new competitors" will continue to prosper by supplying and exploiting the seemingly endless need of the American public for illegal products and services."[27] And as Patrick Healy, a member of the Chicago Crime Commission, observed, "There will always be someone to step forward and say, 'I'll provide the criminal services.'"[28]

Chapter 10

The Heroin Connection: Generals, Warlords, and Guerrillas of South Asia

"When you get to the stage where traffickers have more money than the government, it's going to take remarkable effort and remarkable people to turn it around."
— Pakistan-based Western official

"Although U.S. heroin control programs in Southeast Asian countries other than Burma have had some limited success, U.S. efforts have not reduced the flow of heroin from the region because producers and traffickers shift transportation routes and growing areas into countries with inadequate law enforcement capacity or political will."
— U.S. General Accounting Office

William Brown, former U.S. ambassador to Thailand, once described Khun Sa as the "the worst enemy the world has," while other officials have been no less kind, labeling the Myanmar warlord the "Prince of Darkness" and the "Pablo Escobar of southeast Asia."[1] Khun Sa has defended himself, telling Western reporters, "I'm a revolutionary leader, not a drug trafficker."[2] His defiance of the central Myanmar government has made him a hero to many people in the Shan State of Myanmar, but the evidence shows that, for nearly three decades, he helped make Myanmar one of the largest opium- and heroin-producing countries in the world. With his Shan United Army of 10,000, Khun Sa used his base in northeastern Myanmar to turn refined opium

into pressed heroin in secret jungle laboratories and transport the narcotic drug to the streets of the United States and Europe. In 1984 the
U.S. General Accounting Office (GAO) reported that Myanmar
accounted for 87 percent of the heroin produced in southeast Asia, with
one part of the country accounting for nearly 90 percent of the opium
produced in the area known as the Golden Triangle.[3]

The Golden Triangle and the Golden Crescent, the other huge drug-
producing area of southern Asia, have made the region the principal
source of the world's heroin supply and a major target of U.S. antidrug
efforts for nearly three decades. The Golden Triangle is an area of rugged
terrain of about 150 square miles, occupying parts of Laos, Myanmar,
and Thailand and consisting of thick jungle, deep valleys, and rising
mountains.[4] Myanmar remains the biggest source country, while opium
production has declined in recent years in Thailand, as tourism and foreign trade have grown. Laos, the only country in the Golden Triangle
where it is legal to raise opium, is a minor producer of opium.

It should be noted that many experts add the People's Republic of
China (Red China) to the Golden Triangle because they believe opium
is being grown illegally for export in the country's Yunnan Province.[5]
Red China has a strict policy against opium use, but, since the country
opened up to the West in the late 1970s, it has been easy for the country to serve as a transport point for drugs bound to the United States
and other Western countries. The Golden Triangle's drug cultivators
produce an estimated 1,500 tons of opium a year, which is refined into
about 100 tons of pure heroin and then distributed worldwide by the
Chinese Triads and Nigerian couriers.[6]

The Golden Crescent, which consists of the major opium-producing areas of Iran, Pakistan, and Afghanistan, and to a lesser extent India
and Turkey, has been a major source of illegal drugs since the late 1970s.
The bulk of the opium comes from Afghanistan, where traffickers transport the drug by mules and camels through the higher passes to the
heroin-producing labs of Pakistan's northwest province.[7] Pakistan's role
in the Golden Crescent's heroin trade is that of refiner because it is
believed that the country's estimated one million addicts consume most
of the heroin the country produces.[8] Iran also has an estimated 1 million heroin addicts, who are also believed to consume most of the country's opium production.[9]

The Golden Triangle and Golden Crescent have alternated as the
world's principal source of heroin. The Golden Crescent, for instance,
became the main source of heroin in southern Asia after the Golden

Triangle experienced major crop failures in the mid 1970s. The situation began to change by the mid 1980s, when experts determined that supply in the Golden Triangle was on the rise again. In 1990 the DEA reported that at least 55 percent of the heroin smuggled into the United States came from the Golden Triangle, as compared to only 18 percent in 1987.[10]

Heroin comes from opium, a substance derived from the sap of the opium poppy, a plant that has been in existence for thousands of years. As early as 5,000 BC, people in the area now occupied by the country of Iraq cultivated opium. Priests in Egypt and other countries in the Middle East used opium for religious ceremonies, and later opium was popular among the citizens of the Greek and Roman civilizations. Up until the twelfth century, opium was used for its medicinal qualities. Christian and Moslem doctors, for example, used it for the treatment of dysentery, although in their zeal to use the drug, several patients apparently died of overdoses. By the sixteenth century, it is believed that the upper classes of Persia and India were using opium for "recreational" purposes.[11]

Opium did not become a big addiction problem until the seventeenth century, when the European powers, most notably Great Britain, began to finance their colonial ambitions with money from the opium trade, establishing opium monopolies for themselves in Burma (modern Myanmar), Thailand, and other countries of southeast Asia. As writer Gerald Posner explained, "The British led the drive in Asia. They established a government monopoly over the large poppy tracts in northern India and targeted China's inhabitants as the most profitable market. Moral objections were overwhelmed by the enormous profits, almost twenty percent of the British revenues."[12]

Concern about the Asian drug problem grew and spawned the worldwide anti-opium movement of the twentieth century, discussed earlier, but the damage had been done. "In Southeast Asia, not only did the British and French opium monopolies create massive addict populations, but they also inadvertently fueled a smuggling network that was crucial to the post World War II heroin epidemic," writes Posner.[13] That is because the intelligence services of the United States and France would form alliances with drug traffickers of the region, a development that fueled the growth of the Asian narcotics trade.

The United States has been particularly concerned about heroin trafficking since the late 1980s, when the worldwide production of heroin nearly doubled and the emergency-room cases relating to heroin overdoses increased 50 percent.[14] The U.S. General Accounting Office estimated that opium production worldwide grew from 2,242 metric tons in 1987 to 3,409 metric tons in 1994, and that by 1996 Americans were using 10 to 15 metric tons of heroin annually, as compared to 5 tons annually in the mid 1980s.[15]

By 1997 the press was reporting that a new generation of drug abusers had sprung up in the United States, and did not buy the argument that the drug was harmful. "Heroin is back," complained Barry McCaffrey, director of the White House Office of National Drug Control Policy. "It's more potent, and it's more deadly than ever. A new generation of kids has come along and they simply haven't got the message."[17]

The Golden Triangle has become an integral part of the U.S. heroin problem for several reasons. As Jay Robert Nash explained, "From the hill farmer's perspective, opium is a perfect crop. With an average yield of two kilos an acre, the harvest is non-perishable and easy to sell. The growers do not go to market; the drug traffickers and opium warlords send their agents to buy at source. Many farmers are addicts — a further incentive to replant — and are bound into economic servitude by accepting loans. Sometimes their payment is in kind with goods like salt and matches. For cash, the crop fetches about $40 a kilo."[17]

One U.S. official explained how the setting of the Golden Triangle has served a dual purpose: "On one hand, the topographical and climatic conditions are ideal for the production of opium, and the demographic characteristics of the region ensure the kind of division of labor necessary to sustain a widespread economic system rooted in opium cultivation, narcotics refining and trafficking. On the other hand, these conditions all mitigate against the extension of the control measures which would enforce the law against opium cultivation, or the development initiatives which might offer an alternative to opium culture."[18] Moreover, the three countries composing the Golden Triangle, most notably Myanmar, have shown little willingness or commitment to combat the lucrative heroin trade.

The United States and its allies in southeast Asia, as well as key international organizations, have tried to put a stop to the drug trafficking in the region, but have had little success. Indeed, the U.S. government has candidly admitted its failure. "Although U.S. heroin control programs in Southeast Asian countries other than Burma have had some limited success, U.S. efforts have not reduced the flow of heroin from the region because producers and traffickers shift transportation routes and growing areas into countries with inadequate law enforcement capacity or political will," conceded the watchdog U.S. General Accounting Office (GAO) in a 1996 report that investigated drug trafficking in the Golden Triangle.[20]

In Myanmar, several types of groups are involved in drug trafficking: revolutionary movements trying to overthrow the central government of Myanmar; ethnic insurgents seeking some form of autonomy from the central government; and groups headed by so-called warlords like Khun Sa. Such groups become involved in heroin production and distribution and join trafficking syndicates that have the political power to protect heroin refineries from police raids and serve to facilitate the movement of heroin internationally.[20]

Historically, these elements have been helped in the heroin trade by the corrupt Myanmar government, which has been willing to accept bribes to ignore the heroin production going on within its borders. The problem of corruption became so serious that in 1981 the U.S. government removed Myanmar from the list of countries eligible to receive U.S foreign aid targeted to fight drug trafficking because of its inability — or unwillingness — to stop the drugs leaving the country.[21] Nine years later, the United States cut off eradication assistance to Myanmar because the country's government had virtually suppressed the country's prodemocracy movement, began establishing a record of human rights abuses, and refused to recognize the results of national elections in 1990 that removed the military government from power.[22] The U.S. General Accounting Office admitted that "more importantly, because of the complex Burmese political environment, U.S. assistance is unlikely to be effective until the Burmese government demonstrates improvement in its democracy and human rights policies and proves its legitimacy to ethnic minority groups in opium-producing areas."[23]

Unlike Myanmar, neighboring Thailand had some success with heroin-control efforts. Opium production was as high as 150 to 200 metric tons in the 1970s but had dropped to 17 metric tons by 1994. The GAO attributes this success to U.S. assistance, mainly in the form of law-enforcement training programs funded primarily by the U.S. Drug Enforcement Agency (DEA). The total cost to the United States was a relatively modest $16.5 million.

The GAO admits, however, that the Golden Triangle experience has mirrored the familiar pattern that has occurred in other parts of the world. In response to the Thai crackdown, the drug traffickers have established new trafficking routes that have moved heroin via the southern provinces of China to Taiwan and Hong Kong and on through Laos,

Cambodia, and Vietnam to markets in Europe and North America.[24] In fact, the GAO predicted that until "law enforcement efforts aimed at heroin-trafficking organizations and drug-trafficking routes can be coordinated regionally, the flow of Southeast Asia heroin to the United States will continue unabated."[25]

The Golden Crescent has also thrived as a major player in international drug trafficking since the late 1970s and may actually be the world's biggest producer of heroine.[26] The cheapness and high purity of its heroin, as well as the region's huge addict population, are important factors that help explain the growth of the Golden Crescent as a major drug-producing region.[27] Two other important reasons for its growth include the complicity of the local governments in drug trafficking and the U.S. government's inability — or unwillingness — to do anything about it.

We have read how suspected CIA involvement with Mujahideen guerrillas in the late 1970s may have led to a heroin epidemic in the United States. The Afghan guerrillas were believed to be heavily involved in drug trafficking to finance their war against the Soviet-backed national government.

The Pakistani army has also been accused of heavy involvement in the heroin trade, largely the result of the country's covert support for Afghanistan guerrillas. In 1988 Lawrence Lifschultz wrote that "the local Pakistani press, led by a courageous English-language newspaper, the *Herald*, reported on a number of occasions that the main conduit by which weapons reached the Afghan insurgents is also one the principal routes for the transport of heroin to Karachi for shipment to Europe and the United States."[28]

According to Lifschultz, the Pakistani heroin connection has been allowed to flourish because of "conflicting agendas of U.S. policy in Pakistan in which concerns about drug trafficking are superseded by national security concerns."[29] In other words, Pakistan may be involved in the drug trade, but its government has long been allies of the United States, helping Uncle Sam meet its strategic foreign policy objectives.

Lifschultz noted that "George Bush's handling of the drug issue raises serious concerns about his objectives in Pakistan," and he described how, at a banquet in Pakistan in 1988 in George Bush's honor, the vice president heaped praise on General Zia Ul-Haq's (then Pakistan's president) antinarcotics program. Bush noted that drug control was a matter of "personal interest" and that Pakistan's efforts are the source of the greatest satisfaction to him. Among the guests listening to his remarks were a number of prominent individuals allegedly linked to the most lucrative heroin syndicates in the world."[30]

Critics of the U.S. drug policy see Pakistan as another graphic example of how, in the words of Alfred W. McCoy, "America's heroin plague is of its own making." Some U.S. officials have wondered out loud what impact the heroin trade will have on Pakistan. "It's become a serious domestic problem with all kinds of implications for Pakistan's security," one Pakistan-based official said. "And it's a problem Pakistan authorities still seem either unwilling or unable to cope with."[31]

Many of the powerful drug traffickers in the Golden Crescent operate in the remote border regions ruled by tribal warlords and outside the control of the central government, where the Pakistani authorities have limited resources to combat the well-armed tribesmen who can operate along a largely unpatrolled 1,400-mile border. In 1992, for example, Pakistan spent only $1.8 million on its antinarcotics efforts. The ineffectiveness of the Pakistani government combined with the growing power of the drug lords has spawned concern that Pakistan might become another Colombia. "Many narco-traffickers are going to be in a position where they control everything," according to one Pakistan-based Western official. "When you get to the stage where traffickers have more money than the government, it's going to take remarkable effort and remarkable people to turn it around."[32]

Amidst the gloom, however, the United States and its allies in southern Asia garnered one stunning victory in the War on Drugs. In 1996 Khun Sa surrendered to Myanmar authorities with most of his 10,000-man army, ending his long war with the central government. Myanmar turned down a U.S. request to extradite Khun Sa to the United States for trial. The United States took the warlord's elimination from the international drug-trafficking scene as an encouraging sign, but nobody is about to say that the tide had turned against drug trafficking in southern Asia. Statistics make that clear. Just as Khun Sa's long reign as the "the Escobar of southeast Asia" was coming to an end, Myanmar was growing enough poppy to produce a bumper supply of 230 tons of heroin, about 23 times the U.S. demand of 10 tons.[33]

Chapter 11

The Chinese Connection: Triads, Tongs, and Street Gangs

"It's impossible to attack the Triads as a whole organization … It's really like fighting hundreds of street gangs."
— Hong Kong law enforcement official

"The wave of corruption has already occurred. They have already filtered out the money into the U.S. High-level Triads are already here, and they are spreading out a lot of money, gathering their forces."
— Tom Perdue, detective,
San Francisco Police Department.

Southern Asia is the world's biggest producer of raw opium and its refined product, heroin, but to get the heroin from the remote jungle laboratories of southern Asia to the transshipment points in Bangkok, Taiwan, and Hong Kong onto the streets of the United States and Europe is the job of well-organized ethnic Chinese criminal groups, as well as African drug couriers, primarily under the control of Nigerian crime syndicates.[1] Most of the heroin shipments, which can range in size from fifty to many thousands of kilograms, are hidden in containerized freight aboard cargo airlines and commercial maritime vessels. Chinese and African couriers also smuggle heroin by either concealing the drug in their luggage, swallowing it, or hiding it in their bodies.[2]

The Chinese connection in international drug trafficking came to public attention in the mid 1980s, when Chinese criminal gangs began to replace the Italian crime syndicates as the dominant force in heroin trafficking. In New York City, the country's biggest heroin market, federal prosecution of mob leaders in the famous Pizza Connection case weakened the Italian mob's hold of the wholesale distribution of the drug and allowed the Chinese to grab control of 65 to 85 percent of the market.

Beginning in 1986, customs officials at international airports in cities like New York, Los Angeles, and San Francisco began to notice a huge increase in heroin trafficking involving Chinese nationals arriving from Thailand, Taiwan, Hong Kong, and mainland China. By September of that year, the modus operandi was changing, as the Chinese traffickers began to shift from the use of couriers to the use of cargo ships to smuggle heroin. Within the next six months, the authorities intercepted shipments totaling 133 pounds of heroin.[3] By February 1989 one investigation was being called the biggest heroin bust in U.S. history. Twenty-six people who worked for a powerful Hong Kong–based international heroin ring were arrested and 800 pounds of pure high-grade heroine seized.[4] The following year, cases implicating Chinese traffickers had become routine, and law enforcement agencies around the world were confiscating many thousands of pounds of heroin.[5]

"This is clearly one of the most dramatic changes in drug trafficking patterns that I have seen," said Robert M. Stutman, a special agent in charge of the federal Drug Enforcement Administration's office in New York. "It is important because it makes our enforcement job much more difficult — particularly in penetrating a culture that is essentially unknown to us."[6]

Who are the Chinese criminal entrepreneurs responsible for transporting and distributing hundreds of pounds of heroin to consumers in the United States, Europe, and other parts of the world? According to extensive research conducted by the Center for the Study of Asian Organized Crime, the global infrastructure for the distribution of heroin has been set up by the Taiwanese and the remnants of the KMT army that fled to Laos, Myanmar, Cambodia, and Thailand after the Communists under Mao Tse Tung took control of mainland China in 1949. "When we look at the heroine producing labs that are moving out of the Burmese states and across the border into Yunnan province, and stretching in an area all the way to Southeast Asia, these labs are controlled by Taiwanese," Willard H. Myers, head of the Center for the Study of Asian Organized Crime, explained in testimony before the U.S. Senate Subcommittee on Terrorism and Narcotics in 1994.[7]

Many of the Taiwanese leaders in the international drug-trafficking business are members of the Triads, Chinese secret societies that organized in China in the early seventeenth century as resistance groups to the Manchu dynasty that ruled China from the seventeenth century to 1911.[8] After the Manchus were deposed, some Triad members moved into crime, including the lucrative opiate trade from the Golden Triangle.[9] The nationalists under Dr. Sun Yat-Sen tried to disband the Triads but were unsuccessful. When the Communists took over mainland China in 1949, a large group of Triads followed General Chiang Kai Shek to Taiwan; others moved to Hong Kong, strengthening the large Triad population in what was then a British colony.[10]

The remnants of the Kuomintang Army (KMT) boosted opium production from 50 tons to 350 tons a decade after arriving in the Shan State of Myanmar in 1949. "The Chinese nationalists and their Taiwanese connections brought the Triads into every stage of the heroin business, from the source to the refinement to the distribution and sale," writer Gerald Posner explains. "Hong Kong Triads sent chemists to KMT heroin labs, and the Chinese armies reserved the best narcotics and lowest prices for the Hong Kong syndicates."[11]

Today, Hong Kong is the nerve center for the Triad organization, which has spread all over the world and is involved not only in drug trafficking but also protection, loan sharking, illegal gambling, and extortion rackets, among other criminal activities. The Triads have a tradition, organization, initiations, and rituals that remind many law-enforcement officials of the Italian Mafia.[12] For example, to be a Triad, new members must be recommended by existing members in good standing, and, if admitted, they must go through a complicated initiation ceremony and observe many rituals.[13] The Triads, however, differ from the Cosa Nostra in that they have no bosses or no ruling council and are decentralized in nature. "It's impossible to attack the Triad society as a whole organization," one Hong Kong law enforcement official explained. "It's really like fighting hundreds of street gangs."[14]

The Triads, though, have grown into one of the world's biggest criminal organizations with as many as fifty gangs and a membership anywhere from 50,000 to 180,000, according to various estimates.[15] In 1994 the Center for the Study of Asian Organized Crime put Triad earning from the international heroin trade at a staggering $200 billion a year.[16] Major markets for the Triad drug distribution pipeline include Taiwan, the Netherlands, Asia, and the United States.

In the 1970s Triad gang leaders began to see the new criminal opportunity presented by the growing Chinese communities in the United

States. Between 1970 to 1980, the number of Chinese immigrants to the United States jumped 85 percent, from 435,062 to 806,027, thanks to the changes in the 1965 Immigration Act, which helped make the Chinese the second-largest immigrant group in the United States after the Mexicans.[17] This does not include the estimated 100,000-plus Chinese who are smuggled into the United States annually, which according to William H. Myers, shows that the ethnic Chinese transnational criminal organizations can "in the face of mounting (law) enforcement, bring anything into or out of the U.S. anytime, anywhere."[18]

According to many law-enforcement officials, when setting up their operations in the United States, the Triads have infiltrated local Chinese groups and community associations in Chinese communities throughout the country. The extent of Triad involvement in drug trafficking in the United States has been a contentious issue among experts. Some FBI and DEA officials concealed that individual gang members had come from Hong Kong to the U.S., but they have insisted that there is no organized Triad criminal activity. Ko-lin Chin, a noted scholar of Chinese subculture, believes that the "Chinese mafia" does not exist and has maintained that "there was little evidence to support the contention that Hong Kong Triad societies are responsible for the bulk of heroin smuggled into the United States."[19] Law-enforcement officials in the streets have disagreed with the skeptics and warned that it would be a mistake to underestimate the Triad presence in the United States. "The wave of corruption has already occurred," Sergeant Tom Perdue of the San Francisco Police Department explained. The Triads "have already filtered out the money into the U.S. High-level Triads are already here, and they are spreading out a lot of money, gathering their forces."[20]

Analysis by the U.S. Department of Justice appears to back up what many of the police operating in the streets are saying. According to one government agency's report, "Some ordinary Triad members are entering the U.S. and some of their former leaders are moving significant portions of their assets here as a hedge against the future. Both of these trends should accelerate in the next ten years."[21] Reports indicated that the Triads were established in many U.S. cities with large Chinese populations, including Chicago, New York, San Francisco, Boston, and Monterey Park, California.

Most of the Triads emigrating to the United States came from Hong Kong. When Hong Kong authorities launched an anticorruption drive in the 1970s, five former Hong Kong police sergeants, known as the Five Dragons, fled the colony, each reportedly carrying as much as $1 million.

One of the five was Eddie Chan, who became a successful businessman in New York City's Chinatown, a force in the Triads, and a leader of the Tong group known as On Leong.[22]

Given the U.S. connection, Hong Kong became a major heroin transshipment point in the mid 1980s; the amount of number 4 heroin seized by Hong Kong authorities jumped dramatically from 12.4 kilograms in 1985 to 79.24 kilograms in 1986 to 157.2 kilograms in 1987 and 161 kilograms in 1988. "Because local heroin addicts consume only the smokable form (number 3 heroin), the increase in number 4 heroin seizures suggests that more heroine is being transported abroad via Hong Kong," explained Ko-lin.[23] By 1989 the Immigration and Naturalization Service (INS) had established special task forces on Chinese criminal gangs in New York City, Boston, Houston, Los Angeles, San Francisco, and Washington, D.C. "We're seeing more and more Chinese organized crime coming here every day," said James Goldman, the INS's organized crime chief.[24]

When the Triads began organizing in the Chinatowns, they had to deal with the pervasive presence of the Tongs, Chinese volunteer associations that first began to appear in the mid nineteenth century to help Chinese immigrants adapt to the United States and to protect weaker members of the Chinese community from the more powerful local residents. More than 30 Tongs with names like Bing Kung, Chih Kung, Hop Sing, Hop Sung, and, of course, On Leong, have been established. Described as a "legitimate mirror image of the Triads," the Tongs' role in the Chinese American community has been highly controversial.[25]

The Tongs have insisted that their activities are above board, but U.S. law enforcement has said that they are involved in organized crime in the Chinese community. "Historically, Tongs have done a lot of good in America's Chinatowns," explained William Kleinknecht "They deal out credit to merchants, find jobs for new immigrants and mediate business disputes. If the average Tong leader's only crime were the operation of gambling casinos, he would be no bigger a villain than the New York real-estate mogul Donald Trump."[26]

Tong criminal activity, however, involves more than just gambling. According to the FBI, Tong members have directed gangs that have been involved in a number of criminal activities, including drug trafficking and money laundering.[27] In February 1996 federal law enforcement officials charged several leaders of the Tongs living in Atlanta, Boston, New York City, Denver, San Francisco, Ellicott City, Maryland, Portland, Oregon, Wheaton, Maryland, and Washington, D.C., with involvement in drug trafficking and money laundering. The charges stemmed from a lengthy federal investigation in which Tong members allegedly agreed to launder more than $50,000 in cash that they believed came from Colombian cartels. Undercover agents had set up a dummy corporation in Atlanta to investigate local Tong activity there.[28]

"Once we advised that we had money available we literally had people knocking at our door seeking to get money from illegal drug trafficking to put into their gambling business," James Delchert, a United States attorney in charge of the Organized Crime Strike Force in Atlanta, explained at a news conference.[29] David W. Johnson, Jr., the special agent in charge of the Atlanta office of the FBI, said, "We are not indicting the Tongs as an organization, however, some of these are criminal-influenced Tongs."[30]

Since the 1960s, some Tongs have helped fuel criminal activity in Chinese American communities by fostering the growth of street gangs to act as bodyguards for their gambling dens. Most of the thugs are immigrants, between 15 and 37 years of age, from Taiwan and Hong Kong. When Taiwan cracked down on its underworld in the 1970s and early 1980s, hundreds of criminal figures fled for the United States, where most settled in Monterey Park, California, a city whose Chinese community is predominantly Taiwanese. Meanwhile, other Chinese street gangs established bases in New York City, Los Angeles, San Francisco, Chicago, Houston, Dallas, Boston, Philadelphia, Oakland, California, and Arlington, Virginia.[31]

According to law-enforcement and media reports, street gangs are playing an increasingly active role in the heroin trade, establishing profitable distribution pipelines to sources in Hong Kong and southeast Asia. As Professor Chin describes the network, "Gang members hire nonmembers to work for them. They travel frequently between the United States and Hong Kong to reestablish their network with drug producers and dealers in southeast Asia. It is not clear, however, what role gang members play in their gang leaders' drug business. Drug-enforcement authorities assume that the gang leaders' involvement in heroin trafficking is not related to their gangs."[32]

For a variety of reasons, law enforcement has had a difficult time penetrating the Triad, Tong, and street-gang organizations and making any headway against their drug-trafficking activities. The groups operate like brotherhoods, and, when caught, members rarely inform on their brothers, willingly going to jail, if need be, for long stretches of time. Very few federal and local law enforcement officials understand

Chinese culture, let alone speak any of the dialects. For example, most Chinese in San Francisco can speak the Cantonese dialect, but one San Francisco police officer, who is an expert on Chinese organized crime, estimated in 1991 that only 1 percent of the San Francisco police force speak the dialect.[33] Moreover, Chinese communities are isolated from mainstream America and distrustful of outsiders because of past racist experience. This makes for an ideal environment in which Chinese criminals can operate. The Chinese have also used the large profits made from heroin trafficking to develop powerful sophisticated organizations for which the authorities with their meager resources are no match.

In 1991 the Permanent Subcommittee on Investigations of the U.S. Congress had hearings on Asian organized crime and found "little evidence to suggest that either U.S. or foreign law enforcement entities are currently equipped to meet the challenge of this new breed of international criminal." Senator Nunn, chairman of the subcommittee, said, "Not enough progress has been made in establishing formal cooperative relationships among law enforcement bodies willing to address this problem. While the rhetoric often is positive…. too often the information is not shared, documents are not accessible, and efforts to locate criminals do not receive international assistance. Their international capabilities make these Asian criminals a world problem and one that we should be eager to address together."[34]

The Chinese connection to heroin traffic is so huge that it would be a mistake to focus just on the Triads, Tongs and street gangs, says Professor Ko-lin Chin. He believes that a new generation of non–Triad Chinese criminals is emerging on the American scene, who "are responsible for the bulk of heroin imported into the United States and "are not committed to the rigid Triad subcultural norms and values, thus enabling them to assemble quickly when the criminal opportunities arise and to dissolve after the criminal conspiracy is carried out."[35] He advises: "What we need to do is to focus our attention on the development of both the Triad subculture and the Chinese drug trafficking subculture simultaneously and to prevent the coalition of these two equally destructive forces."[36]

More bad news — the United States has become an even more attractive place for Chinese criminals in southeast Asia. Great Britain officially turned over control of Hong Kong to the People's Republic of China on July 1, 1997. Meanwhile, fearful of what might happen to themselves and their criminal organizations under Communist rule, the Triads and other

Chinese criminals had begun moving themselves and their assets to the United States and other countries, beginning in the early 1980s. This is not an encouraging trend, given that the Chinese connection dominates the worldwide distribution of heroin.

Linchpin: The Colombian Connection

Described as the linchpin of the Latin American drug trade, Colombian drug trafficking organizations, called cartels, have dominated the cocaine trade since the 1970s. Throughout the 1980s and the early 1990s, experts have put their control of the trade at 70 to 80 percent.[1] In the early 1990s, moreover, the cartels began to move into the heroin market, and, within five years, their activities in their new market had made Colombia one of the world's top three producers of the opium plant.[2] Earnings put at between $2 billion and $5 billion a year have made the leaders of the cartels some of the world's richest individuals and have allowed them to penetrate Colombia's democratic political system and create a virtual state within a state. "The illegal drug industry has had serious corrupting influence on every aspect of Colombian society and its economic and political structures," explained Jorge Graitman, an economist with Colombia's national government.[3]

Colombia's role in the multibillion dollar cocaine trade is to acquire coca leaves from farmers in Peru and Bolivia and process them into cocaine hydrochloride and then transport the finished product to the lucrative U.S. market. In Peru alone, an estimated 50,000 tons of coca leaf are produced each year.[4] About 1.8 million people are employed in the underground coca-leaf production in Peru and Bolivia, which accounts for an estimated $700 million of the first country's illegal exports and $410 million of the second. Another 600,000 Colombians are connected legally or illegally in some way to the cocaine trade, which pumps billions into the Colombian economy.[5]

Several reasons help explain why Colombia has come to dominate the Latin American drug trade. First, the coca plant is easy to grow, even in rugged terrain. The plant has a lifespan of about thirty years and can be harvested up to six times annually, which provides for an endless supply of raw material that makes up for drug seizures by law enforcement.

Geographically, Colombia is well situated to serve as the linchpin that receives the coca leaves from Peru and Bolivia, processes them into cocaine, and then transports the finished product by land and sea to the United States. Colombia is also a large country with vast forested land areas that can hide secretive air strips and laboratories and protect their illegal operations against effective attack by the Colombian military and law enforcement agencies.[6]

Myles Frechette, former U.S. ambassador to Colombia (courtesy U.S. Embassy in Colombia).

The size of some of the drug-producing laboratories can be remarkable. In one 1984 raid, code-named Operation Condor, authorities discovered six cocaine laboratories, including a super lab in the process of being installed. It had pumps, steel vats, a 300-horsepower generator and centrifuges capable of producing up to 60 pounds of cocaine a day. The complex even had a house for pilots, who, as they flew in to pick up the next cocaine shipment for the United States, would see a large inviting sign bearing the words, "Welcome to Tranquilandia."[7]

Other factors that help to explain Colombia's rise to prominence in the illegal drug industry include the country's experience in exporting contraband; the lack of significant government presence in many rural areas of the country; a strong entrepreneurial tradition that it could apply to marketing and distributing illegal drugs; the pervasive corruption in Colombian society; the growth of a large underground economy in the 1970s; a large Colombian population in the United States, segments of which provide cover for drug-trafficking activities and a distribution network once the drugs arrive in the United States; and the ruthless nature of Colombian drug cartels, especially the Medellín cartel, which dominated the cocaine trade until the early 1990s.[8]

"I have heard about the Mafia in the U.S., but compared to ours, they can be described as gentlemen when they kill," explained Juan Ferro, a member of *Espectador*'s editorial board, in describing the modus operandi of the Medellín cartel. The U.S. Mafia "might send a note of apology to the next of kin. A capo [Colombian drug-trafficker boss] will kill you, your wife, your children, your relatives, if he can find them, and even your pets."[9]

There have been as many as 20 Colombian cocaine-trafficking organizations, but since Colombia emerged as a power in the drug trade, two particular groups, the Medellín and Cali cartels, have dominated the drug trade. The Medellín cartel, named after the city of Medellín (pop. 1.5 million), the capital of Antioquía province, took a high-profile approach to drug trafficking and included a number of *capos* who became world famous in the 1980s: Pablo Escobar, Rodríguez Gacha, Carlos Lehder, and the Ochoa brothers (Fabio, José Luis, and Juan David), being the most prominent.

Historically, Medellín had a reputation as a smuggling center for liquor and cigarettes from the United States and stereos, radios, and television sets from the many ports of the Panama Canal zone. Medellín began to play an important role in the international drug trade in 1973 when Chilean General Augusto Pinochet overthrew Marxist president

Andrés Pastrana, current president of
Colombia (courtesy Ron Chepesiuk).

Salvador Allende and either jailed
or deported from Chile numerous
drug traffickers who had made
Chile the center of the emerging
U.S. cocaine trade, although at the
time the market for cocaine was
small. The trade then moved to
Colombia, where criminals like
Pablo Escobar and Fabio Ochoa
(the father of the Ochoa brothers)
were eager to expand the cocaine-
distribution network.

Fabio Ochoa, who got his start
in crime by smuggling whisky and
home electronics, is credited with
founding the Medellín cartel around
1978, when Pablo Escobar convinced Fabio to use his well-estab-
lished and well-connected smuggling
routes for the more profitable drug
business.[10] April 18, 1981, may be
considered the key date for the Medellín cartel's establishment. Several
drug traffickers, including Jorge Luis Ochoa, Fabio Ochoa, Pablo Escobar, and Carlos Lehder met at the estate owned by the Ochoa clan to
discuss ways to transport cocaine to the United States. By the end of the
year, the Medellín cartel had supervised at least 38 shipments to the
United States, containing about 19 tons of cocaine. As business picked
up, other family members and relatives joined the cartel. The three
Ochoa brothers, for example, took over from their father when he
decided to retire in the late 1970s.[11]

What the Medellín cartel needed, though, to expand their operation and stay ahead of the competition was a fast, cheap transportation
system. That was provided by Carlos Lehder, a flamboyant, unpre-
dictable criminal of Colombian-German background, who got his start
in crime in the United States. Lehder revolutionized the way drugs were
smuggled into the United States and established a monopoly for the
Medellín cartel by retaining a fleet of small cargo planes and high-speed
boats that eliminated the middleman or "mule" who had traditionally
smuggled cocaine into the United States. The cartel established routine
air corridors in South and Central America and fuel stops in the islands

of the Caribbean and Mexico. Transit sites included the Bahamas, Turks, Caico Islands, Jamaica, Mexico, and Nicaragua, which were protected by cartel employees or independent organizations, including those headed by local government officials.[12]

The planes blended in with the traffic over the Florida Keys, and upon reaching their destination, they either dropped their drug cargoes to waiting boats or landed at clandestine airstrips in Florida, Georgia, or Alabama. Lehder directed the transportation network from his command post at Norman's Cay in the Bahamas. Once safely in the United States, cocaine shipments were taken to warehouses or stash houses and then distributed and sold to the cartel's clients.[13]

Ernesto Samper, former president of Colombia (courtesy Ernesto Samper).

For a big service fee based on the weight of the shipment, independent dealers not affiliated with the Medellín cartel could use the transportation system to get their drugs to the U.S. Gilberto Rodríguez Orejuela, a founding member of the Cali cartel, used his boyhood friendship with Jorge Luis Ochoa to ship an undetermined amount of cocaine through the system to Florida, where he would hire trucks to ship the cocaine to the Cali cartel's prime market, New York City.[14]

Gilberto Rodríguez Orejuela, his brother Miguel and friend José Santacruz Londono, who eventually became the three highest-ranking members of the Cali cartel, got their criminal start in the 1950s and 1960s as juvenile delinquents, kidnappers, petty criminals, enforcers, and couriers for drug traffickers. The ransom money they made from several kidnappings gave the young criminals the necessary capital to finance their entry in the early 1970s into what was becoming big-time cocaine smuggling.[15]

In the mid 1970s, while the more powerful Medellín cartel was establishing a strong base in Miami, the Cali cartel moved into the New York City market. In 1975 Gilberto Rodríguez sent Hernando Giraldo Soto, a close boyhood friend, to New York City to develop the Cali cartel's Colombian contacts in the borough of Queens, and during the next three years, he refined and enlarged their cocaine distribution line to New

Alphonso Valdivieso (left) and the author (author's collection).

York City.[16] Meanwhile, in September 1975, the names of Gilberto and Miguel Rodríguez had appeared as 58th and 62nd, respectively, on a list of 113 top drug traffickers compiled by the intelligence section of Colombia's Customs Service.[17] The Cali cartel was on its way.

As we read in the prologue, the Medellín and Cali Cartels developed different approaches to drug trafficking. The Medellín cartel was not afraid of violent confrontation with anyone, including the Colombian government, and it would not hesitate to eliminate any threats to its interests. During the 1980s, the Medellín cartel used bombings and terrorism and hired and trained hitmen known as sicarios to kill thousands of people, including some of the most prominent figures in Colombian politics: Rodrigo Lara Bonilla, Colombian justice minister, in 1984; Jaime Gómez Ramírez, head of Colombia's National Police antinarcotics Unit, in 1986; Guillermo Cano Isaza, the respected editor of the *Espectador* newspaper, in 1986; and Luis Carlos Galan, a presidential candidate, in 1989; among others. The Cali cartel, in contrast, diligently cultivated an image as a kinder, gentler Mafia that preferred to use the bribe rather than the bullet in doing business. As James Sutton, a security consultant based in Mexico City, explained, "The saying goes that the Medellín Cartel confronts; Cali corrupts."[18]

No group, however, gets to the top of the criminal underworld on sophisticated style alone. The Cali cartel has shown that it can be as

Colonel Leonardo Gallego of the Colombian Antinarcotics Police (author's collection).

ruthless as any other crime syndicate in international drug trafficking. "They are smart; the authorities never seem to find the bodies," one Bogotá-based journalist explained. "And they always seem to be floating in the river, of course, away from Cali."[19]

Differences aside, the two Colombian cartels revolutionized cocaine trafficking, not just in the way the drug was transported to the U.S., but also in how it was distributed within the United States. The cartels established the drug trade on a business model with efficient, well-oiled smuggling marketing and money-laundering networks operating from coast to coast in the United States. By 1989 an estimated 300 Colombian drug-trafficking groups and 20,000 Colombians were involved in the cocaine

Efraín Hernandez, a drug trafficker killed by unknown assaillants in 1997 (courtesy Colombian Antinarcotics Police).

trade in the United States.[20] At least 5,000 of the Colombians who worked for the cartels lived in the Miami area and another 6,000 in the Los Angeles area.[21]

"The Colombians have the momentum by benefit of their early involvement in the cocaine trade," a presidential commission concluded in 1986. "They have evolved from small, disassociated groups into compartmentalized organizations that are sophisticated and systematized in their approach to the trafficking of cocaine in the U.S."[22]

According to law-enforcement reports, Colombian drug-trafficking groups operate as independent cells of about five to fifty members with only a handful of the "managers" knowing all the cell's members. Top-level managers both in Colombia and in the United States are recruited on the basis of blood and marriage, which helps to minimize the potential for theft or disobedience, since family members in Colombia are held accountable for drug deals gone bad. Middle managers are placed all over the United States and may include individuals who may not be family members, but who may be friends of top-level capos or at least have roots in the region a capo comes from. The third level consists of thousands of workers, both inside and outside the United States — accountants, couriers, chemists, lawyers, stash-house keepers, enforcers, bodyguards, launderers, pilots, wholesale distributors — who perform specialized tasks and may work for different cells at different times. While the cartels are predominantly Colombian in membership, they will go outside their group to hire specialists, such as pilots or lawyers, and will, when need be, cooperate with other criminal groups, including Mexicans, Italians, Jamaicans, and Nigerians.[23]

Despite their brilliance in organizing the cocaine trade, the Medellín cartel's emphasis on violence and narcoterrorism to fulfill its criminal objectives ultimately led to its decline and fall. From 1984 to 1993, the cartel engaged the Colombian state in a war of attrition. The terror and death toll was largely of Pablo Escobar's making. "Every time there is a major assassination in Colombia, they [the Ochoas] send out word that they aren't behind it," revealed María Jimena Duzan, an investigative journalist and columnist with the Bogotá-based *Espectador* newspaper.[24]

The Medellín cartel paid for its violent ways. On February 5, 1987, an elite Colombian police unit captured Carlos Lehder 20 miles outside Medellín, the heart of Colombia's cocaine industry, and quickly extradited him to the United States, where he was convicted of drug trafficking and sentenced to a life sentence plus 135 years in prison.[25] José Gonzalo Rodríguez Gacha, who matched Escobar in ruthlessness, was killed in a shootout with police in December 1989, while the three Ochoa brothers, seeing the writing on the wall, all turned themselves in and were sent to jail. Medellín's dominance of the cocaine trade ended when Colombian police killed Pablo Escobar in 1993. That left the Cali cartel to rule supreme the Empire of Cocaine.

During the late 1980s and early 1990s, as the Colombian government engaged the Medellín cartel in a brutal war of attrition, Cali

Guillermo Cano Isaza, the editor of Bogotá newspaper *El Espectador* until he was murdered in 1986 (courtesy Colombian Antinarcotics Police).

expanded its operation and extended its tentacles deeper into Colombia's tottering democracy in search of greater profits and more power. With the heat on in Colombia, Cali began to move most of its cocaine-refining operations to Peru and Bolivia and their transportation routes through Venezuela and Central America.[26] The cartel also began to muscle into the heroin trade, growing the opium themselves in Colombia and then using their efficient cocaine-distribution network to move the refined product.

The heroin the Cali cartel peddled was both purer and cheaper than its chief competitor, the southeast Asian variety. In 1994 a gram of Colombian heroin was selling for $80 to $150 a gram, compared to $300 to $400 for the brand from southeast Asia.[27] One DEA report revealed that the Cali cartel's share of the New York City heroin market had jumped from 22 to 60 percent during the early 1990s.[28] "In the past five years, there has been a steady increase in the flow and purity of heroin in the U.S., suggesting that the taste for the drug is growing," a U.S. State Department report warned in 1994.[29]

Although the Cali cartel has led the Colombian connection's move into big-time heroin trafficking, many other Colombian criminal organizations are involved as well, indicating that the nature of the drug trade was changing. By 1991 one cartel, led by the brothers Ivan and Julio Urdinola and based in the country's northern Cauca Valley, was making as much money in drug trafficking as the Cali cartel. "By expanding from cocaine to heroin production, the [Urdinola] organization has the capacity to become the first true narcotics conglomerate, and it is already shipping mixed loads of the two drugs to the United States and Europe," the *Washington Post* reported.[30]

Facing increasing competition and knowing that, with the demise of the Medellín cartel, it would be the number-one target of Colombian and U.S. officials, the Cali cartel began to negotiate their exodus from international drug trafficking with the Colombian government. After a meeting with Pacho Herrera, José Olmedo Ocampo, and Juan Carlos Ramírez — three leaders of the Cali Cartel — Colombian attorney general Gustavo de Grieff began pushing the Colombian government to accept an agreement with the cartel that would have led to lenient terms of surrender for the drug traffickers. News of the meeting and what transpired caused a storm of controversy both inside and outside Colombia. The United States charged that de Grieff's office had been infiltrated by the Cali cartel and warned that any such agreement with the cartel would seriously damage U.S.-Colombia relations.[31]

Those relations deteriorated anyway, largely because of accusations that Colombian President Ernesto Samper's 1994 presidential campaign had been infiltrated by the Cali cartel. A stunned Colombia heard a cassette tape in which Cali cartel leader Miguel Rodríguez Orejuela revealed that he had arranged to give $3.5 million to the Samper campaign. The so-called "narco cassettes" were based on police wiretaps and intercepts and confirmed the DEA's longtime suspicions that Samper and key members of his Liberal party were on the Cali payroll. The Colombian Congress, dominated by the Liberal party, eventually declared Samper innocent of any wrongdoing in the scandal, but several associates in the Samper's presidential campaign and in his administration went to jail. U.S.-Colombian relations reached rock bottom on March 1, 1996, the date the United States "decertified" Colombia as a helpful partner in the War on Drugs. The move placed Colombia with such pariahs as Iran, Syria, Nigeria, and Afghanistan.[32]

Despite his problems, Samper remained defiant. "The Colombian Congress cleared me and I have no connection to drug traffickers," Samper explained to the author. "In fact, my record shows that I have provided leadership in the War on Drugs. I plan to serve out my term and have no intention of resigning."[33]

Ironically, while these developments were unfolding, the Colombian government was having stunning success against the Cali cartel. Between June and August 1995, Colombian police, with the help of the CIA and DEA, captured six of the top seven leaders of the Cali cartel, including the brothers Rodríguez Orejuela and José Santracruz Londono. Authorities captured Gilberto Orejuela after searching a house in a middle-class neighborhood of Santa Monica and found him inside a secret vaulted closet with three pistols and $100,000 to $200,000 in cash. One of the arresting officers told the press, "He was half asleep. He was very confused. He did not resist arrest."[34]

Rosso José Serrano, head of Colombian National Police (courtesy Colombian National Police).

U.S. officials predicted that Rodríguez's capture would be a "mortal blow" against the Cali cartel. In October 1996 Gilberto Rodríguez agreed to pay a fine of $105 million to the Colombian state and confessed to crimes involving narcotics trafficking and "illegal enrichment." He faced a maximum penalty of 25 years in jail.[35]

Colombia and its allies in the War on Drugs claimed another victory when Venezuelan police captured Justo Pastor Perafan near the Colombian-Venezuelan border in April 1997 and extradited him to the United States the following month. Colombian authorities said that Perafan was the head of the Bogotá-Cauca cartel and had amassed a fortune of $10 billion in the drug trade, but Perafan insisted that he had made the money in coffee. "He made a fortune because of his close working relationship with the Cali cartel," explained Colonel Leonardo Gallego, head of the antidrug unit of the Colombian National Police. "His capture was especially significant because he was the last of the big name drug capos [lords] not in prison or in jail."[36]

The attack on the drug cartels and the alleged corruption of the Samper administration was led by Colombia's prosecuting attorney general, Alphonso Valdivieso, who became known as "Mr. Clean" because of his reputation for honesty. "Valdivieso has made an enormous difference in the War on Drugs, especially in his role in going after and diffusing the power of the Cali cartel," commented U.S. Ambassador Myles Frechette. "His views coincided with the U.S., but we didn't push him."[37]

In the spring of 1997, Valdivieso resigned to run for president in the 1998 election, and many Colombians were hoping he could salvage Colombia's tarnished international reputation. "I plan to run a moral campaign," Valdivieso explained. "Colombia needs a leader it can trust and who has the determination and clean record to lead it out of its current crisis."[38]

But will the stunning success against the Cali cartel have any impact on Colombia's role as the linchpin in the Latin American drug trade? Just as it was business as usual after Escobar's death, there is no reason to expect that the situation will change because another powerful Colombian cartel's tenure of leadership in the drug trade has ended. Indeed, destroying the Colombian connection might be even more difficult in the future, because instead of one monolithic cartel to deal with, law enforcement will have to confront and try to dismantle several "baby cartels," not just in Colombia, but in Mexico and other Latin American countries as well. Rosso José Serrano, general director of Colombia's National Police, explained, "these smaller cartels won't have the corrupting capacity of the Cali cartel, nor will they easily have the organizational reach that made Cali such an international power."[39]

In early 1997, the demand for cocaine and heroin showed no letup, and as long as world consumers are eager to buy cocaine and heroin, it should be expected that ambitious criminal entrepreneurs in Colombia will be ready to supply the drug. In November 1996, sicarios killed a Colombian drug trafficker named Efraín Hernández Ramírez, whom the Colombian public had never heard of. Yet, with the money from his narco trafficking enterprise, Hernandez was able to buy more than 30 businesses; in fact, Colombia authorities revealed that his criminal operation may have been bigger than that of the Rodríguez Orejuela brothers.[40]

Chapter 13

The Yakuza: Merchants of Speed

"One might think that because the Yakuza is exporting drugs from the U.S. to Japan that they are not contributors to the U.S. drug problem. … [But], as the Yakuza acts as a wholesale customer of local drug manufacturers, thus creating a giant demand for production of the drug as a large drug using population would."

— Michael Lyman, author of *Gangland*

"There is a strong sense of empathy with the Yakuza among the Japanese. These days [the Yakuza] would do anything to make money, and I want other police to realize that they are not a bunch of Robin Hoods anymore."

— Takaji Kunimatsu, head of the Criminal Division, National Police Agency, Japan

Most organized crime syndicates do their best to operate in secrecy out of the public spotlight; the Japanese Yakuza is not one of them. With their semidark sunglasses, white shoes, polyester suits, and short, military-style haircuts, a Yakuza gang member could be picked out in a crowd. Get closer and take a look at their hands and you will notice the missing tips of their little fingers, the result of having been snipped off in one of the gang's initiation rituals. If his shirt is open, you might get a glimpse of the near total body tattoos consisting of elaborate dragons and cherry blossoms, and he may hand you a business card, if you happen to stop and chat with him. Pay him a visit and you will most likely see his name on his office doorplate when you enter.

This high profile, though, has not stopped the Yakuza from being one of organized crime's most successful criminal syndicates. With a membership that has been put between 88,000 and 110,000, the Yakuza may be the world's oldest and largest criminal organization.[1] The term Yakuza is actually a generic name applied to about 2,500 different crime groups operating in Japan and several other countries, including Hawaii and the U.S. West Coast.[2] One scholar of organized crime described them as a "highly disciplined group [that] originated in the sixteenth and seventeenth centuries with a large number of dissident Samurai warriors. The Yakuza was formed by these warriors, who adopted the gang name, which is an expression meaning worthless or losers — paralleling the American outlaw motorcycle gang's adoption of the 1 percent logo."[3]

Like the Cosa Nostra, the Yakuza has a strong tradition and a well-defined structure that is based on hierarchical systems of elders and younger brothers in a kind of familial paternalism. There is great emphasis placed on ritual and ceremonial initiatives, such as the finger snipping practice. The gang's hierarchy includes a "kaicho," a type of boss, who is the absolute authority; the "wakato," a deputy chairman; and the "wakaishu," the soldiers who make up most of the membership.[4] By 1980 in Toyko, Japan, alone, there were 50 drug-trafficking syndicates known as the Tekiya, which had names like Koshu-ya, Kyokuto-rengo, and Hashi-ya and formed a closed, powerful, and well-organized society.[5]

The Yakuza got their big criminal break after Japan's defeat in World War II, when adverse political and economic conditions allowed them to expand into a number of illicit enterprises, including narcotics, pornography, and racketeering. "The very nature of the Yakuza changed after World War II," explained Jay Robert Nash. "Swords were replaced by guns and the Yakuza assumed a more Western appearance. They abandoned traditional folk dress in order to copy their counterparts in the [Italian] Mafia."[6]

Before World War II, Japanese criminals were drug suppliers to the United States, providing huge amounts of heroin to the biggest U.S. drug rings. As David Kaplan and Alec Dubro described their role, "Early in the 1930s, some Japanese in America were driven to the narcotics trade for the simple reason that the Japanese Empire, in its conquest of East Asia, had acquired much of the opium, morphine and heroin business there. Connections between the drug distributors in Asia and America were logical and fairly easily made."[7] The outbreak of the war, however, severed the connection.

There were as many as 70,000 Yakuza in Japan by 1958, but that figure had jumped five years later to 184,000, when the crime organization began its modern expansion. The Yakuza leader Kodama Yoshio is credited with leading the Yakuza into the modern era, reorganizing the group, leading its penetration of mainstream Japanese politics, and forging an alliance in 1972 with two of the most powerful Yakuza gangs, the Inagawa-kai and the Kakuseikai.[8] In the early 1970s, the Yakuza diversified and began moving into the growing international narcotics trade, establishing links with the powerful Chinese Triads and becoming active in Hong Kong, Taiwan, and southeast Asia.[9]

U.S. authorities began to get concerned about the Yakuza in the 1970s after it became apparent that the group had made the United States its prime target for criminal activity. In 1975 a Yakuza named Wataru (Jackson) Inada was arrested for selling $165,000 worth of heroin to an undercover agent, an event that many U.S. law enforcement officials took as a sign that the Yakuza were getting serious about establishing a beachhead in the lucrative U.S. heroin market.[10] In the late 1970s, U.S and Canadian police began monitoring Japanese couriers arriving at Los Angeles and Vancouver, Canada, and other West Coast ports of entry. In 1985 authorities seized 12 pounds of heroin and 52 pounds of methamphetamine in Honolulu and Hong Kong and arrested several Japanese and three Chinese, including two of the highest-ranking bosses of Yamaguchi-Yumi, perhaps the most powerful of the Yakuza organizations.[11] The following year, the President's Commission on Organized Crime published a report in which it noted that the Yakuza "are active in drug trafficking, primarily smuggling amphetamine from the United States to Japan."[12]

But what was said about the Yakuza in the mid 1980s by the U.S. House Committee on Foreign Affairs is still true today. In that year, the committee released a report titled *U.S. Narcotics Program Overseas: An Assessment*, which gave this analysis of Yakuza drug smuggling: "It is impossible to know Japan's significance as a transit point for narcotics, due to the lack of cooperation from the Japanese. The Japanese share very little narcotics intelligence with the United States, refuse to permit 'controlled deliveries' through their territory, [and] will not provide conviction records on their list of names of 100,000 known Yakuza members, or other important information."[13]

Although it is difficult to gather information about the Yakuza, U.S. officials do know that the Yakuza's role in drug trafficking is different from the one played by other organized crime groups that target the huge U.S market for distribution. The Yakuza work primarily as exporters of drugs from the United States to Japan, principally trafficking in amphetamines. Methamphetamine, a type of amphetamine, known as speed or meth in the United States, became hugely popular in Japan in the early 1980s. By 1983 the number of speed-related arrests in Japan tripled, and the number of amphetamine abusers was estimated to be between 300,000 and 600,000.[14]

The Yakuza may focus on exporting drugs from the United States, but this does not mean that it has not contributed to the growth of drug use and abuse in the United States. "One might think that because the Yakuza is exporting drugs from the U.S. to Japan that they are not contributors to the U.S. drug problem," explained criminologist Michael Lyman. "But the Yakuza acts as a wholesale customer of local drug manufacturers, thus creating a giant demand for production of the drug as a large drug using population would."[15]

The demand in Japan for meth is so great and the sales so lucrative that some Japanese authorities believe that the trade in the drug could account for as much as half of the Yakuza's income — an amount believed to be worth billions of dollars. At the 1991 congressional hearings on the new international criminal and Asian organized crime, then-FBI director William Sessions reported that in 1988 the Yakuza grossed almost $10 billion U.S. in revenue, one-third from crystal methamphetamine, according to statistics provided by Japan's National Police Agency.[16]

Kaplan and Dubro explained why: "Markup of the drug, according to police, increased forty or fifty times from the factory to the street. A single gram of the drug sells for as much as $1300, and one 'fix'—.01 to .03 grams—goes for more than $40." Kaplan and Dubro added that injection is the preferred method of getting high on meth. One long-time Tokyo resident told the authorities, "Japan is the type of society that needs methamphetamine. The treadmill is very fast and the people use it to stay on."[17]

Crystal methamphetamine (more popularly known as "ice") is a stimulant that became highly popular in Hawaii and the U.S. West Coast during the 1980s. The drug is cheaper than cocaine, has a long-lasting high, is extremely debilitating, and has been known to put users into a violent, paranoid state.[18] The Yakuza produce ice in secretive labs in Korea and Taiwan, and Filipino criminals help to smuggle the drug into the United States.[19]

What the Yakuza does with its huge amounts of illegally earned income poses a greater threat to the United States than the actual act of drug smuggling. Since the late 1960s, the Yakuza have bought legitimate businesses in the United States to serve as fronts to launder their money and to hide it from the Japanese government. Because money laundering is not a crime in Japan and, as noted earlier, they have not been under close scrutiny by the Japanese authorities, U.S. law enforcement has not received the kind of help it needs to monitor Yakuza activities. "Nobody knows how many billions of dollars they are laundering through the U.S. currency system, or how many of Japan's giant companies they are holding for ransom in New York or California, how many U.S. companies may be falling victim to the provocative wiles of their Sokaiya [corporate intimidation]," writes investigative journalist Claire Sterling. "Investigators have enough evidence to believe the Yakuza have a massive subterranean operation going on America. 'Insurmountable difficulties' lie in the way of proving it, says the Senate Subcommittee on Investigations."[20]

The Yakuza's "investment campaign" began in the 1960s in Hawaii, and by the 1980s the syndicate was buying restaurants, nightclubs, gift shops, tour agencies, nightclubs, and import-export concerns in the Los Angeles area. The President's Commission on Organized Crime identified one Yakuza shell enterprise, the Rondan Doyukai Company, as a shareholder in such major corporations as IBM, Bank of America, General Motors, Dow Chemical, and Atlantic Ritchfield. "In 1981 members of the group [the Yakuza] attended stock holders' meetings of the corporations," noted the commission. "Their presence is significant in that, while Rondan Doyukai publishes books and newspapers and claims to provide a consulting service to Japanese firms, its main function is that of sokaiya, corporate intimidation."[21]

In 1993 a U.S. federal witness known only as "Mr. Bully" told a U.S. Senate subcommittee that in Hawaii alone he knew of at least five money-laundering transactions to buy property. The FBI estimated that the Yakuza may have laundered as much as $1 billion in the United States in the 1980s. Jim G. Moody, chief of the FBI's organized-crime and drug section, told *Business Week* magazine that "there are more money laundering activity by them [the Yakuza] than drug trafficking."[22]

In the early 1990s, the Japanese authorities began to crack down on the Yakuza and reverse Japan's long tradition of "official" toleration of organized crime, which had led to a high level of corruption in Japanese society. One 1990 police survey of 2,016 Toyko businesses found that 41 percent of them were making extortion payments to the Yakuza.

New anti-Yakuza laws went into effect in March 1992, and the police began an aggressive campaign to identify Japanese citizens who had been victims of Yakuza's extortion attempts. "There is a strong sense of empathy with the Yakuza among the Japanese," Takaji Kunimatsu, head of the Criminal Investigation Bureau of Japan's National Police Agency, told the press. "These days [the Yakuza] would do anything to make money, and I want other police to realize that they are not a bunch of Robin Hoods anymore"[23]

Despite the recent concerted anti–Yakuza campaign, Japanese authorities continue to worry about the corrupting threat of the Yakuza on Japanese society, especially the gang's efforts to take over the country's far right-wing organizations. Masayuki Takagi, a professor of sociology at Teikyo University and an expert on Japan's political right wing, told one newspaper that the Yakuza had taken over 80 to 90 percent of the country's extreme right-wing groups, although police have put the figure at between 25 and 50 percent. The professor also attributed 39 incidents of terrorism and guerrilla activity to such groups in the previous three years.[24]

The Yakuza, no doubt, remain a potent force in Japanese society and international crime, and there is no indication that, like the Italian American Mafia, the gang is in decline. The U.S. government has been skeptical of Japanese law enforcement's willingness to seriously investigate the Yakuza. "While the Japanese Government has recently adopted new anti-organized crime laws, the effect of these laws remains to be seen," concluded the 1991 congressional hearings on Asian organized crime. "What is clear is that heretofore anemic Japanese law enforcement efforts against Boryokudan [Yakuza] gangs have had an adverse impact on the United States and other countries where the Boryokudan have begun to extend their influence and investments. The failure of Japanese law enforcement officials to share information and intelligence about the Boryokudan members in a timely fashion and in a form which is legally admissible has severely handicapped U.S. law-enforcement efforts."[25]

So the Yakuza will probably continue to be active in drug trafficking activities in the United States and Asia, making billions from the trade in amphetamines; however, at the moment, the Yakuza have given no indication that they intend moving into the more lucrative heroin trade in a big way. Given the Yakuza's ambition, though, the gang may still use its money, resources, and power to expand its organization. After all, the world's huge appetite for illegal drugs shows there is always room for another major player.

Chapter 14

Jamaican Posses:
Kings of Crack

"They have come farther and faster than any other criminal group in the country."

— Al Lamberti, Broward County
(Florida) Sheriff's Department

"You cherish your gun. That's what keeps you alive....You can't trust anybody."

— posse gang member

When the Jamaicans began arriving in Kansas City in 1986, they stuck to themselves and tried to keep a low profile, but city residents couldn't help but notice the different-looking newcomers. The Jamaicans wore dreadlocks, spoke with lilting Caribbean accents, and dressed as if they had arrived from another planet. The Kansas City police were well aware of the sudden Jamaican influx but didn't really know why the strangers had come to town. The authorities certainly didn't think it was to push and sell drugs. They thought, like many local residents, that cocaine and crack use were drug problems found in other parts of the country, not in a solid Midwest metropolis like Kansas City.

Soon, however, crack houses began popping up all over the city, and, in no time, it seemed, the deadly drug could be bought at more than 100 sites in the Kansas City metropolitan area. "We had one drug house that must have made a million dollars before we knew anything about it," marveled one Kansas City narcotics officer.[1] Then the dead bodies started to pile up at the drug houses and the murder rate skyrocketed from 91 in 1985 to 116 in 1986 to 131 in 1987. The Kansas City police have become well aware of the Jamaican criminal presence, estimating that they control 70 percent of the city's crack market.[2]

159

A decade later, the Jamaican criminal gangs, which are known as posses, are one of the most powerful drug-trafficking organizations in American crime, dominating the crack cocaine trade in cities all over the American landscape. Initially based in Jamaican immigrant communities on the East Coast in Miami, New York City, and Washington, D.C., the posses have since spread to other large cities, such as Dallas, Chicago, Cleveland, Denver, Rochester, Boston, and Buffalo and to Long Island as well as many smaller locations in the Midwest and elsewhere in the country. Suspected posse members have been spotted as far from Jamaica as Anchorage, Alaska.[3]

On June 9, 1991, the bodies of Robert Lee Cooper, 20, and Wejewn Briston Byers, 16, were found dead in a fenced-in lane near the Atando industrial area of Charlotte, North Carolina. Police investigators said that the two young men had been tortured and shot as many as 50 times. The murders were two more incidents, said Charlotte police, that indicated that the city was being infiltrated by a formidable and dangerous breed of criminal organization, the Jamaican possess.[4] "We have identified Jamaican gangs as part of an organized crime effort," revealed Lieutenant Tommy Barnes, head of vice and narcotics for the Charlotte Police Department, "They have been here for several years. The local media just hadn't taken much notice of them yet."[5]

All Jamaican posses are believed to be the offshoots of two original gangs named Shower and Spangler. Other posses names are Tel-Aviv, Super Banton, and Waterhouse Riverton City, the last two of which are named after Jamaican neighborhoods. The Shower is said to have gotten its name from its "showering" of its enemies with gunfire, while the Waterhouse posse's grizzly habit of setting its victims on fire earned it the nickname of Firehouse.[6]

Posse members are natives of parts of Kingston, West Kingston, and other tough Jamaican urban shantytowns, and their migration to the U.S. and their powerful role in the country's drug trade can largely be attributed to Jamaican politics. In the 1970s the island's politicians recruited young thugs from the shantytowns to coerce and intimidate voters, as local politics became increasingly divided along two party lines: the People's National Party (PNP) under Michael Manley and the Jamaican Labor Party (JLP) under Edward Seaga.[7] The violence in Jamaican politics reached its zenith in the 1980 elections in which 700 people were killed. Seaga's Jamaican Labor Party (JLP) won the election, but Seaga was left with the potentially explosive situation of having well-armed enforcers milling around with no jobs and nothing to do. The

JLP had no money to keep them on the payroll, so the party began sending their hired help to the United States. As the Jamaican economy continued to decline in the early 1980s, more and more of the young thugs from both political parties made their way to the United States and began organizing themselves into posses.[8]

Ironically, the United States helped facilitate the migration by making it easy for the soon-to-be posse members to get visas.[9] The United States wanted to help Seaga, who was a strong supporter of U.S. policy in the Caribbean. Once again the War on Drugs took second place to other foreign policy considerations. "The United States wanted to help Seaga stabilize Jamaica, and one of the ways to stabilize the country was to get rid of the undesirables," Laurie Gunst, a journalist who has written extensively on Jamaican posses, suggested.[10] In effect, what could have been a crime problem in Jamaica became a crime problem in the United States.

Fifteen years later, did the Jamaican posses still have ties to political parties back home? Opinion remains divided on that question. Many law-enforcement officials have charged that posses have channeled guns and drug money to Jamaica's two major political parties, while Jamaican officials have denied any connection.[11] Faced with a potentially serious political rift, U.S. officials have been careful in their dealings with Jamaican leaders, often making a special effort to praise them for their "cooperation" in the antidrug fight.

The posses began their criminal careers in the United States smuggling marijuana. In 1984 the U.S. government persuaded Colombia to implement a marijuana eradication program, which led to marijuana supplies drying up. The enterprising posses stepped in with potent sinsemilla, a type of marijuana that could be purchased in Jamaica for $20 a pound and sold in the United States for $1,200 a pound. The ambitious criminal entrepreneurs discovered that more money could be made from selling crack cocaine, a new and lucrative source of illegal drug revenue.

They quickly gained a large share of the crack cocaine market and established themselves as major drug traffickers. Federal authorities have estimated that the posses now control 40 percent of the country's cocaine distribution, principally crack. In describing their meteoric rise among the criminal ranks, Al Lamberti of the Broward County (Florida) Sheriff's Department has said, "They have come further faster than any other criminal group in the country."[12]

Michael D. Lyman, an expert on organized crime, described the posse impact on the crack cocaine business: "The evolution of this group was first observed around 1985 and up until then the criminal interest in crack sales was thought to be somewhat of a 'cottage industry,' meaning that organized involvement was on a small, isolated scale. It was, however, the Jamaicans who literally carved out a notch for themselves in this industry, which was previously considered as a user enterprise, but which, in fact, presented tremendous financial resources not yet tapped by other organized crime groups."[13]

The number of Jamaican posses or gangs has been put at 30 to 40 and total membership at about 10,000, although the Jamaican government has questioned these figures, saying that some posse members may actually be other West Indians mistakenly thought to be Jamaicans. Federal authorities, however, have stood by their statistics.

Law-enforcement officials call the posses as cunning and vicious a criminal organization as is presently operating in international drug trafficking and say that, between the mid 1980s and 1990, they may be responsible for more than 1,400 murders nationwide.[14] A 1990 Pennsylvania Crime Commission report assessed that the posses have "a well-deserved reputation for violence, even by the standards of an unusually violent business. This brutality stems in part from their belief that violence is an occupational necessity. Their choice of name 'Posse' testifies to their fascination with the Hollywood image of the outlaw gunslingers of the 'Wild West.'"[15]

Disciplined as well as violent, the posses are a tightknit group and, like the Italian Mafia, shrouded in secrecy and bound by old-country ties. Since members of a particular gang come from the same neighborhood and are often related by blood and marriage, they can be kept in line easily by the posse threat to loved ones back home. The posses hire local helpers to open a crack house in a new city. The core group, however, is always from the island and no outsiders are allowed to penetrate its higher echelons. Masters of forged documentation, the posses give new members entering the United States illegally authentic-looking fake passports, social security numbers, and driver's licenses. The police have difficulty tracking the posses because they are highly mobile and will move their members every few months. When detained, posse members will use Rastafarian argot to confuse the police. (Examples of their argot are "Babylon" to refer to the outside world, "baldness" for an undesirable outsider, and "beast" for police.[16])

The posses form a hands-on criminal enterprise, controlling the importation of cocaine, its conversion into crack, and distribution on the streets in the United States, thus ensuring for themselves a high profit margin. As Lyman explained, "This system of control over all levels of distribution means that Posse members never have to exchange money with outsiders until the drugs are sold on the streets by local dealers (who are sometimes posse members). Profits are then channeled back up the ladder which results in a profit margin some 1,000 percent higher than other trafficking organizations."[17]

The posses have exhibited sophisticated business skills that help explain their rapid rise in the criminal underworld. They have their own airplanes for shipping cocaine into the United States and use a variety of legitimate businesses, such as travel and rental car agencies, to coordinate the transportation of the drugs throughout the country, and they are reported to have a rental fleet of sixty-four cars and ten trucks for distribution purposes. Before setting up an operation in a city, posse leaders send scouts to conduct "market surveys" to assess the demand for drugs and the possible degree of resistance from local criminals. Once in business, they make a point of selling the highest-quality drug available to corner the market, but if that isn't enough to establish themselves, they resort to ruthless violence.[18]

The posses have developed a number of clever and sophisticated techniques to outfox law enforcement. They use cellular phones because police can tap regular phones, and they like to move around in cars as they make their deals. They use predesignated dropoff points to exchange information. Not big on the trappings of drug lord success, the posses use apartments in poor neighborhoods for their offices from which they can sell drugs. They recruit young children to sell drugs in the streets, taking advantage of the lenient U.S. laws toward minors in the United States.[19]

It is the posses' penchant for violence that makes them feared by law-enforcement officials and residents in the neighborhoods in which they operate. One gang member, who called himself Trevor, described life as a posse member: "Guns are more important than women. You cherish your gun. That's what keeps you alive. I never went to sleep without my gun on my chest and my finger on the trigger. I'll doze ten to twenty minutes. I'd rest my back ... If I wanted to get a good sleep, I'd go to a hotel. I'll do that on a regular basis. You can't trust anybody."[20]

In a 1986 nationwide sweep of posse members, federal authorities confiscated 400 automatic weapons, including 200 Uzis that had been altered to fire 100 rounds a minute. "They seem to have a fascination for fire arms," Tom Truman, the agent in charge of the Kansas City office of the Bureau of Alcohol, Tobacco and Firearms Control, told the press. "I don't know what the reason is or what it is about their culture that causes that, but in 131 prosecutions in federal court and forty-three in state court, we confiscated 230 firearms. That's more than one per defendant."[21]

The posse fascination for guns and violence has created terror and mayhem as a way of life in some neighborhoods, particularly in the African American community. There have been many spectacular incidents attesting to the posse propensity for violence. In one shootout between rival posse gangs in Oakland, New Jersey, six people were left dead and thirteen wounded. In Fort Lauderdale, Florida, Shower posse members emptied their automatic weapons into a crowd of 300 attending a reggae concert. A Jamaican gang leader sat in his Mercedes-Benz on a Cleveland, Ohio, street, when an off-duty bus driver accidentally backed into him. Witnesses testify that the gang leader got out of his car, calmly pulled out a handgun and squeezed four shots, killing the bus driver. Colin Forbes was a talented Jamaican soccer star who was shot dead during a soccer match in Miami. Police believe that posse members mistook Forbes for someone else. "The posses "actually try to take people out in public places," immigration special agent William D. West explained. "They don't care if people get caught in the crossfire."[22]

Given the posses' growing power and reputation, many Jamaican Americans and immigrants worry that they are being stereotyped and are becoming the targets of hostility and discrimination from other Americans. Leaders in the Jamaican American community point out that the crimes perpetuated by Jamaican gangs involve only a small number of their countrymen living in the United States, and that the overwhelming majority are hardworking legal immigrants who have come to the United States for an education or an opportunity to improve their lot.

Some Jamaican Americans have charged racism. In February 1986 in Washington, D.C., police conducted a crackdown on the posses. Known as Operation Caribbean Cruise, it targeted alleged drug dealers from Jamaica and other Caribbean countries. Thirty-three people whose houses were raided during the operation sued the Washington, D.C., government in district court for "a vicious and unwanted attack on innocent members of the black community."[23] Ransford W. Palmer, a Jamaican who teaches economics at Harvard University, complained that "We are concerned about the media's quickness to attribute crimes to

Jamaicans, to blame an expatriate group for this antisocial behavior. But when you look at the history of immigration here, pick out one group, the Italians. We all know about the violence and (Mario) Cuomo."[24] It is interesting that Operation Caribbean Cruise netted only 27 arrests, 233 weapons, and $27 worth of drugs.[25]

Amid the charges of racism, law enforcement has moved ahead in the past decade in their effort to crack down on the posses. In October 1988, for example, after conducting a two-year investigation, a federal task force launched a nationwide sweep of posses known as "Operation Rum Punch." The bust led to the arrest of more than 200 posse members in 20 cities in Florida and several other states on charges of cocaine trafficking, illegal immigration, and the possession of illegal firearms. Thirty-four members of Shower were indicted on racketeering charges. The then U.S. attorney general, Richard Thornburgh, said that the raids and arrests were designed to send a message; namely that "drug dealing and other criminal activities by Jamaican gangs would not be tolerated."[26]

Some authorities believe the indictment significantly weakened the posse network, but others note that other posses with names like Red Kerchief and Magenta moved in to fill the void. "The posses continue to pose a serious law-enforcement problem," Lieutenant Barnes explained. "They aren't going to go away."[27]

Meanwhile, the long criminal arm of the Jamaican posses has continued to grow. Scotland Yard has reported increased posse activity in England, where they are known by the name of "Yardies."

The Nigerian Connection: The Mules of the Drug Trade

"When you talk to law enforcement people and you mention Nigerians, that's almost synonymous with heroin. Nigerians have developed a worldwide reputation."

— DEA agent

"Nigerian nationals have been identified as the architects of a complex network of couriers that smuggle heroin into the United States and Europe from Southeast and Southwest Asia ... they are sophisticated organizations capable of quickly adapting to changes in U.S. law enforcement."

— Kelvin Levitsky, Board of International Narcotics, Department of State

Colombian customs officials grew suspicious of the Africans who began coming to Colombia in increasingly large numbers during the early months of 1996. The Africans looked disoriented and unhealthy and didn't have much money, so customs alerted the police, who raided three hotels where the Africans were staying and found 180 pounds of cocaine in their shirts, shoes, jackets, and even their stomachs. Twenty-two Nigerians and thirty-one citizens of other African countries were arrested for drug trafficking. The Africans insisted they were tourists who had come to Colombia to relax and have a good time, but when the authorities asked them what they came to see in Bogotá, a city nearly 8,000 feet above sea level and 2,00 miles from the Pacific coast, the "tourists" said they wanted to visit Bogotá's beaches.[1]

The Africans were actually couriers for Nigerian drug traffickers, who during the last decade have become an important link in the world-wide distribution of narcotics. A report by DAS (Department of Administrative Security), Colombia's equivalent of the FBI, indicates that Nigerian drug traffickers are establishing a drug pipeline to Latin America's huge cocaine and heroin markets in order to transport illegal drugs to hungry consumers in the United States, Europe, and Asia. They are not trying to muscle in on the territory of the powerful Colombian drug cartels, U.S. and Colombian officials say, but they have carved for themselves an important and profitable niche in the international drug distribution network. In the United States, the prime target for Nigerian drug-smuggling activities, they have established links with inner-city crime organizations, as well as Chinese and Jamaican gangs.[2]

"Nigerian nationals have been identified as the architects of a complex network of couriers that smuggle heroin into the United States and Europe from Southeast and Southwest Asia," Kelvin Levitsky, the assistant secretary on the Board of International Narcotics of the Department of State, testified recently before the Committee on Foreign Relations of the U.S. Senate. "We are beginning to see an increase in Nigerian smuggling of cocaine from South America to markets in Africa and Europe. As far as we can tell, the Nigerian trafficking organizations are more loosely organized than their American counterparts, and therefore more difficult to penetrate. There are no clear hierarchies and no unambiguous chain of command. Nevertheless, they are sophisticated organizations capable of quickly adapting to changes in U.S. law enforcement activities."[3]

A tendency on the part of U.S. law enforcement to underestimate the Nigerian connection may explain why Nigerian organized crime has been successful in avoiding arrest and building its drug distribution network. According to Craig Chretien, the DEA's chief of International Operations, "In the over all scheme of things, [Nigerian drug trafficking] is serious, but pales in comparison to larger problems as orchestrated by Colombian and Mexican organizations."[4]

Such analysis not only underestimates the Nigerian connection, it also ignores reality. At a time when the United States is seeing a resurgence in heroin use, Nigerian drug traffickers are, by most estimates, responsible for as much as 50 percent of the heroin entering the United States and are firmly entrenched in such American cities as Atlanta, Chicago, Baltimore, and Washington, D.C.[5]

From 1979 to September 1991, more than 15,000 Nigerians worldwide were arrested for drug trafficking.[6] Nigerian traffickers and their associates accounted for most of the heroin seized at U.S. airports.[7] In one year alone, fiscal 1991, 31 percent of the 756 heroin seizures at U.S. airports by the U.S. Customs Service involved Nigerian nationals and 11 percent other Africans, most likely couriers working for Nigerian drug traffickers.[8] Another DEA agent put the Nigerian connection's role in proper perspective. "When you talk to law enforcement people and you mention Nigerians, that's almost synonymous with heroin. Nigerians have developed a worldwide reputation."[9]

On why the Nigerians have become so prominent in the international drug trade in such a relatively short period of time, the *Economist* wrote, "The most obvious reason is that they are willing to take risks at a lower price than their compatriots. Despite the dangers there is no lack of recruits, particularly from the coastal trading communities. Family or village-based groups are impenetrable to outsiders, speaking dialects that defy interrogators and police taps. Their loyalty to each other is absolute. They are smart. American officials speak respectfully of their abilities."[10]

Experts on African history and culture reveal that organized crime in Nigeria and other African countries was unheard of until the early 1970s. That is when the African continent began to undergo a profound change and experience a rapid growth in criminal activity. Experts attribute the growth of organized crime in Africa to several factors, including the introduction of a monied economy, the prevalence of political instability, rapid urbanization, the growth of international trade, and chronic and widespread unemployment. "The introduction of European money (as a result of colonialism) has had a relatively gradual but far-reaching effect on African values, especially among the educated and entrepreneurial classes," writes scholar James S. E. Opolot. "In this respect, what Africa has been going through is reminiscent of Europe in the seventeenth and eighteenth centuries."[11]

By the early 1970s, Africa watchers began to notice that "lone [criminal] operations are giving way to gangs. In most cases these groups and gangs are still loosely organized."[12] That changed in the late 1970s and 1980s when organized African crime groups got involved in ivory and diamond smuggling and urban crime became more sophisticated, using guns instead of the panga, a traditional long-bladed bush knife, and automobiles for getaways in robberies.[13]

By 1984, as the international narcotics trade began to mushroom, an increasing number of Africans, most notably Nigerians, were being arrested for drug trafficking. E. Kibaka, a scholar in African politics, gave this profile of the African courier at the time and an assessment of the development of the African drug-trafficking connection: "According to an analysis made by Interpol, African couriers belong to all socio professional categories: immigrant workers, students, businessmen, civil servants, etc. Their ages vary between 25 and 45, and the majority are men, although now we are seeing the frequent presence of women among couriers. Traffickers often carry or use one of several false passports, sometimes even diplomatic ones. At their arrival in Europe, couriers possess round-trip tickets, as well as small quantities of foreign currency."[14]

This profile of the Nigerian courier and other African couriers has changed little in the last decade, and neither has the way Nigerian organized crime transports drugs to their destinations. The Nigerians buy the heroin in the Golden Crescent of India, Pakistan, and Afghanistan and the Golden Triangle of Laos, Myanmar, and Thailand, where there is a large Nigerian and West African population. The Nigerians control all facets of the trade — the purchase, transportation, and distribution — from their suppliers in Asia to the dealers on the streets of the United States and European countries. Often, the drugs are shipped in freighters hidden in their containers to Lagos, Nigeria's capital, where they are stored and later transported to their destination. The Nigerians have begun using other African countries as transit points as well, including Ghana, Benin, Senegal, and South Africa.[15]

During the last decade, this network and method of transporting drugs has been extensive, efficient, and sophisticated. "In the early 1980s we saw mom-and-pop gangs," one DEA agent explained. "A group of five or six people raised enough money to go to the source country, get the heroin and bring it back for ultimate transportation to the U.S. As far as growth, I can sum it up in one word: tremendous."[16]

U.S. Customs knows full well that the Nigerian mob will try to smuggle drugs into the country and is always on the lookout for their couriers. John E. Hensley, assistant commissioner with the Office of Enforcement, U.S. Customs, told the Senate, "U.S. authorities look for "routing tickets that do not match up; people that do not have the right amount of luggage for a purported trip they took, short stops in transit countries ... so we use a number of targeting techniques."[17]

Hensley went on to explain some of the techniques: "What the inspector then does is start looking at physical characteristics — individuals who have a raised temperature ... we will see a lot of sweating on some.... We then go to the X-ray, if they do not answer a profile series of questions correctly. It is an acceleration based on the suspicions of the trained investigator, or the inspector — until we finally reach a point that we have identified the heroin inside by X-ray."[18]

The couriers use everything imaginable, including their own bodies, to smuggle the drugs into the United States: shampoo, deodorant, children's toys, cans of food, even coat hangers (broken and then relaquered). Most are "swallowers," who carry the drugs in their digestive systems, or "stuffers," who hide the drugs in their body cavities.[19] Swallowers put the drugs in condoms, which are often wrapped in carbon paper or black electrical tape, making it difficult to spot in an X-ray machine because the carbon looks like any other body part.[20]

"The appearance of African 'mules' on the drug trafficking scene is a good example of the adaptability of the drug entrepreneurs to the changing international environment," explained Victor T. Le Vine, professor of political science at Washington University in St. Louis, Missouri, and author of *Political Corruption: The Ghana Case.* "When it became increasingly difficult to move drugs in and out of Europe and the Mid East, Africa became a transit zone because of the ease with which couriers could be recruited and moved."[21]

Nigerian W.A. Ayeki arrived at the New York's Kennedy International Airport with a suitcase that looked like it contained nothing out of the ordinary — clothes, a Bible, some candles, and a letter of accreditation from a local Christian sect that informed those concerned that Mr. Ayeki was an engineer and honorary church evangelist. When Ayeki reached customs, he was nervous and wouldn't make eye contact, arousing the suspicions of the vigilant customs official. Ayeki was asked if he would submit to an X-ray exam and he agreed. It turned out Ayeki was a swallower, who, in the morning before his flight, had spent three days in a hotel room near the airport, forcing down 3.65 pounds of heroin in 152 condoms. Ayeki was to receive $7,000 when he delivered the heroin to a Brooklyn address. Given the time involved and the amount of heroin he was carrying, Ayeki was lucky he didn't die from a burst condom.[22]

In another incident, a Nigerian arrived by plane in South Africa with terrible stomach cramps. Customs officials found out that one of the 30 cocaine-filled condoms in his stomach broke. This courier was also fortunate to live.[23] Le Vine sums up the impact of the Nigerians on U.S. Customs: "Nigerian mules have been a plague on American points of entry."[24]

For some Africans, being a courier has become much like a regular job. In Ghana, authorities arrested three Ghanaians and gave them a purgative. The three discharged 134 oval balls of cocaine worth about $5,000. The trio had arrived from Bogotá, Colombia, and were planning to return to Caracas, Venezuela, to pick up some cocaine for Amsterdam and travel on to the United States.[25]

Flight attendants on American and European airlines have been told to be on the lookout for Nigerian-controlled couriers, and they have helped law enforcement. On one flight from Lagos to the United States, for example, 14 passengers refused beverages and food during the flight. The flight attendant became suspicious and notified ahead. Customs was waiting for the heroin couriers when the airplane landed.[26]

Given the poverty and unemployment in Africa, the Nigerian traffickers have no trouble recruiting couriers like W. A. Ayeki, who are willing to risk death. "There are thousands of thousands of couriers," Levitsky told the Senate. "You can arrest couriers from now until kingdom come — and there will be other couriers to take their place."[27]

The techniques used by authorities have led to charges of racism — that Africans are being targeted or singled out, but U.S. officials have insisted that their techniques are free of ethnic, racial, or national bias. Hensley said in his testimony that "arriving and departing passengers have itineraries that include travel from known source or transit countries such as Nigeria, who share characteristics found to be associated with drug smuggling. These are routinely subjected to intense scrutiny by U.S. Customs officers."[28]

The development of sophisticated detection procedures and techniques used by U.S. law enforcement has created a cat-and-mouse game with the Nigerian drug traffickers. Often, the Nigerians will fill an airplane with couriers, assuming that many will get caught, but some will get through. They use decoys, "shot guns," who are put on the airplane to distract customs agents and help the real couriers get through. In 1990 U.S. Customs checked an airplane from Lagos to New York City and found out that 19 of the 21 Nigerians aboard carried heroin and only two were clear. Authorities assumed that the two were supervising the drug haul. This is a smuggling technique that appears to pay dividends for the traffickers. If caught, couriers seldom inform on their colleagues and, for every one arrested, U.S. Customs admits, many more get through.[29] The Nigerians are also starting to use white couriers to put the authorities off the scent. For example, in March 1992, six white Americans controlled by a Nigerian group in Dallas, Texas, were caught in Vienna, Austria, carrying 12.5 pounds of heroin.[30]

The growing influence of the Nigerian connection in international drug trafficking has created serious drug-related problems for many African countries. "Drug couriers have come to include Zaireans, Ghanaians, Sierra Leoneans and Cameroonians, among other African countries," Le Vine explained. "There isn't much drug cultivation in Africa itself that I know of, not on the scale of Latin America and the Middle East, but it appears to be a cottage industry in several African countries, including, of course, Nigeria."[31]

Not only has drug trafficking taken root in Africa, but drug dependence, as well as drug-related crime, such as prostitution, robbery, and even gang warfare, has become widespread in such African countries as Liberia, Benin, Senegal, and South Africa, transit countries for drugs destined to the United States and Europe. South African police estimate that as many as 120 gangs in South Africa may be involved in drug trafficking.[32]

In Liberia a heroin-laced cigarette known as "dugee" is now popular. "Today, it's all over the place," said Edward Grant, a psychiatrist and drug counselor at the John F. Kennedy Memorial Hospital in Monrovia. "You can get heroin, you can get cocaine. Our national boundaries are porous now. There are no national customs officers to man the borders. Our drug market is highly saturated."[33]

Corruption has been a big factor in Nigeria's rise as a major conduit for drug trafficking. The federal military government of Nigeria has taken a strong public stance against narcotics trafficking, but U.S. officials acknowledge that its effort leaves a lot to be desired. "The single largest issue facing the government of Nigeria is the presence of general apathy toward police corruption," Hensley told the U.S. Senate. "On the surface, the Nigerian government continues to create the illusion that they are serious about making effective counter-narcotic programs. Our team witnessed first hand that, presently, the government of Nigeria lacks the 'political and social will' necessary to begin addressing the narcotics program in Nigeria."[34]

Two years later, Bill Olsen, former deputy assistant secretary of state for narcotics, told Congress, "Nigerian public institutions are thoroughly penetrated by criminal groups who operate into and through Nigeria and through West Africa with virtually no effort by government to control them."[35]

The corruption in Nigeria has taken many forms. Couriers, for example, have been able to obtain A-2 visas, which make them diplomatically "untouchable" as they move through customs. Many government officials are suspected of taking a percentage of the value of the drugs making their way through the country, while several drug-trafficking suspects have escaped from jail before they went to trial, thanks to the bribes given officials. Compounding the problem are lax banking regulations and an economy that relies on cash transactions, a practice that facilitates money laundering.[36]

In 1989 the Nigerian government created the National Drug Law Enforcement Agency, which is modeled after the DEA, but the agency has been corrupted. In 1992 about 350 of its employees had to be fired because of corruption, and the head of the agency was replaced on suspicion of having accepted bribes to stop pursuing drug traffickers.[37]

The U.S. government has moved to assist Nigeria to clean up its act and make a dent in the narcotics trade by helping to improve the legal and investigative capabilities of Nigerian law-enforcement and providing it with some law enforcement equipment and training. In 1991 and 1992, for example, the United States provided $100,000 in communication assistance and an additional $20,700 in DEA- and U.S. Customs–assisted law-enforcement training. In 1989 Nigeria sent a ten-member interagency delegation to the United States to meet with the DEA, Customs, and U.S. State Department about drug-related issues.[38] Nigeria has also cooperated in the extradition of suspected drug traffickers from Nigeria to the United States to face drug-related charges, but U.S. officials admit that the Nigerian government has moved much more slowly than they would like.[39]

As is often the case in its War on Drugs, Uncle Sam has trodden gently because of foreign policy considerations. Nigeria is either the third- or fourth-largest U.S. supplier of imported petroleum, depending on the year, and U.S. investment to Nigeria is more than $200 million annually. With a population of almost 90 million, about one-fourth the total population of Africa, Nigeria represents a huge market for the U.S.[40]

But in 1994 the United States placed Nigeria on a list of nations it said were "not fully cooperating" in the U.S. antidrug efforts and announced that penalties would be imposed against the country. In a U.S. State Department report, the United States noted that in 1993, "Nigeria ignored repeated appeals of the [U.S.] Administration to crack down on traffickers and failed to apprehend and extradite several major fugitive traffickers indicted in the United States."[41]

U.S. officials have concluded that the Nigerian connection will continue to play a significant role in international drug trafficking in the years ahead. Nigerian organized crime is expanding to South America, not only to Colombia, but also to Brazil, Peru, and Bolivia, and it is becoming an important link in the cocaine and heroin pipeline to the United States and Europe. As one DEA official conceded, "The Nigerians are everywhere. They're diversified and they're beating us."[42]

Chapter 16

The Russians
Are Coming

"We can honestly say that our two nations have more in common than ever before.... Together, we're invincible."
— Sergei Stephasin, head of the
Russian Federal Security Service

"You're going to see more bloodletting as people vie for control. There is just too much money to be made."
— New York City police detective

It was a proud moment for the Russian Security Ministry's anti-smuggling unit. As customs officials watched, St. Petersburg police officers patiently used can openers to pry the lids off 20 tons of cans marked "meat and potatoes," which had been shipped from Colombia, South America. The Russian authorities found a ton of cocaine in what turned out to be the biggest cocaine bust they had ever uncovered.

The Russian authorities, though, were puzzled. They had intercepted large drug shipments before (hashish from Afghanistan and opium from Central Asia, for example), but never a quantity this large. It would take years for the small number of cocaine addicts in Russia to use an amount of cocaine that size. Then the authorities figured it out. Most of the cocaine was on its way to Western Europe, where they estimated it would be worth a staggering $200 million. If cocaine shipments of that size were getting through, the Russian authorities surmised, then perhaps as much 40 percent of the capital moving through Russia was linked to drug trafficking.[1] So amid the elation was the sobering realization that the drug bust represented a trend.

Welcome to the former Soviet Union — a region that has become an emerging force on the international drug-trafficking scene. As President George Bush watched the disintegration of the Soviet Union in the late

1980s, he expressed the optimism of the West when he praised what he
believed was "the New World Order." What has happened since Bush
made his bold announcement, however, has not gone exactly according
to script. The struggle to move from a rigid totalitarian regime to a sta-
ble and viable capitalist society has been a difficult one; in fact, since
the breakup of the Soviet Union, Russia had changed from one of the
world's safest and most orderly societies to a country that has been
almost overwhelmed with crime. Indeed, the range of criminal activity
is astounding: forgery, arms trafficking, smuggling, extortion, bank
fraud, the movement of all kinds of contraband, and, of course, international drug trafficking.

As a result, Russian society had become one of the world's most
violent. Beginning in 1988, the murder rate rose 25 percent each year
during the next five years, reaching 29,200 murders in 1993.[2] Moscow
and other large Russian cities have been the scene of vicious street violence and gangland wars. In 1996 there were 500 contract killings in Russia, up from 100 in 1992. The killings included at least three members
of parliament and 35 bankers.[3] Local hoodlums extort money from
businesses, both Russian and foreign, which have to protect themselves
with electronic fences and around-the-clock security. Former Communist officials make huge fortunes smuggling all kinds of goods
through Russia's porous borders and to get anything done now often
requires a bribe to the right government official. The situation got so
bad so quickly that in 1993, two years after the breakup of the Soviet
Union, organized crime controlled as much as 40 percent of the movement of goods and services in Russia, according to the country's Ministry of Internal Affairs.[4]

Even hard drugs have begun to get a foothold in a society where
vodka has been the Russian drug of choice for centuries. Russia's increasing function as a transshipment point for Colombian cocaine has created a growing domestic market for drugs. Russian police told the press
that Russians were using 15 times as many narcotics in 1992 as they did
in 1987.[5] As one expert testified before Congress, "Highly skilled
chemists, graduates of medical institutions made destitute by wrench-
ing economic changes associated with the reform process, these people
are now, many of them, working under contract to organized crime syndicates, turning out sophisticated synthetic drugs such as LSD, amphetamines and synthetic opiates that are said to be many times more
powerful than heroine."[6] What adds to this chilling scenario is that the
former Soviet Union has huge resources for the production of narcotic

drugs, for example, the vast poppy fields in former Soviet republics, such as Kazakhstan, Uzbekistan, Tajikistan, Turkmenistan, the Ukraine, and southern European Russia, and millions of hectares of wild hemp, including four million in Kazakhstan alone. As Rensselaer Lee writes, "the country is virtually self-sufficient in producing narcotics."[7] The deteriorating situation — the crime, the violence, the drug trafficking, the drug abuse — has caused an exasperated Russian president Boris Yeltsin to say that "organized crime is trying to take the country by the throat."[8] That is not to say that organized crime and drug trafficking emerged in the former Soviet Union overnight. The old Communist system was one of total corruption, involving bribes, thefts, and organized crime on a vast scale. The Mafia was the Communist party and crime was a necessary part of doing business in the Soviet Union.[9] After the emergence of the black market in the 1960s, large criminal organizations developed in many Russian cities, led by powerful mobsters known as Thieves in Law, who began to work with government officials in the pursuit of criminal activities. By the time the Soviet communist system collapsed, an estimated 600 such groups were operating throughout the former empire, and the illegal underground economy accounted for as much as 50 percent of its personal income.[10]

"The apparatchicks and black marketeers profited the most," wrote Robert I. Friedman. "They lived like feudal lords in ornate hill top sanitariums and summer villas, shopped in special stores bulging with Japanese consumer goods, and traveled abroad — the most coveted privilege in the Soviet Union."[11]

Now that Russians can travel freely, crime has been the country's biggest export. Journalist Claire Sterling's investigation of organized crime revealed that, within two or three years of the dissolution of the Soviet empire, "leaders (had) established contact with their Western counterparts, and thousands of its members had expanded operations in the United States and Western Europe. It was moving into international drug trafficking and had mastered the complexities of shady international finance."[12]

Soon after the dissolution of the Soviet empire, Russian criminal groups were active in many major European cities, including Paris, Amsterdam, and London, and their reach extended around the world to cities with growing communities of Russian émigrés. According to the Russian Interior Ministry, by the mid 1990s an estimated 200 or more Russian organized crime groups were operating in 29 cities in Europe, the United States, and such farflung places as Macao in East Asia.[13]

So who are these criminal entrepreneurs? Experts reveal that Russian organized crime, includes about 5,000 gangs, with a membership of about 3 million, and a reach that, in the words of Claire Sterling, "extends into all fifteen of the former Soviet Republics, across five time zones and one-sixth of the earth's land mass."[14] Instead, the number of crimes committed by Russian gangs had jumped 94 percent since 1992.[15] Among its members are many former KGB officers, Communist party members and military officers, who have given the Russian criminal gangs inside access to the workings and wealth of the former Soviet Union.

The term "Russian mafia" may actually be a misnomer, because there is no capo di capi or ruling council, and often the groups are independent organizations that may have as few as two members. Moreover, most of the groups are not Russian at all; in fact, the most powerful and best-organized groups are the Chechens from the Caucasian mountain region, with the Georgians a close second.[16]

The international growth of these criminal organizations has been explosive. In Poland heroin seizures jumped tenfold between 1992 and 1994 after one mega seizure of 1,750 pounds of cocaine.[17] Polish law enforcement reportedly has only 35 full-time drug enforcement officials for the entire country, and its annual budget was a paltry $100,000 to $200,000 a year.[18] During the early 1990s, Poland also began to play an important role in the amphetamine drug trade, moving what was described as "currently the highest quality drug in Europe, with purity levels often ranging from ninety-seven to almost one hundred percent."[19]

Between August and December 1994, about $1 billion a month was deposited in offshore accounts set up by Russian companies, according to Russian Central Bank estimates.[20] "In the CIS (Commonwealth of Independent States) and most East European states, money laundering is not illegal," write Lee and MacDonald. "Banks are not legally required to report deposits, transfers or withdrawals, and banking authorities have no incentive to screen their clients or report suspicious transactions. In Poland the convertibility of local currency and the absence of control on importing and exporting foreign exchange generate additional incentives to launder drug profits there."[21]

The Russian mob's money-laundering activities are not confined to Eastern Europe, for they have also used the United States and Great Britain to move huge profits.[22] In 1993 British intelligence reports identified 200 money-laundering cases that had East European connections. One FBI official investigating Russian organized crime revealed in 1995 that "a lot of money is coming in from overseas and being pushed through United States banks. They run it through various banks and businesses here, and then sent it back there, and it comes back ... looking like legitimate money."[23] In 1993 alone, Russian organized crime transferred an estimated $25 billion from Russia to Western banks.[24]

What disturbs many Western law-enforcement officials is the evidence that the Russian Mafia is looking to expand its base of operation by forging alliances with other powerful criminal organizations around the world. As the bust in St. Petersburg in 1993 revealed, Russian groups have been involved with the Colombian cartels, and other reports indicate that criminal gangs in Russia and some of the other former Soviet republics were holding "summits" with the Sicilian Mafia. According to Claire Sterling, "America's Russian criminals were returning to their homeland to work a whole new set of crooked deals, often in partnership with their American Sicilian counterparts."[25]

The emergence of Russian criminal gangs on the American scene happened a long time before the collapse of the Soviet empire. According to the President's Commission on Organized Crime, the first indication of Russian organized crime activity in the United States came in 1975 when a Russian criminal gang began to operate a con game on Russian émigrés living in the United States. This group of con artists, "Potato Bag Gang," were convincing naive émigrés that they were buying a bag of coins when, in fact, they were getting a sack of potatoes.[26]

In the next decade and half, Russian organized crime got more sophisticated and became involved in drug trafficking as well as fraud, extortion, and counterfeiting. In 1984 the President's Commission estimated that there were 12 Russian organized criminal groups in New York, the city with the largest Russian immigrant population (a total membership between 400,000 and 500,000). Other cities reporting gang activity were Boston, Chicago, Miami, Cleveland, Dallas, and San Francisco.[27]

Russian emigrants continued to come to the United States in large numbers during the 1980s, thanks to a 1974 immigration law that favored Soviet political refugees. Among the immigrants were many hard-core criminals the Soviet government released from its jails.[28] The Russian Communist government relaxed travel restrictions in 1988 and larger numbers of emigrants began to come to the United States, so that by 1991 some 61,000 Russian Jews were offered entry.[29] Most of the Russian immigrants settled in the Brighton Beach area of Brooklyn in the neighborhood of Little Odessa.

In 1994 the FBI and police in various U.S. cities revealed that Vyacheslav Ivankov, a powerful figure in the Russian criminal underworld, had come to the United States, probably as an emissary to some power-ful Russian criminal gangs looking to expand their reach. In reference to Ivankov's arrival, one New York police detective commented, "You're going to see more bloodletting as people vie for control. There is just too much money to be made."[30] In June 1995 Ivankov was charged with attempting to extort $3.5 million from two Russian-born owners of the Summit International Corporation.

Ivankov and the other mob bosses were part of an established two-way traffic of organized criminals between Russia and the United States, which involved "contract killers ... flying in from Moscow or St. Peters-burg or the Caucasus to do a quick and expensive turnaround job — flying in, hit, fly out — for the Organization [Russian mob] or the American or Sicilian Mafia, or even ordinary Russian émigrés."[31]

In May 1997 President Yeltsin moved to counter the growing crim-inal threat by implementing an anticrime measure that called for new laws, improved monitoring of banking transactions, and the strength-ening of law enforcement. A month later, he signed another measure that expanded the investigative powers of the police, allowing them to do such things as detain suspects for thirty days without filing charges.[32]

Initially, U.S. law enforcement was slow to react to the growth of Russian criminal activity within its borders. In 1990 the *Washington Post* columnist James Rosenthal concluded that "Since the [U.S.] Justice Department does not consider the Russian mob to be organized crime, it doesn't treat it with the seriousness that it reserves for more VIP crim-inals."[33] In conducting a strategic assessment of Russian organized crime in 1991, the U.S. Immigration and Naturalization Service reportedly relied not on official investigations but on information obtained from the *New York Times*.[34]

Internationally, however, it was different story. Beginning in 1988, the United States signed a series of antidrug agreements with the Russ-ian government, and the DEA began to help organize seminars for Soviet customs and law-enforcement officials. In 1990 the Russian government invited DEA officials to go on a helicopter tour of the huge marijuana fields in Kazakhstan.[35]

In April 1994 Rensselaer Lee testified before Congress that the "influence of organized crime in the FSU [former Soviet Union] cuts across many aspects of Soviet-West relations."[36] Four months later, FBI director Louis Freeh was in Moscow to sign an agreement with the Russ-ian government to fight Russian-based organized crime more effectively. The agreement allowed FBI agents to gather records and evidence in the former Soviet Union and to interview witnesses, while trying to solve and prevent a variety of crimes, including drug trafficking. Freeh netted similar agreements with Poland, Lithuania, Slovakia, Hungary, Latvia, the Ukraine, and Germany during his ten-day visit to Europe.[37]

"We can honestly say that our two nations have more in common than ever before," Sergei V. Stephasin, head of the Russian Federal Counter Intelligence Service, the successor to the KGB, told the press at a conference to celebrate the Russian–U.S. agreement. "Together, we're invincible."[38]

That remains to be seen. The Russian Mafia is now an important part of the international drug-trafficking network, one of many illegal activities that has made it a powerhouse on the world's criminal scene. In the United States the Russian gangs are expanding their influence after learning much from the Italian Mafia, although, so far, they have been content to play second fiddle to the Cosa Nostra. That relationship, however, has a good chance of changing. "They are now like the (Italian) Mafia was back in the Twenties and Thirties, but I think that they'll far surpass it," predicted Terry Minton of the Los Angeles Police Department's organized crime intelligence division.[39]

Chapter 17

Vietnamese Gangs:
New Kids on the Block

"I have seen signs in the windows of Vietnamese non–drug stores advertising in Vietnamese the sale of prescription drugs without prescriptions. This is done openly since most law enforcement officials can't read Vietnamese."
— James A. Badey, detective, Arlington
County, Virginia, Police Department

"Large numbers of young Vietnamese have difficulty assimilating into American life. This has contributed to a rise in gang membership and gang-related violence."
— U.S. House Committee on Government Affairs.
Permanent Subcommittee on Investigations

Vietnamese gangs are among the fastest-growing ethnic criminal groups in America today and could become a major force in the lucrative world of international drug trafficking. The gangs are as ruthless and violent as any criminal group currently operating in the United States, and this trait, combined with their constant mobility, have made them a difficult target for U.S. law enforcement. According to testimony before U.S. Congress on October 3, 1991, Sergeant Douglas Zwemke of the San Jose Police Department said that the Vietnamese criminal gangs have left "virtually no illegal stone undisturbed" and identified their major criminal activities as narcotics trafficking, fraud, extortion, prostitution, gambling, home-invasion robberies, high-tech theft, and political and criminal terrorism.[1]

Vietnamese criminal gang activity in the United States has its roots in the Vietnam War and the fall of Saigon in 1975, when many Vietnamese criminals with experience in drug trafficking and other criminal activities fled Vietnam and became part of a massive influx of 650,000

Asian immigrants to the United States.[2] Writer Peter Huston has described the exodus: "Although many of the Vietnamese refugees are either freedom-loving people who found life under Communism intolerable or ordinary people who have too many ties to the former government or the capitalist system to be tolerated by the current government of Vietnam, there are exceptions. Like Cuba, the Socialist Republic of Vietnam simply allowed many of its petty and minor-league criminals and undesirables to leave if they wanted, thereby saving the cost of incarceration and causing problems for the United States in the process."[3]

The 1986 President's Commission on Organized Crime identified seven cities in California with active Vietnamese gangs, four in Texas, three in Louisiana, two in Alabama, and one each in New York, Oregon, Colorado, Florida, Washington, Hawaii, Virginia, Massachusetts, and Pennsylvania.[4] Scholar Ko-Lin Chin says that by 1980, about 110,000 Vietnamese refugees settled in southern California, concentrating mainly in the cities of Los Angeles, Anaheim, Westminster, Santa Ana, and Garden Grove, where gangs with names such as Frogmen, the Thunder Tigers, and the Pink Knights have since become active.[5] The U.S. government has estimated that more than 80 different Vietnamese gangs are operating in Orange County alone.

According to a congressional investigation, "Large numbers of young Vietnamese have difficulty assimilating into American life. This has contributed to a rise in gang membership and gang-related violence."[6]

Although not willing to describe Vietnamese criminal activity as organized crime, witnesses at the 1986 President's Commission hearings said that there was some networking among gangs and that "this pattern could accommodate the development of a true Vietnamese criminal cartel."[7]

Many law enforcement experts believe that the oligarchy that ruled South Vietnam before the Communist takeover also has played a role in the development of Vietnam criminal activity in the U.S. Marshall Nguyen Cao Ky, the former Prime Minister of the Republic of Vietnam who settled in California, was accused of involvement in drug trafficking during the Vietnam War and then working as a head of an international organization of Vietnamese gangs in the U.S. after his immigration. Ky has strongly denied the charges and the 1984 President's Commission on Organized Crime went on record as saying, "We accept this denial."[8]

The Vietnamese gangs got their criminal start in the United States in the 1970s preying on their fellow countrymen in numerous violent and often brutal home-invasion robberies. In their 1992 study of home-invasion robberies, law-enforcement officials Phil Hannum and Al Lotz described many of the robberies committed between 1987 and 1992 and noted that "for the United States and Canada, the home invasion robbery phenomenon took on new dimensions with the fall of Vietnam and the exodus of Vietnamese refugees to the United States and Canada from 1974 to the present."[9]

By the mid 1980s, articles about an emerging criminal pattern across the United States began appearing in the newspapers. In November 1985 the *New York Times* reported that the home-invasion robberies were being committed against Vietnamese families in Florida and other southern states, while the following year, the *Dallas Morning News* ran a story revealing that "Asian organized crime was growing in Dallas and described how Vietnamese and other Asians were being preyed upon by young Asians."[10]

According to federal intelligence reports, "those criminal organizations rooted in New York, Los Angeles, Seattle, Hong Kong and Taiwan form a loose national and, in some cases, an international network of burglary and extortion rings, 'safe houses' and money laundering schemes that often defy traditional law enforcement."[11]

Detective James R. Badey of the Arlington County, Virginia, Police Department described how Vietnamese gangs operate: "The roving bands travel from one Vietnam community to another throughout the United States committing serious and dangerous crimes. They have no names and no permanent leader. Their membership is very fluid, and there is no group loyalty. As they travel, some members drop out and go their separate ways while new members join the band.... Members of those bands are usually male, ranging in age from sixteen to twenty-five, and travel in bands of three to ten. They have few language skills, offer little or no job skills, and often have no nuclear family in this country."[12]

By the 1980s Vietnamese criminal gangs were diversifying and becoming heavily involved in a number of illegal activities, including drug trafficking. Law-enforcement officials suspected that Vietnamese criminals are involved in the illegal importation and distribution of prescription drugs, including codeine and valium, which they smuggle in from France and sell illegally in the Vietnamese community, either on the street or in unlicensed businesses. "I have seen signs in the windows of Vietnamese non–drug stores advertising in Vietnamese the sale of prescription drugs without prescriptions," said detective James R. Badey. "This is done openly since most law enforcement officials can't read

Vietnamese."[13] Badey described one incident involving the interception by U.S. Customs of three packages of valium from France, which were being sent to three Vietnamese addresses in the Arlington, Virginia, area: "Upon investigation, I learned that the packages had been sent to the same people several times before and that the packages eventually ended up in the hands of one person."[14]

By the 1980s, Vietnamese gangs began earning such a fearsome reputation that Chinese criminal organizations were recruiting them to work as enforcers. Smart, bold, and ruthless, a number of Vietnamese began to rise in the Chinese organizations and some even held top posts. In the mid 1980s, for example, one Vietnamese named Van Huey Huynh became a top heroin dealer in a Chinese gang in New York City's Chinatown as Ping On Gang, even though he was just twenty-two years old.[15] In New York City, Boston, and Toronto, war broke out between rival Chinese and Vietnamese gangs, but rather than openly confront the Vietnamese, some Chinese Triad gangs from Toronto moved their operations into Chinese communities in the city's suburbs. "Chinatown's street-level rackets were essentially handed over to the Vietnamese groups," writes William Kleinknecht.[16]

Although Vietnamese gangs are known for their decentralized nature, the Vietnamese gang Born to Kill rose to notoriety in New York City with strong leadership and well-defined structure. Born to Kill was founded in 1988 by David Thai, who had left another gang known as the Vietnamese Flying Dragons. At its zenith, the gang, also known as the Canal Street Boys, had about 50 to 100 members and branches in other cities in New York State, as well as New Jersey, Connecticut, and Canada. Even though David Thai and six of his top assistants in the gang were convicted on March 30, 1992, of committing numerous violent crimes, U.S. law enforcement believes the gang is still active.[17]

Vietnamese gangs appear to becoming more organized and structured, and law enforcement worries that they will become an increasingly powerful criminal threat in the future. They point out that law enforcement faces many of the same problems they face in investigating Chinese criminal organizations, including the language barrier, lack of resources, and poor interagency and police department coordination. Moreover, their ambition and criminal talent means that they will want a greater share of the tremendous amount of money to be made from international drug trafficking.

Chapter 18

The Mexican Connection: The Emerging Linchpin of International Drug Trafficking

"Mexican drug traffickers today are the premier organized drug crime group in the world. What we've seen recently is the Mexicans moving into markets that have been traditionally Colombian markets; for example, New York City."
— James Milford, deputy director, DEA

"There is not one organization, not one group in law enforcement within Mexico that we [the U.S.] have been able to work with and have total trust in."
— James Milford, deputy director, DEA

In June 1995, the private jet appeared as a blip on the military radar screen and then crashed into the mountains near Guadalajara, Mexico. General José Gutierrez Rebello, the military commander in Guadalajara, learned that among the passengers aboard the plane was Hector Luis "El Guero" Palma, one of Mexico's most powerful drug traffickers. Within hours, he had sent federal agents into the mountains to find the place and El Guero. The agents tracked the drug trafficker to an upscale mansion in a Guadalajara neighborhood, where heavily armed federal police were protecting him. Gutierrez brought in reinforcements, surrounded the house, and arrested Palma and his three police bodyguards — all without firing a shot. Mexican and U.S. officials hailed Palma's speedy capture as one of the most successful and impressive antidrug operations in Mexican history.[1]

The operation also helped get Gutierrez appointed commissioner of Mexico's key government antidrug agency: the National Institute for Combating Drugs, the country's equivalent of the U.S. Drug Enforcement Agency (DEA). Historically, the position was given to well-connected politicians, but Gutierrez's success made him the first career military officer to hold the post. Mexico, whose much-maligned antidrug program had been plagued by corruption in the past, looked to be on the right track.

"Gutierrez has a public reputation of absolute integrity," enthused U.S. drug czar Barry McCaffrey. "He is strong leader. This is clearly a focused high energy man. But the important thing is the Mexicans are confident in him."[2]

Within two months of his appointment, Gutierrez was under arrest on corruption charges, Mexico's antidrug program was in disarray, the country was facing what one Mexican official described as "the worst law enforcement crisis in the history of modern Mexico," and U.S.-Mexico relations were at their lowest point in years.[3] Gutierrez was accused of being on the payroll of Amado Carrillo Fuentes, one of Mexico's most powerful drug traffickers. It seemed that Mexico's former top antidrug official lived in the same apartment complex as Carillo, and the police said that they had evidence that the two were on intimate terms. From his jail cell, Gutierrez vehemently insisted that he was just trying to get close to the drug trafficker.[4]

The Mexico government quickly replaced Gutierrez with Mariano Herran Salvatti, a former Mexico City prosecutor who had no experience in fighting drug trafficking and a mere two years experience in law enforcement. "My first priority is restructuring the Institute," Herran told the press. "Then we will deepen the investigations into drug trafficking organizations and go after whomever we must break."[5]

The scandal underscored the depth of drug corruption in Mexico and came at a time when the country was emerging as the linchpin in the Latin American drug trade. No country in the world poses a more immediate narcotics threat to the U.S. than does Mexico, declared the U.S. State Department, which said that its research showed that, by 1996, Mexico was supplying up to 80 percent of the foreign-grown marijuana consumed in the United States, 20 to 30 percent of the heroin, and 80 percent of the methamphetamines.[6]

Mexico is not a big producer of cocaine, and, in the past, it has mainly supplied the couriers for the powerful Colombian cartels, smuggling the drugs into the United States, where the Colombians would retake and distribute them through their local organization. With the successful crackdown against Colombia's Medellín and Cali cartels in the early 1990s, however, Mexican drug-trafficking organizations began to finance Colombian drug shipments, take over drug smuggling routes between Colombia and the United States, and coordinate Colombian drug-trafficking rings within the United States.

"The Mexican drug cartels are now holding their own with the Colombians and the center of the Latin American drug trade may be shifting," revealed Rosso José Serrano, general director of the Colombian National Police.[7] So confident were the Mexicans of their new role that by 1997 reports indicated they that they were contacting guerrillas in Colombia who operate near coca fields and cocaine laboratories and showing signs that they had plans of taking control of the coca fields in Colombia as well as Peru and Bolivia.

"Mexican drug traffickers today are the premier organized drug crime group in the world," James Milford deputy direction of the U.S. DEA, told the *Miami Herald*. "What we've seen recently is the Mexicans moving into markets that have been traditionally Colombian markets; for example, New York City."[8]

In February 1997, U.S. authorities became aware of the extent of Mexico's growing drug-trafficking presence in New York City when it intercepted an 18-wheel tractor-trailer parked near La Guardia Airport and found it packed with cocaine hidden in a shipment of carrots.[9]

Some Mexican organizations can be as powerful as their Colombian counterparts, according to the DEA.[10] In fact, reports indicated that by the mid 1990s, the Mexican cartels were earning almost as much money as the Colombians. For example, in 1994 the Colombian Cali cartel's earnings were put at $30 billion; Mexico's Gulf cartel, between $10 and $20 billion.[11]

Colombian officials told the *Miami Herald* that at least one Mexican drug lord, Amado Carrillo Fuentes, was even loaning money to the Cali cartel, whose leaders were in jail and short of the cash they needed to finance drug shipments and to wage a retaliatory terrorist campaign in Colombia if the country adopted its proposed law allowing extradition to the United States. "When you have one drug lord asking a favor from another, and when the favor is a $20 million loan, that indicates clear subordination," one Colombian official told the *Miami Herald*. "The Mexicans are now clearly in charge."[13]

Mexico had not suddenly become a problem for the United States in its battle against international drug trafficking. Smuggling drugs

across the 1,933-mile U.S.-Mexican border has a history that goes back
to the 1930s, when Mexico first became a major transshipment point for
opium.[14] In the 1930s Cosa Nostra mobster Meyer Lansky worked with
Mexican drug trafficking syndicates to smuggle heroin and marijuana
into the United States.[15] In 1945 U.S. drug-enforcement officials seized
Mexican brown heroin for the first time.[16]

After World War II the demand for Mexican opium and heroin
declined, but marijuana production continued to climb until the 1960s,
when demand skyrocketed. The Nixon administration became so concerned about marijuana smuggling from Mexico that it launched Operation Intercept, which mandated closing the U.S.-Mexican border and
trying to search every car. Chaos ensued; U.S.-Mexican relations chilled;
and the U.S. Congress began looking for alternative ways to stop illegal
drugs from flowing across the border.[17]

In the early 1970s, when the famous French Connection heroin-dis-
tribution network was destroyed and the Turkish government carried
out a successful opium-eradication program, Mexico emerged as the
major U.S. source of heroin, and by the late 1970s it had captured nearly
90 percent of the market while maintaining a 70 percent share of the
U.S. marijuana market. The Mexican government, however, also launched
a successful crackdown on opium and marijuana cultivation and drug
trafficking, and by the early 1980s, the country was supplying less than
30 percent of the heroin and marijuana consumed by the United States.[18]

That situation began changing again by 1987, when the growing
demand for heroin led to a sharp increase in the production of opium
around the world. The biggest increase came from Mexico and the
Golden Triangle region of southeast Asia. Mexico began to capture an
increasing share of the U.S. heroin market after their drug traffickers
introduced a cheaper, purer, and more readily available heroin product
known as black tar. Largely because of black tar's introduction, Mexico
opium production more than doubled between 1984 and 1988, going
from 21 metric tons to between 45 and 55 metric tons.[19]

Opium and marijuana crops are grown in ten Mexican states, including Jalisco, Oaxaca, Sinoa, and Veracruz, and are believed to support at
least 138,000 workers. Mexican opium farmers can make more money
than their counterparts in the Golden Triangle and Golden Crescent
regions of Asia, but as drug-policy analyst Mary H. Cooper notes, Mexican farmers have higher overhead costs than other opium growers,
which means that even those higher profits are not enough to improve
their living standards.[20] Cooper also points out that "climate and soil

conditions require Mexican growers to use costly irrigation techniques" and that in Mexico "cultivators also spend large amounts of money bribing drug-enforcement agents to escape the country's aggressive opium drug eradication program."[21]

In 1995 alone, Mexican authorities used 110,000 soldiers to destroy 15,389.2 hectares of opium and 21,573.3 of marijuana, according to the U.S. General Accounting Office (GAO), but the agency also noted that the amount of cocaine seized and the number of drug-related arrests declined between 1992 and 1995.[22]

Although Mexico remains the biggest supplier of United States heroin, the country claims that it is having success in its drug eradication program. A *Miami Herald* article in November 1996 quoted Mexican drug agents who said they expected to wipe out nearly 100,000 acres of marijuana and poppy plants by the end of the year.[23] No statistics were given, however, and a cynic might have concluded that the report was part of Mexico's public relations campaign to convince the U.S. government that it should be recertified as fully cooperating in the War on Drugs.[24]

In the 1970s, the major cartels operating in Mexico today entrenched themselves in the big business of international drug trafficking. Three cartels dominate Mexican drug trafficking: the Juárez or Chihuahua cartel, which until his mysterious death in 1997 was headed by Amado Carrillo Fuentes and traffics mainly in cocaine across the western border, from Tijuana to Ciudad Juárez; the Tijuana cartel, which is run by the Arellano Felix brothers and covers the Pacific Coast, smuggling mainly heroin and marijuana; and the Gulf cartel, which controls a huge area extending along the eastern part of the U.S.-Mexican border from Ciudad Juárez to Matamoros, along the Mexican Gulf Coast through the Yucatán Peninsula to the border with Belize.[25]

The Gulf and Tijuana cartels are among the world's most violent drug-trafficking organizations. The Mexican government believes that the capo of the Tijuana cartel, Benjamin Arellano, was responsible for the murder of Cardinal Juan Jesús Posadas Ocampo at Guadalajara's international airport in January 1993. According to reports, after Cardinal Posadas Ocampo and six others were killed, the gunmen boarded a Tijuana-bound Air Mexico jet that had been held for twenty minutes awaiting their arrival, even though they had no boarding pass. Mexican prosecutors later accused four state police officers of acting as the killers' bodyguards.[26]

The Tijuana cartel has tortured and killed several federal law enforcement officials and at least two chief prosecutors from Tijuana and are suspected of arranging the killing of reform-minded presidential candidate Donaldo Colasio in March 1994. So dangerous does the Mexican government consider the Arellano Felix brothers that it placed a $1 million reward on each of their heads. "It reminds me of Wyatt Earp and those big gunslingers — wanted dead or alive," Tijuana police chief Jorge Álvarez Barriere told reporters. "What I don't know (in the Arellano case) is if the reward is for dead or alive."[27]

In contrast to the violent Arellano brothers, Amado Corrillo Fuentes, who was considered Mexico's most powerful drug lord until his death, liked to keep a low profile and fancied himself as a businessman who would rather buy off competitors than kill them. "Amado has tried to be a peacemaker," one well-placed U.S. law-enforcement official told the *Dallas Morning News*. "He has influence. I think his value is that he is more like the Cali Cartel people. He tries to keep it that way and not provoke acts of violence."[28]

Not much was known about Carrillo Fuentes — not his exact age, his height, or the color of his hair. His nickname was "Lord of the Skies," reportedly because of his success in using huge passenger jets like Boeing 727s to handle large loads of cocaine.[29] On September 28, 1989, the Juárez cartel became the target of the biggest cocaine bust in history, when U.S. law-enforcement officials discovered 21.3 tons of cocaine and more than $12 million in cash in a warehouse near Los Angeles.[30]

Carrillo solidified his position as the Pablo Escobar of Mexico after the capture and extradition to the United States of Juan Garcia Abrego, the Gulf cartel head, the only drug trafficker ever placed on the FBI's most wanted list. In October 1996, Garcia was found guilty by a Houston jury of 22 counts of conspiracy, drug trafficking, money laundering, and operating a criminal enterprise and sentenced him to a minimum of ten years in jail for each of the offenses. Jurors also decided that the U.S. government could seize $350 million of the drug lord's fortune, which was estimated to be as high as $15 billion.[31]

But long before his troubles with the U.S. authorities, competitors were moving into Garcia Abrego's territory. In fact, U.S. law-enforcement officials conceded that, at the time of his arrest, Abregon had probably been inactive as a drug trafficker for some time. That would help to explain his capture, for the Mexican system is so corrupt that drug kingpins can operate with virtual impunity and have little fear of arrest. Drug lords like Carrillo and the Arellano brothers have thousands of government and law-enforcement officials at all levels on their payroll, who provide the traffickers with information and use their authority to help them to move and protect their drugs.

The official corruption in Mexico began to make international headlines in 1985 when Mexican drug traffickers kidnapped, tortured, and murdered DEA special agent Enrique Camarena Salazar and his pilot Alfredo Zavalar Avelar in Guadalajara. Six Mexican police were later charged with complicity in the murders, but still the corruption worsened and continued unabated, as the increasingly powerful drug traffickers have spent billions of dollars for payoffs.[32]

"The emergence of Mexico's drug trafficking elite could not have occurred without the collaboration of high ranking officials, the country's law enforcement and national security agencies who provided intelligence and on occasion the logistical infrastructure, as well as the required security," writes security consultant James Sutton. "At one time or another, members of most drug trafficking organizations in Mexico possessed official credentials from a number of police."[33]

Here are some graphic examples to illustrate how widespread the drug corruption in Mexico is:

> • Cuauhtemoc Herrara Suastequi, the chief prosecutor for Tijuana, estimates that perhaps as much as 15 percent of the 1,200 officers under his command may be crooked.[34]
>
> • In a two-month period (February–March 1997), two high-ranking Mexican generals are charged with bribery, drug trafficking, and criminal conspiracy. One of the two, Brigadier General Alfredo Navarro, is accused of offering $1 million a month to a top federal agent to protect the Juárez cartel's Amado Carrillo Fuentes.[35]
>
> • In February 1997 the *New York Times* accuses Jorge Carrillo Olea, governor of the state of Morelos, and Manlio Fabio Betrones Rivera, governor of the state of Sonora, of having ties with Mexican drug lords and allowing huge quantities of drugs to pass through their territory.[36]
>
> • In August 1996 Attorney General Antonio Lozano Garcia announced the mass firing of 737 agents; that is, nearly one-fifth of the federal police force.[37] The northern state of Tamaulipas is so corrupt that the Mexican government announces that it will replace federal police there with military officers.[38] "Federal agents act as the drug traffickers' department of Intelligence and Quality Control," disgusted police commander Juan José Tafoya González told the press before resigning.[39]

• In November 1995 the sister-in-law of former Mexican president Carlos Salinas de Gortari is linked to allegations of drug trafficking and money laundering after she used a false name to withdraw funds from a bank account containing $84 million. Carlos's brother Raul is already in jail, charged with conspiracy in the killing of politician José Francisco Ruiz Massieu, a conspiracy that is believed to involve Mexican drug traffickers.[40]

• Former deputy attorney general Mario Ruiz Massieu, the brother of José Francisco, is charged in the United States with the murder of José Francisco and taking bribes from drug traffickers in exchange for protection. Mario Ruiz was arrested in Newark, New Jersey, after he had fled from Mexico with more than $40,000 in cash and a reported $9 million stashed away in bank accounts.[41]

"There is not one organization, not one group in law enforcement within Mexico that we [the U.S.] have been able to work with and have total trust in," complained James Milford, the DEA's deputy director.[42]

Despite the pervasive corruption and concerns about Mexico's effort in the War on Drugs, the Clinton administration once again certified Mexico has a cooperative ally in the War on Drugs in March 1997. Some members of the U.S. Congress objected. They wanted to send Mexico a stern message — namely, that it risks sanctions if it fails to clean up its antidrug act. Clinton administration officials said decertifying Mexico would, among other things, destabilize its financial markets, weaken the peso, hurt the North American Free Trade Association (NAFTA), and create new immigration problems.[43] "We must always remember the following thing: that (we) have a 2,000 mile border with Mexico," the new secretary of state, Madeleine Albright, told a Senate committee.[44]

In April 1997 Mexico moved to reform its discredited antidrug program, establishing a new crime unit to replace the corruption-ridden National Institute to Combat Drugs and strengthening its field operations. To show that it now meant business in the War on Drugs, Mexican police confiscated 10.7 tons of cocaine found in a truck heading towards the U.S.-Mexican border.[45] Then in May, the United States and Mexico signed an antidrug alliance that provided for a new protocol for extradition and increased the number of personnel used to fight drug trafficking along the U.S.-Mexican border.[46]

The United States expressed its pleasure and its support for the reform measures, but without any real U.S. pressure being put on Mexico to change its corrupt ways, nothing much is likely to change in the country's battle against drug trafficking. As the GAO reported, "Mexico has been plagued by numerous other problems besides corruption, which has hindered its anti drug efforts. Serious economic and political problems that include focusing funds and resources on a strong insurgency movement, the lack of basic legislative tools (wire tapping, confidential informants, witness protection programs, for example) to combat drug trafficking and inadequately trained and poorly maintained aircraft."[47] The report also noted that the U.S. has cut the size of its counternarcotics program, which has hindered U.S. efforts to monitor how its aid is being used by Mexico.[48]

The U.S. government might have been expected to be outraged at the murder of Colosio, but on the day of his assassination President Clinton's first question to his aides was, how will it affect NAFTA?[49] That anecdote, as much as any, reveals the true U.S. priorities when it comes to fighting international drug trafficking.

Section 4
Impact

Chapter 19

Going Multinational: The Globalization of International Drug Trafficking

"We must play by the books, while they listen to nothing and … are run by nothing, in terms of laws."
— Carol Boyd Hallet, U.S. ambassador to the Bahamas

"We are going to need a new arsenal of foreign policy tools and organizational responses to cope with the complex challenges arising from the former Soviet crime groups and the types of malevolent non state actors in the modern international environment."
— Rensselaer Lee III, president, Global Advisory Services and co-author of *The Andean Cocaine Industry*

Colombian drug cartels serve as the linchpin of the South American drug trade, while the Italian Mafia coordinate the international flow of heroin. The Chinese Triads move the heroin from southeast Asia to markets all around the world; Nigerians work as their couriers. The Jamaican posses dominate the U.S. crack trade. The Japanese specialize in "ice." The Mexicans have muscled their way into the amphetamine trade and are about to become the new linchpins of the Latin American drug trade. The fall of the Soviet Union has unleashed the Russian Mafia, which is spreading over the globe as an emerging force in international drug trafficking. Koreans, Peruvians, Dominicans, Pakistanis, and other ethnic criminal groups are working hard to buy, sell, and distribute the heroin, cocaine, marijuana, amphetamines, and other illegal drugs marketed by the major international drug-trafficking syndicates.

Not only are more criminal organizations than ever before involved in international drug trade, but the huge worldwide appetite for drugs has given rise to an international criminal network of unprecedented scope and sophistication. New patterns of cooperation have emerged between the drug-trafficking organizations, which is allowing them to address "business issues" of common concern, such as production, security, marketing logistics, and the laundering and investment of illicit drug profits. This cooperation has been a prime reason that the international drug trade is the fastest-growing industry — legal or illegal — in the world.

Making it difficult for law enforcement to combat this trend is the fact that the major drug syndicates can no longer be thought of as mere criminal organizations, for in terms of their size, resources, and sophistication, they operate like giant multinationals on the scale of many Fortune 500 companies. "The major ICOs (the International Criminal Organizations) have all the same characteristics and features of the more traditional, nationally based criminal organizations," Goodson and Olson explained. "What distinguishes their ability to conduct global operations on the scale of a major multinational cooperation is their transnational scale and their ability to challenge national and international authority. Disposing of large quantities of ready cash, diversified into a wide range of activities and employing a work force spread around the globe, the ICO represents a different order of magnitude in criminal operations."[1]

We have seen how the Cali cartel used big-business methods to transform itself into what many law-enforcement experts call the most powerful criminal organization in history.[2] The Cali cartel has been only the most visible example of how this business dynamic is transforming organized crime. "The drug trade has created a breed of shady billionaires who seem as canny in business as they are vicious," writes Louis Kraar. "They stay ahead of market conditions, constantly change operating methods to avoid arrest, and invest their earnings in legitimate business ... in short, a huge multinational commodity business with a fast-moving top management, and price-sensitive customers."[3] Scholar Stephen Flynn agrees that the drug syndicates pattern themselves after the multinational corporation but points out, "Unlike traders in oil, automobiles or microchips, traders in illicit drugs must outwit a dynamic enforcement environment designed to defeat them. Consequently, over the past two decades the drug trade has undergone something of a Darwinian evolution, the survivors of which had developed into sophisticated and highly flexible organizations."[4]

As the powerful crime syndicates forge alliances in pursuit of power and profit, they become even more dangerous to corrupt governments, manipulating national currencies and buying their way into legitimate governments to disguise their illicit activities. "In general, international narco cooperation opens new markets for narcotics and other illegal products, exploits economics of scale for selling in these markets, enhances organized crime's penetration of legal economic and financial systems and generally increases the power of criminal formations relative to national governments," explains Rensselaer Lee, president of Global Advisory Services and coauthor of *The Andean Cocaine Industry*.[5]

Many experts now see the globalization of international crime, especially in its drug-trafficking form, as an example of how organized crime has replaced the Soviet Union and global communism as the new threat to the United States and other democracies around the world. They have warned that governments themselves must begin to cooperate more seriously, if they are to begin to ward off this threat.

This view is held by respected and long-established institutions around the world. In 1990 Italy's Parliamentary Anti-Mafia Commission told the UN General Assembly that "international criminal organizations have reached agreements and understandings to divide up geographical areas, develop new market strategies, work out forms of mutual assistance and the settlement of conflicts" and warned that this new force "was capable of imposing its will on legitimate states, of undermining institutions and forces of law and order, of uprooting delicate economic and financial equilibrium and destroying democratic life."[6]

The globalization of international drug trafficking is a trend that has taken strong root in Latin America, according to José Leonardo Gallego, counternarcotics director of the Colombian National Police. "Alliances have formed between Colombian cartels and drug traffickers in many other countries all over the region," Gallego revealed. "The degree of cooperation is remarkably sophisticated, which makes it difficult for law enforcement in particular countries like Colombia to combat the criminal problem."[7]

Alliances and cooperation among organized crime syndicates is not an entirely new trend. There has always been some form of cooperation because criminals cannot move a commodity like drugs by themselves.

The Italian American La Cosa Nostra had an established relationship with the Sicilian mob to transport heroin from the Golden Triangle and the Golden Crescent. The Sicilian organizations supplied heroin to their American affiliates, which then distributed the drug themselves or sold it in large quantities to major distributors, as witnessed in the Pizza Connection case of the early 1980s, which involved the Sicilian and Italian American Mafias.

Over the years, the Italian Mafia has sought out Asian connections in southeast Asia to move heroin from the Golden Triangle. The mob has also been dealing with the Yakuza since the 1960s.[8] "The two have always traded in guns and dope," investigative journalist Claire Sterling writes. "American guns sell for ten to fifteen times their cost in Japan, where they are banned. 'Ice,' or crystal methamphetamine, the Yakuza's specialty, comes back in exchange by way of Honolulu, where it is now the drug of choice. Yakuza traffickers are bringing in [to Japan] heroine and cocaine, too."[9]

Collaboration between drug traffickers, however, has accelerated in the 1990s. Cocaine, for instance, started to make inroads in Japan, mainly because the Yakuza were forming liaisons with South American drug lords, most notably the Colombians, to expand drug imports to the country. The Colombians are also working with the Russian Mafia to move cocaine to Eastern Europe through the former Soviet bloc countries, an inviting distribution corridor that lacks sophisticated customs methods and has poorly paid and poorly equipped law enforcement. Russian criminal organizations have also met with syndicates from other countries to map out strategy.[10]

The growing relationship between the Sicilian Mafia and the Colombian cartels is the most striking example of how organized crime is collaborating to expand its influence and power in international drug trafficking. The Sicilian-Colombian connection began in the late 1980s when the North American cocaine market was becoming saturated. Prosperous, untapped Western Europe looked ready to exploit as an illegal drug market. "My research shows that the Colombian-Sicilian relationship is on a very firm footing," Rensselaer Lee explained.[11]

An alliance offers many advantages to the Colombians. For starters, the Sicilian Mafia knew the European market and has a sophisticated distribution network that the Colombians couldn't possibly match. Not knowing their way around Europe, moreover, was costing the Colombians a lot of money. "Because they were losing loads, they were beginning to look at allowing the Sicilians to play a larger role," reported Greg

Passic, head of Financial Investigations for the U.S. Drug Enforcement Agency (DEA).[13]

The Colombian-Sicilian Mafia set up a "financial" arrangement that allowed the Colombians to sell to European buyers outside Italy. That an alliance did form was verified in the "Green Ice" money-laundering case of September 1992, in which U.S., Italian, and European law enforcement arrested 164 drug traffickers and seized $51 million in traffickers' assets.[13] Since then, other investigations have shown that Italian-Colombian collaboration is still in place and thriving. One such investigation was Operation Dinero, which involved establishing and operating a bank in 1994 to uncover money-laundering activities.[14]

In February 1997 Italian authorities captured Trivello Silvano, an important figure in the Italian-Colombian connection. General Rosso José Serrano, director of the Colombian National Police, said that, since 1985, Silvano had directed the international traffic of cocaine from South America to such European countries as Italy, Germany, Belgium, Switzerland, France, and Holland.[15] The Italian police have also released evidence showing that Colombian and Italian syndicates were collaborating in using shipments of coffee from Colombia to distribute cocaine through Russia and other Eastern European countries.[16]

Several factors have created the setting that has allowed Colombian cartel–Sicilian Mafia and other forms of international trafficking cooperation to flourish. First of all, like legitimate multinationals, international drug-trafficking syndicates have been able to take advantage of the revolution in global communication and transportation. Traffickers now use sophisticated technology such as sign interceptors to plot radar and avoid monitoring, and they can now move their illicit drug profits in seconds to almost any place in the world and use computers, faxes, and cellular phones to coordinate their activities and make their businesses run smoothly. The Italian Mafia reportedly encrypts its computer files using the free and popular PGP (Pretty Good Privacy), an Internet security program. The Cali cartel has even used scanners to monitor the movements of DEA agents.[17]

"The speed at which you can move money around the world with electronic-funds transfers makes it difficult to trace launderers," explained Dennis Lynch, dean of the University of Denver Law School.[18]

To survive in a very competitive, high-tech environment, drug traffickers must also be able to innovate and adapt to changing law-enforcement tactics. A four-year secret investigation of the Cali cartel, code-named Operation El Cid, revealed that the cartel's operation included a fleet of 20 specialized submarinelike boats that could move mostly submerged to evade radar. Made by a boat builder in Colombia, each boat measured 26 feet by 30 feet and could carry two people and up to a ton of cocaine.[19]

Another factor has been the spectacular collapse of communism. In the words of Boutros Boutros-Ghali, former secretary-general of the United Nations, this development "has led to a weakening of institutional structures and a loss of social and ideological benchmarks in Eastern Europe."[20] According to Robert Moroni, interior minister of Italy, immediately after the fall of the Berlin Wall the first links that were established between East and West were those of organized crime. "West Europe crime groups are better organized than those in the East, and they forged alliances for certain activities," Moroni explained.[21]

The drug traffickers have been able to exploit the power vacuum fully. For example, the sudden shift from communism to private capitalism throughout the former communist world has fostered the organization of numerous front companies that have allowed drug traffickers to hide their money in legitimate enterprises.

As we have read, the former Soviet Union and Eastern Europe are being used both as markets for drugs and as conduits for distributing heroin and cocaine to Western European and other markets. Russia is

A captured helicopter is inspected by a member of the Colombian National Police (courtesy Colombian National Police).

now growing and producing opium, marijuana, and other drugs, while local criminal organizations are linking with their counterparts from other countries to improve their own organizational alliances and marketing contacts. While communism has collapsed in the former Soviet Union, it is changing in the People's Republic of China, where the profit motive and market economy have become increasingly important. With these changes, however, have come crime, corruption, and the increasing importance of the country as a drug producing, consuming, and distribution center.

The declining importance of national borders has also fostered the globalization of international drug trafficking. "As late as the 1960s, the Japanese were not allowed to travel around for pleasure," *Newsweek* explained in a cover story in 1993. "Just a few years ago, exit visas for those living in the Soviet Union, Eastern Europe and China were a prized rarity. Now Czech prostitutes work the Italian Riviera; Chinese immigrants to America are transshipped through Hungary; and South American drug lords recruit traffickers in Nigeria. In Western Europe, people, goods, money and arms swirl around in an all but bottomless space."[22]

The European Union (EC), the North American Free Trade Association, and the other regional organizations that have moved into this "bottomless space" have weakened customs controls and other security safeguards, making it easy for the international organized crime connection to move into new markets, distribute drugs, and shift money. It is no big challenge for drug traffickers to smuggle cash out of the United States and move it through the international financial system elsewhere. As the Center for Strategic Studies explained in a 1993 report: "These recent trade initiatives ... portend an upward trend in cross-border trading so that collectively ... [they] largely neutralize drug interdiction efforts and create unparalleled opportunities for the drug trade's [chemical] precursors, products and profits to move throughout the international system."[23] Countries around the world are eager to serve as safe havens for cash deposits and other laundered transactions.

The era of free trade has been widely praised, but in the changing international marketplace there are few rules. What has happened was expressed aptly by former United Nations Secretary-General Boutros Boutros-Ghali in an address to the World Ministerial Conference on Organized Transnational Crime in Naples, Italy, in November 1994. Ghali told his audience, "A sociologist recently posed the question: what does a market without a state and without rules of law resemble? The Jungle. And what organization is born of the jungle? The mafia."[24]

As national borders decrease in importance, more and more people from all parts of the world are migrating — searching for a better life, trying to avoid ethnic turmoil, or for a variety of other reasons. With the immigrants are coming criminals who are exploiting immigrant communities for illegal means and are using those communities as strong bases from which to launch their drug-trafficking activities. It's not a new trend. Criminal groups like the Triads, Russian Mafia, and the Vietnamese gangs have done this in the past. But the trend should accelerate in the future, given the growth of international drug trafficking.

International drug syndicates are seeking out alliances because the international market for drugs is booming, thanks to big increases in worldwide drug use. "The countries that are not suffering from the harmful consequences of drug abuse are the exception rather than the rule," the International Narcotics Control Board reported in 1993.[25] The number of addicts in the former Soviet Union, for example, has been estimated at 1.5 to 7.5 million, while most neighboring East European countries have drug problems. In Poland, for instance, two-thirds of the drug abusers are under 21 years of age.[26]

"For the populations of the former Eastern Bloc, the collapse of Communist regimes has meant an end to the state's monopoly on information and has allowed almost entirely unfettered domestic and international travel," the Center for Strategic and International Studies explained. "When increased awareness and travel and a surge in drug production and trafficking are combined with the communications revolution, then the word that a particular drug has acquired popularity somewhere will inevitably spread."[27]

Law enforcement agencies worldwide have shown that they are ill equipped to meet the challenge. In fact, states acting on their own can do little to stop the growth of international drug trafficking. What's more, it is much easier for criminals to operate illegally across borders than it is for law enforcement agencies to coordinate their activities across those borders. Carol Boyd Hallett, U.S. ambassador to the Bahamas, has compared drug trafficking syndicates to guerrilla organizations and the efforts of the United States and other countries to stop the bad guys as being more like the " regular army." The ambassador noted, "We must play by the books while they listen to nothing and ... are run by nothing, in terms of laws."[28]

Ernest Samper, former president of Colombia, stressed in an interview that "the power and sophistication of drug-trafficking organizations at the international level makes it imperative that countries around the world begin thinking in terms of global strategies and not bilateral or regional approaches to combating the drug threat."[29]

Countries have been slow to react to the globalization of international drug trafficking. Many countries, in fact, still do not have laws against fraud, money laundering, and organized crime, and when there are laws, they often conflict with each other. In the European Community, for example, each country has its own law on extortion, wiretaps, sharing of intelligence information, and the invasion of privacy in databanks. "Standardizing the regulations could take a lifetime," Claire Sterling points out. "Indeed, hardly any have been standardized up to now."[30]

The European problem is replicated in other parts of the world. In March 1997, a panel of Western European experts issued a report that said the disparate legal systems of the Caribbean region, which are based on Dutch, English, French, and Spanish law, make for weak implementation of laws against drug trafficking. It advised that more effort be made to establish bilateral and multinational treaties and agreements against narcotics smuggling.[31]

In Mexico, money laundering is a tax violation, not a criminal offense, and the country does not have the same kinds of requirements for reporting money transactions as does its neighbor, the United States. This discrepancy has allowed drug cartels to use Mexico's official banking system and the mostly unregulated dollar exchange houses to launder their cash.[32]

The sobering reality that drug lords are so powerful and rich that they can corrupt and manipulate the system for their ends has compounded the problem. Witness what has happened in Colombia, Russia, and Mexico. At the domestic level in many countries, such as the United States, law enforcement is hampered by competition between agencies having jurisdiction over drug trafficking. Turf wars have resulted in actions that do not necessarily have to do with what it is going to take to "win" the drug war, but rather with promoting individual agendas and protecting budgets. "Like agencies in other bureaucracies, each drug agency is concerned about its discrete mission — seizing shipments, arresting smugglers, prosecuting dealers — not with the policy as a whole," Eva Bartram, the co-author of *Drug War Politics,* has pointed out.[33]

Whether countries can show the same kind of flexibility that the enemy exhibits is still an open question. It's one, though, that will have to be answered soon. As Rensselaer Lee explained in testimony before Congress, "We are going to need a new arsenal of foreign policy tools and organizational responses to cope with the complex challenges arising from the former Soviet crime groups and the other malevolent non state actors in the modern international environment."[34]

Chapter 20

Dirty Laundry: Cleaning the Profits of Illicit Enterprise

"Not all money laundering involves cash from drug sales. However, almost all drug sales require some form of money laundering."

— Robert E. Powis, author

"We have had some moderate success against money launderers, but it is nearly an impossible job for enforcers, given cyber transfers and the many other new methods of moving cash. The best the authorities can hope to do is to keep up with the launderers, much less catch and prosecute them."

— Charles Intriago, publisher of
Money Laundering Alert newsletter

In the fall of 1994, Robert Hirsch, a New York City banking and entertainment lawyer, was in serious trouble with the drug trade's most powerful trafficking organization. An angry woman had called Hirsch to tell him that the Cali cartel wanted its $425,000 or it was going to send hit men from Colombia to cut him and his family up into nice little pieces. Fortunately for Hirsch, federal agents had wiretapped his phones, and they came to the rescue, hustling him away to a safehouse.

It was the beginning of the end of what had become the biggest money-laundering operation in New York history. Hirsch was part of an extensive international network of at least 30 individuals, which included Hirsh's colleague at his law firm, a firefighter, two Hasidic rabbis, a bank manager, a police officer, a beer distributor, a Belgian honorary consul living in Los Angeles, officials from two banks in Zurich, Switzerland, and a man named Carlos from South America. Before U.S.

federal authorities uncovered the network, it had used couriers, wire transfers, and cash drops to launder more than $100 million in drug profits from deals in several cities in the U.S., Europe, and Canada, to the head offices of their bosses in Cali, Colombia. The cartel paid the operation's three New York city leaders — Hirsch, colleague Harvey Weining, and beer distributor Richard Spence — 7 percent of any amount of money moved successfully through the network. They, in turn, paid their couriers $1,000 for each cash pickup.

Unfortunately for Hirsch and his associates, they started to lose lots of the laundered money through theft, arrests, and, at times, outright incompetence, and the cartel began demanding with threats that the group replace the money. The three ringleaders developed a scam designed to fool the Cali cartel and get them out of the money-laundering business. The Cali cartel, however, was not fooled. After being taken to the safe house, Hirsch agreed to wear a wire to save his skin, and 14 people were eventually charged in the case. The three ringleaders all pleaded guilty.[1]

The case was a classic example of how drug trafficking had made money laundering an extensive global enterprise and a big law-enforcement problem around the world. "Drug trafficking has brought money laundering to the fore of law enforcement's attention because it is such a lucrative business," explains Charles Intriago, publisher of the Miami-based newsletter, *Money Laundering Alert.* "Money laundering is a complicated global problem involving numerous countries, and it has only been recently that countries like the United States and those in Western Europe.[2]

The U.S. General Accounting Office defines money laundering as "the process through which the existence, illegal source and unlawful application of illegal gains is concealed or disguised to make the gains appear legitimate, thereby helping to evade detection, prosecution, seizure and taxation."[3] No one knows for sure how much dirty drug money is laundered through the world's banking system, but the FBI has put the annual figure at $300 billion worldwide, one-third of which is collected in the U.S.[4] Virtually all payments for drugs are made in cash and must be laundered or cleaned so that drug traffickers can create the illusion that the money comes from legitimate sources. Money laundering is the nervous system of the international drug trade. "Not all money laundering involves cash from drug sales," explained author Robert Powis. "However, almost all drug sales require some form of money laundering."[5]

Money laundering is not an easy task, considering the huge amounts of cash involved. In fact, moving the cash can be a lot harder than moving the drugs, given the weight and sheer bulk of it. Four hundred fifty paper bills weigh one pound, and the money made from a cocaine deal can weigh 30 times as much as the drugs it bought. "To move cash around the world in the quantities and with the speed demanded by the operation of the major cartels is, therefore, difficult, if not impossible," noted financial expert David Andelman.[6]

In the 1960s and 1970s, when the profits were not as huge as they would become later, drug traffickers used couriers known as smurfs, a nickname taken from popular cartoon characters that reflected the couriers' relative unimportance in the Colombian cocaine trade. The smurfs simply deposited the money, most of which was made from street-level deals, in a nearby bank. In 1970 the U.S. government made its first effort to detect large cash deposits by passing the Bank Secrecy Act of 1970, which requires bank and other financial institutions to report large domestic transactions of more than $10,000 to the U.S. Department of the Treasury. Failure to do so by a financial institution can lead to prosecution and confiscation of the money. Since 1970 the act's provisions have been progressively tightened. In 1980, for example, the Treasury rules were changed, requiring all banks to file reports involving currency transactions with foreign institutions.

Not until the mid 1980s, however, did the financial institutions begin to take the legal change seriously. That happened after several highly publicized cases, most of which involved drug money, gave prominent banks wide notoriety. In 1985 the Bank of Boston pleaded guilty and was fined $500,000 for failure to file reports on transactions with international banks and for financial involvement with an organized crime figure, who would boldly bring shopping carts full of cash to the bank and made deposits or used the cash to buy cashier's checks of more than $10,000 without the bank filling out currency transaction forms. The federal government charged that the Bank of Boston had failed to report some 1,163 cash transactions totaling $1.22 billion. The bank claimed ignorance of the law but, as Powis pointed out, "Frankly, there was no excuse. The bank certainly should have known and understood the reporting requirements."[7] Forty-three other major banks — including Chemical Bank, Bank of England and Manufacturers Hanover's Trust — were penalized for failing to report similar violations, evidence that financial institutions from all over the country were ignoring the reporting requirements.

Remarkably, money laundering was not a crime until 1986, a water-

shed year in the history of money laundering, when as part of the Anti
Drug Abuse Act, the U.S. Congress passed the Money Laundering Control Act of 1986, in an effort to close the loophole that allowed financial
institutions to avoid the reporting of any deposits over $10,000. Also in
1986, President Ronald Reagan stepped up his offensive against drug
trafficking by signing the National Security Decision Directive 221, which
made drug enforcement a national security issue and made drug
trafficking an international policy concern. Banks, corporations, and individuals who operated in money-laundering-haven countries like Panama,
Aruba, Hong Kong, and the Turks and Caicos Islands learned that their
assets could be frozen or confiscated. Two years later, the so called Kerry
Amendment to the Anti Drug Abuse Act of 1988 brought all financial
institutions, wherever located, under the umbrella of the U.S. currency
transactions reporting system set up under the 1970 Bank Security Act.[8]

Between 1986 to 1992, 290 accountants, 151 chartered public accountants, and 225 attorneys were charged with laundering drug money.[9]
Most were convicted, and the U.S. banking community realized that,
under the new money laundering legislation, they could still get in trouble if they failed to recognize or allowed transactions that might involve
money laundering activity. Consequently, banks became more vigilant,
training employees to spot suspicious transactions and developing deterrence measures like "Know Your Customer" programs that provide for
identification of individuals who make use of the bank's services. By
1992 it was costing U.S. banks as much as $136 million annually to com-
plete currency transaction reports for the government. The tougher legislation was costing drug traffickers, too. Experts estimated that by the
mid 1980s the cost of full-service money laundering of drug money had
risen from 6 percent to a high of 26 percent.[10]

The crackdown forced the drug traffickers to become more sophisticated in their money laundering practices. No longer did the traffickers
boldly haul sacks of money into banks. "Guys with duffel bags — I haven't
seen that for a long time," said one U.S. attorney. "The banks, I must
say, have shown not only increased compliance but increased willingness to cooperate on the issue. I'm not saying that money laundering
has ended, but I'm saying it has been reduced."[11]

Once again, U.S. law enforcement underestimated the drug syndicates. Being the innovative entrepreneurs they are, the drug lords
simply changed their method of doing business. The major drug
trafficking organizations began to turn to money laundering specialists, money brokers, or independent contractors, who had the tech-

Confiscated packets of cocaine and other contraband (courtesy Colombian National Police).

niques to move large amounts of cash. Many of these specialists are white-collar professionals like Hirsch and his associate Weining — bankers, lawyers, accountants — who often don't have criminal records and don't consider themselves as being a part of a criminal drug-trafficking syndicate.

The Cali cartel now use ambitious money brokers in Colombia who bid competitively for the right to move large amounts of cash from cocaine sales to Colombia. The brokers have to show that they are "bonded;" that is, they have enough financial resources to reimburse the drug traffickers if their cash load is stolen by competitors or seized by the police. The cartel will often send a few members to stay with the broker's family until the deal is consummated.[12]

David Andelman describes how a typical contract might work: "Each time a million dollars has to be moved from a particular city in the United States, bids are taken. For a lot of $1 million, the money launderers guarantee the cartel's accountant $900,000, or whatever bid is fixed. The launderer delivers the $900,000 to Bogotá, generally in Colombian pesos or perhaps in merchandise that is quickly sold for pesos, and later takes possession of the dollars in New York or Los Angeles or Miami. It is then up to the launderer to get the full million dollars out of the U.S. His profit is $100,000 minus expenses."[13]

By the late 1980s, the drug traffickers were using many money-laundering schemes, many of which were able to avoid banks. They included dummy corporations at home and abroad, postal money orders, international transfer of funds, letters of credit for offshore banks, *casas de cambio*, and a shadow banking system of cash laundering outlets. Drug traffickers, moreover, are now electronically laundering much of their money. "The online revolution has undoubtedly been of major import," explained Victor T. Le Vine, professor of political science at Washington University in St. Louis, Missouri, and an expert on the economic and political impact of money laundering. "Transfers are now instantaneous from account to account, and the trick is to do it without leaving a trace or conceal the transfers under legitimate trading labels, all of which is relatively easy to do."[14]

Keeping track of this movement of money is complicated, given the size and scope of the transactions. In 1990 the Clearing House Interbank Payment System, the primary wholesale international electronic funds transfer system, processed about 37 million money transfers valued at $222 trillion between the U.S. and international banks.[15] "Ultimately, the degree of sophistication and complexity in a money laundering scheme is virtually infinite, and is limited only by the creative imagination and expertise of the criminal entrepreneurs who devise such schemes," observed the President's Commission on Organized Crime.[16]

One of the first big money-laundering schemes uncovered by U.S. authorities involved Eduardo Orozco-Prada, the owner of Cirex International, a Colombian coffee-exporting company in New York City. From 1978 to 1992, Orozco-Prada successfully laundered approximately $150 million, using 18 banks to hide money in United States accounts and at offshore banks in Panama, the Bahamas, and the Cayman Islands. The money launderer used several methods to hide the sources and the amount of the money, including the deposit of sums of money just under $10,000 to avoid filing currency transaction reports, setting up dummy corporations, using fake bills of lading and converting small-denomination bills into larger-denomination bills. Despite his clever ways, Orozco was caught and found guilty.[17]

Since Orozco's arrest, the Colombian cartels have used a wide variety of schemes involving U.S. business to launder cash. In 1995 law-enforcement investigations in Los Angeles, Miami, Houston, and New York City uncovered a range of complex trade-related schemes that had moved a staggering $3 billion through U.S. companies. In one single New York investigation, federal customs officials identified 105 American companies that accepted drug money for electronics, auto parts, and other goods shipped to Colombia. "What makes [the schemes] so difficult to detect is that those operations are cloaked in what appear to be legitimate businesses," revealed Eric Friedberg, the chief of narcotics prosecution in the U.S. Attorney's office in Brooklyn. "The drug money is easily mixed in the legal sales of the company."[18]

The Japanese Yakuza is adept at using the U.S. economic system to launder money. According to the FBI, the Yakuza have used country clubs and other real-estate ventures to channel more than $1 billion to the United States during the 1980s. The money moved in several ways, but one of the Yakuza's favorite schemes was to lend dirty money to a private investment company, which then used the cash to buy a golf club or resort in the United States. The resort property then collected the large fees from its members, which, as "clean" money, was then channeled back to investors. Eventually, the investment company would sell the property, sometimes at a loss.[19]

The reality is that a country's economic system can serve the money-laundering needs of a drug-trafficking syndicate. "Before the passage of anti drug money laundering laws in the U.S. and the setting of various oversight rules for banks, most of the money went to U.S. banks, their affiliates abroad, and their correspondent banks," explained Intriago. "Since then, the amounts have dropped appreciably, mainly because the drug traffickers and their agents have increasingly taken to moving bulk lots from the U.S. to overseas destinations, bypassing banks."[20]

Mexico has been the most significant conduit for the money-laundering activities of Latin American drug-trafficking syndicates. It borders the United States, it has a high level of corruption, and money laundering is not a crime there. Traffickers have used aging airplanes to fly money out of the United States to Mexico, slipped money through tunnels under the border, employed trucks and cars that bring drugs into the United States to transport laundered cash from stash houses to Mexico, and exploited the numerous, mostly unregulated Mexican dollar-exchange houses — the *casas de cambio* — which are located along the border. According to the U.S. Treasury Department's Financial Crime Enforcement Network (FINCEN), as much as $10 billion — 75 to 90 percent of the Latin American drug traffickers' annual revenue — passes through Mexico annually.[21] Representative Spencer Bachus (R–Ala.), chairman of the U.S. House Banking Committee's Financial Services Subcommittee, said that "the amount of cash laundered through Mexico ranges from six billion to thirty billion" dollars a year.[22]

Nearby Caribbean countries — Aruba, the Bahamas, and the Cayman Islands, for example — have long been the target of U.S. scrutiny and investigation. As early as 1985, the amount of money flowing to the Cayman Islands annually was estimated to be between $3 and $10 billion.[23] Meanwhile, Aruba's wide-open banking system has apparently attracted the attention of the Russian Mafia, which is using the country to establish bank accounts to transfer money to legitimate accounts elsewhere.[24] Money transfers from Aruba (pop. 83,000) to the United States have amounted to more than $1.4 billion since 1993, according to U.S. officials.[25]

George Meller, an international banking expert, said that Antigua had "the loosest banking system in the Western world."[26] Antigua has reacted angrily to the characterization, saying that its alleged "loose" banking rules do not prove that it is a money-laundering haven. In a nationalistic pique, an Antigua newspaper charged that "the U.S. banks rank among the biggest launderers anywhere … It is America who started money laundering. It is they who must solve it."[27]

Several islands in other parts of the world, including the Channel Islands and the Isle of Man off the British coast, operate as money-laundering havens for drug traffickers. According to Charles Intriago, at least 50 countries have tight secrecy on their financial transactions, a feature that makes them prime havens for money laundering.[28] As big changes such as free trade, the breakup of communism and the communications evolution have swept the globe in the 1990s, many other countries, especially those in Eastern Europe, have become easy sources of money laundering for drug traffickers. In 1992 money launderers flooded the central bank of Estonia with deposits shortly before the country was to establish a new currency.[29] The Sicilian Mafia has been particularly active in laundering their money through Germany to cash-poor Eastern Europe, while Cali cartel operatives have been found in Poland, Hungary, and the former Czechoslovakia.

Although tight bank secrecy has been a problem in combating money laundering, at least one major banking country has changed its policy. In 1994 Switzerland's parliament passed a law that would allow the country's banks to report suspected illegal transactions without fear of breaking bank secrecy laws.[30] The case of Raul Salinas de Gortari, the brother of Mexico's ex-president Carlos, has shown that Switzerland is serious about cracking down on the use of the country's banks to launder drug money. The Swiss froze more $100 million in a Raul Salinas account after finding out that it had been opened under a false name and suspecting the money came from drug trafficking. The Swiss have also cooperated with Mexican and U.S. officials in the Salinas investigation.[31]

Despite the difficulty in stopping the lifeblood of international drug trafficking, the U.S. decision to focus its law-enforcement efforts on money laundering has led to some successful results.

Two major investigations were mentioned earlier. Operation Greenback was a U.S. Treasury Department program that, beginning in 1980, targeted suspected money-laundering activities in Florida. By 1984 Operation Greenback had documented the laundering of $2.6 million in U.S. currency through sixteen drug-trafficking syndicates.[32] The second investigation, the Pizza Connection, involved a distribution ring that operated in the midwestern and northeastern United States between 1979 and 1984. After a 17-month trial, 21 people associated with the Sicilian and Italian American Mafias were found guilty.[33]

In 1989 the DEA launched a massive three-month sting against money launderers who were using phony leather-goods companies in major U.S. cities to hide international money transfers. Authorities seized more than $50 million in drug money, arrested 192 people in six countries, and exposed the close links between the Sicilian Mafia and the Colombian cartels.[34]

In several cases the U.S. federal authorities have managed to position themselves inside a money-laundering organization, where they have been able to apprehend the criminals who were both sending and receiving the laundered funds. Through the FBI Operation Cashweb and the DEA's Operation Pisces, for instance, agents penetrated a Colombian drug-trafficking and money-laundering network that extended from the United States to Canada, Mexico, Panama, Colombia, Bahamas, Aruba, the Cayman Islands, and the Turks and Caicos Islands. The U.S. Customs Operation C-CHASE resulted in the indictment of 85 people, including several officials of international banks.[35]

U.S. federal agents have even run phony banks themselves to penetrate sophisticated money-laundering rings. In 1994 the DEA's Operation Dinero resulted in the arrest of 88 individuals and the seizure of $54 million in cash and nine tons of cocaine and showed once again the emerging alliances between Colombian, Italian, and Russian drug-trafficking syndicates.[36] In history's biggest money-laundering investigation, the DEA, IRS, FBI, and Customs launched Operation Polar Cap in 1987, a three-year undercover probe of a Los Angeles money-laundering operation known as La Mina (the mine), which was run by Colombian drug traffickers. Federal authorities set up their own

Gilberto Rodríguez Orejuela, the cofounder of Colombia's powerful Cali drug cartel (courtesy Colombian Antinarcotic Police).

undercover laundry, and through the help of an informant uncovered La Mina.[37]

In stepping up their attack on the nervous system of drug-trafficking syndicates, the U.S. government ratified the 1988 United Nations Convention against Illegal Traffic in Narcotic Drugs and Psychotropic Substances, which requires countries adopting the convention to make money laundering a crime. A year later, the U.S. government established the Financial Crimes Enforcement Network (FINCEN), an agency of the Department of the Treasury that was established to provide law enforcement help in identifying, investigating, and prosecuting domestic and international money-laundering activity.

In 1989 the Group of Seven (G-7) Economic Summit in Paris established the Financial Action Task Force (FATF) as a major forum to promote the adoption and implementation of anti-money-laundering measures. In 1994 34 leaders of the Summit of the Americas met in Miami, Florida, and signed a Declaration of Principles that included a commitment to fight money laundering. The following year, President Bill Clinton announced that he would consider imposing sanctions against nations that encouraged money laundering and work to prevent them from doing business in the United States.

Since the 1980s, the United States has also established bilateral treaties and arrangements with several countries, which has led to the exchange of valuable information for money-laundering investigations. In October 1996 Mexico and Texas signed a unique agreement in which they pledged to combat money laundering together. Among other measures, the agreement designated Mexican representatives in Texas to serve as official liaisons with Texas authorities. The agreement reflected the growing concern of Mexico and the United States about the challenges they were going to have to face in the years ahead, as the remaining trade barriers between the two countries are phased out under the North American Free Trade Agreement (NAFTA).[38]

In October 1995 the United States announced that it would move to freeze assets of U.S. companies that it had identified as being associated with the Cali cartel. In 1995, under President Bill Clinton's executive order, the United States identified four principal figures in the Cali cartel, three businesses, and 43 other individuals whose assets could be subject to freezing. By April 1997 the United States had identified 416 businesses and individuals it said were connected to the Cali Cartel. "Criminal entrepreneurs are moving vast sums of ill-gotten gains through the international financial system with absolute impunity," Clinton said, in explaining the government's move. "We must not allow them to wash the blood off profits from the sale of drugs from terror or organized crimes."[39]

For years, the United States suspected the Colombian cartels operating in New York City of sending millions of dollars a year back to Colombia through the storefront shops known as *casas de cambio*. The U.S. government looked upon the federal requirement that transactions of more than $10,000 be reported as a hindrance to its efforts to combat money laundering. In May 1997, the government therefore announced that the 25,000 *casas de cambio* in the United States would have to inform the federal government of any transaction that was over $750.[40]

The United States has also joined with other countries to seize assets and shut down operations of banks suspected of being involved with money laundering. That happened in 1991 when U.S. banking authorities in collaboration with their counterparts in France, Italy, Spain, Canada, Luxembourg, and the Cayman Islands moved against the Bank of Credit and Commerce International SA (BCCI), which operated in 69 countries and had assets of $20 billion. The BCCI had been implicated in money laundering for ex–Panamanian dictator Manuel Noriega, and two branches of the bank had pleaded guilty in 1990 in Tampa Bay, Florida, of laundering $14 million as part of a $32 million money-laundering case.[41]

The U.S. lead has certainly influenced the international community to move forcefully against drug money laundering and has led to more effective cooperation among law-enforcement agencies internationally than there was a decade earlier. The cost of doing business for the drug cartels, moreover, has gone up substantially. Still, the criminal entrepreneurs have managed to adapt to tougher times, using the new technology and cyberspace to track their drug profits and launder it more efficiently. "The drug trafficking entrepreneurs are extraordinarily adept at evading, by-passing and negating domestic and international money laundering laws," explained Le Vine. "You close one loop hole, they open ten others through which to pass the laundry."[42]

When will the international community turn the tide against the money launderers? Probably not soon and probably not ever. "We have had some moderate success against money launderers, but it is nearly an impossible job for enforcers, given cyber transfers and the many other new methods of moving cash," conceded Intriago. "The best the authorities can hope to do is to keep up with the leaders, much less catch and prosecute them."[43]

In the face of the formidable challenge, some authorities are scaling down their ambitions about dealing with money laundering. "There is still much work to be done," wrote John C. Kenney, acting assistant attorney general in a letter to the U.S. General Accounting Office in 1996. "We must increase our interagency efforts, focus on proactive targeting and the sharing of intelligence, law enforcement and regulatory information." But Kenney added, "This strategy will not eradicate either domestic or international money laundering. It will, however, create an increasingly hostile and inhospitable environment for the money launderers and afford new elements of protection to political and economic systems."[44]

Chapter 21

Global Reach: The Economic, Political, and Social Impact

"Corruption caused by drug trafficking is certainly one of the most widespread forms of corruption found in the world today."
— Victor T. Le Vine, professor of political science,
Washington University, St. Louis, Missouri

"The argument that coca and poppy cultivation is immoral has had little effect on the farmers of the Andean region, since growing the crops has a long tradition for them, and they can't really see the ill effects. The situation is not much different from the tobacco farmers in the Carolinas of the U.S., who know what they cultivate can kill people, but that doesn't stop them from growing it."

Bruce Wyrick, professor of economics,
University of San Francisco

San Andresitos is one of Bogotá's most popular shopping centers, where, each day, throngs of people come to buy a large variety of goods at ridiculously low prices: authentic Nike sneakers for $35 a pair, José Cuervo tequila at $6 to $7 a bottle, fashionable Levis for $30 or less, prices that are much lower than prices for similar goods at other stores in Bogotá. The true purpose of San Andresitos and the identity of the entrepreneurs who operate the market are no secret to Colombians: to serve as a money laundry for the billions of dollars the country's hardworking drug cartels are making from the global drug trade. Traffickers buy U.S. and foreign goods like Nikes and Levis with American dollars and then "smuggle" the goods into Colombia where they are sold at below-market prices. According to estimates, Colombian drug

traffickers are repatriating between $2 to $5 billion a year from drug
exports, an amount equal to about 4 to 9 percent of the gross national
product, or about $55 billion annually.[1] The fact the goods are sold
openly is indicative of the power of the drug lords and the scale of corruption in Colombia.

The cash flow from international drug trafficking is evident everywhere in Bogotá, most notably in the construction trade. Apartment
complexes, shopping centers, luxury flats, and office buildings are still
being built, even though many stand nearly empty, a striking example
that, while the Colombian economy is expanding, narco dollars are dis-
torting the economy and hurting its legitimate sector. Between 1991 and
1994, for example, the value of urban property in Colombia appreciated
by 40 to 60 percent, while the average rate of inflation was 22 percent.
"The local markets and manufacturers can't compete with contraband,
so it creates numerous business failures and high unemployment,"
explained Alejandro Saenz de Santamaria, an economics professor at
the Bogotá-based University of the Andes. "Besides, the drug traffickers
pay no taxes on the contraband they smuggle into Colombia."[2]

Economic Impact

Colombia is an example of the economic impact that the international drug trade has had on the economies of countries around the
world. Indeed, it has been one of the major consequences of the War on
Drugs. The Pablo Escobars, Khun Sas, and brothers Rodríguez Orejuela,
the drug kingpins of international drug trade, dominate the news headlines, but the drug trade employs hundreds of thousands of people
worldwide who are dependent on the drug trafficking for their livelihood.
After all, coca and poppy crops have to be planted, grown, harvested,
and transported to the market; precursor chemicals supplied and delivered for the production process; laboratories built, staffed, and guarded;
airports constructed and maintained; airplanes flown and serviced;
workers paid; profits invested; local officials bought off; and records
kept. There is much indirect employment as well, since many people sell
good, services, and labor to drug traffickers. "The drug trade's impact
on the Andean region is significant and crippling it could have serious
economic, political and social consequences," explained Santamaria.[3]

Mauricio Guzmán, the mayor of Cali, estimated in 1996 that drug-
related business accounted for 25 percent of the Cali economy. After the

Colombian government put the Cali cartel's leadership in jail, unemployment in Cali jumped to 15 percent. Economists estimate that the drug trade employs about 1 million people in the Andean region, with the Colombia cartels alone having collectively an estimated 100,000 workers on their payrolls. The Sun Ye On Triad, the biggest criminal group in Hong Kong, employs an estimated 25,000 people, while a 1997 São Paulo, Brazil, police study revealed that the city's drug traffickers employ more people than the country's auto industry, that is, 50,000 versus 40,000.[4]

"Trying to eradicate the global problem of international drug trafficking quickly may create worse problems by throwing people out of work and destabilizing governments," warned Rensselaer Lee, coauthor of *The Andean Cocaine Economy*.[5]

Dr. Alfredo Vásquez Carrizosa, a former Colombian defense minister and now a columnist with *El Espectador* newspaper, points out that "coca and poppy crops are grown in the very poor regions of the Andes. In some areas, growing illegal drug crops is often the only economic type of activity taking place. When the drug traffickers show up with huge amounts of money — money that the farmers haven't seen in their lives, it's impossible to stop the planting of illegal crops."[6]

The farmers in the Andes, moreover, have created powerful lobbies to protect their interests. In Bolivia the 70,000 coca-growing farmers are organized into eight regional federations consisting of several hundred syndicates. These farmers are "highly organized and sometimes well armed, and they can exert tremendous pressure on the government," explained Rensselaer Lee.[7] In Colombia, the farmers are influenced and often protected by the country's increasingly powerful guerrilla groups.

At times, the farmers have reacted aggressively and even violently against government antidrug policies. In 1991, for instance, Bolivian peasants from the Chapare region marched in protest against the involvement of the U.S.-trained Bolivian army in the War on Drugs, because they believed, despite Bolivian government assurances, that the army would pursue the peasants who grew the coca and try to root out their coca plants. When the price of tin plummeted on the international market in the 1980s, the Bolivian economy collapsed, and growing coca became a means of survival for many of Bolivia's 300,000 peasants.[8] In August 1996, soldiers clashed with Colombian farmers protesting their government's decision to eradicate their coca and opium crops. Colombia has tried to make the farmers switch to legal crops like maiz, yuca, and potatoes, but the farmers can make more money growing coca and poppy plants and selling them to drug traffickers. Coca, for example, can earn up to $10,000 an acre; maiz perhaps $200.[9]

"The argument that coca and poppy cultivation is immoral has had little effect on the farmers of the Andean region, since growing the crops has been a long tradition for them, and they can't really see the ill effects," explained Bruce Wyrick, a professor of economics at the University of San Francisco, who has done research on Latin American economic development. "The situation is not much different from the tobacco farmers in the Carolinas of the U.S., who know what they cultivate can kill people, but that doesn't stop them from growing it."[10]

The U.S. and international agencies have not been successful in stopping the cultivation of drug crops in other parts of the world, particularly in southeast Asia's Golden Triangle, still the world's principle source of the poppy crop. According to one U.S. Government Accounting Office report, "The United States has been a major donor for UNCP drug control projects, providing about $2.5 million for fiscal year 1992 to 1994. However ... these projects have not significantly reduced opium production."[11] Earlier, it was discussed how U.S. efforts to eradicate the marijuana crop led to a shift of production from Mexico to Colombia to Jamaica and then full circle to Mexico.[12]

Illegal drug cultivation is directly tied to the world's economy, many experts believe. A study by the Center for Strategic and International Studies pointed out that drug production takes place where there are few economic alternatives and where governments are unable to exercise sovereignty because of limited resources and political instability.[13] "I believe that eradication may be the only way to get rid of the illegal drug business," explained Rensselaer Lee, who added, "The problem is trying to find a way to do that without causing a massive social and economic upheaval."[14]

While coca and poppy farmers struggle to eke out a living, the drug traffickers have accrued tremendous economic power. Cartel bosses in Colombia have built huge business empires by buying radio stations, pharmacies, discotheques, horse ranches, dairy farms, construction companies, banks and financial institutions, and even two higher educational institutions. Drug traffickers have spent some of their money on social welfare programs, a shrewd move that has garnered them support from the poor. It is said that the late Pablo Escobar built more public housing in Medellín than the government did, which helps to explain the outpouring of grief at his funeral in December 1993.[15]

Cartel kingpins have become some of Colombia's biggest landown-

Juan B. Tokatlian, University of the Andes, Bogotá (author's collection).

ers. In 1988 the Bogotá-based Institute of Liberal Studies reported that drug traffickers had bought nearly one million hectares of the country's best land.[16] "A piece of land may be worth $1,000, but along comes a drug trafficker who wants to buy the land as an investment or because the river runs through it, making it good for cocaine processing," explained Julio Orlando Gómez, a press officer for the Colombian Institute for Agricultural Reform (INCORA). "He offers the campesino $1,000. What do you think he is going to do?"[17]

Between 1993 and 1996 alone, the Colombian drug lords increased their landholdings by another million hectares, giving them a total between two and four million acres and a presence in 400 municipalities, according to INCORA. The institute reported that the aggregation of land was having a profound effect on the cost of land and the level of agricultural production and was contributing to the country's frequent violence.[18]

The Colombian government has moved to expropriate the landholdings and other properties of dead and convicted drug traffickers. In December 1996 the Colombian congress approved a law that it hoped would lead to land reform and the redistribution of wealth, strengthen the government's ability to fight organized crime, and to help rehabilitate Colombian society.[19] The law eventually passed, but only after death threats and bribes, five months of heated debate, and the U.S. threat of unspecified sanctions. The process was a vivid example of how drug traffickers have used their money and power to penetrate and corrupt the established order and grow at the expense of legitimate state authority.

Many observers believe that agrarian reform is the only way to diffuse the power and influence of the Colombian guerrilla movement and its influence on the coca and poppy growers. "In my two and a half years here, I have not seen the Colombian government move to develop a strategy to deal with the guerrillas," U.S. ambassador Myles Frechette told this author in 1997. "They need one because a guerrilla movement in Latin America has never been defeated by military force alone."[20]

Corruption

Drug-trafficking-related corruption is a worldwide phenomenon that has involved the highest political levels, including heads of state, military leaders, judges, and police chiefs in every country touched by drug trade. Corruption has particularly affected Bolivia, Mexico, Myanmar, Pakistan, and Colombia, which all have thriving narcotics industries.

In the early 1980s, the Bolivian military under General Luis Garcia Meza joined with the country's drug traffickers to organize what has been described as the country's first official "narcocracy." Journalist Simon Strong described what subsequently happened: "Colonel Luis Arce Gómez, the head of military intelligence and relative of Roberto Suarez, then Bolivia's biggest coca-paste trafficker and supplier of Pablo Escobar, was appointed minister of the interior. Not only did he and General Garcia Meza organize the army's systematic extortion of protection money from major drug traffickers — recalcitrants were murdered

—but they also used paramilitary squads to stamp out the smallest dealers in Santa Cruz, the commercial heart of the cocaine trade. The squads were set up with the assistance of Nazi Klaus Barbie."[21]

Colombia was called a "narco democracy" after strong evidence suggested that the Cali cartel financed Ernesto Samper's successful 1994 political campaign with millions of dollars.[22] Mexican-U.S. relations were seriously strained after the United States learned about the widespread corruption that has riddled Mexico's top drug-fighting unit.[23] In the 1990s, many top Italian officials, including Giulio Andreotti, seven times a prime minister, went on trial on charges of conspiring with the Mafia. Meanwhile, 50 municipal councils in four regions of Sicily have had to be dissolved on the grounds that they had been infiltrated by the Mafia.[24] Corruption is widespread among law-enforcement officials in Myanmar, the world's largest producer of opium, and international narcotics agents have warned that Pakistan could become another Colombia because the meager resources of the Pakistani state are no match for the power and wealth of the country's drug traffickers.[25]

Not only are countries that grow and process narcotics becoming corrupt, many other countries are also getting caught in the net of international drug trafficking as money-laundering centers and transit points in smuggling routes leading to the United States and Europe. For example, in several cases drug shipments to Russia and Eastern Europe have used Peru, Venezuela, and other Latin American countries in order to take advantage of the lax customs regulations and weak law enforcement in the region.

Attempts to stamp out the drug traffic often exacerbate the problem and make hard-fought gains in the War on Drugs short-lived. This is because cocaine, heroin, and marijuana are easy to produce, refine, transport, and sell, and the profits are enormous, which means that an ambitious criminal or criminal organization will always be willing to try to get the illegal product to the market.

The cultivation of opium is no longer confined to Mexico, the Golden Triangle, and the Golden Crescent. It is now also grown in Colombia and Guatemala, Poland and the Ukraine, and the central highland republics of the former Soviet Union (Kazakhstan, Turkmenistan, and Tajikistan). Today, coca is cultivated in Brazil, Ecuador, and Venezuela as well as Peru, Bolivia, and Colombia. Law enforcement now busts cocaine-processing laboratories in Italy, Spain, and Portugal as well as Latin America. New areas of marijuana cultivation include Brazil, Siberia in the former Soviet Union, and Togo, Rwanda, and Nigeria in Africa.

To meet the surging demand for synthetic drugs, secret laboratories have sprung up to manufacture amphetamine in Poland, "ice" in Taiwan and South Korea, and methaqualone or mandrax in India and South Africa.[26] U.S. drug official Brian Stickney warned in November 1996 that the growing popularity of Exstasy and other synthetic drugs constitute a permanent problem.[27]

In 1996 the DEA reported that the Mexican cartels had taken over the U.S. methamphetamine trade, expanding their reach into the country by setting up operations in several major U.S. cities, notably Denver, Houston, Phoenix, Seattle, and St. Louis. According to U.S. and Mexican officials, the Mexican cartels produce the drug in labs based in Mexico but prefer making it in the United States because of harsh penalties if they are caught transporting it across the border.[28] Methamphetamine today rivals cocaine as the drug of choice in the larger cities of Nebraska and North and South Dakota, the U.S. heartland, where it is made in small "mom and pop" labs in motels and abandoned farmhouses. According to one police chief, "Anybody with a chemistry book and the ability to experiment can make meth."[29]

Experts expect this trend in drug production to continue indefinitely. As one report explained, "The increasing drug supplies and opportunities to service and develop new markets can be sustained only if there is a market for narcotics. The bulk of the evidence on global trafficking suggests that drug producers and traffickers have little to worry about."[30]

Earlier, it was noted that increasing drug consumption and abuse was helping to fuel the globalization of international drug trafficking.[31] Here are some more examples to illustrate the trend. In 1996 the Colombian press began reporting about a new type of cocaine that was so pure that it was killing addicts. Crack has spread to Europe from the inner cities of the United States, while opiates from the Golden Triangle have led to a resurgence of drug addiction in China, where, in Yunnan province, a major conduit for Golden Triangle heroin, 50 percent of the population of some villages have become addicted to heroin. The Triads have made Vancouver, Canada (pop. 450,000), the major destination point of heroin entering the U.S. and Canadian markets and the city with the highest overdose rate in North America. The Italian port of Naples (pop. 3 million) is reported to have 20,000 heroin addicts — one in every 150 inhabitants, compared to one in 500 for the United States. The strict Muslim countries of Iran and Pakistan have 1 million and 1.7 million drug users, respectively, while Thailand, according to scholar

Alison Jamieson, "has between 100,000 and 300,00 adults who ingest pure heroin in doses which would be fatal for the Western consumer."[32]

Since 1982 and the beginning of the modern crusade against international drug trafficking, every country in the Caribbean region and Latin America has become involved in some way in the drug trade. In the early 1990s, when authorities began to put pressure on transportation routes through Mexico and Central America, the drug traffickers shifted their routes to go through Barbados, Antigua, Montserrat, and the other small countries of the eastern Caribbean. By 1996 the United Nations Drug Control Program's Caribbean regional office was estimating that Barbados was accounting for 180 tons or 10 to 20 percent of Europe's supply of cocaine.[33]

A 1996 report by eight European experts called drug trafficking "the single biggest threat to the economic and social development of the countries of the region" and concluded, "With their weak economies, high unemployment, meager resources and inadequate law enforcement, the islands of the eastern Caribbean provide easy targets for the international drug traffickers."[34] It may be too late, however, to stop the assault. Various U.S. officials have said that drug-trafficking-induced corruption is widespread throughout the Caribbean, where poorly paid public servants find it difficult to resist payoffs and it is also difficult for honest officials to ferret out corruption.

The Caribbean reflects a worldwide pattern. The people who allow traffickers to conduct business without problems or fear of arrest are everywhere in the drug distribution chain. They could be a top government official like the prime minister of Barbados or the presidents of Panama and Colombia or customs officers on the U.S.-Mexican border or the Burma-Thailand border or a police officer in Palermo, Sicily, or Managua, Nicaragua. Invariably, the drug traffickers find a way to get their help through bribes or intimidation. Manuel Noriega reportedly made millions for helping drug traffickers launder their money, while in Bolivia, drug traffickers reportedly paid police officers between $20,000 and $25,000 for a "seventy-two hour window of opportunity" for moving major drug shipments by air, land, and sea.[35]

A study by the National Autonomous University of Mexico estimates that Mexican drug cartels spend $500 million a year in bribes, an amount that goes a long way considering that a military commander in the Mexican army makes only $900 a month and a regular policeman $300.[36] A customs official on the U.S.-Mexican border can now command as much as $1 million for simply looking the other way when drug traffickers try to sneak a truckload of drugs across the border to the United States. In testifying before the U.S. Senate in 1997, DEA Director Thomas Constantine revealed that a Mexican general had offered a Tijuana judicial official $1.5 million if he would scale back his efforts against drug trafficking.[37]

"Corruption caused by drug trafficking is certainly one of the most widespread forms of corruption found in the world today," explained Victor T. LeVine, professor of political science at Washington University, St. Louis Missouri, and author of *Political Corruption: The Ghana Case*.[38]

Violence

If drug traffickers can't get their way through the bribe, they resort to the bullet, or, as the practice has become known in Colombia, "Plomo o Plata (lead or money)." As discussed in Section Three, drug traffickers will kill anyone who gets in their way, whether it be law-enforcement officials, members of the judiciary, the press, a good citizen, or even a clergyman. In 1974 an Italian priest in Naples was murdered in his church while preparing for mass by drug traffickers angry that he was telling his parishioners to shun their criminal organization.[39]

In protecting their interests, syndicates have undermined democratic states, attacking them at their core. Since the early 1980s, for example, drug traffickers have launched a violent assault on the press in numerous Latin American countries. The drug-related violence has taken many forms: murders, bombings, kidnappings, and intimidation. In Colombia alone, 67 journalists have been murdered as of April 1997.[40]

The judiciary — another cornerstone of the democratic state — has been under assault as well. In Colombia, 350 judicial personnel, including 50 judges, were murdered between 1980 and 1992, and a survey indicated that 25 percent of the Colombian judges had been threatened.[41] Today in Colombia, suspected drug traffickers appear before "faceless" judges who have their identities concealed.

In some drug-growing countries, most notably Colombia, there has been concern about a possible alliance between drug traffickers, the military, and landowners, who share a rabid anticommunism and hatred of leftists and are willing to work together to establish a reactionary social order. In 1989 the Washington Office of Latin America charged that a "marriage of convenience" had formed between the three groups in which "all are bent on eliminating subversive elements," and that "this alliance manifests itself in death squads that have the power of mini-armies, and is the driving force behind Colombia's escalating political violence."[42]

Amnesty International, a human-rights group, has charged that Colombian armed forces and paramilitary units linked to the military have been responsible for the death of some 20,000 suspected leftists since 1986. Amnesty obtained three documents in 1996 that it said supported its claim that the U.S. military equipment intended for Colombian antidrug operations have been used instead to combat insurgency, a development that has led to the deaths of thousands. The leaked documents, said William F. Schultz, Amnesty International director, offered proof that U.S. tax dollars had indeed been used to supply the Colombian armed forces with military equipment that "equipped thugs in uniform who murdered other people who were simply inconvenient to the Colombian military."[43]

Ambassador Frechette said the United States has an "in-use monitoring program to keep a check on the military equipment given to the Colombian military," but he conceded that the program is not completely secure. That would be unrealistic, although we remain satisfied that the aid we give is being used for anti narcotics efforts."[44]

Guerrillas and Insurgents

The highly profitable drug-trafficking business has helped leftist insurgents and guerrilla groups as well as right-wing groups to increase their power and extend their influence at the expense of legitimate state power. Since the early 1970s, insurgents and guerrilla movements have expanded their role in the drug trade as it has spread its tentacles across the globe. This has been especially true in southeast Asia (Myanmar), the Middle East (Lebanon), western Asia (Turkey), and Latin America (Peru and Colombia).

In Colombia in the mid 1990s, self-styled Marxist guerrillas helped fill the vacuum left by the dismantling of the Medellin cartel. They not only support coca and poppy farmers but also impose a 10 percent tax on traffickers who move drugs through their territory, often guard the drug laboratories for a fee, supervise coca and opium cultivation, and even run their own cocaine-producing and distribution operations in remote parts of the country.[45] Analysts say that the money and influence garnered from drug trafficking has helped guerrillas control as much as 40 to 50 percent of the country.

"In some areas of the country, the guerrillas are the law and authority," explained Juan B. Tokatlian, a Bogotá-based sociologist and professor at the National University of the Andes, who has written extensively on the drug trade.[46] Rensselaer Lee added, "Many strategists have written off large parts of Colombia as being ungovernable."[47]

Beginning in the 1980s, the Peruvian guerrilla group Sendero Luminoso (Shining Path) began to expand its presence in the large coca-growing area of the upper Huallaga Valley, where it appears that, while not participating directly in the drug trade, the guerrilla group has extracted "taxes" from peasants who grow and process the coca crop for traffickers. "Aware of the benefits to be gained from cooperation, the coca and cocaine-paste producers and Sendero Luminoso have formed a business relationship in which each side uses the other to achieve its respective goals," explained Gabriela Tarazona-Sevillano.[48]

Elsewhere in the world, the U.S. State Department reported that in 1996 Turkey's Kurdish Worker's Party (KWP) was receiving money to protect drug labs in eastern Turkey, the crossroads and production center for Afghan heroin on its way to Europe and North America. The KWP uses the money, which estimates put at $500 million annually, to buy guns for its struggle to establish an autonomous state in the Kurdish area of Turkey.[49]

The KWP is one of the insurgent groups that most of the world community classifies as a terrorist group. Many experts believe that, with the end of the Cold War, the KWP and other groups involved with global terrorism have turned to the international drug trade to finance their activities. Since the early 1980s, the United States has talked of the existence of "narcoterrorism" and has tried to portray such countries as Cuba, Nicaragua, and Syria as outlaw states that have used the drug trade to finance and inspire terrorism in an effort to undermine U.S. society. Until the breakup of the Soviet Union, many observers believed that the drug trafficker–terrorist link was overstated and that while the two shared some short-term goals, their long-term aims were in opposition.

Donald Mabry, a scholar who has published extensively on Mexican politics and the drug trade, believes there is some evidence implicating Cuba and Nicaragua in the drug trade, but added, "It is difficult to see the validity and importance of the charges in light of the fact that the U.S. government has consistently sought to blame non U.S. persons for the drug trade."[50]

Violence has been one of the byproducts of the international drug trade (courtesy Colombian National Police).

In an interview, Colombian president Ernesto Samper charged that "The U.S. has long practiced a double standard on the War on the Drugs. Through its certification program, the U.S. has passed judgment on countries like Colombia, but have done nothing to curb their own supply of marijuana," Samper explained. "In fact, the U.S. is the world's number one grower of the drug."[51]

The U.S.'s International Drug War Strategy

Even though the drug trade continued to expand and thrive between 1982 and 1987, the United States has steadfastly stuck to a strategy that has tried to stop the flow of drugs before they reach the country. Uncle Sam has supplied weapons, advisers, aircraft, and intelligence under the terms of bilateral agreements with drug-producing countries, but the aid has never seemed to be enough and the strategy has always been questioned. In 1997, for example, Representative Bill McCollum (R–Fla.) criticized President Bill Clinton for budget cuts in the War on Drugs and for a shift of emphasis from interdiction to trying to stop drug production at its source, a move that the congressman charged was allowing the eastern Caribbean to flourish as a cocaine-distribution pipeline to the United States.[52]

The United States has used its power and influence to persuade many other countries to sign bilateral and multilateral antidrug agreements. In 1997, for example, the United States and Colombia signed a maritime accord after two and a half years of negotiations, which allows the U.S. military personnel in Colombia territorial waters to interdict drug trafficking. The agreement came a short time before the United States was to decide whether to certify Colombia as a country that had done enough in the War on Drugs the previous year.[53]

Often the pressure to sign antidrug agreements has led to friction. For instance, many countries have balked at U.S. efforts to get them to sign agreements that would allow U.S. aircraft to pursue suspicious aircraft into the country's airspace and force them to land, complaining that they would give up more than they would receive. "We will not stand accused of not cooperating with our partners, but neither will we allow our hard-fought sovereignty to be sacrificed in the tug-of-war between the moral and social imperative to curtail demand and the need to reduce supply," explained Barbados Foreign Minister Billy Miller.[54]

In light of recent developments, the effectiveness of U.S. major supply-side policies in the War on Drugs can be questioned. Only a few countries actually accept U.S. aid to implement narcotics eradication programs, and, in the countries that do cooperate, little evidence exists that such programs are making a difference. As pointed out earlier, the economic incentives are just not present; poor farmers can make more money growing the illegal coca and poppy crops than they can from legal crops. Besides, there are suspicions that the money the United States often provides in cash payments for eradication is being used to finance the cost of planting new drug crops in other locations. Furthermore, the use of herbicides and the methods of eradication employed have been criticized as being harmful to the environment. Coca cultivation is blamed for the deforestation of at least 700,000 hectares of land in the Amazon region of the Andes (an area almost 40 percent larger than the state of Delaware), the pollution of waterways, the killing of wildlife, and the disappearance of several fish species.[55]

Boliva signed an extradition agreement with the United States in early 1997 that will enable the United States for the first time to extradite Bolivian nationals wanted on U.S. drug-trafficking offenses.[56] Then in May 1997, the United States and Mexico signed an accord against drug trafficking, which included a new protocol for extradition, and six presidents of six Central American countries and the Dominican Republic promised the U.S. that they would "modernize their extradition treaties and apply them vigorously."[57] The next month, the Colombian legislature passed a measure that moved the country close to passing a historic law that would make extradition retroactive. This meant that drug lords like Helmer "Pacho" Herrera and the Rodríguez Orejuela brothers now in Colombian jail could be extradited to the United States for trial.[58]

Most countries, however, view extradition as an affront to their sovereignty and independence, even though most of them concede that drug traffickers would face a greater likelihood of conviction as well as tougher sentences in the United States.

Certification as an instrument of supply-side antidrug policy has been controversial since it was first implemented as part of the Anti-Drug Abuse Act of 1986. The law requires that the U.S. government apply sanctions on countries unless the president reports to Congress that they are cooperating fully with U.S. antinarcotics efforts. Loss of certification status leads to a loss of foreign aid, requires the United States to vote against extending loans to decertified countries by multinational institutions like the World Bank, and could lead to trade sanctions and suspension of commercial airline service to these countries. "Some nationalists in the affected countries object to the certification process," Mabry explained. "Some believe that the process means the U.S. is passing a moral judgment on their nations."[59]

At the Group of Rio's sixteenth annual ministerial meeting in Asunción, Paraguay, in May 1997, 14 countries made a declaration critical of the U.S.'s use of certification in dealing with member states in the War on Drugs.[60]

There are many critics, both in the United States and in foreign countries, who believe that the United States has treated some countries by different standards and have often used other foreign policy considerations in determining certification status. Historically, there has been strong evidence to support the critics. In 1997, for example, the United States decertified Colombia and not Mexico, even though strong evidence suggested that the later was as corrupted by drug money as the former. In an editorial, the *Miami Herald* newspaper summed up the feelings of U.S. allies affected by the U.S. certification program: "Congress would do better to focus its legislative powers on the cumbersome certification law that — rather than discouraging drug trafficking — most effectively hamstrings U.S. policy by making it reek of hypocrisy."[61]

The Future

The United States, however, has given no indication that it will abandon its current policy initiatives or stop looking outside its borders for answers to its drug problem. Most likely, Uncle Sam will continue to pressure producing countries to destroy drug crops at their source, wipe out drug laboratories wherever they exist, and help it interdict drugs before they enter the country, even while the price of narcotics, no doubt, stays low, the drug supply remains abundant, and the international market expands.

In light of current U.S. antidrug policy, foreign countries involved in the War on Drugs will continue to view the superpower's antinarcotics policy as unfair, complaining that Uncle Sam has not made an effort to solve its own drug problem and keeps blaming other countries with a lot fewer resources. They will also continue to point out that the United States is the world's largest consumer of illegal drugs, and if there wasn't such a high U.S. demand, drug crops would not be grown and marketed in other countries.

Chapter 22

A Changing Nation:
The Price of War
for Uncle Sam

"I found it difficult to believe that drug testing … violates the Fourth Amendment. It's just inconceivable that people who are going to head up the government of this state cannot be checked at least one time."
— Michael J. Bowers, Georgia state attorney general

"If there is major change in Connecticut, it won't be because politicians are more enlightened. It's because we don't have enough money to spend on current policy."
— Mitch Laylor, Connecticut state representative

Irvin Rosenfeld is a stockbroker by profession and a conservative by nature, and, under normal circumstances, he would not even consider smoking a marijuana cigarette. Rosenfeld's life, though, is far from normal, for each day for the rest of his life he must bear the pain from a rare congenital disease that has led to several operations and the removal of 40 tumors. Rosenfeld is one of eight select people in the United States who receive regular monthly supplies of marijuana in the form of 300 freeze-dried joints delivered in tins from the U.S. government. "I feel that, without the marijuana, I would be dead," Rosenfeld explained. " And I'm still a good, productive member of society."[1]

Jim Montgomery broke his back and is now confined to a wheelchair. He discovered that marijuana could relieve his back pain, but the United States did not supply him with the drug, so he had to go on the street find a dealer who would. Following up on an anonymous tip, police raided Montgomery's house, discovered his stash of pot, and arrested him. In 1992 a jury convicted him to life plus 16 years in prison for possession with intent to distribute two ounces of marijuana, an amount equal to the tobacco in two packs of cigarettes. The judge reduced Montgomery's sentence to ten years, but he is now serving time with murderers and rapists who could be released before he is. The case cost Montgomery $30,000 in attorney's fees, and the U.S. government tried to seize his home, which he shared with his widowed mother, but was unsuccessful. "My worst violation is a speeding ticket," Montgomery told ABC News in 1995. "That's about as out of hand as I get."[2]

Rosenfeld and Montgomery are at the center of a controversy surrounding marijuana laws that cuts to the heart of the issue of how the United States is waging its war against illegal drugs. The issue flared up on election day 1996, when voters in California and Arizona voted to ease restrictions on the medical use of marijuana just when President Clinton was moving to step up the U.S. assault on its War on Drugs and amid reports that marijuana use was increasing among U.S. teenagers. The University of Michigan's 1996 nationwide survey of 50,000 students in grades 8, 10, and 12 revealed that the use of drugs, both marijuana and harder drugs, was on the rise once again, after declining through much of the 1980s. U.S. drug czar Barry McCaffrey called the trend a "disaster" and U.S. Health and Human Affairs Secretary Donna Shalala denounced the trend as "unacceptable."[3]

McCaffrey and Shalala are highly vocal advocates of the Clinton administration's view that the California and Arizona initiatives represented a significant threat to the U.S. drug-control strategy, because, at a time when marijuana use was increasing among teenagers, the measures were sending the wrong message, that marijuana may be less than harmful; it may actually be medically beneficial. Shalala, who oversees the National Institutes of Health, contended that all available research has concluded that marijuana is dangerous to human health and harms the brain, heart, lungs, and immune system."[4]

That assessment of marijuana, however, does not really mesh with reality. It is true that several experts have said that there is no proven medical use for smoking marijuana and that better drugs exist to treat patients suffering from cancer, glaucoma, and AIDS, diseases from whose suffering marijuana is supposed to offer relief. It is also true, however, that many experts have said that marijuana has medical value and should be prescribed. A 1990 survey, for example, found that 44 percent of oncologists have recommended that a patient smoke marijuana for relief of nausea induced by chemical therapy.[5] At a news conference in February 1997, a panel of medical experts spoke of interesting "hints" that "marijuana smoking has helped patients with AIDS, glaucoma and cancer. For at least some indications [medical uses], it looks promising enough that there should be some new controlled studies," said Dr. William T. Beaver, the panel's chair and a professor of pharmacology at Georgetown University School of Medicine.[6]

That assessment has not stopped the U.S. government from reacting in typical fashion to any group or individual who has dared to question the official view of marijuana or the law-and-order paradigm that has served as the U.S. drug-control strategy since Ronald Reagan declared war on drugs in the early 1980s. In 1996 the Clinton administration warned doctors not to prescribe marijuana because to do so would be illegal under federal law and threatened to move against those doctors who did both by revoking their U.S. Drug Enforcement Administration registration, which they need to prescribe drugs, and if need be, by prosecuting them. "We will not turn a blind eye to our responsibility," warned Janet Reno, the U.S. attorney general.[7]

Leaders in the movement to ease restrictions on medical marijuana pointed out that the California and Arizona laws had been written so as not to contradict and violate federal law, but the clarification fell on deaf ears. McCaffrey stepped up the government attack, calling marijuana "a gateway drug that would lead young people to use harder drugs like cocaine and heroin."[8] Such sweeping assessments of medical marijuana have angered many experts. "Advocates of medical use of marijuana ... are sometimes charged with using medicine as a wedge to open a way for recreational use," wrote Lester Grinspoon and James B. Balakar, two doctors who have studied marijuana for several years. "The accusation is false as applied to its target, but expresses in a disturbed form a truth about some opponents of medical marijuana: They will not admit that it can be safe and effective medicine largely because they are stubbornly committed to exaggerating its dangers when used for medical purposes."[9]

The furor over medical marijuana has shown that U.S. political leaders have no intention of rethinking or revising their antidrug strategy. As noted earlier, the United States has pursued an aggressive policy to curb the supply of drugs from abroad, while trying to limit the demand for drugs within its borders by punishing users with sanctions that have included fines, stiff jail terms, and the loss of jobs, driving licenses, and even housing. A stream of media ads continue to warn American viewers, especially the young, about the dangers of illegal drug use. Each year, the federal government spends about $12 billion and state and local government another $8 billion in an effort to turn the tide.[10] The War on Drugs now costs the U.S. government more than it spends for the Commerce, Interior, and State departments combined.[11]

The media is filled with reports about how illegal drugs are eroding the country's institutions — family, schools, the workplace — and how the United States with about 6 percent of the world's population consumes about 60 percent of the world's drug supply, the sale of which has been put at more than $100 billion. But while as many illegal drugs are entering the country as ever before and there is no indication that drug use will drop sharply any time soon, few U.S. leaders have questioned the increasingly costly punitive strategy and its effect on American society. Indeed, the response has been to call for tougher laws, more police, more prisons, and more restrictions of personal freedoms, as well as a tougher stance abroad.

The calls for legislative reform by the growing number of critics of U.S. drug policy are ignored by the politicians who seem afraid to challenge the conventional wisdom even in the face of statistics and media reports that show policy as usual is not working and that crime is rising. And they would rather shoot the messenger than heed the message. "Policy makers have requested numerous studies to assess the progress and prospects for the drug war," Bertram and her coauthors revealed. "Yet when their findings are negative, even those international reports are met with denial."[12]

Those who do question the official party line face the threat of attacks and censure from their colleagues and leaders. When the former U.S. surgeon general Jocelyn Elders told the National Press Club in 1993 that the U.S. government should conduct some studies to see whether drug legalization would reduce crime, she received widespread condemnation, both outside and inside the government, including some from the White House. "The President is against legalization," press secretary Dee Dee Myers assured the nation.[13]

Yet this lack of vision, responsibility, and often political courage is having a profound impact on U.S. society. Unbending adherence to the drug strategy in place since the early 1980s is costing the United States dearly. The annual bill to the American taxpayers from illegal drug use has been put at $67 billion.[14] There are other costs as well, which give strong evidence that the punitive strategy is actually exacerbating the problems it is intended to solve and damaging the society it is suppose to protect.

"The drug war, like any war, inflicts collateral damage," explained

Bertram and her coauthors. "In military conflicts, collateral damage mounts when civilians are unintentionally killed, injured or displaced and when schools and hospitals are inadvertently destroyed. The collateral costs of the drug war are the unintended harms imposed on innocent citizens and valued institutions."[15]

Due Process and Civil Liberties

The undermining of the U.S. Constitution has been one of the most significant effects of the increasing U.S. militarization of the drug war. The United States is a democracy — a free, open society — but those qualities, which much of the world admires, are being seen by an increasing number of Americans as a liability in the war against international drug trafficking. "There is little public concern over civil rights violations in the drug war, because generally the public views drug traffickers with horror," wrote William Weir.[16]

The protections guaranteed Americans under the Fourth Amendment, which protects against unreasonable search and seizure, have been seriously eroded. Millions of Americans, most of whom do not use illegal drugs, must now undergo drug tests. Police can now routinely stop motorists on highways for drug checks. Police now use "courier profiles" to detain and question travelers without probable cause, even though no one in law enforcement has been able to describe what a typical drug trafficker or courier looks like, and, as critics have charged, Blacks, Hispanics, and other minorities have been singled out for harassment through drug courier profiles. Police take advantage of "no knock laws" that allow them to break down doors when they bring search warrants. The U.S. Drug Enforcement Agency now keeps files on hundreds of thousands of citizens, most of whom are not under investigation for suspected drug trafficking, and these files are available to other law enforcement agencies, such as the FBI, IRS, and U.S. Customs. "These files can be the source of abuse," Blachman and Sharpe explained. "For instance, the IRS could, as it did during the Nixon administration, selectively audit (i.e. harass) those who appear in the files, even if they are not under investigation. Names might also be selectively leaked, with considerable damage to individuals' reputations."[17]

Is the American public worried about such threats to their basic liberties? "In the crisis atmosphere of the drug war, neither the public nor the mainstream media has asked whether the ephemeral effectiveness of such police action is really worth compromising a key element of the Constitution," wrote Alfred J. McCoy.[18]

The U.S. government has determined that an effective way to fight drug trafficking is to go after the assets used to facilitate the trade. In 1984 the U.S. government inserted a section in the Controlled Substances Act that now allows for the civil forfeiture of a broad range of property, including residences, taverns, apartment and office buildings, undeveloped land, and improvements built on land. In 1985 the U.S. Department of Justice created the National Assets Seizure and Forfeiture fund, which by 1990 had grown to $500 million. By that year, an additional $1.4 billion in real and personal property had been seized and was awaiting forfeiture.[19]

Asset forfeiture, however, has raised questions about drug war tactics because it appears to be in conflict with the Fifth Amendment's protection against seizing property without due process. It has also been criticized as a graphic example of how federal and statement government power could be widely abused. In 1993 Richard Lyle Austin was convicted of cocaine possession with intent to distribute and sentenced to seven years in jail by a South Dakota court. While the offense in South Dakota can lead to a fine of $10,000 maximum, the court assessed Austin a fine 40 to 50 times larger. Moreover, the federal government confiscated Austin's mobile home and auto body shop, which was appraised at $400,000.[20]

The federal government has confiscated property even in cases where the owner has been ignorant of the use to which the property was put and even if no criminal charges had been filed. The U.S. House Judiciary Committee has noted that in more than 80 percent of the civil asset forfeiture cases the property owner is not charged with a crime. Nevertheless, the government can keep the seized property.[21] In December 1993, the U.S. Supreme Court gave a ruling that guaranteed owners the right to protest the property seizure in court before it is confiscated. In an editorial, the *Christian Science Monitor* noted that "the closeness of the 5-4 decision indicates "both the reluctance to weaken an anti crime measure that has been at least somewhat successful, and the acknowledgment that seizure by law enforcement agencies of assets even suspected to be contraband may have been carried out in some instances with too little regard for basic civil liberties."[22]

By the mid 1990s, many federal and local government agencies had grown fat on the cash obtained from forfeiture using it for staff, equipment, and even for basic operating expenses. A 1992 U.S. General Accounting Office study revealed that one police department relied on forfeiture for 10 percent of its budget.[23]

The U.S. Supreme Court has also ruled that the government's right to forfeiture extends to drug assets needed or used by a defendant to pay attorney's fees, and so, since the 1980s, government has used forfeiture laws to go after drug traffickers and their lawyers in an effort to destroy their criminal organizations. Critics have charged that forfeiture may prevent defendants in drug cases from being able to pay fees to their attorneys, thus preventing them from receiving a fair trial. Many defendants in drug cases, moreover, have been able to negotiate lighter sentences by giving up hidden property or agreeing not to challenge forfeiture in court. Groups like the American Civil Liberties Union and the National Association of Criminal Defense lawyers have said that the practice favors the successful, powerful criminal over the lesser one.[24]

Drug Testing

Drug testing has been the most controversial issue to affect civil liberties. In 1986 President Ronald Reagan, in his crusade to have a drugfree workplace, issued an executive order requiring all federal workers to be tested for illegal drugs. The U.S. Army and the Transportation Department had to initiate drug-testing programs immediately while other federal departments were required to "devise appropriate policies to identify jobs that were sufficiently sensitive, for reason of public safety or national security, to warrant screening."[25] The following year, the U.S. Senate overwhelmingly approved a bill that required random drug testing of airline pilots, citing a figure that was bound to cause public alarm: the number of near misses in the air had ostensibly more than doubled since 1987. But as journalist Dan Baum pointed out, "That happened to have been the year that Ronald Reagan fired — on a single day — every qualified air traffic controller in the country for participating in a strike."[26]

In 1989 the U.S. Supreme Court upheld the government's right to demand urine tests from workers in "sensitive" positions. By that time, most private U.S. employers had implemented programs — nearly half of which involved drug testing — to identify drug use and abuse among its employees.[27] In 1995 the U.S. Supreme Court upheld the drug testing of student athletes in public schools because of the national concern over drug use by youngsters.

In handing down one drug-testing decision, the Supreme Court explained, "We must balance the nature and quality of the intrusion on the individual's Fourth Amendment interests against the importance of the governmental interest alleged to justify the intrusion."[28] Many prominent Americans like Senator Edward Kennedy of Massachusetts have disagreed, warning that this kind of intrusion into an individual's privacy is leading to the creation of "a drug exception" to the Fourth Amendment."[29]

In light of the court's rulings on drug testing, government, both at the national and at the state level, has attempted to extend the practice, but the courts have put a check on its zeal. In 1992 the state of Georgia required that candidates for state office had to certify that they had taken and passed a drug test before their names could appear on the ballot. But in an 8–1 decision the U.S. Supreme Court ruled that Georgia's drug-testing law violated the Constitution's ban on unreasonable searches, and the state couldn't just force political candidates to take a drug test to prove how tough it was on the War on Drugs. The perplexed Georgia state attorney, Michael J. Bowers, said, "I found it difficult to believe that drug testing candidates for high office violates the Fourth Amendment. It's just inconceivable that people who are going to head up the government of this state cannot be checked at least one time."[30]

In 1997 a measure in Florida to allow random drug testing of middle and high school students was defeated in a 6–0 vote by the state house criminal justice committee. Initially, the bill would have required drug tests for youths applying for driving licenses as well.

Attitudes toward drug testing have certainly changed in the past decade. What was controversial is now an accepted measure of American society to protect itself against the scourge of drugs. Even Senator Ted Kennedy, the renowned champion of civil liberties, now agrees that drug testing "is appropriate when based on reasonable suspicion, such as after a worksite accident."[31]

Impact on the Judicial System

During its War on Drugs, the United States has taken a great many prisoners — literally; in fact, the United States has never had more people incarcerated, nor more inmates doing time for drug offenses. By October 1994 the nation's state and federal prison populations had topped 1 million for the first time in history. The national incarceration rates for whites grew from 116 per 100,00 in 1984 to 203 in 1993, while the rate for African Americans during the same period rose from 723 per 100,000 to 1,432.[32]

In California statewide felony drug arrests increased more than 180 percent between 1980 and 1989, from 57,682 to 163,742, a figure that represented about one-third of all felony arrests in 1989, compared to about one-fifth in 1980. In Atlanta, the number of drug arrests grew nearly 136 percent, from 1986 to 1989 (3,790 to 8,985).[33] By 1989 the U.S. Senate was estimating that 70 percent of all violent crime in the United States was related to drugs. From 1980 to 1993, the number of drug offenders as a percentage of inmates in the federal prisons increased by 25 percent in 1980 to 61 percent in 1993.[34]

As the country moved to get tough on drugs during Ronald Reagan's presidential administration, new state and federal laws required the courts to impose definite mandatory prison sentences on drug offenders, whether they were major dealers or casual users. Indeed, many of the arrests and tough sentences that followed have been for mere possession of drugs, mainly marijuana. This trend has put a tremendous burden on the judicial system, exacerbating serious overcrowding in prisons, creating huge backlogs in courts, and costing the taxpayers millions of dollars that could have been used for social and educational programs.

By the late 1980s the War on Drugs was causing serious logjams in both the federal and state court systems, a development that is making it difficult for justice to be served. "The overload of the criminal justice system generates the distortion of justice," Bertram and her coauthors have pointed out, because "mandatory minimums force judges to jail guilty drug offenders, [and] those who have committed more serious crimes [including murder and rape] may end with lighter sentences. There is simply not enough space for everyone convicted, and those receiving mandatory sentences are given spaces first. Between 1980 and 1990 the average sentence imposed for robbery, rape and kidnapping fell, while the average drug sentence almost doubled, and the proportion of persons imprisoned for drug offenses increased while those imprisoned for violent crimes decreased."[35]

Also, as the U.S. General Accounting Office's study of judicial systems in eight cities revealed: "Overcrowded jails and prisons have resulted in more offenders being placed in the probation and parole systems in the eight cities we reviewed. This, in turn, has generally decreased the level of supervision of probationers and parolees."[36]

Incarceration is costly and getting costlier. The average annual cost for each federal prisoner is now estimated between $20,000 and $25,000, which means it costs the taxpayer at least $6 billion annually to incarcerate the estimated 300,000 Americans who are behind bars for nonviolent drug offenses.[37] The cost for operating just one federal facility, the Marianna Federal Correctional Institution in Florida, where three-fourths of the inmates are incarcerated for drug-related offenses, is $21 million annually. It has an 803-prisoner capacity but now has more than 1,200 inmates, forcing some prisoners to sleep in bunkbeds in lobbies. "We're locking up drug offenders for much longer terms than we put away armed robbers, rapists and murderers," commented Todd Clear, a professor of criminal justice at Rutgers University. "I don't think you can explain why this is a good idea."[38]

The War on Drugs has had another effect on the judicial system as well. In May 1997 the *USA Today* reported on the rising incidence of witness intimidation, a trend that is threatening the integrity of the criminal justice system. Each year, threats from powerful drug traffickers are discouraging frightened witnesses from showing up in court and testifying. As a result, thousands of cases are being thrown out of court and many criminals are going free. The situation has become so serious that several states have begun implementing their own witness-protection programs.[39]

Corruption

An increasing number of Americans being incarcerated are the officials and law-enforcement officers on the front lines of the war. Like their counterparts in foreign countries, many police officers have been bought off by drug traffickers. Paul Eddy and his coauthors estimated that one out of ten Miami police officers were on the take.[40] In one of the latest cases, three Miami police officers and two U.S. Customs agents were arrested in early 1997 for drug dealing and other charges that included the theft of narcotics and extortion of drug dealers. According to prosecutors, one of the officers, a 25-year veteran Customs official, used his authority to direct cocaine shipments through the inspection process. All five defendants pleaded guilty and faced prison terms that could reach 35 years.[41] In Miami, Chicago, Atlanta, New York, Philadelphia, and New Orleans, many drug cases have been overturned or thrown out of court because testifying officers have been convicted of corruption charges. As a result of one corruption investigation in Philadelphia, the police commissioner transferred some 200 officers to new positions in the 6,000-member department and reassigned 7 top internal affairs commanders.[42]

Corruption has been especially serious along the U.S.-Mexican border, where, during the mid 1990s, at least 39 U.S. local, state, and federal officials had been convicted in federal court on drug corruption charges, according to the U.S. Justice Department.[43] Speaking before the U.S. Senate in May 1997, Thomas Constantine, the head of the U.S. Drug Enforcement Agency (DEA), revealed that drug traffickers had offered one U.S. official working along the U.S.-Mexican border an $18 million bribe.[44]

The U.S. federal government and a number of states have moved to address the problem. In 1997 two congressional panels conducted hearings on drug-related corruption of U.S. border officials, while the FBI had asked Congress for 67 more prisons so that it could conduct more border corruption investigations. In 1996 California formed an anticorruption task force, and several other states are considering similar groups. In February 1997 Arizona announced the creation of a task force of three federal agencies in the state to combat drug corruption.[45]

Lawyers and judges are being corrupted as well. Several lawyers were arrested in 1995 on a drug-smuggling conspiracy involving the Cali cartel in which charges included obstruction of justice, money laundering, and conspiracy to import cocaine. "Lawyers have a license to practice law, but they don't have a license to be above the law," James Milford, special agent in charge of the DEA's field office, told the press.[46]

Cynicism and Distrust of the System

Bad cops, crooked lawyers, distorted jail sentences and a malfunctioning criminal-justice system have created distrust of American institutions and a cynicism about their ability to work fairly and efficiently. Many African Americans, for example, have come to view drug laws and their enforcement as racist because a disproportionate number of their ethnic group have been arrested and convicted of drug offenses under the banner of the War on Drugs. They point out the disparity in the sentencing for crack and cocaine offenses, noting that almost all those sentenced for crack have been black, although whites are now users of both drugs.

Blacks, in fact, are now three to four times as likely to be arrested on drug charges as are whites.[47] A report by the Sentencing Project, a Washington, D.C., research group, found that between 1979 and 1988, a period when the overall crime rate increased by only 2 percent, the number of African Americans in prison doubled.[48]

Many Americans find it grossly unfair that users of marijuana can get a life sentence in some states and that a rapist or murderer could serve less time in jail than a nonviolent drug offender. Workers are spending millions of dollars to find schemes that they hope can beat the ever-widening use of workplace drug tests. Experts estimate that 1 to 2 percent of workers who must submit to drug tests now drink fluids to weaken or contaminate their urine samples.[49] "So many Americans have tried or used drugs like marijuana or cocaine casually — and see nothing objectionable about this — that increased sanctions will not have the legitimacy to make them work," Blackman and Sharpe explained.[50]

Economic and Social Costs

The War on Drugs has strapped local budgets, forcing states and cities to spend increasing amounts of money for prisons, courts, and law enforcement. Taxpayers have to pay, too, for the increasing numbers of AIDS cases and drug-addicted babies. By 1993 one-third of the 37,900 AIDS cases reported to the U.S. Centers for Disease Control were associated directly or indirectly with injecting heroin or cocaine or both.[51] Many experts contend that the drug prohibition has led to an epidemic of violence, the natural result of outlawing items like narcotics that consumers want. "The evidence indicates that, while drug use and violence are increasing on parallel tracks, drug use does not necessarily cause violence," Weir explained. "But the drug trade, which supplies the users, seems to be responsible for a substantial amount of the violence."[52]

As Mary Cooper has pointed out, many children have been casualties of the drug war. "There are social costs involved in the growing number of children and youth who end up in the criminal justice system long before they have completed their education or training for legitimate employment."[53]

The Booming Domestic Illicit Drug Industry

While the U.S. has waged war abroad, the domestic production of some illicit drugs — most notably marijuana and methamphetamines —

has flourished. The amount of marijuana seized between 1991 and 1995 jumped from 400 to 529 tons. "Because of the drug's relative low market price and the increased risk of interdiction at the border, the profitability of marijuana trafficking from foreign suppliers has diminished, explaining in large part the boom in marijuana production in the United States during the late 1980s," wrote Cooper.[54]

The American market for marijuana is huge and traffickers have no problem finding customers to buy their illegal product. According to one report, 17 million Americans smoked marijuana in 1992, with at least 3 million of them using it daily. An estimated one-third of all Americans over the age of 11 have smoked pot at least once. The value of the U.S. marijuana crop has been put at between $4 and $24 billion, making it the country's largest cash crop, legal or illegal.[55] In 1995 the top five marijuana-producing states in order were Tennessee, Kentucky, Hawaii, California, and New York.[56]

Given the money involved, many U.S. marijuana farmers have been willing to use all kinds of devices to protect their investments, including high-powered firearms, explosives, and booby traps.[57] Today, more American are incarcerated in the federal penal system for marijuana-related offenses than for any other drug.[58]

The U.S. government's marijuana policy and the tactics it has used to suppress the drug's distribution and use has sparked widespread criticism. "In order to eliminate marijuana use, state and federal legislators have sanctioned an enormous increase in prosecutorial power, the emergence of a class of professional informers, and the widespread confiscation of private property by the government without trial — legal weapons reminiscent of those used in former Soviet-bloc countries," wrote Eric Schlosser.[59]

Alternatives to Militarization

Indeed, the high cost of the war on international drug trafficking and its many negative impacts on the American system and U.S. foreign policy has led an increasing number of Americans to question not only the U.S. marijuana policy but its overall antidrug strategy. The dissenters represent a wide range of approaches. Some respected experts such as Ethan Nadelmann, director of Lindsmith Institute, says the strategy has not diminished the American appetite for drugs, and so legalization should be given serious consideration as a policy option. Nadelmann admits that legalization may pose risks, but he argues that "the risks of legalization may well be less than most people assume, particularly if independent alternative measures are implemented."[60]

Others opponents of the current system, like Baltimore mayor Kurt Schmoke, favor decriminalization but not the legalization of all drugs. "Decriminalization is in effect 'medicalization,' a broad public health strategy — led by the surgeon general, not the attorney general — designed to reduce the harm caused by drugs by putting addicts into the public health system," Schmoke has explained.[61] The approach has also been called "harm reduction" — a middle way between the extremes of legalization and prohibition, in which an effort is made to reduce the risk to drug addicts and society. Examples of this approach include giving treatment to nonviolent users rather than long prison sentences, pushing legislative measures that will make marijuana available for medical purposes, and moving to make clean needles available to heroin addicts and small amounts of cocaine and heroin to drug users in an effort to divert them from crime.

Harm-reduction advocates say that, if their strategy is adopted, law enforcement would not be eliminated, nor the amount of money targeted for the War on Drugs decreased. Rather, the war would be demilitarized, with the emphasis and money redirected toward treatment. According to one 1994 RAND Corporation study, by diverting 25 percent of the money now applied to the punitive approach to treating 100 percent of the drug users each year, cocaine consumption could be cut in half over a 12-year period, saving American taxpayers $12 billion annually."[62]

Some American cities have begun trying alternative approaches. For instance, in August 1996 Andrew Sonner, the chief prosecutor for Montgomery County, Maryland, announced that he would prosecute only those drug offenses that occurred in high-crime areas or that involved violent or repeat offenders. In explaining his decision, Sonner said that small-time drug offenders belonged in treatment, not in jail, and were not dangerous criminals.[63]

New Haven, Connecticut, has a program in place in which police officers accompany health officials in door-to-door visits in high-crime areas to help publicize treatment services.[64] In 1997 the state of Connecticut began considering a major revision of its drug laws to reduce the costs and make drug abuse primarily a public health problem, not a law-enforcement matter. "By this year (1997), Connecticut will have re-shaped its drug policy," predicted Mitch Laylor, Connecticut state representative and chairman of the judiciary committee, who added, "If there is major change in Connecticut, it won't be because politicians are more enlightened. It's because we don't have enough money to spend on current policy."[65]

Section 5
Assessment

Chapter 23

The Summing Up:
Lessons from the
War on Drugs

"It's like hitting mercury with a hammer."
— U.S. State Department official

"Stop the traffic on the ground and they take to the air. Control the air and they go by sea. It's a battle with no end."
— Enrique Salgado Cordero, chief of the Mexican Police

In chronicling and analyzing the background and development of U.S. antinarcotics policy in the period 1982 to 1997, this book has shown how the Reagan, Bush, and Clinton administrations steadily militarized the War on Drugs and made it a central component of U.S. foreign policy. By 1997 the U.S. military and a host of federal agencies were deeply involved in an antidrug strategy that has focused on keeping illegal drugs from entering the United States. The battle plan has had two main objectives: reduce supply from abroad so that American consumers will find illegal drugs like heroin, cocaine, and marijuana difficult to buy and afford, and discourage domestic consumption through stiff penalties and sanctions.

As Eva Bertram and her coauthors explained the rationale: "If law enforcement can restrict the growing, manufacture and distribution and sale of illegal drugs ... these illicit drugs will become scarce, their prices will soar and drug consumption will drop. The policy mix often changes — at times emphasizing a crackdown on domestic dealers and traffickers; at other times concentrating on foreign growers and international traffickers — but the underlying logic has remained constant."[1]

But, as the analysis herein of international drug trafficking has shown, the battle plan has not gone according to the script. The United States has scored some successes — Operation Greenback, the overthrow of the Noriega regime in Panama, the killing of violent drug trafficker Pablo Escobar, the capture and surrender of the Cali cartel's top leadership, and the surrender of Myanmar war lord Khu Sa are prominent examples — but despite spending billions of dollars ($38 billion between 1989 and 1993 alone), the creation of a huge drug-fighting bureaucracy, and the engagement of its allies around the world, the antidrug strategy has failed to attain its objective. The hope has been that if enough force was used against international drug trafficking, drug use would eventually taper off in the United States, but the country's huge market continues to make international drug trafficking the world's fastest-growing industry, with profits of some $400 billion annually.

Despite concerted attempts to disrupt supply in the 1980s, the price of cocaine, heroin, and marijuana has remained largely unchanged during the 1990s. Heroin was less expensive in 1997 than it was when Ronald Reagan declared War in Drugs in 1981, and, while the U.S. market for cocaine has stabilized since the boom of the 1980s, Europe has become a big market for the drug. Meanwhile, heroin use in the United States has surged, the drug's supply on the streets nearly doubling in the past two decades.[2]

Many Americans, moreover, have rejected the strong message of the U.S. antidrug campaign and believe, according to public officials, that certain types of drug may be relatively harmless. In the mid 1990s, there was growing concern that marijuana use among the nation's youth was climbing once again, that drug emergencies in hospitals were rising sharply, and that different and more potent kinds of drugs — Ice, PCP, LSD, Ecstasy, methamphetamine, amphetamine, and methaqualone (Mandrax) — were more available than ever before. Some experts were blaming parents and the media for the increase in drug use among the young, but few called for a reevaluation of the U.S. antidrug policy. Initially, the use of crack, one of the most addictive of drugs, which made its appearance in the mid 1980s, was limited mainly to minorities, particularly African Americans in the poor inner cities, but by the early 1990s its use and abuse had spread to the white U.S. population and to European countries.

Law enforcement in producing countries expressed frustration with these developments. "Interdicting the supply of illegal drugs in the producing countries and reducing demand in the consuming nations are both important in fighting drug trafficking," explained Rosso José Serrano. "The equation has to be balanced, but so far consuming countries haven't done enough to reduce demand."[3]

While the United States remains the world's biggest consumer of illegal drugs, drug consumption has become a growing problem for rich and poor countries in all parts of the world, with the booming market fueling the expansion of international drug trafficking. By 1997 the drug trade's traditional crime syndicates (Triads, Sicilian Mafia, and Colombian cartels)—were more powerful than ever before, and the up and coming syndicates (Jamaican Posses, the Russian Mafia, and the Mexican cartels) more numerous. Moreover, these criminal enterprises were using their fortunes, entrepreneurial skill, and enormous power and reach to take advantage of several global trends (free trade, fall of communism, and the communications revolution) to threaten international development and the political stability of many countries.

The transformation of international drug trade into a multinational enterprise has been one of the most remarkable international developments since the early 1980s. The pioneers of the drug trade enjoyed the trappings of their illegally earned wealth but were not really interested in developing the business skills that could help them maximize profits and protect their business interests. The use of "smurfs" who would launder drug money in the early 1980s by simply walking into Miami banks with sacks full of cash is a good example of the lack of sophistication of the early drug syndicates. Since then, however, drug syndicates have adapted brilliantly to the changing international business and law enforcement environments, and by 1997 they were operating well-oiled production, distribution, and money-laundering networks. Today, the CEOs of the world's biggest multinationals could pick up some management tips from the leaders of the Triads, Russian Mafia, and Mexican and Colombian cartels.

History shows that the supply-focused interdiction strategy of the War on Drugs has spurred the growth of international drug trafficking. When the United States shut down the French Connection in the early 1970s, heroin production shifted to Asia and the countries of Myanmar, Pakistan, and eventually Afghanistan. Marijuana became the largest U.S. cash crop in the 1980s after the successful efforts to eradicate the herb abroad in Mexico, Jamaica, and Colombia — so successful were they, in fact, that, as Rensselaer Lee explained, "Many people in those countries still believe that the marijuana eradication campaigns were a deliberate ploy to expand and exploit the U.S. domestic market."[4]

The Medellín cartel was dismantled with the death of Escobar in

1993, but a more skillful criminal organization, the Cali cartel, filled the vacuum. The Cali cartel — perhaps history's most powerful criminal organization — has become the prime example of the drug syndicate as the multinational that is willing to adapt and diversify in search of profit and viability. In the late 1980s, the Cali cartel began applying the same entrepreneurial skill in marketing heroin as it had earlier with cocaine, making Colombia in less than a decade a major source of the narcotic. In 1995 60 percent of the heroin seized at U.S. airports came from Colombia; two years later, the cartel controlled 80 percent of the New York heroin market.[5] With the successful offensive against the Cali cartel in the mid 1990s, the Mexican cartels began to rise to dominance, surely a more ominous development, given Mexico's proximity to the United States.

The chances of the United States winning its war against international drug trafficking is bleaker today than it has ever been since Ronald Reagan launched the antidrug offensive, largely because of the problem's scope. For example, more than 100 countries are now involved in the international drug trade. Opium cultivation can be found in Guatemala as well as the Golden Triangle, marijuana in Brazil as well as Mexico and the United States, cocaine laboratories in Italy as well as the Amazon, and synthetic drug labs in the United States as well as Thailand, Poland, and India. Even within countries, drug interdiction has made the situation worse. When the Bush administration finally convinced Bolivia to eradicate coca plants on the eastern slopes of the Andean mountains, cultivation spread into Bolivia's Amazon basin, and then into Brazil. The same thing happened in Peru, where opium cultivation has spread from the Upper Huallaga Valley into the Puno, Pasco, Cuzco, and Ayacucho departments.

Efforts to disrupt the drug distribution pipeline to the United States has forced the drug syndicates to be more innovative and shift their routes and change their means of smuggling. The successful interdiction efforts in South Florida in the early 1980s, for instance, forced the Latin American cartels to shift their routes to the southeast border region. The means shifted as well — from aircraft and maritime vessels to tractor-trailers, containers and private vehicles. U.S. authorities now have a 2,000-mile border, 38 points of entry, and 640,000 pedestrians and 240,000 trucks and other vehicles to worry about, most definitely a change for the worse in the War on Drugs.[6]

"Stop the traffic on the ground and they take to the air," said Enrique Salgado Cordero, chief of the Mexican police. "Control the air and they go by sea. It's a battle with no end."[7] Or as one state department official put it: "It's like hitting mercury with a hammer."[8]

The cat-and-mouse game is played domestically as well. When the DEA launched an interdiction campaign against U.S. marijuana growers in 1982, many growers moved their operations indoors or underground to avoid detection. The authorities have often attempted to "sweep" drug-infested neighborhoods of small-time drug dealers, but they have simply moved their operations to nearby neighborhoods.

Law enforcement has continually refined their surveillance techniques and taken advantage of the communications revolution, but so have the drug-trafficking syndicates, who now use pagers, fax machines, cellular phones, and express mail to make the deal, sophisticated satellite technology and state-of-the-art high-powered motorboats to move their product, and cyberspace to hide the profits. This trend will surely accelerate. "As the communications and transportation revolutions acquire greater reach, most national police authorities will find themselves hopelessly outgunned by technologies that are relatively cheap for organized crime, but may be financially out of the reach for the law enforcement community," predicted the Center for Strategic and International Studies.[9]

The many countries that have been corrupted by the international drug trade are certainly worse off than they were in the early 1980s, when, for example, the Bahamas were about the only country in the Caribbean that had officials on the take from drug traffickers. The drug trade then was simple in scope and dominated by the Medellín cartel; the route more direct. With the intensification of U.S. drug interdiction, however, the entire Caribbean has been caught in the net of international drug trafficking, and the fear is that they will become corrupted, mini narcodemocracies, overwhelmed by the drug traffickers' money and power.

As the drug war has widened in Latin America, countries like Nicaragua, Puerto Rico, and the Dominican Republic have become important transit points on the routes to U.S. and European markets. In Asia, the Triads opened new opium production centers and mapped out new transportation routes from the Golden Triangle, and the southern region of the People's Republic of China got hooked on the drug trade. Today, China has thriving opium fields and a drug problem. Corruption has been rampant in Russia and Eastern European countries since the collapse of the Soviet Union, making them easy marks for the marketing and money-laundering activities of the drug syndicates.

Many corrupt officials have succumbed to greed and may be making lots of money from the bribes they have accepted from drug traffickers, but most people involved in the drug trade are barely scratching out a living. The drug trade employs millions and plays an important role in the economic and political survival of many countries, for example, helping countries to meet debt payment schedules and to pacify potentially explosive sectors of the public. Crippling the trade, therefore, could have serious political and economic consequences.

That illicit drug production has taken root in some of the poorest places on the planet — South America's Amazon region, Africa's Subsahara, Central Asia, and northeastern Brazil, for example — is another significant development in the War on Drugs that offers the United States both a challenge and the opportunity for constructive change. Many experts feel that a solution to the international drug problem lies not in pursuing a military solution, but in developing meaningful economic and social programs. Yet the United States has shown no indication that it has recognized this opportunity to change its flawed antidrug policy, and it continues to focus on supplying its drug war allies with military equipment, hardware, money, and expertise instead of promoting economic development.

It is no wonder then that, as the drug war has intensified, many countries, especially those on the front lines that are directly feeling its impact, have questioned Uncle Sam's sincerity, objectives, and commitment. For nearly two decades, Noriega was a valuable ally to the United States as a CIA informer, but he outlived his usefulness and became expendable. Colombia is decertified as a helpful partner in the War on Drugs, but not Mexico, because it is the biggest U.S. trading partner and considered vital to Uncle Sam's security and economic interests. In the late 1990s President Bush praised Pakistani leader General Zia for his country's role in the War on Drugs even though the president must have been aware of the suspicions that the country's military has been corrupted by drug money. Under the guise of anticommunism, the CIA facilitated the drug trade in Southeast Asia in the 1960s, Afghanistan in the late 1970s, Central America in the mid 1980s and Venezuela in the early 1990s. But while there have been investigations, nothing has been done to make the agency accountable for its operations.

In 1992 Bush announced that he had established an "aggressive new agenda for the rest of the century" for battling drugs, but a close look at the budget details revealed that the drug war was being widened on the same budget and that he had failed to heed the pleas of his Latin

American neighbors to include more money and assistance in the budget so that they could establish alternatives to the drug trade for their citizens. Clinton decimated the budget of his drug czar Lee Brown, radically reduced his staff, and then announced to the media without blushing that he is behind his drug czar in an all-out war against drugs. Meanwhile, Clinton quietly cut 277 DEA agent positions between 1992 and 1995.[10]

While U.S. legislators talk tough and play politics with the War on Drugs, producing countries have been told to fight the battle with less. In 1990 the United States gave $3 million in antidrug aid to Thailand, down from $3.5 million the previous year, even while reports indicated that heroin use was beginning to increase in the United States.

While failing to reduce supply and demand in any appreciable way, the punitive U.S. antidrug strategy has changed the American system, destabilizing certain institutions and creating dangerous repercussions for the democracy and the basic rights of its citizens. Escalation has led to seriously overcrowded prisons, which has strained the budgets of federal, state, and local governments, while jamming the courts with drug cases and putting an enormous burden on the legal system. U.S. leaders have touted the virtues and benefits of small government and tight budgets, but governmental drug-fighting bureaucracies continue to grow and government continues to hire more police, more judges, and more prosecutors to fight the drug war, the logic being that drug strategy may not be working because more money and resources are needed. Law enforcement now has more power than ever before and more opportunity to abuse the rights of American citizens, thanks to forfeiture, drug testing, and other laws. Yet violence, crime, and disintegration of social institutions continue. As Bachman and Sharpe explained, "The inability of many policy makers to see the structural flaws of the punitive law enforcement approach to the drug problem, mistakenly leads them to respond with the same logic used to confront the failure of militarization: escalation."[11]

Chapter 24

Getting Control: Twelve Practical Options for U.S. Antidrug Strategy

"It would be more prudent to establish objectives that appear to be reasonable than to raise expectations for degrees of control of the drug trade that are beyond the resources or capabilities of the United States ... or other nations."
— Bruce Bagley, University of Miami

"We have bits and pieces but we have no overall list of objectives and no serious planning measures that are likely to lead to success in the attainment of these objectives."
Roy Godson, president, National
Strategy Center, Washington, D.C.

So how should the United States proceed in its battle against international drug trafficking? If, as the lessons of war show, Uncle Sam has failed to meet its objectives, and the punitive law-and-order strategy in place since the early 1980s has not worked, and, as the analysis herein makes clear, will never work, what alternatives are there to counter the scourge of international drug trafficking? What can the United States do to help itself and its allies alleviate the debilitating effects of the drug trade?

The situation is not hopeless if the United States critically examines its strategy and priorities and begins to show more flexibility and resourcefulness in defining and implementing its antidrug strategy than it has shown in the past. Most American leaders and its citizens have supported the U.S. antidrug policy unequivocally and, given the present political climate, few decision makers have dared offered new initiatives or approaches to the issue. The U.S., though, does have alternatives that can ameliorate the effects of illegal drugs, if it chooses its objectives real-istically and seeks to achieve them by practical means.

Be Realistic

Policy objectives that try to achieve "zero tolerance" and attempts to seal the borders against drug trafficking have been counterproduc-tive. History shows that the desire to change one's mood or conscious-ness is inborn in the human species. Whether it be drugs, alcohol, fasting, meditation, chanting, or whatever, man has always felt, for a variety of reasons, the desire to escape himself or herself, at least tem-porarily. If this reality is accepted, then the U.S. strategy should have as its objective not prohibition but the reduction of the harm caused by illegal drugs to the individual and society.

The United States, for example, can lift the current ban on fund-ing AIDS programs that allow drug users to swap dirty needles for clean ones. In the United States, AIDS infections are occurring more frequently among drug users who inject than among any other group.[1] The jour-nal *Lancet* reported that 10,000 Americans could have avoided HIV infec-tion between 1987 and 1995 if needle-exchange programs had been in place. Meanwhile, caring for those sick people cost U.S. taxpayers $500 million.[2] "Needle exchange is not some abstract issue to be consigned to the whims of spin doctors obsessed over political damage control," wrote Dr. Peter Lurie and Dr. Ernest Drucker in an op-ed article. "Rather exchange is a proven public-health intervention [that] leads to pre-ventable suffering and death."[3]

Holland, Switzerland, Great Britain and other countries have, to varying degrees, accepted this analysis and implemented drug policies that reflect it; the United States and much of the world, because of the U.S. lead, has not. Professor Bruce Bagley of the University of Miami believed that "It would be more prudent to establish objectives that appear to be reasonable than to raise expectations for degrees of control of the drug trade that are beyond the resources or capabilities of the United States ... or other nations."[4]

Change the Metaphor

The term War on Drugs makes it sound like the United States means business, but it leads to an "us against them" climate and feeds the illu-

Federal Counterdrug Research and Development Spending, FY 1992–97

(Dollars in millions) Federal agency	1992	1993	1994	1995	1996	1997 request	Total
Agriculture Research Service	$6.5	$6.5	$6.5	$6.5	$4.2	$4.7	$34.9
U.S. Forest Service	0.5	0.5	0.5	0.1	0.1	0.1	1.8
Department of Defense	91.6	34.1	44.7	54.0	51.4	29.4	305.2
Bureau of Indian Affairs	0.0	0.0	1.0	0.9	0.5	0.5	2.9
Drug Enforcement Administration	0.0	0.0	2.4	2.3	2.7	3.2	10.6
Federal Bureau of Investigation	3.8	6.8	2.8	4.5	12.9	12.9	43.7
Federal Aviation Administration	0.7	1.0	1.0	1.1	1.0	1.0	5.8
Financial Crimes Enforcement Network	1.0	1.2	0.0	0.0	0.0	0.0	2.2
Immigration and Naturalization Service	0.5	0.4	0.5	0.9	0.5	0.5	3.3
Office of Justice Programs	16.7	18.1	20.6	15.0	16.4	17.6	104.4
Interagency Crime and Drug Enforcement†	0.4	0.4	0.3	0.4	0.4	0.4	2.3
U.S. Coast Guard	5.2	2.4	1.2	1.0	0.7	0.5	11.0
National Highway Traffic Safety Administration	0.5	0.8	1.0	0.3	0.5	0.2	3.3
U.S. Customs Service	3.7	3.7	0.0	0.0	0.0	0.0	7.4
ADAMHA-Prevention	157.5	0.0	0.0	0.0	0.0	0.0	157.5
NIDA-Prevention	0.0	164.3	174.8	179.6	188.5	191.7	898.9
ADAMHA-Treatment	191.8	0.0	0.0	0.0	0.0	0.0	191.8
NIDA-Treatment	0.0	239.9	250.4	257.3	269.9	274.6	1,292.1
Office of Veterans Affairs Treatment	2.7	2.1	3.2	3.9	3.9	3.9	19.7
Counterdrug Technology Assessment Center	21.0	15.0	8.5§	8.0	16.0	18.0	86.5§
Office of National Drug Control Policy	0.5	0.9	0.9	6.4	0.0	1.0	9.7
Total $	504.6	498.1	520.3	542.2	569.6	559.2	3,194.0

* The 1997 figures reflect those requested but not spent.

† Formerly the Organized Crime Drug Enforcement Task Forces.

† Total includes $1 million in funding received from the ONDCP Director's discretionary fund account in fiscal year 1994. Therefore, the total of CTAC's spending is $1 million more than CTAC's total appropriation.

Source: 1996 National Drug Control Safety.

sion that illegal drug trafficking and drug use can be stopped and that "victory" can be achieved. Drugs and drug abusers have always been with us and they won't go away. The metaphor, furthermore, makes the United States treat as its enemy the victims of illegal drugs and seduces it into policies against the real enemies (the drug traffickers) that are counterproductive.

Seek Accountability

The United States has pursued its antidrug policy since the early 1980s without evaluating or assessing objectives, analyzing the impact, or examining the various components of the strategy to see whether its terms were clear and consistent. What is the objective of U.S. antidrug policy and are the results being measured to see if it is successful? To be effective, the policy must have much more substance to it than simply "waging war on drugs," "getting drugs off the street," or some of the other clichés that have defined our strategy. In testimony before the House Committee on Terrorism, Narcotics and International Operations, Roy Godson, president of the Washington-based National Strategy Center, called for a national policy and strategy to counter drug trafficking and organized crime and noted that "we have bits and pieces but we have no overall list of objectives and no serious planning measures that are likely to lead to success in the achievement of these objectives."[5]

The lack of accountability in the War on Drugs is evident in the huge bureaucracy that has grown in response to the thriving international drug trade. Antidrug efforts have been hampered by poor management and bureaucratic in fighting among the many government agencies responsible for drug policy. In 1995, for example, a U.S. General Accounting Office report revealed that the 19 counternarcotics centers operated by various federal agencies duplicated much of each other's drug intelligence activity. Four of the intelligence centers, for example, analyze air traffic activity along the southwest U.S. border. Lack of accountability has allowed this type of unproductive tax waste to flourish.

Meanwhile, the CIA has also been allowed to operate without any accountability for its role in the War on Drugs. Consequently, the allegations are that agency operations during the past forty years have actually fueled the international drug trade and done much damage to U.S. credibility and its leadership in the antidrug battle.

Recently, however, there has been some growing recognition of the importance of accountability in the War on Drugs. In 1994, for example, Drug Strategies, a nonprofit organization, was created to serve as a watchdog to measure the effectiveness of the federal antidrug strategy. Board members included former U.S. defense secretary Robert McNamara, novelist Michael Crichton, and Children's Defense Fund president Marian Wright Edelman.[6]

Have a Real Debate About Drug Strategy and Policy

Once the antidrug strategy is made accountable, its many tenuous assumptions and flaws will become much more evident and a real debate about how the United States should approach the drug issue should ensue. The United States will be able to move beyond the political posturing and self-defeating moralizing that has characterized the drug issue and begin to take a hard look at strategy to see what viable options are available.

So far, the "debate" that has taken place has been artificial and framed in either/or terms. Either we make a tough law-and-order stance against illegal drugs or we should legalize them. "The options have to be discussed," said Rensselaer Lee. "People who support legalization talk to themselves and the people who oppose it talk to themselves. There has been no real dialogue so it's hard to get accurate information."[7]

A real debate — like the meaningful debates we have had in American politics — will lead to a melting away of this polarization and the realization that a middle way called harm reduction is available. It does not mean "surrender," but rather offers us a way to deal more effectively with the drug issue. Otherwise, some of the battles will be won some of the time but the war will continue to be lost. Besides, the United States has had tough debates about welfare, national health care, affirmative action, and immigration reform. Isn't it time for a national debate about drug policy?

Implement an Honest and Fair Policy

The old adage that "truth is the first casualty of war" is no more evident than in the U.S. War on Drugs. In its attack on medical marijuana,

U.S. officials have made many outlandish statements about how marijuana use leads to harder drugs, and the drug harms the brain, lungs, and so on, without providing any evidence to back up the assertions. Marijuana, heroin, and cocaine can indeed be dangerous, but it is also true that they have been used in relatively harmless ways by many people, including those in the medical establishment to treat patients. Research, in fact, has shown that cocaine is relatively harmless if used in moderation.[8] Besides, history shows that many of the drugs that we view as dangerous to society today were actually legal at the turn of the century before the modern antidrug crusade took shape. Doctors actually prescribed cocaine, heroine, and marijuana for a variety of ailments. Marijuana grew wild in many states in nineteenth century America.

Today millions of Americans smoke marijuana, lead normal lives, and are healthy, productive citizens. Many of them find it difficult to believe that a Jim Montgomery can spend more time in prison than a murderer because he used marijuana to relieve back pain. Such injustice can only lead to contempt for U.S. antidrug policy. Distortions and lies can only undermine the best intentions. U.S. antidrug strategy therefore should be both realistic and fair.

Think and Act Globally

Former United Nations Secretary General Boutros Boutros-Ghali has characterized the modern criminal syndicate as "crime multinationals," a term that reflects the fact that the drug issue is a global problem requiring a concerted response from the international community.[9] The products the drug traffickers market and sell are illegal, but the means by which they get to the market follow the best principles, techniques, and practices of modern capitalism. "The identification of drug trafficking as a criminal activity seems to foster the simplistic notion that it can be curbed with sufficient law enforcement," the Center for Strategic and International Studies has noted. "But to confront the problem directly, it is more helpful to view drug trafficking as an international business or, more accurately, as a commodity trade conducted by consortiums. Although illegal, acquiring chemicals, for the production of illegal drugs, transporting the finished contraband to wholesale distributors, and laundering the drug profits are all operations that can be undertaken successfully only by interacting with and blending in already established markets."[10]

The challenge to the United States and its allies, therefore, is to break down the legal, political, economic, and bureaucratic barriers that keep them from cooperating to fight criminal drug operations that now span the globe. The United States should continue to make bilateral agreements a part of its antidrug strategy, but it also needs to coordinate more of its drug control efforts with regional and international organizations like the United Nations the North American Free Trade Association (NAFTA), World Bank, the World Trade Organization and the European Community.

So far, however, there has been more cooperation between criminal organizations than between the United States and its allies. "Colombia believes the fight against international drug trafficking needs a four-prong approach," Colombian President Ernesto Samper explained in an interview. "The international community needs to attack the drug problem's social and industrial roots (that is, the petrochemicals used in the manufacture of narcotics), while recognizing that interdiction efforts must be balanced with a strong effort to reduce the consumer demand for drugs, especially in the industrialized nations. Otherwise, we won't make any progress."[11]

But international efforts to counter the drug trade are still largely in the planning stage. At the World Ministerial Conference on Organized Transnational Crime held in November 1993, Italy announced plans to finance an international center for training law-enforcement personnel to combat transnational crime, while at the second session of the Commission on Crime Prevention and Criminal Justice held in April 1993, there was strong support for a UN convention that would seek more effective ways to counter organized crime.[12]

Such meetings can be useful, but there should be fewer of them and more action. The world community, for instance, needs an international agreement on money laundering. The United States can develop a system that will keep suspicious bank transfers from entering the U.S. banking system, but it won't hurt the drug syndicates, because they can now deposit their funds in U.S. dollars in dozens of countries around the world. "The United States has largely relied on bilateral agreements to reduce money laundering, but there are so many countries in which traffickers can hide their money," explained Charles Intriago, publisher of *Money Laundering Alert*. "It's important, therefore, to stop illicit funds before they enter the international banking system. Otherwise, it's too late. That can only happen with a comprehensive international agreement."[13]

Other drug-trafficking issues need to be addressed internationally: how to stop drug crop cultivation, how better to coordinate law-enforcement activities and resources, and how to facilitate more judicial cooperation. A world center for intelligence would allow police forces around the world to share information, an important move given that most international drug trafficking now cuts across national borders. It is also time for a global criminal court, but although strong support exists in the international community for such a body, several U.S. leaders have opposed the concept, fearing that such a judicial body could infringe upon U.S. sovereignty. No one, however, would deny that the criminal justice systems of individual countries were not designed to meet the challenge of global crime, and so the United States should support the formation of a world court in its own best national interests.

The international community needs to make a concerted effort to deal with the problem of how drug traffickers get the chemicals they need to make illegal drugs. "I really feel the answer to the drug problem is stopping the flow of precursor chemicals to the producing countries," explained Leonardo Gallego, head of Colombia's Antinarcotics Police. "If the world community got serious about the problem, we could stop drug trafficking in its tracks."[14]

Other drug officials feel the same way about the crops that are cultivated to make heroin, cocaine, and marijuana, believing that the money should be redirected toward developing viable crop-substitution programs that offer alternatives to illicit drug cultivation. The United States could help by providing more money and aid for income-substitution programs that resemble the Marshall Plan after World War II, which can provide U.S. drug war allies with hard currency support and agricultural credits and promote investment, area development, and institution building to help the countries govern their national territory and to enforce the law.

"It's time to have an international summit to address the economic roots of the drug problem," explained Juan Tokatlian, a professor of sociology at the National University of Colombia. "We have had summits on the environment, population control and the status of women. Why not one for international drug trafficking and its effects?"[15]

Dr. Alfredo Vásquez Carrizosa, a former Colombian defense minister, said that such a summit should include the international banks and organizations that help Peru, Mexico, and Colombia and other undeveloped countries and stressed that "the summit must not just deal with words and proposals or it will be another failure in the War on Drugs.

The summit will have to approve a plan that would be carried out immediately under international supervision. It will be a start."[16]

The Marshall Plan model could be used in the United States as well to get at the root economic causes of drug abuse and trafficking among a sizable section of the populace, namely the poor and minorities in the inner cities. Kieran Konderich believes that "innercity regeneration should be a top priority and should include aid in starting a small business to tap some of the entrepreneurial skills displayed by drug dealers' and suggests that the aid include "job training and credit for those shut out by banks because of their race or lack of connections."[17]

What Harvard University economist Jeffrey Sachs said in 1989 is true today: "It's a tragedy that what appears to be the most promising alternative hasn't been explored. If there were a U.S. commitment, a couple of billion dollars over three or four years, and if it were shown to lead to a significant cut in the supply of cocaine, it would not be much money."[18] It certainly would not be much money, considering the negative economic impact that the futile U.S. War on Drugs has already had, and given the global impact of international drug trafficking. U.S. allies — the wealthier industrialized countries like Japan, Germany, and Great Britain — should be willing to help foot the bill. It will not cost nearly as much as the $12 billion (or $88 billion in today's terms) that the original Marshall Plan cost the Western allies.

Strengthen Economies and Rebuild Institutions

At the same time, the United States should work to strengthen the economies and institutions of producing and transit countries. The Caribbean — through which up to 40 percent of the cocaine and heroin entering the United States moves — is a case in point. The United States has put strong pressure on the Caribbean nations to cooperate in the drug war without giving much in return besides pep talks. U.S. aid to the Caribbean actually dropped from $225 million in 1995 to $26 million in 1996, while the drug trade in the region mushroomed and continued to take its devastating toll on the nations. The United States should provide financial and technical assistance to fight drug trafficking more effectively and look for ways to build trade in the region. For starters, Uncle Sam can work for the integration of the Caribbean countries into a regional trade zone.

Change the Tenor of the Drug Strategy

U.S. policy toward the Caribbean is an example of how the United States has used rhetoric and bullying tactics as ways to get support for its War on Drugs. The United States has pressured many countries to launch their own antinarcotics programs and to allow U.S. officials to operate on their national territory. The United States needs to respect national sovereignty and to practice more diplomacy if it is to get cooperation from those who are essential in combating drug trafficking. A positive diplomatic move, for example, would be to scrap the certification process, which, as we have read, has been unfairly applied and is counterproductive to U.S. foreign policy interests.

The United States should provide more money and assistance to countries like Colombia and Mexico whose judiciary systems have been badly weakened by the brutal and corruptive power of the drug cartels. In Colombia 350 judicial personnel, including 50 judges, were murdered between 1980 and 1992 alone. In 1990 the U.S. began a six-year, $36 million program to enhance the power and autonomy of the Colombian judiciary and make the court system more efficient and the criminal investigative process more effective. U.S. officials say the judicial program has helped Colombia, so this type of program can and should be used elsewhere.[19]

"It has been an effective program in Colombia, Panama, and other Third World countries," explained Myles Frechette, U.S. ambassador to Colombia. "The U.S. has to help train judges, police and investigators in many countries if their justice systems are to work. It's in the U.S.'s best interests."[20] And as the Center for Strategic and International Studies pointed out in a report, "The longer the drug traffickers are allowed to operate relatively unmolested within a society, the more susceptible are the legal institutions to corrosive forces of greed and intimidation."[21]

Study the Drug Policies of Other Countries

Unlike the United States some countries such as Holland, Switzerland, and Great Britain have been willing to experiment to see what kind of drug programs work best for them. Instead of categorically attacking those countries' drug programs, as the United States has done often in the past, study them to see what it can learn and perhaps borrow. Adopting Holland's antidrug program in toto would probably not work in the

United States for a number of reasons, including differences in their histories, national characters, and population, but adopting a policy that makes distinctions between soft drugs (hashish and marijuana) and hard drugs (heroin and cocaine) might make sense after a thorough and critical investigation.

Promote More Drug Research

The National Drug Control Strategy introduced in 1989 by President George Bush called for a "much better understanding of the structure and infrastructure of trafficking organizations and allied enterprises."[22] It is remarkable, though, how little is still known about the international drug trade, the products it distributes and sells, and their effects on consumers. Yet the United States continues to pursue policies that fail.

More money and resources should be provided to help law enforcement get a fuller and better picture of how the sophisticated drug organizations now work. More accountability is in order here, too. For example, there are no published figures on drug-enforcement spending or activities by state and local police, and taxpayers should know that their money is being spent to counter drug trafficking.[23]

Money should also be spent on medical treatment for addiction, both in the United States and abroad. Fortune magazine has estimated that treating every one of the country's drug abusers would cost about $6.5 billion annually—more than half of the federal government's total spending on the drug war."[24] The United States has given resources to fund drug research within major producing and transit countries, but given the scope of the drug problem, the policy should be expanded to include all countries.

Reduce Global Demand

The United States continues to see the drug problem as being caused by foreign countries. Consequently, it has looked for an answer abroad rather than at home. But many drug-producing and transit counties share the view of Andrés Pastrana, a former mayor of Bogotá, and future Colombian president, "The United States is the main problem in the distribution and consumption of drugs. In other words, production is the result of consumption, which means that the criminal element is attracted by the high profits to be made. So it's impossible to stop entirely the export of drugs from Latin America unless the United States takes strict measures to curb consumption."[25]

More research is needed to identify why Americans use and abuse drugs, to spot drug use earlier, and to develop programs to help children resist drugs. Public education is worthwhile, provided it does not become propaganda, for bombarding the public with misinformation will not help the problem. As one writer explained, "Should a teenager, for example, smoke a marijuana cigarette expecting some kind of overwhelming experience and discover that he feels nothing, he will forever after suspect whatever authorities tell him about the drug."[26]

The United States should work to curb global demand by sharing its drug information, the good and the bad, with other countries through such agencies as the National Institute on Drug Abuse and United States Information Agency. In the view of the Center for Strategic and International Studies, the NIDA "should place the highest priority on multinational research that seeks to isolate the socio-cultural aspect of drug consumption, that is, research that analyzes how the social structure and culture interpret and determine drug consumption and treat and prevent drug dependence."[27]

Accept the Basic Principles of Economics

Law enforcement worldwide, of course, should continue to interdict drugs and try to put the drug syndicates out of business, but the ill effects of 15 years of failed antidrug policy can be reversed only by changing priorities and moving from a punitive law-and-order strategy to one that offers more flexibility and stresses harm reduction, not prohibition; treatment, not punishment; and gets at the economic and social roots of the international drug problem.

Waging war has created a black market for narcotics because drug trafficking, as has been pointed out throughout this book, is a business, dominated by the laws of supply and demand. As long as there are huge profits to be made and a huge demand to satisfy, current U.S. policy will undoubtedly fuel the international drug trade and the problems associated with it. The United States will never be able to disrupt the supply line to the point where criminals will find the risks for drug trafficking not worth the rewards, nor the prices high enough so that consumers cannot afford the product. "When a product is made illegal, or a massive escalation of law enforcement takes place, both suppliers and consumers later alter their strategies and the use of their profits in response to the change," wrote Edward J. Nell. " We can expect them to look for new markets and new ways to offset the police efforts."[28]

It is one of ironies of the War on Drugs that conservative advocates of current U.S. antidrug policy, who are always championing the free market and the virtues of capitalism and how it works best with minimal government intervention, fail to acknowledge or admit the harm that government policy has done to the market forces operating in the business of international drug trafficking.

The United States and its allies have spent billion of dollars the past 15 years, put some of the biggest names in the history of organized crime out of business, and imprisoned thousands for drug-related offenses. Yet cocaine, heroin, and marijuana and other illegal drugs still enter the U.S. freely. What is needed is a strong dose of realism, bold vision, and the political will to change course. The U.S. battle against international drug trafficking will get results when the country begins looking at the drug issue in an entirely different way.

Notes

Chapter 1. The Nature of the Beast

1. Peter Slevin, "Outlaw Cowboy Relished His Fame," *Miami Herald*, Dec. 3, 1993.

2. Post, T. and Douglas Walker. "10 Acres, Valley View: A Drug Lord's Jail," *Newsweek*, July 1, 1991, p. 34.

3. *Ibid.*

4. Simon Strong, *Whitewash: Pablo Escobar and the Cocaine Wars* (London: Macmillan, 1995).

5. Interview with Raphael Santos, Bogotá, Colombia, 1988.

6. Interview with a DEA agent, Bogotá, Colombia, 1989.

7. Mary Speck, "Police Kill Escobar During Gun Battle atop Medellin Roof," *Miami Herald*, Dec. 3, 1994.

8. *Ibid.*

9. Elaine Shannon, "New Kings of Cocaine," *Time*, July 1, 1991, p. 30.

10. Interview with Fernando Brito Ruiz, Bogotá, Colombia, 1994.

11. For background on the Cali cartel, see Linda Robinson, "New Target: Cali Cartel," *U.S. News and World Report*, Dec. 23, 1991, pp. 28–29; Tom Morgenthau and others, "Cocaine's 'Dirty' 300," *Newsweek*, Nov. 13, 1989, pp. 36–41; and Elaine Shannon, "The New Kings of Coke," *Time*, July 1, 1991, p. 30.

12. U.S. Senate Committee on Foreign Relations, Subcommittee on Terrorism, Narcotics and International Operations, *Recent Developments in Transnational Crime Affecting U.S. Law Enforcement and Foreign Policy* (Washington, D.C.: U.S. Superintendent of Documents, 20–21 Apr. 1994).

13. For background on Escobar's career and last days on the run, see Simon Strong, *Whitewash: Pablo Escobar and the Cocaine Wars* (London, Eng.: Macmillan, 1995); Guy Gugliotta and Jeff Leen, *Kings of Cocaine* (New York: Harper, 1990); Robert D. McFadden, "Drug Baron Escobar Killed in Shootout," *Charlotte Observer*, Dec. 3, 1993; James Brooke, "Drug Lord Is Buried As Crowd Wails," *New York Times*, Dec. 4, 1993; Mary Speck, "Crowd Mobs Escobar's Funeral," *Miami Herald*, Dec. 4, 1993; Speck, "Police Kill Escobar During Gun Battle atop Medellin Roof," *Miami Herald*, Dec. 3, 1994; and "Thousands Throng Rites for Escobar," *Chicago Tribune*, Dec. 4, 1993.

14. Stephen Ambrus, "Pablo Escobar Dies in Shootout," *Los Angeles Times*, Dec. 3, 1993.

15. Associated Press, "U.S. Warns of Possible Heroin Epidemic," *Rock Hill* (S.C.) *Herald*, Apr. 4, 1994.

16. *Ibid.*

17. For background on the Cali cartel's contribution to heroin, see especially Robert Sabbage, "The Cartels Would Like a Second Chance," *Rolling Stone*, May 4, 1994, pp. 35–38.

18. Associated Press, "U.S. Warns of Possible Heroin Epidemic," *Rock Hill* (S.C.) *Herald*, Apr. 4, 1994.

19. *Ibid.*

20. *Ibid.*

21. Douglas Ferah, et al. "Illicit Dollars Flow via Unique Network," *Washington Post*, Sept. 19, 1993.

22. McFadden, "Drug Baron Escobar Killed."

23. Joseph H. Teaster, "Officials See Efforts to Curb Drug Flow Worsening," *New York Times*, Dec. 4, 1993.

Chapter 2. Reagan Declares War

1. George Shultz, "The Campaign Against Drugs: The International Dimension," *Dept. of State Bulletin*, Nov. 1984, p. 30; for additional information see President's Commission on Organized Crime, *America's Habit: Drug Trafficking and Organized Crime* (Washington, D.C.: U.S. Government Printing Office, 1986), p. 258; Walter J. Stoessel, Jr., "U.S. Policy on International Narcos Control," *Dept. of State Bulletin*, Sept. 1982, p. 46; and Daniel Courtnay, "International Narcotics Control: The Challenge of Our Decade," *Police Chief*, Oct. 1985, p. 42.

2. James Mills, *The Underground Empire: Where Crime and Justice Embrace* (New York: Doubleday, 1986), p. 1120.

3. Shultz, "Campaign Against Drugs," p. 30.

4. H. Wayne Morgan, *Drugs in America: A Social History, 1800–1980* (Syracuse, N.Y.: Syracuse Univ. Press, 1981), p. 16.

5. James Kelly, "Trouble in Paradise," *Time* Nov. 27, 1981, p. 23.

6. Alfred McCoy and Alan A. Block, eds., *War on Drugs: Studies in the Failure of U.S. Narcotics Policy* (Boulder, Colo.: Westview, 1992), p. 264.

7. President's Commission, *America's Habit*, p. 6.

8. David Goody, "A Rite of Passage More Young People Avoid," *Scholastic Update*, May 10, 1985, p. 15; Steven Wisotsky, "Beyond the War on Drugs," in James A. Inciardi, *The Drug Legislation Debate* (Newbury Park, Calif.: Sage, 1991), p. 103.

9. Goody, "A Rite of Passage More Young People Avoid," p. 14.

10. *Ibid.*

11. Guy Gugliotta and Jeff Leen, *Kings of Cocaine* (New York: Harper, 1990), pp. 68–69; and Brian Freemantle, *The Fix*. (London, Eng.: Corgi, 1985), pp. 98–99.

12. *New York Times*. Dec. 4, 1993.

13. Freemantle, *The Fix*, pp. 98–99.

14. Peter Hellman, "Reagan Gets Tough on Drugs," *Rolling Stone*, Apr. 15, 1982, pp. 13.

15. James Kelly, "Trouble in Paradise," *Time*, Nov. 23, 1981, p. 23.

16. Gugliotta and Leen, *Kings of Cocaine*, p. 89.

17. *Ibid.*, p. 88.

18. Kelly, "Trouble in Paradise," p. 23.

19. Freemantle, *The Fix*, p. 99.

20. Peter B. Bensinger, "World Drug Traffic," *Society*, May–June 1982, pp. 78–79.

21. Freemantle, *The Fix*, pp. 308–9.

22. Kelly, "Trouble in Paradise," p. 31.

23. Freemantle, *The Fix*, p. 98.

24. Courtnay, "International Narcotics Control," p. 74.

25. President's Commission on Organized Crime, *The Cash Connection: Organized Crime, Financial Institutions and Money Laundering* (Washington, D.C.: U.S. Government Printing Office, 1984), pp. 39–40.

26. Kelly, "Trouble in Paradise," p. 31.

27. *Ibid.*

28. Mills, *Underground Empire*, Appendix, p. 6.

29. Gugliotta and Leen, *Kings of Cocaine*, p. 89. The South Florida Task Force was also known as Operation Florida.

30. Paul Eddy, Hugh Sabogal, and Sarah Walden, *The Cocaine Wars* (New York: Norton, 1988), pp. 97–98; Freemantle, *The Fix*, p. 101; and Gugliotta and Leen, *Kings of Cocaine*, p. 89.

31. President's Commission, *Cash Connection*, pp. 260 and 284.

32. Peter Hellman, "Reagan Gets Tough on Drugs," p. 14.

33. Mark Starr, "Reagan's War on Drugs," *Newsweek*, Aug. 9, 1982, p. 15.

34. Freemantle, *The Fix*, pp. 102–3.

35. *Ibid.*, p. 103.

36. *Ibid.*

37. Eddy and others, *Cocaine Wars*, p. 98.

38. Starr, "Reagan's War," p. 15.

39. Jeffrey Robinson, *The Laundrymen* (New York: Simon and Schuster, 1990), p. 192.

40. Orr Kelly, "Feds Versus Drug Runners: Game Gets Trickier," *U.S. News and World Report*, Oct. 4, 1982, p. 54.

41. Starr, "Reagan's War," p. 15.

42. Kelly, "Feds vs. Drug Runners," p. 54.

43. *Ibid.*

44. Starr, "Reagan's War," p. 15.

45. Stoessel, "U.S. Policy," p. 46.

Chapter 3. The Birth of the Underground Empire, 1840–1960

1. AFP, "Las Drogas Ganan Terreno en Europa," *Tiempo*, Oct. 9, 1996; Jorge Cardona Alzate, "Catarsis de una Epidemia," *Espectador* Oct. 20, 1996; "Drugs $400 Billion; Second Only to Arms Trade," *Chicago Tribune*, Dec. 15, 1994.

2. H. Wayne Morgan, *Drugs in America: A Social History, 1800–1980* (Syracuse, N.Y.: Syracuse Univ. Press, 1981), pp. 10–28.

3. *Ibid.*, p. 1.

4. *Ibid.*, p. 35.

5. William Weir, *In the Shadow of the Dope Fiend* (North Haven, Conn.: Archon, 1995), p. 9.

6. Morgan, *Drugs in America*, p. 16.

7. Gail B. Stewart, *Drug Trafficking* (San Diego, Calif.: Lucent, 1990), p. 17.

8. Morgan, *Drugs in America*, p. 94.

9. *Ibid.*, p. 29.

10. *Ibid.*, p. 39.

11. President's Commission on Organized Crime, *America's Habit: Drug Trafficking and Organized Crime* (Washington, D.C.: U.S. Government Printing Office, 1986), pp. 188–89.

12. Morgan, *Drugs in America*, p. 30.

13. *Ibid.*, p. 30.

14. Stewart, *Drug Trafficking*, pp. 21–22.

15. Kieran Konderich, "Cocaine Capitalism," in G. Epstein and others, eds., *A New World Economy: Forces of Change and Plans of Action* (Philadelphia: Temple Univ. Press, 1993), p. 127.

16. Weir, *Shadow of the Dope Fiend*, p. 16.

17. David Musto, *The American Disease: Origins of Narcotics Control* (New York: Oxford Univ. Press, 1987), p. 245.

18. *Ibid.*

19. See chapters 3 and 6 in Morgan, *Drugs in America*, for a good discussion of the impact of the Progressive Era on drug attitudes.

20. President's Commission, *America's Habit*, p. 192.

21. Morgan, *Drugs in America*, p. 196.

22. President's Commission, *America's Habit*, p. 195.

23. *Ibid.*, p. 196.

24. Brian Inglis, *The Forbidden Game: A Social History of Drugs* (New York: Scribner's, 1975), pp. 178–79.

25. Dennis J. Kenney and James O. Finckenauer, *Organized Crime in America* (London,: International Thompson, 1990), p. 144.

26. James Traub, *The Billion Dollar Connection: The International Drug Trade* (New York: Julian Messner, 1983), p. 20.

27. Jill Jones, "Founding Father: One Man Invented the Modern Narcotics Industry," *American Heritage*, Feb.-Mar. 1993, pp. 48–49.

28. *Ibid.*, p. 49.

29. Stephen Walsh, "Some Aspects of the International Drug Trafficking," in Dennis Rowe, ed., *International Drug Trafficking* (Chicago: Univ. of Illinois at Chicago, Office of International Criminal Justice, 1988), p. 102.

30. Morgan, *Drugs in America*, p. 144.

31. Alan Howell Moorhead, "International Narcotics Control, 1939–1946," *Foreign Policy Reports*, July 1, 1946, pp. 94–103.

32. Morgan, *Drugs in America*, p. 144.

33. Weir, *Shadow of the Dope Fiend*, p. 52.

34. Traub, *Billion Dollar Connection*, pp. 26–27.

35. Morgan, *Drugs in America*, p. 145.

36. President's Commission, *America's Habit*, p. 208.

37. President's Commission on Organized Crime, *The Cash Connection: Organized Crime, Financial Institutions and Money Laundering* (Washington, D.C.: U.S. Government Printing Office, 1984), pp. 212–13.

38. Morgan, *Drugs in America*, p. 147.

Chapter 4. America Rediscovers the Drug Habit, 1960–1980

1. Simon Strong, *Whitewash: Pablo Escobar and the Cocaine Wars* (London: Macmillan, 1995), p. 37.

2. Ron Chepesiuk, *Sixties Radicals, Then and Now: Candid Conversations with Those Who Shaped an Era* (Jefferson, N.C.: McFarland, 1995), p. 305.

3. *Ibid.*, pp. 247 and 251.

4. H. Wayne Morgan, *Drugs in America: A Social History, 1800–1980* (Syracuse, N.Y.: Syracuse Univ. Press, 1981), p. 164.

5. President's Commission on Organized Crime, *America's Habit: Drug Trafficking and Organized Crime* (Washington, D.C.: U.S. Government Printing Office, 1986), p. 215.

6. Brian Inglis, *The Forbidden Game: A Social History of Drugs* (New York: Scribner's, 1975), pp. 198–99.

7. President's Commission, *America's Habit*, pp. 216–17.

8. *Ibid.*, p. 220.

9. *Ibid.*, p. 226.

10. Chepesiuk, *Sixties Radicals*, p. 69.

11. Morgan, *Drugs in America*, p. 161.

12. Inglis, *Forbidden Game*, pp. 188–89.

13. Claire Sterling, *Octopus: The Long Rule of the International Sicilian Mafia* (New York: W. W. Norton, 1990), p. 147.

14. Michael Lyman, *Gangland: Drug Trafficking by Organized Criminals* (Springfield, Ill.: Charles C Thomas, 1989), p. 43; President's Commission, *America's Habit*, pp. 111–12.

15. Lyman, *Gangland*, p. 41; President's Commission, *America's Habit*, pp. 111–12.

16. President's Commission, *America's Habit*, pp. 77–78.

17. Jessica de Grazia, *DEA: The War Against Drugs* (London, Eng.: BBC Books, 1991), p. 13.

18. James Traub, *The Billion Dollar Connection: The International Drug Trade* (New York: Julian Messner, 1983), p. 27.

19. *Ibid.*, p. 9.

20. Stanley Karnow, *Vietnam: A History* (New York: Viking, 1983), p. 631.

21. *Ibid.*, p. 440.

22. For an in-depth study of this theme, see Alfred J. McCoy, *The Politics of Heroin: CIA Complicity in the Global Drug Trade* (Brooklyn, N.Y.: Laurence Hill, 1991).

23. Jay Robert Nash, *World Encyclopedia of Organized Crime* (New York: Marlow, 1994), pp. 145–46.

24. Inglis, *Forbidden Game*, pp. 196.

25. William Weir, *In the Shadow of the Dope Fiend* (North Haven, Conn.: Archon, 1995), p. 64.

26. Alfred J. McCoy, "What War on Drugs? The CIA Connection," *Progressive*, July 1991, p. 26.

27. Weir, *Shadow of the Dope Fiend*, p. 65.

28. McCoy, "What War?" p. 26.

29. Catherine Lamour and Michael R. Lamberti, *The International Connection: Opium from Growers to Pushers* (New York: Pantheon, 1974), p. 60.

30. *Ibid.*

31. President's Commission, *America's Habit*, p. 230.

32. *Ibid.*, p. 233.

33. Lamour and Lamberti, *International Connection*, p. 60.

34. *Ibid.*, p. 104.

35. President's Commission, *America's Habit*, p. 234.

36. *Ibid.*, p. 237.

37. Alfred J. McCoy and Alan A. Block, "U.S. Narcotics Policy: An Anatomy of Failure," in McCoy and Block, eds., *War on Drugs: Studies in the Failure of U.S. Narcotics Policy* (Boulder, Colo.: Westview, 1992), p. 14.

38. Traub, *The Billion Dollar Connection*, p. 76.

39. Inglis, *Forbidden Game*, p. 190.

40. James A. Inciardi, *The Drug Legislation Debate* (Newbury Park, Calif.: Sage, 1991), p. 147.

41. Inglis, *Forbidden Game*, p. 190.

42. De Grazia, *DEA*, p. 12.

43. Inciardi, *Drug Legislation*, p. 147.

44. Morgan, *Drugs in America*, p. 155.

45. President's Commission, *America's Habit*, pp. 134–36.

46. *Ibid.*, pp. 136–37.

47. *Ibid.*, p. 137.

48. De Grazia, *DEA*, p. 12.

49. *Ibid.*

50. *Ibid.*

51. McCoy and Block, "U.S. Narcotics Policy," p. 94.

52. McCoy, "What War?" p. 26.

53. *Ibid.*, p. 22.

54. President's Commission, *America's Habit*, p. 229.

Chapter 5. Full of Sound and Fury, 1980–1990

1. "Drug War Begins," *CQ Researcher*, Mar. 19, 1993, p. 251.

2. President's Commission on Organized Crime, *America's Habit: Drug Trafficking and Organized Crime* (Washington, D.C.: U.S. Government Printing Office, 1986), p. 1967.

3. President's Commission on Organized Crime, *America's Habit: Drug*

Trafficking and Organized Crime (Washington, D.C.: U.S. Government Printing Office, 1986), p. 1967.

4. President's Commission, *America's Habit*, pp. 270–71.

5. *Ibid.*, p. 269.

6. *Ibid.*, pp. 272–73, 276–80.

7. *Ibid.*, p. 327.

8. Maura, Christopher, "How the U.S. Battles Drugs on Three Fronts" *Scholastic Update*, May 10, 1985, p. 6.

9. "Drug War Begins," *CO Researcher*, Mar. 19, 1993, p. 251.

10. For insight into the impact on Colombia of this episode in the country's history, see Paul Eddy, Hugh Sabogal, and Sarah Walden, *The Cocaine Wars* (New York: Norton, 1988), pp. 285–301; Guy Gugliotta and Jeff Leen, *Kings of Cocaine* (New York: Harper, 1990), pp. 129–89; and Simon Strong, *Whitewash: Pablo Escobar and the Cocaine Wars* (London, Eng.: Macmillan, 1995), pp. 138–61.

11. Gugliotta and Leen, *Kings of Cocaine*, p. 148.

12. President's Commission, *America's Habit*, Appendix, p. 9.

13. Gugliotta and Leen, *Kings of Cocaine*, p. 156.

14. President's Commission, *America's Habit*, Appendix, p. 9.

15. *Ibid.*

16. Bruce Bagley, "The New Hundred Years War? U.S. National Security and the War on Drugs," *Journal of Interamerican Studies and World Affairs*, Spring 1988, p. 164.

17. William Weir, *In the Shadow of the Dope Fiend* (North Haven, Conn.: Archon, 1995), p. 83.

18. For a detailed and insightful investigation of the Contra chapter in the War on Drugs, see Peter Dale Scott and Johnathan Marshall, *Cocaine Politics, Drugs, Armies and the CIA in Central America* (Los Angeles: Univ. of California Press, 1991).

19. Eddy and others, *Cocaine Wars*, p. 335.

20. U.S. Senate Committee on Foreign Relations, Subcommittee on Terrorism, Narcotics and International Operations, *Report: Drugs, Law Enforcement and Foreign Policy* (Washington, D.C.: U.S. Government Printing Office, 1989), p. 41. (Hereafter cited as the Kerry Report.)

21. Bagley, "New Hundred Years War?" p. 164.

22. Kieran Konderich, "Cocaine Capitalism," in G. Epstein and others, eds., *A New World Economy: Forces of Change and Plans of Action* (Philadelphia: Temple Univ. Press, 1993), p. 122.

23. Bagley, "New Hundred Years War?" p. 168.

24. *Ibid.*, p. 167.

25. *Ibid.*, p. 173.

26. *Ibid.*, p. 161.

27. James A. Inciardi, "American Drug Policy and the Legalization Debate," in Inciardi, *The Drug Legislation Debate* (Newbury Park, Calif.: Sage, 1991), p. 85.

28. Doniphan Blair, "Drug War Delusions, Unrealistic, Infeasible and Logistical Nightmare," *Humanist*, Sept.-Oct. 1990, p. 7.

29. Robert Wagman, "Bennett Shifts Focus of Drug War," *Rock Hill* (S.C.) *Herald*, Aug. 21, 1989.

30. Michael T. Klare, "Fighting Drugs with the Military," *Nation*, Jan. 1, 1990, p. 8.

31. Strong, *Whitewash*, p. 52.

32. Kerry Report, pp. 169–70.

33. Strong, *Whitewash*, p. 52.

34. Charles Edward Anderson, "Fighting the International Drug War," *ABA Journal*, Jan. 1991, p. 24.

35. Stephen J. Hedges and Gordon Witkin, "Kidnapping Drug Lords," *U.S. News and World Report*, May 14, 1990, p. 28.

36. *Ibid*, p. 30.

37. Bruce Bagley, "Dateline Drug Wars: Colombia: The Wrong Strategy," *Foreign Policy*, Winter 1989–1990, p. 155.

38. Jay Robert Nash, *World Encyclopedia of Organized Crime* (New York: Marlow, 1994), p. 159.

39. *Ibid*., p. 160.

40. Bagley, "Dateline Drug Wars," pp. 155–56.

41. David Isenberg, "Military Options in the War on Drugs," *USA Today*, July 7, 1990.

42. Klare, "Fighting Drugs with the Military," p. 8.

43. Isenberg, "Military Options," p. 24.

44. Donald J. Mabry, "The U.S. Military and the War on Drugs," in Bruce Bagley and William O. Walker III, eds., *Drug Trafficking in the Americas* (New Brunswick, N.J.: Transaction, 1994), p. 44.

45. Isenberg, "Military Options," p. 26.

46. Konderich, "Cocaine Capitalism," p. 123.

47. Alfred J. McCoy and Alan A. Block, "U.S. Narcotics Policy: An Anatomy of Failure," in McCoy and Block, eds., *War on Drugs: Studies in the Failure of U.S. Narcotics Policy* (Boulder, Colo.: Westview, 1992), p. 2.

48. *Ibid*., p. 4.

49. Konderich, "Cocaine Capitalism," p. 123.

Chapter 6. The Longest War, 1990–1997

1. James Baker, "Narcotics: Threat to Global Security," *U.S. Dept. of State Dispatch*, Sept. 3, 1990, p. 15.

2. *Ibid*., p. 16.

3. Bruce Bagley, "The New Hundred Years War? U.S. National Security and the War on Drugs," *Journal of Interamerican Studies and World Affairs*, Spring 1988, p. 171.

4. William O. Walker III, "The Bush Administration's Andean Drug Strategy in Historical Perspective," in Bruce Bagley and William O. Walker III, eds., *Drug Trafficking in the Americas* (New Brunswick, N.J.: Transaction, 1994), p. 2.

5. Baker, "Narcotics Threat," p. 16.

6. Todd Lippin, "Drug War Versus Development," *Technology Review*, Jan. 1991, p. 19.

7. "Andean Trade Pact of 1991," *U.S. News and World Report*, Mar. 2, 1992, p. 166.

8. Peter Andreas, "Cocaine Chemistry," *New Republic*, Nov. 20, 1989, p. 12.

9. Linda Feldman, "By Keeping the Chemicals Flowing, American Business Kept the Cocaine Cartels in Business," *Rolling Stone*, Nov. 1, 1990, p. 44.

10. Andreas, "Cocaine Chemistry," p. 13.

11. David J. Hanson, "Chemical Industry, Drug Agency Sort Out Chemical Diversion Issues," *Chemical and Engineering News*, Jan. 29, 1990, p. 18.

12. "Fact Sheet: Controlling Chemicals Used in Drug Trafficking," *U.S. Dept. of State Dispatch*, Mar. 2, 1992, p. 164.

13. Hanson, "Chemical Diversion Issues," p. 18.

14. "CMA Defends Industry on Drug Charges," *Chemical Marketing Reporter*, Feb. 12, 1990, p. 3.

15. Hanson, "Chemical Diversion Issues," p. 18.

16. Joseph B. Teaster, "Federal Agents Track Down a Rural Cocaine Factory," *New York Times*, Oct. 5, 1991.

17. Guy Gugliotta and Jeff Leen, *Kings of Cocaine* (New York: Harper, 1990), p. 66.

18. James Painter, "Colombians Elbow In on Bolivian Drug Trade," *Christian Science Monitor*, Dec. 10, 1991.

19. *Ibid.*

20. Douglas Farah, "Drug Traffickers Build Central American Route to U.S.," *Washington Post*, Mar. 28, 1993.

21. David R. Dye, "Nicaraguan Cocaine Bust Reveals New Cartel Route," *Christian Science Monitor*, Jan. 26, 1994.

22. *Ibid.*

23. *Ibid.*

24. Tom Morgenthau and Douglas Waller, "The Widening Drug War," *Newsweek*, July 1, 1991, pp. 32.

25. Gail B. Stewart, *Drug Trafficking* (San Diego, Calif.: Lucent, 1990), p. 59.

26. U.S. General Accounting Office, "Drug Control: Threats and Roles of Explosives and Narcotics Technology: Briefing Report to Congressional Requesters" (Washington, D.C.: General Accounting Office, Mar. 1996), p. 15.

27. President's Commission on Organized Crime, *America's Habit: Drug Trafficking and Organized Crime* (Washington, D.C.: U.S. Government Printing Office, 1986), p. 84.

28. Daniel Machalaba, "Deadly Cargo," *Wall Street Journal*, May 18, 1989.

29. U.S. GAO, "Explosives and Technology," p. 15.

30. *Ibid.*

31. President's Commission, *America's Habit*, p. 97.

32. Abe Dane, "High Tech Drug Busters," *Popular Mechanics*, Feb. 1990, p. 49.

33. John Rhea, "High Technology's Growing Role in War on Drugs," *USA Today*, Nov. 6, 1978.

34. Jim McGhee, "Drug Cartel's Calls Are Key to U.S. Case," *Charlotte Observer*, Jan. 7, 1995.

35. Gordon Witkin, "New Drug Warriors: Lasers, Labs and Coke Eating Bugs," *U.S. News and World Report*, Feb. 19, 1990, p. 21.

36. Bruce Bagley, "After San Antonio," in Bruce Bagley and William O. Walker III, eds., *Drug Trafficking in the Americas* (New Brunswick, N.J.: Transaction, 1994), p. 69.

37. Don Podesta and Douglas Farah, "Drug Policy in the Andes," *Washington Post*, Mar. 27, 1993.

38. Michael Isikoff, "U.S. Considers Shift in Drug War," *Washington Post*, Sept. 16, 1993.

39. Byron York, "Clinton's Phony Drug War," *American Spectator*, Feb. 1994, p. 42.

40. U.S. GAO, "Explosives and Technology," p. 18.

41. Joseph B. Teaster, "Pentagon Plans Shift in War on Drug Traffickers," *New York Times*, Oct. 29, 1993.

42. U.S. GAO, "Explosives and Technology," p. 3.

43. Christopher Wren, "New International Strategy to Combat Drugs," *U.S. Dept. of State Dispatch*, Feb. 21, 1994, p. 89.

44. Joseph B. Teaster, "Exiting Drug Chief Warns of Cartels," *New York Times*, Oct. 31, 1993.

45. Bagley, "After San Antonio," p. 71.

46. York, "Clinton's Phony Drug War," p. 42.

47. *Ibid.*

48. U.S. General Accounting Office, *Drug Control: U.S. Interdiction Efforts in the Caribbean Decline* (Washington, D.C.: General Accounting Office, Apr. 1996), p. 2.

49. Ko-lin Chin, *Chinese Subculture and Criminality* (Westport, Conn.: Greenwood Press, 1990), pp. 112, 148.

50. See chapter 12 for more information on the Colombian cartels.

51. U.S. GAO, "Interdiction Efforts," p. 2.

52. Rachel L. Jones, "Cocaine, Pot Use Soars among Young,"

53. Robin Toner, "Parties Seek to Cast Blame for Rise in Teenage Drug Use," *New York Times*, Aug. 22, 1996; Kevin Johnson, "Political Rhetoric Escalates over Teenage Drug Use," *USA Today*, Sept. 5, 1996.

54. Mauricio Bayona Vargas, "Clinton Reparte los Dolores," *Espectador*, Sept. 25, 1996.

55. George J. Church, "The War Against Drugs Turns Nasty," *Time*, Sept. 30, 1996, p. 23.

56. Toner, "Cast Blame."

57. Andre Cavelier Castro, "Droga: Debate Artificial en E.U.," *Tiempo*, Sept. 14, 1996.

58. Patrick May, "Illicit Drug Trade Booming," *Miami Herald* (International Satellite Edition), Sept. 8, 1996.

59. José de Cordoba, "Ex-General Venezolano: La CIA Aprobó Envío de Cocaína a EE.UU.," *Tiempo*, Nov. 22, 1996; Tim Wener, "Anti-Drug Unit of CIA Sends Tons of Cocaine to U.S.," *New York Times*, Nov. 20, 1993; Geraldo Reyes and Jeff Leen, "One-time Venezuela Guard Chief Indicted on Drug Counts in the U.S.," *Miami Herald* (International Satellite Edition), Nov. 23, 1996.

60. Marcelo Sanchez Fonseca, "CIA: Traficantes de Cocaína," *El Tiempo*, Sept. 22, 1996; Thomas Farragher, "Ex Contra Chief Scoffs at CIA Drug Link," *Miami Herald* (International Satellite Edition), Nov. 27, 1996.

61. Associated Press, "Colombian Pushing Anti-Drug Plan," *Miami Herald* (International Satellite Edition), Dec. 2, 1996.

62. "New Drug Strategy Needed," *Colombian Post*, Nov. 18–24, 1996.

63. Rob Schulteis, "Chinese Junk: My Search for the Red Tiger General," *Mother Jones*, Mar. 1982, pp. 40–41.

Chapter 7. The Changing Face of International Drug Trafficking

1. Claire Sterling, *Thieves' World: The Threat of the New Global Network of Organized Crime* (New York: Simon and Schuster, 1994), p. 142.

2. Michael Lyman, *Gangland: Drug Trafficking by Organized Criminals* (Springfield, Ill.: Charles C Thomas, 1989).

3. President's Commission on Organized Crime, *America's Habit: Drug Trafficking and Organized Crime* (Washington, D.C.: U.S. Government Printing Office, 1986), p. 5.

4. *Ibid.*

5. Dennis Rowe, ed., *International Drug Trafficking* (Chicago: Univ. of Illinois at Chicago, Office of International Criminal Justice, 1988).

6. Robert J. Kelly, "Organized Crime: Past, Present, and Future," *USA Today Magazine*, May 1992, p. 80.

7. William Kleinknecht, *The New Ethnic Mobs: The Changing Face of Organized Crime in America* (New York: Free Press, 1996), p. 6.

8. Jack Seamonds, "Ethnic Groups and Organized Crime," *U.S. News and World Report*, June 18, 1988, p. 30.

9. *Ibid.*, p. 29.

10. Sterling, *Thieves' World*, p. 150.

11. Frank Viviano and Holly Lloyd, "The New Mafia Order," *Mother Jones*, May-June 1995, pp. 44–45.

12. Stephen Handelman, "The Russian Mafia," *Foreign Affairs*, March 19994, p. 86.

13. Stephen Handelman, *Comrade Criminal: Russia's New Mafiai* (New Haven, Conn:, Yale University Press, 1995) p. 49.

14. The term "Russian Mafia" can be misleading, since it includes gangs from the former Soviet republics and Eastern European countries.

15. Sterling, *Thieves' World*, p. 160.

16. Dennis Wagner, "Crackdown Shifted Drug Trafficking to Mexico," *Colombian Post*, Nov. 18–24, 1996.

17. Kleinknecht, *New Ethnic Mobs*, p. 7; Seamonds, "Ethnic Groups," p. 35.

18. Kleinknecht, *New Ethnic Mobs*, p. 11.

19. Estrada, Lows, "Renegades in the Drug World: A Look with Jamaican Posses," *Times of the Americas*, June 26, 1991, p. 17.

20. Journalist Manuel de Dios Unanue was gunned down in a restaurant in Queens, New York, on March 11, 1992. José Santacruz Londono, one of the leaders of the Cali cartel, was later implicated as the mastermind of the killing.

Chapter 8. Octopus: The Powerful Reach of the Sicilian Mafia

1. Italians compare the Sicilian Mafia to the *piovra*, or octopus, in that like the octopus the crime syndicate has the remarkable capacity to regenerate a limb that has been damaged. It should also be noted that Italy is also home to two other major Mafias: the Camorra and the N'Drangheta. In terms of international drug trafficking, especially its impact on the U.S., the Sicilian Mafia is the one that has dominated.

2. Michael Lyman, *Gangland: Drug Trafficking by Organized Criminals* (Springfield, Ill.: Charles C Thomas, 1989), p. 26; Nicholas Gage, "A Tale of Two Mafias," *U.S. News and World Report*, Jan. 18, 1988, p. 36; Sean M. McWeeney, "The Sicilian Mafia and Its Impact on the United States," *FBI Law Enforcement Bulletin*, Feb. 1997, pp. 1–10.

3. Lyman, *Gangland*, p. 26.

4. Pennsylvania Crime Commission, *1985 Report* (Comshohocken, Penn.: Commonwealth of Pennsylvania, 1985), p. 16.

5. McWeeney, "Sicilian Mafia," p. 6.

6. Claire Sterling, *Octopus: The Long Reach of the International Sicilian Mafia* (New York: W. W. Norton, 1990), p. 187.

7. Sterling, *Octopus*, p. 45.

8. John J. Navone, "Italy's Re-Renaissance," *America*, Dec. 9, 1989, p. 417.

9. McWeeney, "Sicilian Mafia," p. 6; Gage, "Two Mafias," p. 36.

10. Lyman, *Gangland*, p. 27.

11. McWeeney, "Sicilian Mafia," pp. 6–7.

12. Sterling, *Octopus*, p. 45.

13. McWeeney, "Sicilian Mafia," p. 8.

14. *Ibid.*, p. 10.

15. Jay Robert Nash, *World Encyclopedia of Organized Crime* (New York: Marlow, 1994), p. 266.

16. Sterling, *Octopus*, p. 49.

17. President's Commission on Organized Crime *The Impact of Organized Crime Today* (Washington, D.C.: U.S. Government Printing Office, 1986), p. 52.

18. Sterling, *Octopus*, p. 53.

19. McWeeney, "Sicilian Mafia," p. 4.

20. *Ibid.*

21. Sterling, *Octopus*, p. 80.

22. *Ibid.*, p. 85.

23. McWeeney, "Sicilian Mafia," p. 5.

24. *Ibid.*

25. President's Commission, *Impact*, pp. 57–58.

26. *Ibid.*, p. 87.

27. McWeeney, "Sicilian Mafia," p. 8.

28. Pino Arlacchi, *Men of Dishonor: Inside the Sicilian Mafia: An Account of Antonio Calderone* (New York: William Morrow, 1993), p. 5.

29. McWeeney, "Sicilian Mafia," p. 9.

30. *Ibid.*

31. Pia Hinckle, "The Grip of the Octopus," *Newsweek*, June 8, 1992, p. 36.

32. Sterling, *Octopus*, p. 288.

33. Hinckle, "Grip of the Octopus," p. 36.

34. Hinckle, "Grip of the Octopus," p. 36; Rachel Ehrenfeld, "The Sicilian," *Newsweek*, June 8, 1992, p. 36.

35. Alexander Stille, "The Mafia's Biggest Mistake," *New Yorker*, Mar. 1, 1993, p. 66.

36. "Roots Run Deep," *Economist*, Jan. 16, 1993, p. 49.

37. John Rossant, "The Cleanup of Italy, Inc.," *Business Week*, Mar. 1, 1993, p. 50.

38. "Is the Mafia in Retreat or in Defeat?" *Economist*, July 29, 1995, p. 33.

39. "The Mafia Again," *Economist*, Mar. 11, 1995, p. 54.

40. Claire Sterling, *Thieves' World: The Threat of the New Global Network of Organized Crime* (New York: Simon and Schuster, 1994), p. 144.

41. *Ibid.*, p. 43.

Chapter 9. The Italian America Mafia: On the Ropes, but Not Out

1. Robert J. Kelly, ed., *Organized Crime: A Global Perspective* (Totowa, N.J.: Rowman and Littlefield, 1986), p. 8.

2. Oliver Cyrix, *Crime: An Encyclopedia* (North Pomfert, Vt.: Trafalgar Square, 1995), p. 248.

3. Cyrix, *Crime*, p. 249.

4. President's Commission on Organized Crime, *The Impact of Organized Crime Today* (Washington, D.C.: U.S. Government Printing Office, 1986), p. 36.

5. *Ibid.*, p. 37.

6. *Ibid.*, p. 45.

7. Arnold H. Lubasch, "Drug Dealing Was Banned by Mob, U.S. Witness Says," *New York Times*, Apr. 15, 1993.

8. Peter Reuter, "The Decline of the American Mafia," *Public Interest*, Summer 1995, p. 91.

9. President's Commission, *Impact*, p. 126.

10. *Ibid.*, p. 124.

11. Reuter, "Decline," p. 92.

12. Michael Massing, "The New Mafia," *New York Review of Books*, Dec. 3, 1992, p. 6.

13. Stephen R. Fox, *Blood and Power: Organized Crime in Twentieth Century America* (New York: William Morrow, 1989), p. 397.

14. President's Commission, *Impact*, p. 126.

15. *Ibid.*

16. *Ibid.*

17. Fox, *Blood and Power*, p. 405.

18. Edward Conlon, "Mob Stories," *American Spectator*, Nov. 1992, p. 78.

19. Jay Robert Nash, *World Encyclopedia of Organized Crime* (New York: Marlow, 1994), p. 195.

20. Conlon, "Mob Stories," p. 33.

21. "The Mob: Hit Hard but Still a Force," *U.S. News and World Report*, May 25, 1996, p. 32.

22. George Anastasia, "That Last Civil War," *Playboy*, Sept. 1994, pp. 68.

23. *Ibid.*, p. 150.

24. Reuter, "Decline," p. 97.

25. *Ibid.*

26. Edward Conlon, "Mob Stories," *American Spectator*, Nov. 1992, p. 78.

27. Kelly, *Organized Crime: A Global Perspective*, p. 8.

28. President's Commission, *Impact*, p. 34.

Chapter 10. The Heroin Connection: Generals, Warlords and Guerrillas of South Asia

1. Bertil Lintner, "Khun Sa: Asian Drug King on the Run," *Far Eastern Economic Review*, Jan. 20, 1994, p. 23.

2. *Ibid.*, p. 22.

3. U.S. General Accounting Office, *Drug Control: U.S. Heroin Program Encounters Many Obstacles in Southeast Asia* (Washington, D.C.: General Accounting Office, Mar. 1, 1996), p. 2; William Branigan, "Sting Snares Asian Drug Ring, but Mass Heroin Flows to U.S.," *Washington Post*, Dec. 12, 1993.

4. Jon A. Wiant, "Narcotics in the Golden Triangle," *Washington Quarterly*, Feb. 1985, pp. 125–26; Jay Robert Nash, *World Encyclopedia of Organized Crime* (New York: Marlow, 1994), p. 145, s.v. "Golden Triangles."

5. See U.S. GAO, *Heroin Program Obstacles*, for a discussion of the Chinese connection.

6. Oliver Cyrix, *Crime: An Encyclopedia* (North Pomfret, Vt.: Trafalgar Square, 1995), p. 47.

7. Mary Cooper, *The Business of Drugs* (Washington, D.C.: Congressional Quarterly, 1990), pp. 50–51.

8. *Ibid.*, p. 52–53.

9. *Ibid.*, p. 52.

10. Mark Pownall, *Heroin* (Oxford, Eng.: Heinemann, 1991), pp. 10–11.

11. Peter Huston, *Tongs, Gangs, and Triads: Chinese Crime Gangs in North America* (Boulder, Colo.: Paladin, 1995), p. 188.

12. Gerald Posner, *Warlords of Crime: Chinese Secret Societies — The New Mafia* (New York: McGraw-Hill, 1988), p. 62.

13. *Ibid.*

14. U.S. GAO, *Heroin Program Obstacles*, p. 3.

15. *Ibid.*

16. Casandra Burrell, "U.S. Demand for Heroin Growing," *Colombian Post*, Feb. 10–16, 1997.

17. Jay Robert Nash, *World Encyclopedia of Organized Crime* (New York: Marlow, 1994), p. 145, s.v. "Golden Triangle."

18. Wiant, "Narcotics in the Golden Triangle," pp. 131–36.

19. U.S. GAO, *Heroin Program Obstacles*, p. 9.

20. Wiant, "Narcotics in the Golden Triangle," pp. 125.

21. Bertil Lintner, "Hooked on the Junta: U.S. Drug Policy Assailed for Links to Burmese Generals," *Far Eastern Economic Review*, Nov. 18, 1993, p. 23.

22. U.S. GAO, *Heroin Program Obstacles*, pp. 8–9.

23. *Ibid.*

24. *Ibid.*

25. *Ibid.*, p. 12.

26. Michael D. Kelley, *Gangland: Drug Trafficking by Organized Criminals.* (Vancouver, Wash.: Charles C Thomas, 1988), p. 114.

27. *Ibid.*

28. Lifschultz, "Bush, Drugs and Pakistan: Inside the Kingdom of Heroin," *Nation*, Nov. 14, 1987, pp. 492, 494–96.

29. *Ibid.*

30. *Ibid.*

31. Marcus W. Brauchli, "Pakistan's Wild Frontier Breeds Trouble," *Wall Street Journal*, June 3, 1993.

32. John Ward Anderson and Molly Moore, "Pervasive Heroin Traffic Putting Production at Risk," *Washington Post*, Apr. 29, 1993.

33. Grant Peck, "McCaffrey Sees Case for Asian Cooperation," *Miami Herald* (International Satellite Edition), Nov. 24, 1996.

Chapter 11. The Chinese Connection: Triads, Tongs, and Street Gangs

1. See chapter 15 for an in-depth discussion of the Nigerian connection to international drug trafficking.

2. U.S. General Accounting Office, *Drug Control: U.S. Heroin Program Encounters Many Obstacles in Southeast Asia* (Washington, D.C.: General Accounting Office, Mar. 1, 1996), p. 12.

3. Stanley Penn, "Asian Connection," *Wall Street Journal*, Mar. 22, 1990.

4. "Chinese Mafia Takes Vice Abroad," *Insight,* Apr. 24, 1989, p. 71.

5. Ko-lin Chin, *Chinese Subculture and Criminality* (Westport, Conn.: Greenwood Press, 1990), pp. 148–49.

6. Peter Kerr, "Chinese Dominate New York Heroin Trade," *New York Times*, Aug. 9, 1987.

7. U.S. Senate Committee on Foreign Relations, Subcommittee on Terrorism, Narcotics and International Operations, *Recent Developments in Transnational Crime Affecting U.S. Law Enforcement and Foreign Policy* (Washington, D.C.: U.S. Superintendent of Documents, 20–21 Apr. 1994).

8. The term "Triad" refers to the triangle symbol used by traditional Chinese secret societies to signify the unity of Man, Earth, and Heaven, the three basic forces of nature for the Chinese.

9. Michael Lyman, *Gangland: Drug Trafficking by Organized Criminals* (Springfield, Ill.: Charles C Thomas, 1989), p. 117; President's Commission on Organized Crime, *The Impact of Organized Crime Today* (Washington, D.C.: U.S. Government Printing Office, 1986), p. 82.

10. President's Commission, *Impact*, p. 82.

11. Gerald Posner, *Warlords of Crime: Chinese Secret Soceites — The New Mafia* (New York: McGraw-Hill, 1988), pp. 72–73.

12. Dennis J. Kenney and James O. Finckenauer, *Organized Crime in America* (London, Eng.: International Thompson, 1990), p. 257.

13. Lyman, *Gangland*, p. 119.

14. "Chinese Mafia Takes Vice Abroad," *Insight*, Apr. 24, 1989, p. 72.

15. *Ibid.*

16. Richard Cole, "Asian Gangs a Rising Threat," *Chicago Tribune*, July 6, 1994; Philippe Pons, "China's Gang of Choice," *World Press Review*, Feb. 1994, p. 51; T. J. English, "Hong Kong Outlaws," *Playboy*, Nov. 1992, p. 169.

17. Fox Butterfield, "Chinese Organized Crime Said to Rise in U.S.," *New York Times*, Jan. 13, 1985.

18. U.S. Senate Committee, *Recent Developments in Transnational Crime*, p. 147.

19. Ko-lin, *Chinese Subculture*, p. 39.

20. Hodding Carter III, "Day of the Triads," *M Inc.*, June 1991, p. 73.

21. "Chinese Triads Pushing the Mafia Aside: Focusing on Heroin Smuggling, Extortion," *Organized Crime Digest*, Aug. 9, 1989, p. 4.

22. President's Commission, *Impact*, p. 83.

23. Ko-lin, *Chinese Subculture*, p. 38.

24. "Chinese Triads Pushing the Mafia Aside," p. 4.

25. Carter, "Day of the Triads," p. 68.

26. William Kleinknecht, *The New Ethnic Mobs: The Changing Face of Organized Crime in America* (New York: Free Press, 1996), p. 47.

27. Kenney and Finckenauer, *Organized Crime in America*, p. 257; Ko-lin, *Chinese Subculture*, p. 215.

28. Kevin Sack, "26 Members of Chinese-American Groups in Atlanta Indicted," *New York Times*, Feb. 6, 1996.

29. *Ibid.*

30. *Ibid.*

31. *Ibid.*, p. 214; R. T. Kelly, *Handbook of Organized Crime in the United States* (Westport, Conn.: Greenwood Press, 1994), p. 214.

32. Ko-lin, *Chinese Subculture*, p. 228.

33. Carter, "Day of the Triads," p. 72.

34. U.S. Senate Committee on Governmental Affairs, *Asian Organized Crime* (Washington, D.C.: U.S. Government Printing Office, 1992), p. 2.

35. Ko-lin, *Chinese Subculture*, pp. 152–53.

36. *Ibid.*, p. 153.

Chapter 12. Linchpin: The Colombian Connection

1. *Time*, *Newsweek*, the *New York Times*, the *Los Angeles Times*, and other major news organizations have quoted these percentages, based on DEA estimates. See also Bruce Bagley, "Dateline Drug Wars: Colombia: The Wrong Strategy," *Foreign Policy*, Winter 1989–1990, p. 154.

2. Associated Press, "U.S. Warns of Possible Heroin Epidemic," *Rock Hill* (S.C.) *Herald*, Apr. 4, 1994.

3. Interview with Jorge Graitman, Bogotá, Colombia, 1987.

4. Michael Lyman, *Gangland: Drug Trafficking by Organized Criminals* (Springfield, Ill.: Charles C Thomas, 1989), p. 38.

5. Edmundo Morales, "The Andean Cocaine Dilemma," in Bruce Bagley and William O. Walker III, eds., *Drug Trafficking in the Americas* (New Brunswick, N.J.: Transaction, 1994), pp. 77–97.

6. Francisco E. Thoumi, "The Size of the Illegal Drug Industry," in Bagley and Walker, eds., *Drug Trafficking*, pp. 37–59.

7. Ron Chepesiuk, "The Colombian Connection: Its Source, Distribution and Impact," *Journal of Defense and Diplomacy*, Sept. 1988, p. 75.

8. Thoumi, "Size of the Illegal Drug Industry," pp. 77–97.

9. Author's interview with Juan Ferro, Bogotá, Colombia, 1987.

10. Lyman, *Gangland*, p. 40.

11. U.S. Army Enforcement Agency, "Reportage on Medellin Cartel's Operation, Nicaragua Link, Activities since 1978" (n.d.), p. 26.

12. *Ibid.*, p. 28.

13. For a solid overview of the history of the Medellín cartel, see Guy Gugliotta and Jeff Leen, *Kings of Cocaine* (New York: Harper, 1990); Simon Strong, *Whitewash: Pablo Escobar and the Cocaine Wars* (London, Eng.: Macmillan, 1995).

14. Fabio Castillo, *Los Jinetes de la Cocaína* (Bogotá, Colombia: Documentos Periodísticos, 1988), p. 43.

15. See Castillo, *Jinetes*, for an informative history of the Cali cartel's drug-smuggling prominence.

16. Castillo, *Jinetes*, p. 45.

17. *Ibid.*, p. 44.

18. Interview with James Sutton, 1994.

19. Interview with a Colombian journalist who wanted to remain anonymous, Bogotá, Colombia, 1994.

20. Tom Morgenthau and Robert Sandza, "Cocaine's Dirty 300," *Newsweek*, July 1, 1991, p. 37.

21. *Ibid.*, p. 39.

22. President's Commission on Organized Crime, *America's Habit: Drug Trafficking and Organized Crime* (Washington, D.C.: U.S. Government Printing Office, 1986), p. 78.

23. James Sutton, "A Brief Overview of the Collaboration Between Colombian and Mexican Drug Trafficking Operations," Unpublished report to the U.S. Department of Justice, ca. 1994, pp. 1B–2B.

24. Ron Chepesiuk, "Kingpin's Trial a Small Win in Losing War on Drugs," *Orlando Sentinel*, Oct. 4, 1987.

25. Mary Matheson, "Kings Jailed but Colombia's Drugs Roll On," *Christian Science Monitor*, July 11, 1995.

26. Sam Vincent Meddis, "Colombians Enter Free-for-all for Heroin Trade," *USA Today*, Feb. 4, 1994.

27. Christopher Wren, "Colombians Taking Over Heroin Trade," *New York Times*, Feb. 11, 1996.

28. AP, "Possible Heroin Epidemic."

29. Douglas Farah, "U.S.-Colombian Split over Cali Cartel," *Washington Post*, Mar. 8, 1994.

30. Farah, "U.S.-Colombian Split."

31. *Ibid.*

32. Ronald J. Ostrow, "Leaders Arrest Called Death of Cali Drug Cartel," *Los Angeles Times*, Aug. 7, 1995.

33. Author's interview with Ernesto Samper, 1997.

34. Mary Beth Sheridan and others, "Colombia Arrests Kingpin of Cali Cartel," *Miami Herald*, June 10, 1995.

35. "Gilberto Rodríguez Quedo Abogado a Pagar $105.00 Millones a la Justicia," *Tiempo*, Oct. 30, 1996.

36. Author's interview with Leonardo Gallego, 1997.

37. Author's interview with Myles Frechette, 1997.

38. Author's interview with Alphonso Valdivieso, 1997.

39. Author's interview with Rosso José Serrano, 1987.

40. See "El Dossier de Efraín Hernández Ramírez," *Espectador*, Nov. 7, 1996; "Asesinado Narco Alias 'Don Efra.'" *Espectador*, Nov. 7, 1996; "La Fortuna de El Señor de los Mares," *Tiempo*, Nov. 8, 1996; "La Fortuna de 'Don Efra.'" *Espectador*, Nov. 8, 1996; "Los Hombres de 'Don Efra,'" *Espectador*, Nov. 10, 1906.

Chapter 13. The Yakuza:
Merchants of Speed

1. See Robert J. Kelly, ed., *Organized Crime: A Global Perspective* (Totowa, N.J.: Rowman and Littlefield, 1986), p. 208; Karen Lowry Miller, "Suddenly, the Japanese Mob Is Out of the Shadows," *Business Week*, July 8, 1991, p. 29; President's Commission on Organized Crime, *The Impact of Organized Crime Today* (Washington, D.C.: U.S. Government Printing Office, 1986), p. 97; Oliver Cyrix, *Crime: An Encyclopedia*. North Pomfret, Vt.: Trafalgar Square, 1995).

2. Dennis J. Kenney and James O. Finckenauer, *Organized Crime in America* (London, Eng.: International Thompson, 1990), p. 260. Note that the Japanese National Police Agency refers to Japanese criminal groups as the "Boryokudan."

3. Michael Lyman, *Gangland: Drug Trafficking by Organized Criminals* (Springfield, Ill.: Charles C Thomas, 1989), p. 121.

4. *Ibid.*, p. 122.

5. Kelly, *Organized Crime: A Global Perspective*, p. 213.

6. Jay Robert Nash, *World Encyclopedia of Organized Crime* (New York: Marlow, 1994), p. 411.

7. David E. Kaplan and Alec Dubro, *Yakuza: The Explosive Account of Japan's Criminal Underworld* (Reading, Mass.: Addison-Wesley, 1986), p. 232.

8. Nash, *World Encyclopedia of Organized Crime*, p. 229.

9. *Ibid.*, p. 411.

10. Lyman, *Gangland*, p. 121.

11. Kaplan and Dubro, *Yakuza*, p. 236.

12. President's Commission, *Impact*, p. 100. Quoted in DEA Report to the Committee on Foreign Affairs "U.S. Narcotics Control Efforts: An Assessment," February 22, 1985.

13. Kaplan and Dubro, *Yakuza*, p. 268.

14. *Ibid.*, p. 199.

15. Lyman, *Gangland*, p. 121.

16. U.S. Senate Committee on Government Affairs, *Asian Organized Crime* (Washington, D.C.: U.S. Government Printing Office, 1992), p. 30.

17. Kaplan and Dubro, *Yakuza*, p. 191.

18. U.S. Senate, *Asian Organized Crime*, p. 30.

19. *Ibid.*, pp. 30–31.

20. Claire Sterling, *Thieves' World: The Threat of the New Global Network of Organized Crime* (New York: Simon and Schuster, 1994), p. 155.

21. President's Commission, *Impact*, p. 103.

22. Ronald Grover, "A Japanese Laundry Worth $1 Billion," *Business Week*, May 24, 1993, p. 38.

23. Miller, "Japanese Mob Out of Shadows," p. 29.

24. Charles A. Radin, "Japan's Political Gangsters," *Charlotte Observer*, June 10, 1994.

25. U.S. Senate, *Asian Organized Crime*, p. 54.

Chapter 14. Jamaican Posses: The Kings of Crack

1. Eric Harrison, "Jamaicans: New Face of U.S. Crime," *Los Angeles Times*, Jan. 3, 1989.

2. Ingwerson Marshall, "Jamaican Drug Gangs Stake Out Turf in U.S.," *Christian Science Monitor*, Aug. 13, 1987.

3. William Kleinknecht, *The New Ethnic Mobs: The Changing Face of Organized Crime in America* (New York: Free Press, 1996), p. 229; Joseph B. Teaster, "Jamaican Gangs Take Root in U.S.," *New York Times*, Nov. 13, 1988.

4. Harvey Burgess, "Drug Ring Suspected in Double Slaying," *Rock Hill (S.C.) Herald*, June 6, 1991.

5. Interview with Lieutenant Tommy Barnes, Charlotte Police Department, 1991.

6. For an overview of the Jamaican posses, see Michael Lyman, *Gangland: Drug Trafficking by Organized Criminals* (Springfield, Ill.: Charles C Thomas, 1989), pp. 86–93; Mary Cooper, *The Business of Drugs* (Washington, D.C.: Congressional Quarterly, 1990), pp. 36–38.

7. W. Hampton Sides, "This Is War: In the Shadowy World of Drugs, Police Battle Violent Jamaican Posses," *Washingtonian*, Apr. 1988, pp. 139.

8. Louis Estrada, "Renegades in the Drug World: A Look at the Jamaican Posses," *Times of the Americas*, June 26, 1991.

9. *Ibid.*

10. *Ibid.*

11. Marshall, "Jamaican Drug Gangs."

12. *Ibid.*

13. Lyman, *Gangland*, pp. 85–86.

14. Kleinknecht, *New Ethnic Mobs*, p. 227; Laurie Gunst, "Johnny-Too-Bad and the Sufferers," *Nation*, Nov. 13, 1989, p. 54.

15. Estrada, "Renegades."

16. Harrison, "Jamaicans: New Face."

17. Lyman, *Gangland*, pp. 85–86.

18. William Weir, *In the Shadow of the Dope Fiend* (North Haven, Conn.: Archon, 1995), pp. 189–90.

19. Cooper, *Business of Drugs*, p. 38.

20. "True Confessions: A Gang Member's Story," *U.S. News and World Report*, Jan. 18, 1988, p. 34.

21. Harrison, "Jamaicans: New Face."

22. Dana Priest, "Officials Face Challenge in Stemming Jamaican Drug Trade," Feb. 23, 1988.

23. Sue Anne Pressley, "Area Jamaicans Struggle Against Drug-Crime Image," *Washington Post*, Jan. 29, 1988.

24. *Ibid.*

25. Priest, "Officials Face Challenge."

26. Robert L. Jackson, "219 Jamaicans Held in Gang Arrest," *Los Angeles Times*, Oct. 14, 1988.

27. Interview with Tommy Barnes.

Chapter 15. The Nigerian Connection: The Mules of the Drug Trade

1. Douglas Farah, "Nigerian Cartels Widening Drug Operations," *Charlotte Observer*, June 23, 1996.

2. *Ibid.*; see also Danielle Pletka, "Heroin, Inc.: The Nigerian Connection (Drug Trafficking Through Nigeria)," *Insight on the News*, Sept. 30, 1991, p. 24.

3. U.S. Senate Committee on Foreign Relations, Treaty Between the U.S. and the Federal Republic of Nigeria on Mutual Legal Assistance in Criminal Matters Treaty Doc. 10226 (Washington, D.C.: U.S. Superintendent of Documents, 20 May 1992), p. 7.

4. Farah, "Nigerian Cartels Widening Drug Operations."

5. For statistics on heroin entering the U.S., see "Nigerian Drugs: International Trade," *Economist*, Aug. 26, 1995; U.S. Senate, see #B, p. 7; U.S. Senate Committee on Foreign Relations, Subcommittee on Terrorism, Narcotics and International Operations, *Recent Developments in Transnational Crime Affecting U.S. Law Enforcement and Foreign Policy* (Washington, D.C.: U.S. Superintendent of Documents, 20–21 Apr. 1994), p. 124.

6. Pletka, "Heroin, Inc.," p. 22.

7. U.S. Senate, See #3, p. 15.

8. *Ibid.*

9. Pletka, "Heroin, Inc.," p. 22.

10. "Nigerian Drugs," p. 36.

11. James S. E. Opolot, "Organized Crime As It Emerges in Sections of Africa," in R. T. Kelly, ed., *Organized Crime: A Global Perspective* (Totowa, N.J.: Rowman and Littlefield, 1986), p. 196.

12. *Ibid.*, p. 193.

13. *Ibid.*, p. 198.

14. E. Kibaka, "Crime in African Countries," *International Review of Criminal Policy* 35 (1974): 18.

15. Allan Bake and others, "Drugged to the Eyeballs," *New African*, June 1995, p. 17.

16. Pletka, "Heroin, Inc.," p. 23.

17. U.S. Senate [see note 3], p. 15.

18. *Ibid.*, p. 14.

19. Pletka, "Heroin, Inc.," p. 23.

20. Farah, "Nigerian Cartels Widening Drug Operations."

21. Author's interview with Victor T. Le Vine, 1997.

22. Pletka, "Heroin, Inc.," p. 23.

23. Bake and others, "Drugged to the Eyeballs," p. 18.

24. Author's interview with Victor Le Vine.

25. *Ibid.*, p. 18.

26. *Ibid.*, p. 15.

27. *Ibid.*, p. 6.

28. *Ibid.*, p. 24.

29. Pletka, "Heroin, Inc.," p. 24.

30. U.S. Senate, [see note 3], p. 13.

31. Author's interview with Victor Le Vine.

32. Peter Maser, "Africa Joins the Narcotics Pipeline," *Toronto Star*, Aug. 15, 1995.

33. Cindy Shiner, "Nigerian Drug Traders Ply the Liberian Connection," *Christian Science Monitor*, Jan. 29, 1996.

34. U.S. Senate, [see note 3], p. 28.

35. U.S. Senate, *Recent Developments in Transnational Crime*, p. 124.

36. *Ibid.*, p. 3–4.

37. "Nigerian Drugs," p. 34.

38. U.S. Senate, [see note 3], p. 7.

39. *Ibid.*, p. 8.

40. *Ibid.*, p. 7.

41. Elaine Sciolino, "State Department Report Labels Nigeria Major Trafficker of Drugs to U.S.," *New York Times*, Apr. 5, 1994.

42. Maser, "Africa Joins."

Chapter 16. The Russians Are Coming

1. Stephen Handelman, *Comrade Criminal: Russia's New Mafia* (New Haven, Conn.: Yale Univ. Press, 1995), p. 47; Carey Goldberg, "Russian Police Warn of Cocaine Blizzard," *Los Angeles Times*, Feb. 27, 1993.

2. John Gray, "The Rise of Russia's Crime Commissars," *World Press Review*, June 1994, p. 13.

3. Jack Kelly, "Mafia Has Death Grip on Russia," *USA Today*, Nov. 4, 1996.

4. Stephen Handelman, "The Russian 'Mafiya.'" *Foreign Affairs*, Mar. 1994, p. 84.

5. Goldberg, "Russian Police."

6. U.S. Senate Committee on Foreign Relations, Subcommittee on Terrorism, Narcotics and International Operations, *Recent Developments in Transnational Crime Affecting U.S. Law Enforcement and Foreign Policy* (Washington, D.C.: U.S. Superintendent of Documents, 20–21 Apr. 1994).

7. Rensselaer W. Lee III, "Soviet Narcotics Trade," *Society*, Aug. 1991, p. 47.

8. Jack Kelly, "Mafia Has Death Grip on Russia, *USA Today*, Nov. 7, 1996.

9. See Jim Leitzel, Clifford Gaddy, and Michael Alexeev, "Mafiosi and Matrioshki," *Brookings Review*, Winter 1995, pp. 26–29, for a good discussion of this subject.

10. Handelman, "Russian 'Mafiya,'" p. 86; Robert I. Friedman, "Brighton, Beach Goodfellows," *Vanity Fair*, Jan. 1993, p. 35.

11. Friedman, "Brighton Beach Goodfellows," p. 35.

12. Claire Sterling, *Thieves' World: The Threat of the New Global Network of Organized Crime* (New York: Simon and Schuster, 1994), p. 95.

13. Neela Banerjee, "Russian Organized Crime Goes Global," *Wall Street Journal*, Dec. 22, 1994.

14. Julio Fuentes, "Russia Se Convierte en Reino del Crimen Organizado," *Tiempo*, June 16, 1997.

15. Claire Sterling, "Redfellas," *New Republic*, Apr. 11, 1994, pp. 19–22.

16. Paul Klebnikov, "Joe Stalin's Heirs," *Forbes*, Sept. 27, 1993, pp. 128.

17. Gregory Katz, "East Europe's Underworld Flexes Might," *Dallas Morning News*, Dec. 17, 1995.

18. Rensselaer W. Lee III and Scott B. MacDonald, "Drugs in the East," *Foreign Policy*, Spring 1993, p. 93.

19. *Ibid.*, p. 95.

20. Banerjee, "Russian Organized Crime Goes Global."

21. Lee and MacDonald, "Drugs in the East," pp. 93–94.

22. "Britian Foresees East Block Crime," *Wall Street Journal*, July 26, 1995.

23. Adam Tanner and Pam Grier, "Russia's Notorious Mafia Spreads Tentacles of Crime Around Globe," *Christian Science Monitor*, Jan. 11, 1995.

24. Handelman, "Russian 'Mafiya,'" p. 95.

25. Sterling, *Thieves' World*, p. 165.

26. President's Commission on Organized Crime, *The Impact of Organized Crime Today* (Washington, D.C.: U.S. Government Printing Office, 1986), p. 122.

27. *Ibid.*, pp. 122–23.

28. Friedman, "Brighton Beach Goodfellows," p. 28.

29. Robert J. Kelly, *Handbook of Organized Crime in the United States* (Westport, Conn.: Greenwood Press, 1994), p. 252.

30. Banerjee, "Russian Organized Crime Goes Global."

31. Sterling, *Thieves' World*, p. 165.

32. Linnea P. Raine and Frank J. Clilluffo, *Global Organized Crime: The New*

Empire of Evil (Washington, D.C.: Center for Strategic and International Studies, 1994), p. 143.

33. Kelly, *Handbook of Organized Crime*, p. 258. James Rosenthal, "Russia's New Expect the Mob," *The Washington Post* June 14, 1990, p. 1.

34. *Ibid.*, p. 210.

35. Lee, "Soviet Narcotics Trade," p. 52.

36. U.S. Senate, *Recent Developments in Transnational Crime*, p. 153.

37. Richard Boudreaux, "Russian Police Back Plan for Joint Anti-Mob Effort," *Los Angeles Times*, July 5, 1994; Stephen Erlanger, "Old Enemies Now Allied Against Crime," *New York Times*, July 6, 1994.

38. William Norman Grigg, "Russia's Global Crime Cartel," *New American*, May 27, 1996, p. 4.

39. Robert Cullen, "Comrades in Crime," *Playboy*, Apr. 1994, pp. 70–72.

Chapter 17. Vietnamese Gangs: New Kids on the Block

1. Peter Auston, *Tongs, Gangs and Triads: Chinese Crime Gangs in North America*, p. 217.

2. President's Commission on Organized Crime, *The Impact of Organized Crime Today* (Washington, D.C.: U.S. Government Printing Office, 1986), p. 93.

3. Peter Huston, *Tongs, Gangs, and Triads: Chinese Crime Gangs in North America* (Boulder, Colo.: Paladin, 1995), p. 226.

4. President's Commission, *Impact*, p. 95.

5. Ko-lin Chin, *Chinese Subculture and Criminality* (Westport, Conn.: Greenwood Press, 1990), p. 74.

6. Peter Huston, *Tongs, Gangs, and Triads: Chinese Crime Gangs in North America*, p. 22.

7. President's Commission, *Impact*, p. 96.

8. *Ibid.*

9. Phil Hannun, with Al Lotz, *Nightmare: Vietnamese House Invasion Robberies* (Falls Church, Va.: International Association of Asian Crime Investigators, 1991), p. 1.

10. Allen Pusey, "Asian Organized Crime Growing in Dallas," *Dallas Morning News*, Sept. 14, 1986; "Vietnamese Gangs Active in Florida," *New York Times*, Nov. 25, 1985.

11. Allen Pusey, "Asian Organized Crime Growing in Dallas," *Dallas Morning News*, Sept. 14, 1986.

12. James R. Badey, "Federal Coordination Is Needed to Head Off Growing Threat from Vietnamese Criminals," *Organized Crime Digest*, Mar. 11, 1967, p. 5.

13. *Ibid.*

14. *Ibid.*

15. William Kleinknecht, *The New Ethnic Mobs: The Changing Face of Organized Crime in America* (New York: Free Press, 1996), p. 178.

16. *Ibid.*, p. 202.

17. James R. Badey, "Federal Coordination is Needed to Head Off Growing Threat from Vietnamese Criminals," *Organized Crime Digest*, Mar. 11, 1967, p. 202.

Chapter 18. The Mexican Connection: The Emerging Linchpin of International Drug Trafficking

1. Mark Fineman, "Mexico's Drug Czar Called Man of Integrity," *Miami Herald* (International Satellite Edition), Dec. 6, 1996.

2. *Ibid.*

3. Tim Padgett, "Getting Off Drugs?" *Time*, Mar. 10, 1997, p. 14.

4. Martha Brant, "Most Wanted Kingpin?" *Newsweek*, Mar. 10, 1997, p. 12.

5. Philip True, "Mexico's New Anti-Drug Czar Vows to Reorganize, Deepen Investigation," *Miami Herald* (International Satellite Edition), Mar. 23, 1997.

6. U.S. General Accounting Office, *Drug Control: Counter Narcotics Efforts in Mexico* (Washington, D.C.: General Accounting Office, June 1996), p. 2.

7. Author's interview with Rosso José Serrano, 1997.

8. Andres Oppenheimer, "New Cartels Muscle In: Mexico, Not Colombia," *Miami Herald* (International Satellite Edition), Mar. 15, 1997.

9. Clifford Krauss, "Mexico Joins Drug Underworld in New York," *Colombian Post*, Apr. 23–May 4, 1997.

10. U.S. GAO, *Counter Narcotics Effort in Mexico*, p. 3.

11. Silvana Paternostro, "Mexico as a Narco Democracy," *World Policy*, Spring 1995, p. 42.

12. Augusta Dwyer, "Economics of the Narcotics Trade," *Financiero International*, Aug. 28, 1993.

13. Oppenheimer, "New Cartels Muscle In."

14. Peter A. Lupsha, "Drug Trafficking: Mexico and Colombia in Comparative Perspective," *Journal of International Affairs*, Spring/Summer 1981, pp. 95.

15. Jorge Mejia Prieto, *México y Narcotréfica* (Mexico, D.F.: Editorial Universo, 1988), p. 12.

16. U.S. Drug Enforcement Administration, Washington, D.C. U.S. Drug Enforcement, *Drug Enforcement and the Early Years* 7,2 (Dec. 1980) : 33.

17. Lupsha, "Drug Trafficking," p. 96.

18. President's Commission on Organized Crime, *America's Habit: Drug Trafficking and Organized Crime* (Washington, D.C.: U.S. Government Printing Office, 1986), p. 107.

19. Mary H. Cooper, *The Business of Drugs* (Washington, D.C.: Congressional Quarterly, 1990), pp. 48–49.

20. *Ibid.*, p. 49.

21. *Ibid.*

22. "El Negocio de la Droga Se Extiende en México," *Tiempo*, Dec. 10, 1996; U.S. GAO, *Counter Narcotics Effort in Mexico*, pp. 3–4.

23. Tracy Eaton, "Mexico's Drug Eradication Agents Hail Success Against Pot, Poppies," *Miami Herald* (International Satellite Edition), Nov. 23, 1996.

24. *Ibid.*

25. Paternostro, "Mexico as a Narco Democracy," p. 45; Andrew Reding, "The Fall and Rise of the Cartels," *Washington Post*, Sept. 17, 1995.

26. Frank Viviano and Holly Lloyd, "The New Mafia Order," *Mother Jones*, May–June 1995, p. 51. Carillo Fuentes died in Mexico City on July 7, 1997, after plastic surgery. It has not been determined if foul play was involved.

27. Dan Trotta, "U.S.-Mexican Border Becomes Fertile New Killing Ground," *Reuters*, Oct. 24, 1996.

28. Tracy Eaton, "Mexico Drug Lords Infecting Southwest," *Dallas Morning News*, Oct. 12, 1996. p. 1A, YA.

29. *Ibid.*; Ana Arana, "El Pablo Escobar, de México," *Tiempo*, Oct. 20, 1996.

30. Eaton, "Mexico Drug Lords Infecting Southwest."

31. Deborah Tedford and Jo Ann Zuniga, "Cocaine Kingpin Is Guilty, Cartel Chief Could Get Life," *Houston Chronicle*, Oct. 17, 1996; "E.U. No Se la Rebaja a Capo Mexicano," *Espectador*, Oct. 17, 1996.

32. In April 1997 a Mexican tribunal overturned on a technicality the sentence of Rafael Caro Quintero, the man convicted of killing Camarena. See Elaine Shannon, *Desperadoes* (New York: NAl-Dutton, 1989), for background on this subject.

33. James Sutton, "A Brief Overview of the Collaboration Between Colombian and Mexican Drug Trafficking Operations," Unpublished report to the U.S. Department of Justice, ca. 1994, p. 1.

34. Trotta, "U.S.–Mexican Border."

35. Anita Snow, "Mexico Drug Scandal Widens with Arrest of Second General," *Miami Herald* (International Satellite Edition), Mar. 19, 1997.

36. "México, Minado por los Narcos," *Espectador*, Feb. 24, 1997.

37. Tracy Eaton, "Mexico Fights Its Own Police in Drug War," *Dallas Morning News*, Aug. 18, 1996.

38. Associated Press, "Mexican Military to Fight Drugs," *Miami Herald* (International Satellite Edition), Dec. 15, 1996.

39. Eaton, "Mexico Fights Its Own Police."

40. Tod Robberson, "Salinas In-Laws Linked to Drug Allegations," *Washington Post*, Nov. 25, 1995.

41. Viviano and Lloyd, "The New Mafia Order," p. 51; Terri Langford, "Ruiz Massieu: No Drug Bribes on My Watch," *Miami Herald* (International Satellite Edition), Mar. 15, 1997.

42. Sutton, "A Brief Overview," p. 15.

43. David Lyons, "DEA Officer Faults Police in Mexico," *Miami Herald* (International Satellite Edition), Mar. 14, 1997.

44. Peter Slevin, "Clinton Rebuffed on Mexico," *Miami Herald* (International Satellite Edition), Mar. 7, 1997.

45. Anita Snow, "Mexico Overhauls Drug Fight," *Miami Herald* (International Satellite Edition), Apr. 29, 1997.

46. "E.U. y México Firmaron Aliano contra las Drogas," *Tiempo*, May 7, 1997.

47. Paternostro, "Mexico as a Narco Democracy," p. 45.

48. U.S. GAO, *Counter Narcotics Effort in Mexico*, p. 4.

49. *Ibid.*, p. 5.

Chapter 19. Going Multinational:
The Globalization of International
Drug Trafficking

1. Roy Goodson and William J. Olson, "International Organized Crime," *Society*, Jan. 1995, p. 22.

2. See chapter 12 for background on the Cali cartel.

3. Louis Kraar, "The Drug Trade," *Fortune*, June 20, 1988, p. 27.

4. Steven Flynn, "Worldwide Drug Scourge: The Expanding Traffic in Illicit Drugs," *Brookings Review*, Winter 1993, p. 9.

5. Rensselaer W. Lee III, "Global Reach: The Threat of International Drug Trafficking," *Current History*, May 1995, p. 210.

6. Anti-Mafia Commission report.

7. Author's interview with José Leonardo Gallego, 1997.

8. See chapters 8 and 9 for background on the Sicilian and Italian-American Mafias and chapter 13 on the Yakuza.

9. Claire Sterling, *Thieves' World: The Threat of the New Global Network of Organized Crime* (New York: Simon and Schuster, 1994), p. 66.

10. *Ibid.*, p. 72.

11. Author's interview with Rensselaer Lee III, 1997.

12. "The Mob: Hit Hard But Still a Force," *U.S. News and World Report*, May 25, 1998, p. 33.

13. Sterling, *Thieves' World*, p. 51.

14. Gordon Witkin, "Cocaine Kings and Mafia Dons," *U.S. News and World Report*, Oct. 19, 1992, p. 53.

15. Author's interview with Rosso José Serrano, 1987.

16. "Duros Golpes a Mafia Colombianol-Italiano," *El Tiempo*, Feb. 9, 1997.

17. Joshua Cooper Ramo, "Crime Online," *Time Canada*, Sept. 30, 1996, p. 28.

18. Dean Foust, "The New, Improved Money Launderers," *Business Week*, June 28, 1993, pp. 90–91.

19. David Reed, "Cocaine Boats Evade Radar by Sailing Low in Water," *Miami Herald* (International Satellite Edition), Feb. 27, 1997.

20. Boutros Boutros-Ghali, "Transnational Crime: The Market and the Rule of Law," *Vital Speeches*, Dec. 15, 1991, p. 131.

21. National Public Radio, Morning Edition, "UN Conference in Naples Focuses on International Crime," Nov. 21, 1994. [Transcript: NPR, Washington, DC.]

22. Michael Elliott, "Global Mafia," *Newsweek*, Dec. 13, 1993, pp. 22–31.

23. Center for Strategic and International Studies, *The Transnational Drug Challenge* (Washington, D.C.: Center for Strategic and International Studies, 1993), p. 16.

24. Boutros-Ghali, "Transnational Crime," p. 131.

25. "International Cartels Expand Influence," *UN Chronicle*, June 1994, p. 68.

26. Flynn, "Worldwide Drug Scourge," p. 10.

27. Center for Strategic and International Studies, *Transnational Drug Challenge*, p. 16.

28. The World This Week, "Fighting International Organized Crime," Oct. 14, 1993. Transcript: Journal Graphics, Denver, Colo.

29. Author's interview with Ernesto Samper, 1997.

30. Sterling, *Thieves' World*, p. 41.

31. "Caribbean: Differing Legal Systems Complicate Drug Control," *Miami Herald* (International Satellite Edition), Mar. 20, 1997.

32. See chapter 20 for an in-depth discussion of money laundering.

33. Eva Bertram and others, *Drug War Politics: The Price of Denial* (Berkeley: Univ. of California Press, 1996), p. 131.

34. U.S. Senate Committee on Foreign Relations, Subcommittee on Terrorism, Narcotics and International Operations, *Recent Developments in Transnational Crime Affecting U.S. Law Enforcement and Foreign Policy* (Washington, D.C.: U.S. Superintendent of Documents, 20–21 Apr. 1994), p. 151.

Chapter 20. Dirty Laundry: Cleaning the Profits of Illicit Enterprise

1. For background on the case, see "Lawyer Admitted He Laundered Drug Money," *New York Times*, Sept. 22, 1995; Joseph B. Teaster, "U.S. Says It Uncovered $100 Million Drug-Money Laundry," *New York Times*, Dec. 1, 1994; Timothy L. O'Brien, "Law Firm's Downfall Exposes New Methods of Money Laundering," *Wall Street Journal* (Eastern Edition), May 26, 1995.

2. Author's interview with Charles Intriago, 1997.

3. U.S. General Accounting Office, *Money Laundering: The U.S. Government Is Responding to the Problem* (Washington, D.C.: U.S. Government Printing Office, 1991).

4. Carl P. Florenz and Bernardette Boyce, "Laundering Drug Money," *FBI Law Enforcement Bulletin,* Apr. 1990, p. 23.

5. Robert E. Powis, *The Money Launderers* (New York: Probus, 1992), p. 239.

6. David A. Andelman, "The Drug Money Maze," *Foreign Affairs*, July 1994, pp. 94–108.

7. Robert E. Powis, "Money Laundering: Problems and Solutions," *Banker's Magazine*, Nov.–Dec. 1992, p. 72.

8. Jeffrey Robinson, *The Laundrymen* (New York: Simon and Schuster, 1990), p. 31.

9. Rachel Ehrenfeld, *Evil Money* (New York: Harper Collins, 1992), p. 217.

10. Andelman, "Drug Money Race," p. 98.

11. David Satterfield, "Banks Tighten Cash Control," *Miami Herald*, Mar. 29, 1986.

12. Douglas Farah and others, "Illicit Dollars Flow via Unique Network," *Washington Post*, Sept. 19, 1993.

13. Andelman, "Drug Money Race," p. 99.

14. Author's interview with Victor T. Le Vine, 1997.

15. U.S. General Accounting Office, *Money Laundering: The U.S. Government Is Responding to the Problem* (Washington, D.C.: U.S. Government Printing Office, 1991), p. 13.

16. President's Commission on Organized Crime, *The Cash Connection: Organized Crime, Financial Institutions and Money Laundering* (Washington, D.C.: U.S. Government Printing Office, 1984), p. 8.

17. Ehrenfeld, *Evil Money*, p. 218; President's Commission, *Cash Connection*, pp. 35–39.

18. Clifford Krauss and Douglas Frantz, "Cali Drug Cartel Using U.S. Business to Launder Cash," *New York Times*, Oct. 30, 1985.

19. Ronald Grover, "A Japanese Laundry Worth $1 Billion," *Business Week*, May 24, 1993, p. 38.

20. Author's interview with Charles Intriago, 1997.

21. Elaine Shannon, "Narco-Gnomes of Mexico: Where Drug Money Goes to Hide," *Washington Post*, Mar. 17, 1996.

22. Stanley Meisler, "Mexico Called Laundering Haven," *Miami Herald* (International Satellite Edition), Sept. 8, 1996.

23. Anthony P. Maingot, "Offshore Secret Centers and the Necessary Role of States: Bucking the Trend," *Journal of Interamerican Studies and World Affairs*, Winter 1995, p. 9.

24. Gregory Katz, "Antigua's Lax Banking Laws Invite Russian Mafia Money," *Miami Herald* (International Satellite Edition), Feb. 19, 1997.

25. Juan Tamayo, "Aruba Called Budding Drug Haven," *Miami Herald* (International Satellite Edition), Feb. 24, 1997.

26. Katz, "Antigua's Lax Banking Laws."

27. Don Bohning, "Antigua Chief: U.S. Giving Drug War a Bum Rap," *Miami Herald* (International Satellite Edition), Nov. 21, 1996.

28. Author's interview with Charles Intriago, 1997.

29. Center for Strategic and International Studies, *The Transnational Drug Challenge* (Washington, D.C.: Center for Strategic and International Studies, 1993), p. viii.

30. "Change in Swiss Bank Laws," *New York Times*, Mar. 3, 1994.

31. Mark Fineman, "Swiss Link Raul Salinas to $100 Million," *Los Angeles Times*, Dec. 7, 1995.

32. President's Commission, *Cash Connection*, p. 20.

33. Powis, *Money Launderers*, pp. 1–30.

34. Farah and others, "Illicit Dollars."

35. Florenz and Boyce, "Laundering Drug Money," p. 22.

36. John J. Fialka, "DEA's Sting Bank in the Caribbean Uncovers Laundering of Drug Money," *Wall Street Journal*, Dec. 19, 1994; Jim McGee, "Fake DEA Bank Stings Cali Cartel," *Washington Post*, Dec. 17, 1994; Michael Janofsky, "Fake Bank Set Up by U.S. Agents Snare Drug Money Launderers," *New York Times*, Dec. 17, 1994.

37. See Ann Woolner, *Washed in Gold: The Story Behind the Biggest Money-Laundering Investigation* (New York: Simon and Schuster, 1994).

38. "Mexico, Texas Sign Antidrug Laundering Pact," *Reuters*, Oct. 15, 1996.

39. Alison Mitchell, "U.S. Freezes Assets of Cartel in New Effort Against Drugs," *New York Times*, Oct. 23, 1995.

40. "U.S. Puts Squeeze on Cash Transfers," *Colombian Post*, Mar. 17–23, 1997.

41. Associated Press, "Eight Countries Seize Bank Tied to Money Laundering Schemes," *Charlotte Observer*, July 6, 1991; "U.S. Freezes Colombian Assets," *Miami Herald* (International Satellite Edition), Apr. 18, 1997.

42. Author's interview with Victor T. Le Vine, 1997.

43. Author's interview with Charles Intriago, 1997.

44. U.S. General Accounting Office, *Money Laundering: A Framework for Understanding U.S. Efforts Overseas* (Washington, D.C.: U.S. Government Printing Office, 1996), p. 48.

Chapter 21. Global Reach: The Economic, Political and Social Impact

1. Rensselaer W. Lee III, "Global Reach: The Threat of International Drug Trafficking," *Current History*, May 1995, pp. 208.

2. Author's interview with Alejandro Saenz de Santamaria, 1997.

3. *Ibid.*

4. William J. Olson and Samuel Francis, "Question: Should Crime Fighting Be Foreign Policy Priority?" *Insight on the News*, July 17, 1995, p. 20; "Drug Trade Bigger Than the Andes," *Miami Herald* (International Satellite Edition), May 12, 1997; Diana Jean Schemo, "As Drug Money Dries Up, Cali Struggles to Rebuild Economy," *Colombian Post*, Dec. 16–22, 1997.

5. Author's interview with Rensselaer W. Lee III, 1997.

6. Author's interview with Alfredo Vásquez Carrizosa, 1994.

7. Rensselaer W. Lee III, "South American Cocaine: Why the U.S. Can't Stop It," *Current History*, June 1989, p. 23.

8. Leslie Wirpsa, "U.S. Militarization of Antidrug Campaign in Bolivia Fires More Peasant Opposition," *National Catholic Reporter*, Mar. 26, 1993, p. 15.

9. *Ibid.*

10. Author's interview with Bruce Wyrick, 1997.

11. U.S. General Accounting Office, *Drug Control: U.S. Heroin Program Encounters Many Obstacles in Southeast Asia* (Washington, D.C.: General Accounting Office, Mar. 1, 1996), p. 16.

12. See chapter 4.

13. Center for Strategic and International Studies, *The Transnational Drug Challenge* (Washington, D.C.: Center for Strategic and International Studies, 1993), p. 8.

14. Author's interview with Rensselaer W. Lee III, 1997.

15. See chapter 1, "The Nature of the Beast."

16. Simon Strong, *Whitewash: Pablo Escobar and the Cocaine Wars* (London, Eng.: Macmillan, 1995), p. 162.

17. Author's interview with Julio Orlando Gómez, 1997.

18. "Narcos Avanzan en el Sector Agrario," *Tiempo*, Nov. 30, 1996.

19. Frank Bajak, "Colombia Okays Law Enabling Seizure of Drug Assets," *Miami Herald* (International Satellite Edition), Dec. 14, 1996.

20. Author's interview with Myles Frechette, 1987.

21. Richard B. Craig, "Are Drug Kingdoms South America's New Wave?" *World and I*, Nov. 1989, p. 160; "The Mafia Again," *Economist*, Mar. 11, 1995, p. 53.

22. "Birth of Narco Democracy," *Time*, Apr. 11, 1994, p. 19.

23. See chapter 18.

24. "The Sicilian Mafia: A State Within a State," *Economist*, Apr. 24, 1993, p. 21; "Mafia Again," p. 53.

25. John Ward Anderson and Sally Moore, "Pervasive Heroin Traffic Putting Pakistan at Risk," *Washington Post*, Apr. 29, 1993.

26. Center for Strategic and International Studies, *Transnational Drug Challenge*, pp. 5–6.

27. "El Narcotráfico Amenaza con Destabilizar a Europa," *Tiempo*, Nov. 27, 1996.

28. John Ward Anderson, "Mexican Cartels Diversify: Drug Dealers Concerning U.S. Speed Market," *Washington Post*, Aug. 12, 1996; Philip Brasher, "U.S. Drugs Made in America," *Colombian Post*, Sept. 30–Oct. 6, 1996.

29. Louis Kraar, "How to Win the Drug War," *Fortune*, Mar. 12, 1990, p. 79.

30. Center for Strategic and International Studies, *Transnational Drug Challenge*, pp. 5–6.

31. See chapter 19.

32. Claire Sterling, *Octopus: The Long Reach of the International Mafia* (New York: W. W. Norton, 1990), p. 312; "Nuevo Clase de Cocaína," *Espectador*, Oct. 19, 1996; David J. Hanson, "Narcotics Commission: Novel Initiatives for Growing Crisis," *UN Chronicle*, Sept. 1992, p. 86; Center for Strategic and International Studies, *Transnational Drug Challenge*, pp. ix, 15; Alison Jamieson, *Terrorism and Drug Trafficking in the 1990s* (Aldershot, Eng.: Dartmouth, 1994), p. 142.

33. U.S. General Accounting Office, *Drug Control: U.S. Interdiction Efforts in the Caribbean Decline* (Washington, D.C.: General Accounting Office, Apr. 1996), pp. 11–12.

34. Lee, "South American Cocaine," p. 25.

35. Linda Robinson, "An Inferno Next Door," *U.S. News and World Report*, Feb. 24, 1997, pp. 37–38.

36. *Ibid.*

37. "E.U. Teme al Poder Corruptor de los Narcos," *El Tiempo*, May 15, 1997, p. A1, 47.

38. Author's interview with Victor T. Le Vine, 1997.

39. Linnea P. Raine and Frank J. Cilluffo, *Global Organized Crime: The New Empire of Evil* (Washington, D.C: Center for Strategic and International Studies, 1994), p. 139.

40. Ron Chepesiuk, "Undermining Democracy: Drug Lords Versus the Press," *New Leader*, Apr. 30, 1990, pp. 9–11.

41. Mary Cooper, *The Business of Drugs* (Washington, D.C.: Congressional Quarterly, 1990), p. 5.

42. See Washington Office of Latin America, *Colombia Besieged: Political Violence and State Responsibility* (Washington, D.C.: Washington Office of Latin America, 1989).

43. George Gedda, "Amnesty: U.S. Military Aid to Colombia Used for Repression," *Miami Herald* (International Satellite Edition), Oct. 30, 1996.

44. Author's interview with Myles Frechette, 1997.

45. Ron Chepesiuk, "Colombia's Guerrillas Cultivate a Different Kind of Power Base," *Orlando Sentinel*, Jan. 26, 1996.

46. Author's interview with Juan B. Tokatlian, 1997.

47. Author's interview with Rensselaer W. Lee III, 1997.

48. Gabriela Tarazona-Sevillano, *Sendero Luminoso and the Threat of Narcotterorism* (Westport, Conn.: Praeger, 1990), p. 100.

49. Richard Cole, "Heroin Trade Helps Kurdish Rebels, among World's Deadliest Terrorists," *Colombian Post*, Dec. 23–29, 1996.

50. Donald J. Mabry, *Latin American Narcotics Control and U.S. National Security* (Westport, Conn.: Greenwood Press, 1989), p. 5.

51. Author's interview with Ernesto Samper, 1997.

52. Don Bohning, "U.S.-Colombian Drug Agreement Falters," *Miami Herald* (International Satellite Edition), Nov. 29, 1996.

53. "Colombia-U.S. to Sign Maritime Accord," *Colombian Post,* Feb. 10–16, 1997.

54. *Ibid.*

55. "International Narcotics Control," *U.S. Dept. of State Dispatch*, Sept. 3, 1990, p. 15.

56. "Extradition Treaty Signed with U.S.," *Miami Herald* (International Satellite Edition), Apr. 28, 1997.

57. "E.U. y México Firmaron Alianza contra las Drogas," *El Tiempo*, May 7, 1997; "Promesa de Extradición en San José," *Tiempo*, May 9, 1997.

58. "La Historia Jurídica de la Extradición," *El Tiempo*, June 20, 1997.

59. Mabry, *Latin American Narcotics Control*, p. 7.

60. José María Amarilla, "Grupo de Río Asume Postura Crítica contra 'Certificaciones,'" *Cartagena* (Colombia) *Universal*, May 18, 1997.

61. "Congress, Heal Thyself," *Miami Herald* (International Satellite Edition), Mar. 10, 1997.

Chapter 22. A Changing Nation:
The Price of War for Uncle Sam

1. Stephen Smith, "Two Who Smoke It Legally Tell of Medical Benefits of Pot," *Miami Herald* (International Satellite Edition), Mar. 3, 1997.

2. ABC News, "America's War on Drugs — Searching for Solutions," Apr. 7, 1995 (Transcript: Journal Graphics, Denver, Colo.), p. 2.

3. "Teenage Wasteland," *USA Today*, Dec. 24, 1996.

4. Harry Rosenthal, "U.S. Tells Doctors Not to Prescribe Pot," *Miami Herald* (International Satellite Edition), Dec. 31, 1996.

5. Lester Grinspoon and James Balakar, "Marijuana as Medicine," *Colombian Post*, Nov. 18–24, 1996.

6. Paul Racer, "NIH Panel: Medical Use of Pot Worth More Study," *Miami Herald* (International Satellite Edition), Feb. 21, 1997.

7. Rosenthal, "U.S. Tells Doctors."

8. *Ibid.*

9. Grinspoon and Balakar, "Marijuana as Medicine."

10. Eva Bertram and others, *The Politics of the War Against Drugs: The Price of Denial* (Berkeley: Univ. of California Press, 1996), p. 32.

11. Dan Baum, *Smoke and Mirrors — The War Against Drugs and the Politics of Failure* (Boston: Little, Brown, 1996), p. xii.

12. Bertramand others, *Politics*, p. 153.

13. Baum, *War Against Drugs*, p. 334.

14. ABC News, "America's War on Drugs," p. 2.

15. Bertram and others, *Politics*, p. 32.

16. William Weir, *In the Shadow of the Dope Fiend* (North Haven, Conn.: Archon, 1975), p. 227.

17. Morris Blackman and Kenneth Sharpe, "The War on Drugs: American Democracy under Assault," *World Policy Journal*, Winter 1989, p. 141.

18. Alfred J. McCoy and Alan A. Block, eds., *War on Drugs: Studies in the Failure of U.S. Narcotics Policy* (Boulder, Colo.: Westview, 1992), p. 7.

19. Thomas W. Kukura, "Civil Forfeiture: Real Property Used in Drug Trafficking," *FBI Law Enforcement Bulletin*, Oct. 1991, pp. 26–31.

20. Stephen Chapman, "A Weapon of the Drug War Provokes Growing Disgust," *Chicago Tribune*, July 1, 1993.

21. Dale McFeatters, "Civil Seizure Laws Should Be Reformed," *Rock Hill* (S.C.) *Herald*, July 30, 1996.

22. "Drugs and Civil Rights," *Christian Science Monitor*, Dec. 16, 1993.

23. Kimberly Kingston, "Forfeiture of Attorney's Fees," *FBI Law Enforcement Bulletin*, Apr. 1, 1990, p. 27.

24. Mireya Navarro, "When Drug Kingpins Fall, Illicit Assets But a Cushion," *New York Times*, Mar. 19, 1996.

25. Mary Cooper, *The Business of Drugs* (Washington, D.C.: Congressional Quarterly, 1990), p. 119.

26. Baum, *War Against Drugs*, pp. 237–38.

27. Cooper, *Business of Drugs*, p. 137.

28. Blackman and Sharpe, "The War on Drugs" p. 140.

29. Edward Kennedy, "The War on Drugs Threatens Civil Liberties," in Karen Swisher, ed., *Drug Trafficking* (San Diego, Calif.: Greenhaven, 1991), p. 57.

30. "Drug Testing of Candidates Struck Down," *Miami Herald* (International Satellite Edition), Apr. 16, 1997.

31. Kennedy, "The War on Drugs Threatens Civil Liberties," p. 57.

32. "U.S. Prison Population Exceeds 1 Million," *Charlotte Observer*, Oct. 28, 1994.

33. U.S. General Accounting Office, *War on Drugs: Arrests Burdening Local Criminal Justice System* (Washington, D.C.: General Accounting Office, 1996), p. 18.

34. *Ibid.*, p. 37.

35. Bertram and others, *Politics*, p. 51.

36. U.S. GAO, *War on Drugs*, p. 10.

37. ABC News, "America's War on Drugs," p. 2.

38. William Booth, "Drug War Locks Up Prisons," *Washington Post*, July 7, 1993.

39. Gary Fields, "Justice Is Threatened When the Public Is Afraid to Testify," *USA Today*, July 22, 1997.

40. Paul Eddy, Hugh Sabogal, and Sarah Walden, *The Cocaine Wars* (New York: Norton, 1988), p. 73.

41. "The Tarnished Badges," *Miami Herald* (International Satellite Edition), May 17, 1997.

42. Jennifer Brown, "Police Corruption on the Streets Eroding Trust in Court Rooms," *Miami Herald* (International Satellite Edition), Mar. 21, 1997.

43. Andres Oppenheimer, "Witness: Corruption on Both Sides of the Border," *Miami Herald* (International Satellite Edition), Mar. 24, 1997.

44. "E.U. Teme al Poder Corruptor de los Narcos," *El Tiempo*, May 15, 1997.

45. *Ibid.*; see also Dan Freedman, "Congress to Probe U.S.–Mexican Border Corruption," *Miami Herald* (International Satellite Edition), Nov. 22, 1996.

46. Will Lester, "Lawyers among Sixty Charged in Drug Smuggling Case Conspiracy," *Charlotte Observer*, June 6, 1995.

47. Tom McNichol, "The Drug Fix," *USA Weekend*, Apr. 8–10, 1994.

48. McCoy and Block, *War on Drugs*, p. 6.

49. Deb Reichman, "Schemes to Beat Drug Tests Increasing with Workplace Testing," *Colombian Post*, Mar. 10–16, 1997.

50. Blackman and Sharpe, "The War on Drugs" p. 55.

51. Bertram and others, *Politics*, p. 75.

52. Weir, *Shadow of the Dope Fiend*, p. 171.

53. Cooper, *Business of Drugs*, p. 100.

54. *Ibid.*, p. 117.

55. Eric Schlosser, "Reefer Madness," *Atlantic Monthly,* Aug. 1994, p. 46.

56. Kevin Johnson, "The Violent Drug War Within," *USA Today*, Oct. 4, 1996.

57. *Ibid.*

58. Schlosser, "Reefer Madness," p. 42.

59. Eric Schlosser, "Reefer Madness," *Charlotte Observer*, Apr. 16, 1997. (Reprint $55)

60. Nathan Nadelmann, "Drug Prohibition in the United States: Costs, Consequences and Alternatives," *Science*, Sept. 1989, p. 139.

61. Kurt Schmoke, "Back to the Future," *Humanist*, Sept.–Oct. 1990, p. 28.

62. McNichol, "Drug Fix," p. 5.

63. Jayson T. Blair, "Prosecutor to Ignore Petty Drug Crimes," *Charlotte Observer,* July 29, 1996.

64. Robert Scheer, "Fighting the Wrong War," *Playboy*, Oct. 1994, p. 49.

65. Christopher Wren, "Hartford Mulls Overhaul of Drug Laws," *Miami Herald* (International Satellite Edition), Apr. 24, 1997.

Chapter 23. Summing Up:
Lessons from the War on Drugs

1. Eva Bertram and others, *The Politics of the War Against Drugs: The Price of Denial* (Berkeley: Univ. of California Press, 1996), p. 3.

2. Cassandra Burrell, "The Demand for Heroin Said to Be Growing," *Colombian Post*, Feb. 10–16, 1997.

3. Author's interview with Rosso José Serrano, 1997.

4. Author's interview with Rensselaer W. Lee III, 1997.

5. Christopher Torchia, "Dominant in Cocaine, Making U.S. Foray with Heroin," *Colombian Post*, Apr. 17–23, 1997.

6. U.S. General Accounting Office, "Drug Control: Threats and Roles of Explosives and Narcotics Technology: Briefing Report to Congressional Requesters" (Washington, D.C.: General Accounting Office, Mar. 1996), p. 15.

7. Clifford Krauss, "Fighting the Drug War with Boomerangs," *Colombian Post*, May 19–25, 1997.

8. Eva Bertram and Kenneth Sharpe, "The Unwinnable Drug War: What Clausewitz Would Tell Us — Part II," *Colombian Post*, Mar. 17–23, 1997.

9. Center for Strategic and International Studies, *The Transnational Drug Challenge* (Washington, D.C.: Center for Strategic and International Studies, 1993), p. 11.

10. Michael Hedges, "Mexicans Seen Muscling In on Colombian Drug Trade," Scripps Howard News Service, Dec. 19, 1995.

11. Morris Blackman and Kenneth Sharpe, "The War on Drugs: American Democracy under Assault," *World Policy Journal*, Winter 1989, p. 155.

Chapter 24. Getting Control: Twelve Practical Options for U.S. Antidrug Strategy

1. Peter Lurie and Ernest Drucker, "Fight AIDS Through Needle-Exchange Program," *Miami Herald* (International Satellite Edition), May 30, 1997.

2. Steve Sternberg, "Funding Urged for Needle Exchanges," *USA Today*, June 13, 1997.

3. Lurie and Drucker, "Fight AIDS."

4. Bruce Bagley, "The New hundred Years War? U.S. National Security and the War on Drugs," *Journal of Interamerican Studies and World Affairs*, Spring 1988, p. 179.

5. U.S. Senate Committee on Foreign Relations, Subcommittee on Terrorism, Narcotics and International Operations, *Recent Developments in Transnational Crime Affecting U.S. Law Enforcement and Foreign Policy* (Washington, D.C.: U.S. Superintendent of Documents, 20–21 Apr. 1994), p. 156.

6. Tom McNichol, "The Drug Fix," *USA Weekend*, Apr. 8–10, 1994.

7. Author's interview with Rensselaer W. Lee III, 1997.

8. Bruce K. Alexander, "Alternatives to the War on Drugs," *Journal of Drug Issues*, Winter 1990, p. 7.

9. Boutros Boutros-Ghali, "Transnational Crime: The Market and the Rule of Law," *Vital Speeches*, Dec. 15, 1991, p. 130.

10. Center for Strategic and International Studies, *The Transnational Drug Challenge* (Washington, D.C.: Center for Strategic and International Studies, 1993), p. 9.

11. Author's interview with Ernesto Samper, 1997.

12. Tim Wall, "Transnational Crime Busters Agree on New Action Plan," *UN Chronicle*, Mar. 1985, p. 89; "World Conference on Organized Crime, Money Laundering to Be Hosted by Italy," *UN Chronicle*, Sept. 1993, p. 71.

13. Author's interview with Charles Intriago, 1997.

14. Author's interview with Leonardo Gallego, 1997.

15. Author's interview with Juan Tokatlian, 1997.

16. Author's interview with Alfredo Vásquez Carrizosa, 1997.

17. Kiaran Konderich, "Cocaine Capitalism," in G. Epstein and others, eds., *A New World Economy: Forces of Change and Plans of Action* (Philadelphia: Temple Univ. Press, 1993), p. 136.

18. Gustavo Gorriti, "How to Fight the Drug War," *Atlantic Monthly*, July 1989, p. 76.

19. See U.S. General Accounting Office, *Foreign Assistance Promising Approach to Judicial Reform in Colombia* (Washington, D.C.: General Accounting Office, Sept. 1993).

20. Author's interview with Myles Frechette, 1997.

21. Center Strategic and International Studies, *Transnational Drug Challenge*, p. xi.

22. John M. Martin and Anne T. Romano, *Multinational Crime: The Challenge of Terrorism, Espionage, Drugs and Arms Trafficking* (Newbury Park, Calif.: Sage, 1992), p. 67.

23. Robert J. Kelly, Ko-Lin Chin and Rufus Schatzberg. *Handbook of Organized Crime in the United States* (Westport, Conn.: Greenwood Press, 1994), p. 409.

24. Louis Kraar, "How to Win the Drug War," *Fortune*, Mar. 12, 1990, p. 71.

25. Author's interview with Andres Pastrana, 1997.

26. John Rublowsky, *The Stoned Age: Drugs in America* (New York: Putnam, 1974), pp. 205–6.

27. Center for Strategic and International Studies, *Transnational Drug Challenge*, p. 22.

28. Edward Nell, "The Dynamics of the Drug Market," *Challenge*, Mar.–Apr. 1994, p. 19.

Selected Bibliography

ABC News. "America's War on Drugs — Searching for Solutions," Apr. 7, 1995. Transcript: Journal Graphics, Denver, Colo.

Abrams, Elliott. "Drug Wars: The New Alliance Against Traffickers and Terrorists." *Dept. of State Bulletin*, Apr. 1986, pp. 89–92.

Abrams, Jim. "U.S. Drug Czar Defends Mexico Certification." *Miami Herald* (International Satellite Edition), Mar. 4, 1997.

Adams, James. *The Financing of Terrorism*. New York: Simon and Schuster, 1986.

Adams, James Ring. "Losing the Drug War." *American Spectator*, Sept. 1988, pp. 20–24.

_____. "Medellín's New Generation." *American Spectator*. Dec. 1991, p. 22.

AFP. "Los Drugs Ganan Terreno en Europa." *El Tiempo*, Oct. 9, 1996.

Agency for International Development and the Foundation for Higher Education. *Justice Sector Reform Program*. Bogotá, Colombia: Agency for International Development, L. 1996.

Albini, Joseph, *The American Mafia: Genesis of a Legend*. New York: Appleton-Century-Crofts, 1971.

Albor, Teresa. "Burma's Heroin Trade Picks Up Despite U.S. Isolation Policy." *Christian Science Monitor*, July 29, 1992.

Alexander, Bruce K. "Alternatives to the War on Drugs." *Journal of Drug Issues*, Winter 1990, pp. 1–27.

Alzate, Jorge Cardona. "Catarsis de una Epidemia." *El Espectador*, Oct. 20, 1996.

Amado Carrillo Fuentes. "El Pablo Escobar de Mexico." *El Tiempo*, Feb. 20, 1997.

Ambrus, Stephen. "Pablo Escobar Dies in Shootout." *Los Angeles Times*, Dec. 3, 1993.

"American Express Unit found Official Guilty in U.S. Case." *Wall Street Journal*, June 3, 1994.

Anastasia, George. "That Last Civil War." *Playboy*, Sept. 1994, pp. 66–68.

"Andean Trade Pact of 1991." *U.S. News and World Report*, Mar. 2, 1992, p. 166.

Andelman, David A. "The Drug Money Maze." *Foreign Affairs*, July 1994, pp. 94–108.

Anderson, John Ward. "Mexican Cartels Diversify: Drug Dealers Cornering U.S. Speed Market." *Washington Post*, Aug. 12, 1996.

"Annals of a Permanent War, The." *U.S. News and World Report*, Aug. 28, 1989, p. 21.

Anslinger, Harold Jacob. *The Protectors*. New York: Farrar, Straus, 1964.

Anslinger, Harold Jacob, and Will Oursler. *The Murderers: The Story of the Narcotics Gangs.* New York: Farrar, Straus and Culahy, 1961.

_____, and W. F. Tomkins. *The Traffic in Narcotics.* New York: Funk and Wagnalls, 1953.

"Antigua and Barbados Combat Drug Trafficking." *Americas*, Mar. 1996, pp. 52–53.

Arana, Ana. "El Pablo Escobar, de México." *El Tiempo*, Oct. 20, 1996.

_____. "Saul Sanchez Sabía Demasiado." *El Tiempo*, Oct. 22, 1996.

Arlacchi, Pino. *The Mafia Ethic and the Spirit of Capitalism.* New York: Verso, 1987.

_____. *Men of Dishonor: Inside the Sicilian Mafia: An Account of Antonio Calderone.* New York: William Morrow, 1993.

Aronson, Bernard W. "Andean Trade Preference Pact: Essential to Combating Narcotics Traffic." *U.S. Dept. of State Dispatch*, Aug. 5, 1991, pp. 584–86.

"Asesinado Narco Alias 'Don Efra.'" *El Espectador*, Nov. 7, 1996.

"Asian Gangs Move into Drugs." *Newsday*, Sept. 29, 1987.

Assad, Hafex Al-, and Charles R. Schwab. "Syria." *Wall Street Journal.* Nov. 23, 1992.

Associated Press. "Bacchus Asked Why Ex-Prosecutor Not Charged." *Miami Herald* (International Satellite Edition), Mar. 22, 1997.

_____. "Colombian Pushing Anti-Drug Plan." *Miami Herald* (International Satellite Edition), Dec. 2, 1996.

_____. "Mass Exodus of Traids Denied." (Hong Kong) *South Morning Post*, June 8, 1997.

_____. "Mexican Military to Fight Drugs." *Miami Herald* (International Satellite Edition), Dec. 15, 1996.

_____. "Mexico's Lozano Defends Tenure." *Miami Herald* (International Satellite Edition), Mar. 5, 1997.

_____. "Upheaval Won't Stop War on Drugs, McCaffrey Says." *Miami Herald* (International Satellite Edition), Dec. 8, 1996.

_____. "U.S. Warns of Possible Heroin Epidemic." *Rock Hill* (S.C.) *Herald*, Apr. 4, 1994.

Badey, James R. "Federal Coordination Is Needed to Head Off Growing Threat from Vietnamese Criminals." *Organized Crime Digest*, Mar. 11, 1967, pp. 1–6.

Bagley, Bruce. "Dateline Drug Wars: Colombia: The Wrong Strategy." *Foreign Policy*, Winter 1989–1990, p. 154.

_____. "The New Hundred Years War? U.S. National Security and the War on Drugs." *Journal of Interamerican Studies and World Affairs*, Spring 1988, p. 164.

_____. "U.S. Foreign Policy and the War on Drugs: An Analysis of Policy Failure." *Journal of Interamerican Studies and World Affairs*, Summer/Fall 1988, pp. 189–212.

_____, and William O. Walker III. "Special Issue: Drug Trafficking Research Update." *Journal of Interamerican Studies and World Affairs*, Fall 1992, p. 35+.

_____, and _____, eds. *Drug Trafficking in the Americas.* New Brunswick, N.J.: Transaction, 1994.

Bak, David J., and Robert C. Fourier. "New Weapons in the War on Drugs." *Design News*, Sept. 4, 1989, p. 117+.

Bake, Allan, and others. "Drugged to the Eyeballs." *New African*, June 1995, pp. 16–19.

Baker, James. "Narcotics: Threat to Global Security." *U.S. Dept. of State Dispatch*, Sept. 3, 1990, p. 15.

Bakesley, Christopher. *Terrorism, Drugs, International Law and the Protection of Human Liberty*. New Brunswick, N.J.: Transaction, 1991.

Bandow, Doug. "Perverse Effects of the War on Drugs." *New York Times*, Aug. 23, 1992.

"Banker Pleads Innocent to Laundering Charges." *Wall Street Journal*, Jan. 17, 1994.

Bastone, William. "The Mob Is Dead! Long Live the Mob!" *Village Voice*, Sept. 21, 1993, pp. 25–32.

Baum, Dan. *Smoke and Mirrors: The War on Drugs and the Politics of Failure*. Boston: Little, Brown, 1996.

_____. "The War on Civil Liberties." *Nation*, June 29, 1992, pp. 886–88.

Bayona Vargas, Mauricio. "Clinton Reparte los Dolores." *El Espectador*, Sept. 25, 1996.

Beasley, James O. "Forensic Examination of Money Laundering Records." *FBI Enforcement Bulletin*, Mar. 1993, pp. 13–17.

Beaty, Jonathan, and S. C. Gwynne. "Too Many Questions." *Time*, Nov. 11, 1991, p. 42.

Beaty, Johnathan, and Richard Hornick. "A Torment of Dirty Dollars." *Time*, Dec. 18, 1989, p. 50.

Bensinger, Peter B. "World Drug Traffic." *Society*, May–June 1982, pp. 78–79.

Bentsen, Lloyd. "National Can Pull Plug on Money Laundering." *USA Today*, Dec. 8, 1994.

Bertram, Eva, and others. *Drug War Politics: The Price of Denial*. Berkeley: Univ. of California Press, 1996.

"Birth of a Narco Democracy." *Time*, Apr. 11, 1994, p. 19.

Blackman, Morris, and Kenneth Sharpe. "The War on Drugs: American Democracy under Assault." *World Policy Journal*, Winter 1989, p. 135+.

Blair, Doniphan. "Drug War Delusions, Unrealistic, Infeasible and Logistical Nightmare." *Humanist*, Sept.–Oct. 1990, p. 7+.

Blumenthal, Ralph. "How Tapes and Turncoat Helped Win the War Against Gotti." *New York Times*, Apr. 5, 1992.

Bolgar, Catherine. "Colombian Drug Money Distortion." *Wall Street Journal*, Mar. 25, 1994.

Booth, William. "Drug War Locks Up Prisons." *Washington Post*, July 7, 1993.

Boudreaux, Richard. "Russian Police Back Plan for Joint Anti-Mob Effort." *Los Angeles Times*, July 5, 1994.

Boutros-Ghali, Boutros. "Transnational Crime: The Market and the Rule of Law." *Vital Speeches*, Dec. 15, 1991, p. 130+.

Boyce, Daniel. "Narco Terrorism." *FBI Law Enforcement Bulletin*, Oct. 1987, pp. 1–32.

Boyum, David. "No: Swift and Sure Sanctions Work Better." *Insight on the News*, June 12, 1995, p. 19.

Branigan, William. "Sting Snares Asian Drug Ring, but Mass Heroin Flows to U.S." *Washington Post*, Dec. 12, 1993.

Brant, Martha. "Most Wanted Kingpin?" *Newsweek*, Mar. 10, 1997, p. 12.

Brauchli, Marcus W. "Pakistan's Wild Frontier Breeds Trouble." *Wall Street Journal.* June 3, 1993.

Brecher, E. M. *Licit and Illicit Drugs: The Consumer Union Report on Narcotics, Stimulants, Depressants, or Inhalants, Hallucinogens and Marijuana — Including Coffee, Nicotine and Alcohol.* Boston: Little, Brown, 1972.

Brianchon, Pierre. "Russian Mob Scene." *World Press Review*, Oct. 1995, pp. 28–29.

Briscoe, David. "Senators Won't Seek Mexico Vote." *Miami Herald* (International Satellite Edition), Mar. 15, 1997.

Brooke, James. "Crackdown Has Cali Drug Cartel on the Run." *New York Times*, June 27, 1995, p. 1.

Brookes, Stephen. "Drug Money Soils Clean Hands." *Insight on the News*, Aug. 21, 1989, p. 8.

Burgess, Harvey. "Drug Ring Suspected in Double Slaying." *Rock Hill* (S.C.) *Herald*, June 6, 1991.

Burnstein, P. "The Deadly Politics of Heroin." *Macleans*, Dec. 6, 1992, p. 10.

Buruma, Ian, and John McBeth. "Asia's Crime Syndicates." *World Press Review*, Mar. 1985, p. 55.

Butturini, Paula. "Italy Slowly Breaking Mafia's Iron Grip." *Boston Globe*, Jan. 16, 1994.

Byrne, John J. "How the Feds Beat the Money Launderers." *ABA Banking Journal*, Jan. 1995, pp. 55–56.

"Cae Capo de la Mafia Colombo Italiano." *El Espectador*, Feb. 8, 1997.

"Cali Quiere Jubilarse." *La Semana*, May 11, 1993, pp. 44–47.

Carey, Donald J., and H. Indelicarto. "Indications and Warning and the New World Environment: The Drug War Example." *Defense Intelligence*, Spring 1994, pp. 89–105.

Carrigan, Ann. "Victims of the Dirty War." *Progressive*, Nov. 1996, pp. 39–41.

Carter, Hodding III. "Day of the Triads." *M Inc.*, June 1991, p. 68+.

Carter, Mark R. "How to Win the Drug War Quickly." *Wall Street Journal*, Dec. 2, 1992.

"Cash at Any Price." *Economist*, May 9, 1992, p. 100.

Casper, Juliet M. "Review, *Organized Crime in America*, by Dennis Jay Kennedy and James O. Finkenauer." *Journal of Criminal Law and Criminology*, Winter 1995, p. 837.

Cassidy, Peter. "The Banker Who Said No to the CIA." *Progressive*, June 1992, p. 24.

Castillo, Fabio. *Los Jinetes de la Cocaína.* Bogotá, Colombia: Documentos Periodísticos, 1988.

Castro, Janice. "The Cash Cleaners: A Major Bank Is Indicted in Running a Global Drug-Money Network." *Time*, Oct. 24, 1988, p. 65.

_____. "A Worrisome Brand of Japanese Investor." *Time*, Apr. 20, 1992, p. 21.

Center for Strategic and International Studies. *The Transnational Drug Challenge.* Washington, D.C.: Center for Strategic and International Studies, 1993.

"Change in Swiss Bank Laws." *New York Times*, Mar. 3, 1994.

Chapman, Stephen. "The Awful Price of Fighting the War on Drugs." *Chicago Tribune*, May 21, 1992.

_____. "A Weapon of the Drug War Provokes Growing Disgust." *Chicago Tribune*, July 1, 1993.

"Charms of Coca, The." *Economist*, Oct. 28, 1995, p. 52.

Chauvin, Lucien. "Bolivia Farmers Open Markets to Show Coca Is Not a Drug Problem." *National Catholic Reporter*, Mar. 26, 1993, p. 15.

Chepesiuk, Ron. "Are CIA's Hands Clean on Drugs?" *Rock Hill* (S.C.) *Herald*, Jan. 30, 1997.

_____. "America's Other War." *Creative Loafing*, Mar. 16, 1991, p. 1+.

_____. "Colombia: A Nation Descends into Anarchy as Drug-Fueled Violence Escalates." *Defense and Diplomacy*, Sept. 1989, p. 1D+.

_____. "Colombian Connection: Mafia Battles Drug Mafia's Vicious Terror." *Charlotte Observer*, June 14, 1987.

_____. "Colombian Drug Lords Try to Buy Legitimacy." *Orlando Sentinel*, Mar. 18, 1990.

_____. "Colombian Drug Lords Try to Turn Wealth into Respect." *Orlando Sentinel*, Mar. 10, 1989.

_____. "Colombia's Better Run Kingdom." *Orlando Sentinel*, Feb. 7, 1994.

_____. "Colombia's Cocaine Convulsion." *New Leader*, June 27, 1988, pp. 11–14.

_____. "Colombia's Guerrillas Cultivate a Different Kind of Power Base." *Orlando Sentinel*, Jan. 26, 1996.

_____. "Colombia under Siege." *Defense and Diplomacy*, Sept. 1990, pp. 41–45.

_____. "A Country under Siege: Fighting Anarchy in Colombia." *New Leader*, Sept. 18, 1989, pp. 5–8.

_____. "Kingpin's Trial a Small Win in Losing War on Drugs." *Orlando Sentinel*, Oct. 4, 1987.

_____. "The New Drug Threat in Colombia." *Rock Hill* (S.C.) *Herald*, Mar. 15, 1997.

_____. *Sixties Radicals, Then and Now: Candid Conversations with Those Who Shaped an Era*. Jefferson, N.C.: McFarland, 1995.

_____. "Tales of the Drug Wars." *Creative Loafing*, Nov. 11, 1989, pp. 1–2.

_____. "To Live and Die in Colombia." *St. Petersburg Times*, Sept. 24, 1989.

_____. "Undermining Democracy: Drug Lords Versus the Press." *New Leader*, Apr. 30, 1990, pp. 9–10.

_____. "A War of Attrition: Narco-Paralysis in Colombia." *New Leader*, Jan. 13–27, 1997, pp. 6–7.

_____. "War on Drugs: A Government Sham." *Rock Hill* (S.C.) *Herald*, Dec. 21, 1996.

_____. "The War on Drugs: A Latin American Perspective." *Defense and Diplomacy*, Sept. 1989, pp. 48–51.

"Chinese Triads Pushing the Mafia Aside: Focusing on Heroin Smuggling, Extortion." *Organized Crime Digest*, Aug. 9, 1989, pp. 3–4.

Christensen, Mike. "FBI May Help Russia Fight Cocaine Wave." *Atlanta Journal and Atlanta Constitution*, May 28, 1994.

Clawson, Patrick, and Rensselaer Lee III. *The Andean Cocaine Industry*, New York: St. Martin's Press, 1996.

"Clinton Pressured to Decertify Mexico after Drug Arrest." *USA Today*, Feb. 28, 1997.

"CMA Defends Industry on Drug Charges." *Chemical Marketing Reporter*, Feb. 12, 1990, p. 3.

Cohen, Laurie, and Kenneth H. Bacon. "Banker at American Express Affiliate Faces Money-Laundering Investigation." *Wall Street Journal*, Nov. 8, 1993.

Cole, Richard. "Asian Gangs a Rising Threat." *Chicago Tribune*, July 6, 1994.

Collette, Merrill. "The Myth of the Narco Guerrilla." *Nation*, Aug. 1988, p. 130.

"Colombian Terror." *Economist*, Sept. 30, 1995, pp. 50–52.

"Colombian Traffickers Enter Heroin Market." *Rock Hill* (S.C.) *Herald*, Dec. 10, 1990.

"Colombia's Drug Business." *Economist*, Dec. 24, 1994, pp. 21–24.

"Colombia's Other Gangsters." *Economist*, Mar. 25, 1995, p. 48.

Conlon, Edward. "Mob Stories." *American Spectator*, Nov. 1992, p. 78.

Conner, Roger, and L. Burns. "The Winnable Drug War: How Communities Are Eradicating Local Drug Markets." *Brookings Review*, Summer 1992, pp. 26–29.

Cooper, Mary H. *The Business of Drugs*. Washington, D.C.: Congressional Quarterly, 1990.

Córdoba, José de. "Ex-General Venezolano: La CIA Aprobo Envío de Cocaína a EE.UU." *El Tiempo*, Nov. 22, 1996.

_____. "Testimony Says President Knew of Contributions by Cali Cartel." *Wall Street Journal*, Aug. 4, 1995.

Cordtz, Dan. "Dirty Dollars." *Financial World*, Feb. 1, 1994, pp. 20–24.

Cormier, Bill. "Mexicans Bristle over Rebuke of Clinton." *Miami Herald* (International Satellite Edition), Mar. 8, 1997.

_____. "Zedillo Vows to Restore Mexico Confidence, Respect." *Miami Herald* (International Satellite Edition), Mar. 9, 1997.

Cormier, Jim, "Booking the Mafia," *Saturday Night*, Mar. 1990, p. 19+.

Corn, David. "The C.I.A. and the Cocaine Coup." *Nation*, Oct. 7, 1991, p. 404.

Courtnay, Daniel. "Washing Dirty Money." *Police Chief*, Oct. 1985, p. 74.

Courtwright, David T. "Should We Legalize Drugs? History Answers." *American Heritage*, Feb.–Mar. 1993, p. 43.

Cowall, David. "Laundering of Crime Cash Troubles UN." *New York Times*, Nov. 25, 1994.

Cox, Caroline. "Glyphosate." *Journal of Pesticide Reform*, Summer 1991, p. 121+.

Craig, Richard B. "Are Drug Kingdoms South America's New Wave?" *World and I*, Nov. 1989, pp. 160–65.

Crozier, William. "The New World Disorder." *National Review*, Dec. 19, 1994, p. 47.

Cullen, Robert. "Comrades in Crime." *Playboy*, Apr. 1994, pp. 70–72.

Culley, Harriet. "International Narcotics Control." *Dept. of State Bulletin*, Oct. 1984, p. 39.

Cusack, Michael. "Where the Drug Trade Begins, How It Must End." *Scholastic Update*, May 10, 1985, p. 6.

Cyrix, Oliver. *Crime: An Encyclopedia*. North Pomfret, Vt.: Trafalgar Square, 1995.

D'Amato, Alphonse. "How to Stamp Out Money Laundering." *USA Today Magazine*, Sept. 1991, p. 16–18.

Dane, Abe. "High Tech Drug Busters." *Popular Mechanics*, Feb. 1990, p. 49+.

De Borchgrave, Arnaud. "The Bubonic Plague of International Crime." *Insight on the News*, Oct. 23, 1995, p. 40.

DeGeorge, Gail. "Confessions of a Money Launderer." *Business Week*, May 30, 1994, p. 119.

"Democracy and Drugs." *Christian Science Monitor*, Oct. 6, 1995.

De Palma, Anthony. "A $50 Million Payment Fuels Mexican Scandal." *New York Times*, Feb. 1, 1996.

_____. "Drug Traffickers Smuggling Tons of Cash from the U.S. Through Mexico." *New York Times*, Jan. 25, 1996.

Departamento Administrativo de Seguridad Dirección. *Aspectos de Interese sobre el Cultivo de Amapola.* Bogotá, Colombia: Departamento Administrativo de Seguridad, Dirección, Nov. 1991.

"Detecting Illegal Drugs." *USA Today Magazine*, June 1993, p. 8+.

Dolphin, Rick. "A Global Struggle: Drug Police Are Fighting the Odds." *Maclean's*, Apr. 3, 1989, p. 48.

"Don't Wait: Reintegrate." *Economist*, Feb. 29, 1992, pp. 46–47.

"El Dossier de Efraín Hernández Ramírez." *El Espectador*, Nov. 7, 1996.

Drozdiak, William. "European Unit — For Organized Crime." *Washington Post*, Aug. 2, 1994.

"Drug-Linked Currency Irregularities at Florida Banks." *International Currency Review*, 1980, No. 4, pp. 44–49.

"Drugs and Civil Rights." *Christian Science Monitor*, Dec. 16, 1993.

"Drugs $400 Billion; Second Only to Arms Trade." *Chicago Tribune*, Dec. 15, 1994.

"Drug Tale of Two Cities, A." *Economist*, Apr. 6, 1996, pp. 41–42.

"Drug War Begins." *CO Researcher*, Mar. 19, 1993, p. 250.

"Drug Wars." *U.S. News and World Report*, Feb. 11, 1991, p. 12.

"Duros Golpes a Mafia Colombos-Italianos." *El Tiempo*, Feb. 9, 1997.

Duzán, María Jimena. *Death Beat: A Colombia Journalist's Life Inside the Cocaine Wars.* New York: Harper Collins, 1994.

Dvorak, Rich. "Clinton's New Tack in War on Drugs: Reduce Demand." *Chicago Tribune*, Sept. 17, 1993.

Eaton, Tracy. "Mexico Fights Its Own Police in Drug War." *Dallas Morning News*, Aug. 18, 1996.

_____. "Mexico's Drug Eradication Agents Hail Success Against Pot, Poppies." *Miami Herald* (International Satellite Edition), Nov. 23, 1996.

Eddy, Paul, Hugh Sabogal, and Sarah Walden. *The Cocaine Wars.* New York: Norton, 1988.

Editorial Amnistía Internacional. *Violencia Política en Colombia: Mito y Realidad.* Washington, D.C.: Editorial Amnistia Internacional, 1994.

Ehrenfeld, Rachel. *Evil Money.* New York: HarperCollins, 1992.

_____. *Narcoterrorism and the Cuban Circuit.* New York: William Morrow, 1994.

_____. "Narco-Terrorism and the Cuban Connection." *Strategic Review*, Summer 1988, pp. 55–63.

Elliott, Michael. "Global Mafia." *Newsweek*, Dec. 13, 1993, pp. 22–31.

Elliott, Patricia. "A Life in the Drug Trade." *Saturday Night*, Dec. 1993, p. 20.

Ellis, David. "Open Borders, Sealed Accounts." *Time*, Apr. 29, 1991, p. 21.

Elsasser, Glen. "Court Rules U.S. May Abduct Foreigners." *Chicago Tribune*, June 16, 1992.

Emshwiller, John R. "IRS Dispatches Agents on Business in Crackdown on Money Laundering." *Wall Street Journal*, May 2, 1995.

English, T. J. *Born to Kill: America's Most Notorious Gang and the Changing Face of Organized Crime*. New York: William Morrow, 1994.

_____. "Rude Boys." *Playboy*, Oct. 1991, p. 86.

Epstein, G., and others, eds. *A New World Economy: Forces of Change and Plans of Action*. Philadelphia: Temple Univ. Press, 1993.

Erlanger, Stephen. "Southeast Asia Is Now Number One Source of U.S. Heroin." *New York Times*, Feb. 11, 1990, p. 26A.

Estlada, Louis, "Renegades in the Drug War: A Lord of Jamaican Posses" *Times of the Americas*, June 26, 1991, p. 16–19.

"E.U. No Se la Rebaja a Capo Mexicano." *Espectador*, Oct. 17, 1996.

"European Markets in Cocaine." *Contemporary Crisis*, Mar. 1989, pp. 35–52.

"Fact Sheet: Controlling Chemicals Used in Drug Trafficking." *U.S. Dept. of State Dispatch*, Mar. 2, 1992, p. 164.

Farah, Douglas. "Colombian Chain-Saw Gang Pushes Heroin, Prospers." *Washington Post*, July 27, 1992, p. 17.

_____. "Colombia's Jailed Drug Barons Said to Carry On Business." *Washington Post*, Jan. 13, 1996.

_____. "Drug Traffickers Build Central American Route to U.S." *Washington Post*, Mar. 28, 1993.

_____. "U.S.-Bogota: What Went Wrong?" *Washington Post*, Mar. 3, 1996.

_____. "U.S.-Colombian Split over Cali Cartel." *Washington Post*, Mar. 8, 1994.

_____, et al. "Illicit Dollars Flow via Unique Network." *Washington Post*, Sept. 19, 1993.

Farley, Hugh. "To Catch a Drug Kingpin, Follow the Money." *Governing*, Oct. 1990, p. 94.

Farragher, Thomas. "Ex Contra Chief Scoffs at CIA Drug Link." *Miami Herald* (International Satellite Edition), Nov. 27, 1996.

Fay, P. W. *The Opium War, 1840–1842*. Chapel Hill: Univ. of North Carolina Press, 1975.

Fedarko, Kevin. "Outwitting Cali's Professional Moriarty." *Time*, July 17, 1995, pp. 30–31.

Felsenthal, Edward, and Laurie P. Cohen. "Legal Beat: Bank Employees Charged." *Wall Street Journal*, Dec. 22, 1993.

Fialka, John J. "Computers Keep Tabs on Dirty Money." *Wall Street Journal*, May 8, 1995.

_____. "DEA's Sting Bank in the Caribbean Uncovers Laundering of Drug Money." *Wall Street Journal*, Dec. 19, 1994.

_____. "Drug Dealers Export Billions of Dollars to Evade Laws on Currency Reporting." *Wall Street Journal* (Eastern Edition), Apr. 7, 1994.

Fineman, Mark. "Mexico's Drug Czar Called Man of Integrity." *Miami Herald* (International Satellite Edition), Dec. 6, 1996.

_____. "Swiss Link Raul Salinas to $100 Million." *Los Angeles Times*, Dec. 7, 1995.

Fish, Jefferson. "Discontinuous Change and the War on Drugs." *Humanist*, Sept.–Oct. 1994, p. 14+.

Fitz-Simmons, Daniel W. "Sendero Luminoso—Case Study in Insurgency." *Parameters*, Summer 1993, pp. 64–73.

Florez, Carl P., and Bernardette Boyce. "Colombian Organized Crime." *Policy Studies*, 1990, pp. 81–88.

_____, and _____. "Laundering Drug Money." *FBI Law Enforcement Bulletin*, Apr. 1990, pp. 22–25.

Flynn, Steven. "Worldwide Drug Scourge: The Expanding Traffic in Illicit Drugs." *Brookings Review*, Winter 1993, pp. 6–11.

Follain, John. *A Dishonored Society: The Sicilian Mafia Threat to Europe*. New York: Warner, 1976.

"Follow the Money." *Economist*, Oct. 21, 1989, p. 29.

Ford, Jesse T. *Drug Control: U.S. Heroin Efforts in Southeast Asia: Testimony before the Subcommittee on National Security, International Affairs and Criminal Justice*. Washington, D.C.: U.S. Government Printing Office, 1996.

Foreign Affairs Subcommittee on Western Hemisphere Affairs. *Review of the 1992 International Narcotics Control Strategy Report Hearings, March 3–12, 1992*. Washington, D.C.: U.S. Superintendent of Documents, 1992.

"La Fortuna del 'Don Efra.'" *El Espectador*, Nov. 8, 1996.

"La Fortuna de El Señor de los Mares." *El Tiempo*, Nov. 8, 1996.

Foust, Dean. "The New, Improved Money Launderers." *Business Week*, June 28, 1993, pp. 90–91.

Fowler, Thomas B. "Winning the War on Drugs: Can We Get There from Here?" *Journal of Social, Political and Economic Studies*, Winter 1990, pp. 403–21.

Fox, Stephen R. *Blood and Power: Organized Crime in Twentieth Century America*. New York: William Morrow, 1989.

Frankel, Max. "O.K., Call It a Drug War." *New York Times Magazine*, Dec. 18, 1994, p. 30+.

Friedman, Alan. "B.C.C.I.'s Deadly Secrets." *Vanity Fair*, Feb. 1992, p. 36+.

Friedman, Robert I. "The Organizatsiya." *New York*, Nov. 7, 1994, pp. 50–58.

"From the Money Laundering Front." *ABA Banking Journal*, Mar. 1990, p. 16.

Gallego, Leonardo. "Coca Growers and Guerrillas." *Wall Street Journal*, Dec. 15, 1994.

Gambatta, Diego. *The Sicilian Mafia: The Business of Private Protection*. Cambridge, Mass.: Harvard Univ. Press, 1993.

"Gangster's Story, A." *Economist*, Dec. 5, 1992, p. 33.

"García Abrego Attorneys Rest Case." *Miami Herald* (International Satellite Edition), Oct. 11, 1996.

García, G. D. "Running Pot Where It's Not as Hot." *Time*, Nov. 29, 1982, p. 20.

Garrison, Lloyd. "Let Them Shoot Smack." *Time*, Mar. 19, 1984, p. 35.

Gelbard, Robert S. "International Crime Fighting Strategies." *U.S. Dept. of State Dispatch*, Dec. 1995, pp. 924–27.

Gene, J. P. "Losing Battles in the War on Drugs." *World Press Review*, June 1992, pp. 16–17.

"Getting the Boot: Italy, Unfinished Revolution." *Virginia Quarterly Review*, Spring 1996, pp. SS59–SS60.

"Gilberto Rodríguez Quedo Abogado a Pagar $105.00 Millones a la Justicia." *El Tiempo*, Oct. 30, 1996.

Gobierno de la República de Colombia and gobierno de los Estados unidos de América. *Programa para la Modernización de la Administración de Justicia*. Bogotá, Colombia: U.S. Embassy, 1996.

Goldberg, Carey. "Russian Police Warn of Cocaine Blizzard." *Los Angeles Times*, Feb. 27, 1993.

Goldman, Albert. "Outlaw Strongholds of Colombia." *High Times*, July 1978, pp. 45–48.

Goodson, Roy, and William J. Olson. "International Organized Crime." *Society*, Jan. 1995, pp. 18–29.

Gordon, Dinah. *The Return of the Dangerous Classes: Drug Prohibition and Politics.* New York: W. W. Norton, 1994.

Gordon, Michael R. "U.S. Military Long a Part of the Drug Battle." *New York Times*, Aug. 2, 1992.

Gray, John. "The Rise of Russia's Crime Commissars." *World Press Review*, June 1994, pp. 13–15.

Grazia, Jessica de. *DEA: The War Against Drugs.* London, Eng.: BBC Books, 1991.

Greenberger, Robert S. "China Becomes Major Transit Point in Heroin Trade." *Wall Street Journal*, May 20, 1992.

Greenburg, Michael. *British Trade and the Opening of China, 1800–1842.* Cambridge, Eng.: Cambridge Univ. Press, 1951.

Grover, Ronald. "A Japanese Laundry Worth $1 Billion." *Business Week*, May 24, 1993, p. 38.

Gugliotta, Guy, and Jeff Leen. *Kings of Cocaine.* New York: Harper, 1990.

Gunst, Laura. *Born Fi': A Journey Through the Jamaican Posse.* New York: Henry Holt, 1995.

_____. "Johnny-Too-Bad and the Sufferers." *Nation*, Nov. 13, 1989, p. 54.

Guthrie, Steven. "Colombia Enters Heroin Market." *Charlotte Observer*, Oct. 13, 1991.

Hallett, Carol Boyd. "Drugs, Diplomacy, Trade." *Washington Post*, Aug. 27, 1993.

Handelman, Stephen. *Comrade Criminal: Russia's New Mafia.* New Haven, Conn.: Yale Univ. Press, 1995.

_____. "The Russian 'Mafiya.'" *Foreign Affairs*, Mar. 1994, pp. 83–94.

Hannun, Phil, with Al Lotz. *Nightmare: Vietnamese House Invasion Robberies.* Falls Church, Va.: International Association of Asian Crime Investigators, 1991.

Hanson, David J. "Chemical Industry, Drug Agency Sort Out Chemical Diversion Issues." *Chemical and Engineering News*, Jan. 29, 1990, pp. 18–19.

_____. "Industry Rebuts Chemical Diversion Charges." *Chemical and Engineering News*, Feb. 12, 1990, pp. 5–6.

_____. "Narcotics Commission: Novel Initiatives for Growing Crisis." *UN Chronicle*, Sept. 1992, p. 72.

Hargreaves, Claire. *Snowfields: The War on Cocaine on the Andes.* New York: Holmes and Meir, 1992.

Harrison, Eric. "Jamaicans: New Face of U.S. Crime." *Los Angeles Times*, Jan. 3, 1989.

Harrison, Faye V. "Jamaica and the International Drug Economy." *Transafrican Forum*, Fall 1990, pp. 49–57.

Healy, Melissa. "New Anti-Drug Plan Would Use Military." *Los Angeles Times*, June 1, 1992.

Hellman, Peter. "Reagan Gets Tough on Drugs." *Rolling Stone*, Apr. 15, 1982, pp. 13–14.

Herman, E., and G. O'Sullivan. *The Terrorism Industry: The Experts and Institutions That Shape Our View of Terror.* New York: Pantehon, 1989.

"Heroina Colombiana Alarma a la DEA." *El Espectador,* Sept. 14, 1996.

Hertling, Mark P. "Narcoterrorism: The New Unconventional War." *Military Review,* Mar. 1990, pp. 28–45.

"High in the Andes." *Economist,* Feb. 13, 1993, p. 45.

Hinckle, Pia. "The Grip of the Octopus." *Newsweek,* June 8, 1992, p. 32.

Hockstader, Lee. "Russia's Criminal Condition: Gangsters Spreading Web from Moscow to the West." *Washington Post,* Feb. 26, 1995.

Hohler, Bob. "Crime Gangs Imperil Regimes, CIA Says." *Boston Globe,* Apr. 21, 1994.

Holmstrom, David. "War on Drugs, Two Decades Later." *Christian Science Monitor,* Aug. 27, 1992.

"Honorable Mob." *Economist,* Jan. 27, 1990, p. 19.

Horvitz, Leslie Alan. "U.S. Gamble May Pay Off in High Stakes Crime Battle." *Insight on the News,* July 25, 1994, p. 6.

"Hot Money; City of Angels." *U.S. News and World Report,* Apr. 10, 1989, p. 14.

"How BCCI Grew and Grew." *Economist,* Jan. 27, 1990, p. 84.

Hudson, Tim. "South America High: A Geography of Cocaine." *Focus,* Jan. 1985, p. 22.

Huff, Ronald. *Gangs in America.* Newbury Park, Calif.: Sage, 1990.

Huston, Peter. *Tongs, Gangs, and Triads: Chinese Crime Gangs in North America.* Boulder, Colo.: Paladin, 1995.

"In the Land of the Rising Sun." *Economist,* Aug. 26, 1989, p. 23.

Inciardi, James A. *The Drug Legislation Debate.* Newbury Park, Calif.: Sage, 1991.

_____. *History and Crime: Implications for Criminal Justice Policy.* Newbury Park, Calif.: Sage, 1980.

_____. *The War on Drugs: Heroine, Cocaine, Crime and Public Policy.* Palo Alto, Calif.: Mayfield, 1984.

Inglis, Brian. *The Forbidden Game: A Social History on Drugs.* New York: Scribner's, 1975.

"International Assistance for U.S. Police." *Police Chief,* Oct. 1993, p. 40.

"International Cartels Expand Influence." *UN Chronicle,* June 1994, p. 68.

"International Narcotics Control." *U.S. Dept. of State Dispatch,* Sept. 3, 1990, p. 15.

"International Narcotics Control: The Challenge of Our Decade." *Police Chief,* Oct. 1985, p. 42.

Intriago, Charles A. "Money Laundering: New Penalties, Risks, Burdens for Bankers." *Banker's Magazine,* Mar.–Apr. 1990, pp. 50–55.

"Is the Mafia in Retreat or in Defeat?" *Economist,* July 29, 1995, p. 33.

Isikoff, Michael. "U.S. Considers Shift in Drug War." *Washington Post,* Sept. 16, 1993.

_____. "U.S. May Widen Anti-Drug Drive in the Caribbean." *Washington Post,* June 1, 1992.

_____. "U.S. Probes Narcotics Unit Funded by CIA." *Washington Post,* Nov. 20, 1993.

"Italy: Mafia Looks East." *International Management* (European Edition), May 1990, p. 14.

Jackson, Robert L. "219 Jamaicans Held in Gang Arrest." *Los Angeles Times*, Oct. 14, 1988.

James, George. "Suspected Head of Heroin Network Is Arrested." *New York Times*, Mar. 30, 1993.

"Japanese Gangs Invade U.S." *Boston Globe*, Feb. 6, 1994.

Jensen, Holger. "The Laundering Game: Cleaning Dirty Money Is Crucial." *Economist*, June 24, 1989, p. 22.

Johnson, Peyton, and Philip Lealey. "Tackling Drug Trafficking at Its Source." *Ceres*, July–Aug. 1980, pp. 27–35.

Jones, Colin. "What's in a Suitcase?" *Banker* (London), Apr. 1990, p. 12.

Kaplan, David E., and Alec Dubro. *Yakuza: The Explosive Account of Japan's Criminal Underworld*. Reading, Mass.: Addison-Wesley, 1986.

Karnow, Stanley. *Vietnam: A History*. New York: Viking, 1983.

Katz, Gregory. "Russian Underworld Flourished in Police Wake." *Atlanta Journal and Atlanta Constitution*, June 18, 1995.

Kelley, Michael D. *Gangland: Drug Trafficking by Organized Criminals*. Vancouver, Wash.: Charles C Thomas, 1988.

Kelly, Orr. "Feds Versus Drug Runners: Game Gets Trickier." *U.S. News and World Report*, Oct. 4, 1982, p. 54.

Kelly, Robert J. "Organized Crime: Past, Present, and Future." *USA Today Magazine*, May 1992, p. 78.

_____, and Ko-lin Chin and Rufus Schatzberg. *Handbook of Organized Crime in the United States*. Westport, Conn.: Greenwood Press, 1994.

Kelly, Robert S., ed. *Organized Crime: A Global Perspective*. Totowa, N.J.: Rowman and Littlefield, 1986.

Kenney, Dennis J., and James O. Finckenauer. *Organized Crime in America*. London, Eng.: International Thompson, 1990.

Kernovsky, Eva. "Chaos in Colombia." *World Press Review*, Dec. 1996, p. 5.

Kerr, Peter. "Chinese Dominate New York Heroin Trade." *New York Times*, Aug. 9, 1987.

King, R. *The Drug Hang Up: America's Fifty Year Folly*. New York: Norton, 1972.

Kirkpatrick, Sidney. *Turning the Tide: One Man Against the Medellin Cartel*. New York: E. P. Dutton, 1991.

Klare, Michael T. "Fighting Drugs with the Military." *Nation*. Jan. 1, 1990, pp. 8–12.

Klebnikov, Paul. "Joe Stalin's Heirs." *Forbes*, Sept. 27, 1993, pp. 124–34.

Kleiman, Mark A. R. "Snowed in the Cocaine Blizzard." *New Republic*, Apr. 23, 1990, pp. 45–67.

Kleinknecht, William. *The New Ethnic Mobs: The Changing Face of Organized Crime in America*. New York: Free Press, 1996.

Ko-lin Chin. *Chinese Subculture and Criminality*. Westport, Conn.: Greenwood Press, 1990.

_____. "Triad Societies, Tongs, Organized Crime and Street Gangs in Asia and the United States." Unpublished Ph.D. diss., Univ. of Pennsylvania, 1986.

Krauss, Clifford. "One Cartel Dies and the Drugs Go On." *New York Times*. Aug. 13, 1995.

_____. and Douglas Frantz. "Cali Drug Cartel Using U.S. Business to Launder Cash." *New York Times*, Oct. 30, 1985.

Laats, Alexander, and Kevin O'Flaherty. "Colombia's Human Rights Implications of the War on Drugs Control Policy." *Harvard Human Rights Journal*, Spring 1990, p. 87.

_____. "Is U.S. Narcotics Assistance Promoting Human Rights Abuse in Colombia?" *Human Rights Working Paper* 1 (Mar. 1990): 102.

Labaton, Stephen. "Dirty Laundry." *New York Times Book Review*, Dec. 11, 1994, p. 33.

LaFranchi, Howard. "Cali Cartel Shows Drug Fight Isn't Over." *Christian Science Monitor*, Mar. 9, 1995.

_____. "Cali Cartel Stretches Out Tentacles." *Christian Science Monitor*, Feb. 8, 1996.

Lamour, Catherine, and Michael R. Lamberti. *The International Connection: Opium from Growers to Pushers*. New York: Pantehon, 1974.

Langer, John H. "A Preliminary Analysis: Drug Trafficking." *Police Studies*, Spring 1986, pp. 42–56.

Langford, Terri. "Ruiz Massieu: No Drug Bribes on My Watch." *Miami Herald* (International Satellite Edition), Mar. 15, 1997.

_____. "U.S. Gets to Seize $7.9 Million from Mexican Prosecutor." *Miami Herald* (International Satellite Edition), Mar. 16, 1997.

Larmer, Brooke. "A Leap of Faith." *Newsweek*, Mar. 10, 1997, pp. 10–12.

Lasagna, Louis, and Gardner Lindzey. "Marijuana Policy and the Drug Mythology." *Society*, Jan.–Feb. 1983, p. 67.

Lee, Rensselaer W. III. "Global Reach: The Threat of International Drug Trafficking." *Current History*, May 1995, pp. 207–11.

Lehmann-Haupt, Christopher. "Corralling the Brute and Boobs of the Mob." *New York Times*, Feb. 8, 1996.

Leitzel, Jim, Clifford Gaddy, and Michael Alexeev. "Mafiosi and Matrioshki." *Brookings Review*, Winter 1995, pp. 26–29.

Levine, Michael. *Deep Cover*. New York: Delacorte, 1990.

Levitsky, Melvyn. "Progress in the International War Against Illicit Drugs." *U.S. Dept. of State Dispatch*, Mar. 2, 1992, pp. 156–62.

_____. "Review of U.S. Efforts to Combat the Narcotics Trade." *U.S. Dept. of State Dispatch*, May 24, 1993, p. 386–387.

Lewis, Neil A. "In Washington, a Sicilian Mafia Trial Without the Glass Cages." *New York Times*, July 18, 1992.

Lieberman, Howard. "New Cartel Brazil." *Christian Science Monitor*, Feb. 8, 1996.

Lifshultz, L. "Bush, Drugs and Pakistan: Inside the Kingdom of Heroin." *Nation*, Nov. 14, 1987, pp. 492–96.

Lilley, Jeffrey. "Russian Revolution." *Sports Illustrated*, Jan. 10, 1994, pp. 56–61.

Linden, Dana Wechsler. "Closing In." *Forbes*, June 7, 1993, p. 52+.

Linnemann, J. H. "International Narcotics Control Strategy." *Dept. of State Bulletin*, Feb. 1982, pp. 46–51.

Lintner, Bertil. "Hooked on the Junta: U.S. Drug Policy Assailed for Links to Burmese Generals." *Far Eastern Economic Review*, Nov. 18, 1993, pp. 23–24.

_____. "Khun Sa: Asian Drug King on the Run." *Far Eastern Economic Review*, Jan. 20, 1994, pp. 22–24.

_____. "Pusher with a Cause: Khun Sa Stresses His Role as Shah Leader." *Far Eastern Economic Review*, Jan. 20, 1994, p. 24+.

Lippin, Todd. "Drug War Versus Development." *Technology Review*, Jan. 1991, pp. 17–19.

Lubasch, Arnold H. "Drug Dealing Was Banned by Mob, U.S. Witness Says." *New York Times*, Apr. 15, 1993.

Lubin, Nancy. "Central Asia's Drug Bazaar." *New York Times*, Nov. 16, 1992.

Lubove, Seth. "Cash Capital." *Forbes*, Apr. 16, 1993, p. 18.

Lupo, Alan. "A New Breed of Comrade(s) in Arms." *Boston Globe*, Dec. 10, 1995.

Lupsha, Peter A. "Drug Trafficking: Mexico and Colombia in Comparative Perspective." *Journal of International Affairs*, Spring/Summer 1981, pp. 95–115.

_____. *The Political Economy of Drug Trafficking: The Herrera Organization (Mexico and the United States)*. Albuquerque, N.M.: Latin American Institute, Univ. of New Mexico, 1980.

Lyman, Michael. *Organized Crime*. Springfield, Ill. Charles C Thomas, 1990.

Lyons, David. "DEA Officer Faults Police in Mexico." *Miami Herald* (International Satellite Edition), Mar. 14, 1997.

Mabry, Donald J. *Latin American Narcotics Control and U.S. National Security*. Westport, Conn.: Greenwood Press, 1989.

MacCormack, John. "Border Crossing Access Likely to Be Curtailed." *Colombian Post*, Nov. 18–24, 1996.

MacGregor, James. "The Opium War." *Wall Street Journal*, Sept. 29, 1992.

Machalaba, Daniel. "Deadly Cargo." *Wall Street Journal*, May 18, 1989.

Mack, J. A. *The Crime Industry*. Lexington, Mass.: Lexington Books, 1975.

"Mafia Again, The." *Economist*, Mar. 11, 1995, p. 5+.

Maingot, Anthony P. "Offshore Secret Centers and the Necessary Role of States: Bucking the Trend." *Journal of Interamerican Studies and World Affairs*. Winter 1995, pp. 1–24.

Mallowe, Mike. "Disorganized Crime." *Philadelphia Magazine*, Jan. 1993, p. 72.

Marquis, Christopher. "Decertification Could Result in Backlash." *Miami Herald* (International Satellite Edition), Feb. 26, 1997.

_____. "House Rebuffs Mexico 251–175." *Miami Herald* (International Satellite Edition), Mar. 14, 1997.

_____. "Senate Passes Mexico Bill." *Miami Herald* (International Satellite Edition), Mar. 21, 1997.

_____. "U.S. Lawmakers Urge Sending Stern Warning." *Miami Herald* (International Satellite Edition), Feb. 26, 1997.

Marshall, Ingwerson. "Jamaican Drug Gangs Stake Out Turf in U.S." *Christian Science Monitor*, Aug. 13, 1987.

"Marshall Plan in Reverse, A." *UN Chronicle*, Mar. 1990, pp. 20–33.

Martin, John M., and Anne T. Romano. *Multinational Crime: The Challenge of Terrorism, Espionage, Drugs and Arms Trafficking*. Newbury Park, Calif.: Sage, 1992.

Massing, Michael. "The New Mafia." *New York Review of Books*, Dec. 3, 1992, p. 6+.

_____. "There's Always a New Kingpin." *Washington Post*, June 25, 1995.

Matheson, Mary. "Kings Jailed but Colombia's Drugs Roll On." *Christian Science Monitor*, July 11, 1995.

Maura, Christopher. "How the U.S. Battles Drugs on Three Fronts." *Scholastic Update*, May 10, 1985, p. 6.

McCarroll, Thomas. "The Supply Side Scourge: Cocaine Is So Abundant That Interdiction Fails to Affect Prices." *Time*, Nov. 13, 1989, p. 81.

McClintock, David. *Swordfish: A True Story of Ambition, Savagery, and Betrayal.* New York: Pantheon, 1993.

McCoy, Alfred J. *The Politics of Heroin: CIA Complicity in the Global Drug Trade.* Brooklyn, N.Y.: Laurence Hill, 1991.

_____. "What War on Drugs? The CIA Connection." *Progressive*, July 1991, p. 20–26.

_____, and Alan A. Block, eds. *War on Drugs: Studies in the Failure of U.S. Narcotics Policy.* Boulder, Colo.: Westview, 1992.

McDonald, R. Robin. "DEA Says Operation Exposed U.S.-Europe Drug Money Ties." *Atlanta Journal and Atlanta Constitution.* Dec. 17, 1994.

MacDonald, Scott B. *Dancing on a Volcano: The Latin American Drug Trade.* New York: Praeger, 1988.

_____. *Mountain High, White Avalanche: Cocaine and Power in the Andean States and Panama.* Westport, Conn.: Praeger, 1989.

McGarvey, Robert. "Global Organized Crime." *American Legion*, Feb. 1996, pp. 16–17.

_____. "Hard Time for the Mafia." *American Legion*, Apr. 1991, p. 32.

McGee, Jim. "Fake DEA Bank Stings Cali Cartel." *Washington Post*, Dec. 17, 1994.

McWeeney, Sean M. "The Scilian Mafia and Its Impact on the United States." *FBI Law Enforcement Bulletin*, Feb. 1997, pp. 1–10.

Mecham, Michael. "Customs Integrates P-3B Orion into Surveillance Fleet." *Aviation Week and Space Technology*, Jan. 30, 1989, p. 53.

_____. "E-2C Aircraft Are Key to Coast Guard's Antidrug Smuggling Operations." *Aviation Week and Space Technology*, Jan. 30, 1989, p. 37.

_____. "Pentagon Offers P-3As, Utility Helicopters for Anti Drug Effort." *Aviation Week and Space Technology*, Jan. 30, 1989, p. 45.

Meddis, Sam Vincent. "Cocaine Bust Links Mafia, Cali Cartel." *USA Today*, Sept. 29, 1992.

_____. "Colombians Enter Free-for-all for Heroin Trade." *USA Today*, Feb. 4, 1994.

"Mercenary Talks How Drug Links Get Arms." *San Francisco Chronicle*, Feb. 28, 1991.

Mermelstein, Max. *The Man Who Made It Snow.* New York: Simon and Schuster, 1990.

"Merrill Lynch Brokers in Panama Indicted in Laundering Case." *Wall Street Journal*, Mar. 7, 1994.

"Mexico Files New Charges Against Jailed Brother of Ex-Chief." *New York Times*, Dec. 4, 1995.

"México, Minado por los Narcos." *El Espectador*, Feb. 24, 1997.

"México, Principal Amenaza para E.U. en Tráfico de Droga." *El Tiempo*, Nov. 22, 1996.

Meyer, Dan C. "The Myth of Narco Terrorism in Latin America." *Military Review*, Mar. 1990, pp. 64–70.

Michaelis, Laura. "Money-Laundering Bill Passes House." *Congressional Quarterly Weekly Report*, Mar. 26, 1994, p. 725.

"Military's Drug Interception Is Labeled Failure by Study." *New York Times*, Sept. 16, 1993.

Miller, Karen Lowry. "Suddenly, the Japanese Mob Is Out of the Shadows." *Business Week*, July 8, 1991, p. 29.

Mills, James. *The Underground Empire: Where Crime and Justice Embrace*. New York: Doubleday, 1986.

Mitchell, Alison. "U.S. Freezes Assets of Cartel in New Effort Against Drugs." *New York Times*, Oct. 23, 1995.

"Mob, The: Hit Hard but Still a Force." *U.S. News and World Report*, May 25, 1996, p. 32.

"Money Laundering Problems and Solutions." *Banker's Magazine*, Mar.–Apr. 1990, pp. 50–55.

Montgomery, Jim. "Feds Crack Down on Laundering of Narcotics Money." *Wall Street Journal*, Mar. 12, 1981.

Moody, John. "A Day with the Chess Player." *Time*, July 1, 1991, pp. 34–37.

Moore, John W. "Global Reach." *To Grab Drug Smugglers, Stock Swindlers and Tax Cheats. National Journal*, Feb. 11, 1989, pp. 326–31.

Moore, M. H. "Organized Crime as a Business Enterprise" (Unpub. ms., J. F. Kennedy School of Government, Harvard Univ., 1989.

Moorhead, Alan Howell. "International Narcotics Control, 1939–1946." *Foreign Policy Reports*, July 1, 1946, p. 94.

Morales, Edmundo. *White Gold Rush in Peru*. Tucson: Univ. of Arizona Press, 1989.

Morgan, H. Wayne. *Drugs in America: A Social History, 1800–1980*. Syracuse, N.Y.: Syracuse Univ. Press, 1981.

Morgan, Robert. "Knock and Talk: Consent Searches and Civil Liberties." *FBI Law Enforcement Bulletin*, Nov. 1991, pp. 6–10.

Morgenthau, Tom et al. "Cocaine's 'Dirty' 300." *Newsweek*, July 1, 1991, pp. 3–7.

_____, and Douglas Waller. "The Widening Drug War." *Newsweek*, July 1, 1991, pp. 32–34.

Musto, David. *The American Disease: Origins of Narcotics Control*. New York: Oxford Univ. Press, 1987.

_____. "Illicit Price of Cocaine in Two Eras." *Connecticut Medicine*, June 1990, pp. 321–26.

_____. "Opium, Cocaine and Marijuana in American History." *Scientific American*, July 1991, p. 40.

Myerson, Allen R. "American Express Unit Settles Laundering Case." *New York Times*, Nov. 22, 1994.

Nadelmann, Ethan A. "International Drug Trafficking and U.S. Foreign Policy." *Washington Quarterly*, Fall 1985, pp. 86–104.

Nash, Jay Robert. *World Encyclopedia of Organized Crime*. New York: Marlowe, 1994.

Nash, Nathaniel C. "War on Drugs in Peru Shows Limited Gains." *New York Times*, Dec. 6, 1992.

"National and International Drug Problem, The." *Police Chief*, Oct. 1985, p. 28.

National Narcotics Intelligence Consumers Committee. *The Supply of Drugs to the Illicit Market from Foreign and Domestic Sources in* .... Washington, D.C.: The Committee.

Navarro, Mireya. "When Drug Kingpins Fall, Illicit Assets Buy a Cushion." *New York Times*, Mar. 19, 1996.

Navone, John J. "Italy's Re-Renaissance." *America*, Dec. 9, 1989, pp. 417–418, 425.

"El Negocio de la Droga Se Extiende en México." *El Tiempo*, Dec. 19, 1996.

Nell, Edward. "The Dynamics of the Drug Market." *Challenge*, Mar.–Apr. 1994, p. 13.

"New Drug Strategy Needed." *Colombian Post*, Nov. 18–24, 1996.

"New Front on the War on Drugs, A." *Economist*, Apr. 29, 1995, p. 56.

"New UN Crime Commission Created." *UN Chronicle*, Mar. 1992, p. 87.

Nicholl, Charles. *The Fruit Palace*. New York: St. Martin's Press, 1985.

Nielsen, Kirk. "Cali Cartel Stretches Out Tentacles: Miami Remains Corporate Office for Illicit Drug Barons." *Christian Science Monitor*, Dec. 8, 1996.

"Nigerian Connection, The." *Newsweek* (Asian Edition), Oct. 19, 1991, p. 19.

O'Brien, Timothy L. "Law Firm's Downfall Exposes New Methods of Money Laundering." *Wall Street Journal* (Eastern Edition), May 26, 1992.

O'Donnell, Santiago. "Former Nigerian Diplomat Charged in Heathrow-to-Dulles Drug Sting." *Washington Post*, Dec. 13, 1992.

Olson, William J., and Samuel Francis. "Question: Should Crime Fighting Be Foreign Policy Priority?" *Insight on the News*, July 17, 1995, p. 18.

"Opening Up of BCCI, The." *Economist*, Aug. 3, 1991, p. 21.

Oppenheimer, Andres. "Mexican Drug Suspect Freed." *Miami Herald* (International Satellite Edition), Mar. 2, 1997.

_____. "New Cartels Muscle In: Mexico, Not Colombia." *Miami Herald* (International Satellite Edition), Mar. 15, 1997.

_____. "Rift Threatens Drug Probe." *Miami Herald* (International Satellite Edition), Nov. 28, 1996.

_____. "Salinas Inquiry Puts Mexico to the Test." *Miami Herald* (International Satellite Edition), Dec. 1, 1996.

Ormande, Tom. "Cracking Down on the Yakuza." *World Press Review*, May 1992, p. 48.

Ostrow, Ronald J. "Leaders' Arrest Called Death of Cali Drug Cartel." *Los Angeles Times*, Aug. 7, 1995.

Padgett, Tim. "Getting Off Drugs?" *Time*, Mar. 10, 1997, pp. 14–20.

Padilla, Felix M. *The Gang as an American Enterprise*. New Brunswick, N.J.: Rutgers Univ. Press, 1992.

Paternostro, Silvana. "Mexico as a Narco Democracy." *World Policy*, Spring 1995, pp. 41–47.

Patten, Steve. "All-out War on Heroin in Golden Triangle." *U.S. News and World Report*, May 24, 1982, p. 49.

Peck, Grant. "McCaffrey Sees Case for Asian Cooperation." *Miami Herald* (International Satellite Edition), Nov. 24, 1996.

Penn, Stanley. "Asian Connection." *Wall Street Journal*, Mar. 22, 1990.

Perl, Raphael. *Drugs and Foreign Policy: A Critical Review*. Boston: Westview, 1994.

Philipsborn, Chris. "Cocaine Squeeze." *New Statesman and Society*, Feb. 12, 1993, p. 10.

Pletka, Danielle. "Heroin, Inc.: The Nigerian Connection (Drug Trafficking Through Nigeria)." *Insight on the News*, Sept. 30, 1991, p. 22.

_____. "Mafia Warfare Deadlier Than Ever." *Insight on the News*, Oct. 22, 1990, p. 38.

Podesta, Don, and Douglas Farah. "Drug Policy in the Andes." *Washington Post*, Mar. 27, 1993.

"Police Gain Powers Against Crime." *Facts on File*, Mar. 19, 1992, p. 200.

Policía Antinarcoticas (Colombia). *El Glifisato en la Erradicación de Cultivos Illicitos*. Bogotá, Colombia: Policía Nacional de Colombia, 1992.

Polk, Peggy. "Informers Expose the Sicilian Mafia." *Chicago Tribune*, Feb. 6, 1994.

Pons, Philippe. "China's Gang of Choice." *World Press Review*, Feb. 1994, p. 51.

"Por un General, México Se Raja en Lucha Antidroga." *El Espectador*, Feb. 20, 1997.

Posner, Gerald. *Warlords of Crime: Chinese Secret Societies — The New Mafia*. New York: McGraw-Hill, 1988.

Post, T. "10 Acres, Valley View: Drug Lord's Jail" *Newsweek*, July 1, 1991, p. 34.

Powell, Bill. "Japan: The Fall of the Don." *Newsweek*, Oct. 26, 1992, p. 42.

Powis, Robert E. *Money Launderers*. New York: Probus, 1992.

_____. "Money Laundering: Problems and Solutions." *Banker's Magazine*, Nov.–Dec. 1992, p. 72.

Pownall, Mark. *Heroin*. Oxford, Eng.: Heinemann, 1991.

Prager, Karsten. "Drugs, Money and a President's Ruin." *Time*, Feb. 5, 1996, p. 37.

President's Commission on Organized Crime. *America's Habit: Drug Trafficking and Organized Crime*. Washington, D.C.: U.S. Government Printing Office, 1986.

_____. *The Cash Connection: Organized Crime, Financial Institutions and Money Laundering*. Washington, D.C.: U.S. Government Printing Office, 1984.

_____. *The Impact of Organized Crime Today*. Washington, D.C.: U.S. Government Printing Office, 1986.

Press, Robert M. "Drugs Strain U.S.–Nigeria Relations." *Christian Science Monitor*, Aug. 12, 1992.

Preston, Gregory A. "Review, *The New Ethnic Mobs: The Changing Face of Organized Crime*, by William Kleinknecht." *Library Journal*, Feb. 15, 1996, p. 64.

Preston, Julia. "Drug Connection Links Mexican Military to Spate of Abductions." *Colombian Post*, Mar. 17–23, 1997.

Priest, Dana. "Officials Face Challenge in Stemming Jamaican Drug Trade." Feb. 23, 1988.

Pusey, Allen. "Asian Organized Crime Growing in Dallas." *Dallas Morning News*, Sept. 14, 1986.

"Putting an Ear to the Wires." *Time*, Oct. 16, 1989, p. 60.

Raab, Selwyn. "Influx of Russian Gangsters Trouble FBI in Brooklyn." *New York Times*, Aug. 23, 1994.

Radin, Charles A. "Japan's Political Gangsters." *Charlotte Observer*, June 10, 1994.

Raine, Linnea P., and Frank J. Clilluffo. *Global Organized Crime: The New Empire on Evil*. Washington, D.C.: Center for Strategic and International Studies, 1994.

Ramo, Joshua Cooper. "Crime Online." *Time Canada*, Sept. 30, 1996, p. 24.

Reding, Andrew. "The Fall and Rise of the Cartels." *Washington Post*, Sept. 17, 1995.

Reiss, Spencer. "Jim Brown Is Still Dead." *Newsweek*, Apr. 6, 1992, p. 41.

Reuter, Peter. "The Decline of the American Mafia." *Public Interest*, Summer 1995, pp. 89–99.

"Review, *A Dishonored Society: The Sicilian Mafia's Threat to Europe*, by John Follain." *New Statesman and Society*, Jan. 12, 1996, p. 36.

Reyes, Geraldo, and Jeff Leen. "One-time Venezuela Guard Chief Indicted on Drug Counts in the U.S." *Miami Herald* (International Satellite Edition), Nov. 23, 1996.

Richburg, Keith B. "U.S.-Nigerian Relations Soured by Recriminations." *Washington Post*, July 21, 1992.

Riemer, Blanca. "The Drug War — European Style." *Business Week*, Oct. 2, 1989, p. 31.

"Rising Narcotics Danger Says Council." *UN Chronicle*, June 1982, pp. 76–79.

Robberson, Tod. "Mexico's Spreading Drug Stain: Mexican Cartels Expanding Role in Trafficking." *Washington Post*, Mar. 12, 1995.

_____. "Salinas In-Laws Linked to Drug Allegations." *Washington Post*, Nov. 25, 1995.

Robinson, Jeffrey. *The Laundrymen*. New York: Simon and Schuster, 1990.

Robinson, Linda. "New Target: Cali Cartel." *U.S. News and World Report*, Dec. 23, 1991, pp. 28–29.

_____, and Gordon Witkin. "Cracks in the Drug War." *U.S. News and World Report*, Mar. 2, 1992, p. 49.

Rohter, Larry. "Convicting Cali's Drug Boss May Be as Hard as Arresting Him." *New York Times*, June 11, 1995.

Rose, Jonathan. "The Sorry History of Drug Abuse in the U.S." *Scholastic Update*, May 10, 1985, p. 19.

Rosenthal, James. "Russians' New Expert: The Mob," *The Washington Post*, June 14, 1990, p. 1.

Rotella, Sebastian. "U.S., Mexico Join Forces Against Drug Cartels." *Los Angeles Times*, Apr. 4, 1995.

Rowe, Dennis, ed. *International Drug Trafficking*. Chicago: Univ. of Illinois at Chicago, Office of International Criminal Justice, 1988.

Rublowsky, John. *The Stoned Age: Drugs in America*. New York: Putnam, 1974.

Sabbage, Robert. "The Cartels Would Like a Second Chance." *Rolling Stone*, May 4, 1994, pp. 35–38.

Sabourin, Serge. "From the Cold War to the Drug War." *New Perspectives Quarterly*, Fall 1989, pp. 111–132.

Sack, Kevin. "26 Members of Chinese-American Groups in Atlanta Indicted." *New York Times*, Feb. 6, 1996.

Salerno, Ralph. *The Crime Confederation: Cosa Nostra and Allied Operations in Organized Crime*. Garden City, N.Y.: Doubleday, 1969.

Sanchez Fonseca, Marcelo. "CIA: Traficantes de Cocaína." *El Tiempo*, Sept. 22, 1996.

Sanger, David E. "Hemisphere Talks Open; U.S. Is Hedging Its Hopes." *New York Times*, Dec. 10, 1994.

_____. "Money Laundering New and Improved." *New York Times*, Dec. 24, 1995.

Scheer, Robert. "Fighting the Wrong War." *Playboy*, Oct. 1994, p. 49.

Schemann, Serge. "Russian Wise Guys." *New York Times Book Review*, June 4, 1995, p. 7.

Schlosser, Eric. "Reefer Madness." *Atlantic Monthly*, Aug. 1994, p. 45.

Schreiberg, David. "Birth of the Baby Cartels." *Newsweek*, Aug. 21, 1995, p. 37.

Schulteis, Rob. "Chinese Junk: My Search for the Red Tiger General." *Mother Jones*, Mar. 1982, p. 34+.

Sciolino, Elaine. "State Department Report Labels Nigeria Major Trafficker of Drugs to U.S." *New York Times*, Apr. 5, 1994.

Scott, Peter Dale, and Johnathan Marshall. *Cocaine Politics, Drugs, Armies and the CIA in Central America*. Los Angeles: Univ. of California Press, 1991.

"Scourge of Drug Trafficking, The." *New Times*, Dec. 1985, pp. 18–23.

Select Committee on Narcotics Abuse and Control. *International Narcotics Control Study Mission to Hawaii, Hong Kong, Thailand, Burma, Pakistan, Turkey and India*. Washington, D.C.: U.S. Government Printing Office, 1984.

Sene, P. M. "Africa and the Drug Threat." *World Health*, Dec. 1981, pp. 10–13.

Senigallia, Silvio F. "Challenged by the Mafia: Italian Justice on the Run." *New Leader*, Sept. 4, 1989, pp. 10–11.

Serrill, Michael S. "Mexico's Black Mood." *Time*, Oct. 7, 1991, pp. 14–19.

Sessions, William. "Combating Organized Crime: The American Experience." *Vital Speeches*, Feb. 15, 1993, p. 262+.

_____. "International Crime in the 90s and the 21st Century." *Vital Speeches*, Nov. 15, 1990, p. 69.

Shannon, Elaine. *Desperadoes*. New York: NAL-Dutton, 1989.

_____. "Narco-Gnomes of Mexico: Where Drug Money Goes to Hide." *Washington Post*, Mar. 17, 1996.

_____. "New Kings of Cocaine." *Time*, July 1, 1991, pp. 28–33.

Short, M. *Crime Inc.: The Story of Organized Crime*. London, Eng.: Thomas Methuen, 1984.

Shultz, George. "The Campaign Against Drugs: The International Dimension." *Dept. of State Bulletin*, Nov. 1984, pp. 29–34.

"Sicilian Mafia, The: A State Within a State." *Economist*, Apr. 24, 1993, pp. 21–22.

Sides, W. Hampton. "This Is War: In the Shadowy World of Drugs, Police Battle Violent Jamaican Posses." *Washingtonian*, Apr. 1988, pp. 137–39.

Sierra, Sonia. "El Señora de los Narcos. *El Tiempo*, Feb. 23, 1997.

Sifakis, Carl. *The Mafia Encyclopedia*. New York: Facts on File, 1987.

Silberman, Charles. *Criminal Violence, Criminal Justice*. New York: Random House, 1978.

Sinha, Maya. "The New Mafia Order." Review of *Thieves' World: The Threat of the New Global Network of Organized Crime*, by Claire Sterling. *Mother Jones*, May 1995, p. 78.

Slevin, Peter. "Clinton Rebuffed on Mexico." *Miami Herald* (International Satellite Edition), Mar. 7, 1997.

_____. "A One-Sided War on Drugs." *Miami Herald* (International Satellite Edition), Mar. 16, 1997.

_____. "Outlaw Cowboy Relished His Fame." *Miami Herald* (International Satellite Edition), December 3, 1993.

Sloane, Wendy. "FBI's Moscow Mission: The Mob, Nuclear Theft." *Christian Science Monitor*, July 5, 1994.

_____. "Russian Organized Crime Infiltrates Economy, Threatens Foreign Investment." *Christian Science Monitor*, June 14, 1994.

Sloman, L. *Reefer Madness: The History of Marijuana in America*. Indianapolis: Bobbs Merrill, 1979.

Smith, H. E. *Transnational Crime: Investigative Responses*. Chicago: Univ. of Illinois at Chicago, Office of International Criminal Justice, 1989.

"Sniffing Out Illicit Drugs and Explosives." *USA Today Magazine*, June 1993, p. 8.

Snow, Anita. "Mexico Drug Scandal Widens with Arrest of Second General." *Miami Herald* (International Satellite Edition), Mar. 19, 1997.

_____. "Shakeup in Mexico's Ruling Party." *Miami Herald* (International Satellite Edition), Dec. 15, 1996.

Spaeth, Anthony. "When the Barbarians Overrun the Gate." *Time*, Mar. 20, 1995, p. 51.

Spencer, David. "Liability under UN Drug Trafficking Convention: Do the New Measures to Combat Money Laundering Go Far Enough?" *International Financial Review*, Mar. 1990, pp. 16–19.

Stahl, Marc B. "Asset Forfeiture, Burdens of Proof and the War on Drugs." *Criminal Law and Criminology*, Summer 1992, pp. 274–337.

Stares, Paula B. *The Problem of Drugs in a World Without Frontiers*. Washington, D.C.: Brookings Institution, 1996.

Starr, Mark. "Reagan's War on Drugs." *Newsweek*, Aug. 9, 1982, pp. 14–15.

Sterling, Claire. *Crime Without Frontiers*. New York: Little, Brown, 1994.

_____. *Octopus: The Long Reach of the International Sicilian Mafia*. New York: W. W. Norton, 1990.

_____. "Redfellas." *New Republic*, Apr. 11, 1994, pp. 19–22.

_____. *Thieves' World: The Threat of the New Global Network of Organized Crime*. New York: Simon and Schuster, 1994.

Stevenson, Mark. "Ex-Mexico City Prosecutor New Drug Czar." *Miami Herald* (International Satellite Edition), Mar. 11, 1997.

Stewart, Gail B. *Drug Trafficking*. San Diego, Calif.: Lucent, 1990.

Stoessel, Walter J., Jr. "U.S. Policy on International Narcotics Control." *Dept. of State Bulletin*, Sept. 1982, pp. 46–48.

Strong, Simon. *Whitewash: Pablo Escobar and the Cocaine Wars*. London, Eng.: Macmillan, 1995.

Stuttaford, Genevieve. "Review, *Gangland: How the FBI Broke the Mob*, by Howard Blum." *Publisher's Weekly*, Sept. 20, 1993, p. 52.

Sullivan, Mary Ellen. "Drugs: The World Picture." *Current Health*, Feb. 1990, pp. 4–5.

Sutton, James. "A Brief Overview of the Collaboration Between Colombian and Mexican Drug Trafficking Operations." Unpublished report to the U.S. Department of Justice, ca. 1994.

_____. "Colombian Drug Cartels." Unpublished report to the U.S. Department of Justice, ca. 1993.

Swisher, Karen, ed. *Drug Trafficking*. San Diego, Calif.: Greenhaven, 1991.

Symons, William C., and others. "The Sicilian Mafia Is Still Going Strong." *Business Week*, Apr. 18, 1988, p. 43.

Tanner, Adam, and Pam Grier. "Russia's Notorious Mafia Spreads Tentacles of Crime Around Globe." *Christian Science Monitor*, Jan. 11, 1995.

Tarazona-Sevillano, Gabriela. *Sendero Luminoso and the Threat of Narcoterrorism*. Westport, Conn.: Praeger, 1990.

Tarshis, Lauren. "From Coca-Cola to Cartels: Battling Drugs in America." *Scholastic Update*, Nov. 17, 1989, p. 10.

Taylor, A. H. *American Diplomacy and Narcotics Trafficking, 1900–1939*. Durham, N.C.: Duke Univ. Press, 1969.

Taylor, Clyde D. "Links Between International Narcotics Trafficking and Terrorism." *Dept. of State Bulletin*, Aug. 1985, pp. 68–74.

Teaster, Joseph B. "Exiting Drug Chief Warns of Cartels." *New York Times*, Oct. 31, 1993.

Tedford, Deborah, and Jo Ann Zuniga. "Cocaine Kingpin Is Guilty; Cartel Chief Could Get Life." *Houston Chronicle*, Oct. 17, 1996.

Thomas, Jon R. "International Campaign Against Drug Trafficking." *Dept. of State Bulletin*, Jan. 1985, p. 50.

———. "Narcotics Control in Latin America." *Dept. of State Bulletin*, Apr. 1986, pp. 77–80.

Thomas, Pierre. "Rules Target Chemical Sales in Colombia." *Washington Post*, Mar. 18, 1996.

Thornton, Mark. *Economics of Prohibition*. Salt Lake City: Univ. of Utah Press, 1991.

"Time for a Global Criminal Court." *New York Times*, Nov. 21, 1994.

Toro, María C. *Mexico's War on Drugs: Causes on Consequences*. Boulder, Colo.: Lynne Rienner, 1995.

"Tracking the International Drug Trade." *Scholastic Update*, May 10, 1985, pp. 37–41.

Traub, James. *The Billion Dollar Connection: The International Drug Trade*. New York: Julian Messner, 1983.

Trebach, A. S. *The Great Drug War*. New York: Macmillan, 1986.

Trotta, Dan. "U.S.-Mexican Border Becomes Fertile New Killing Ground." *Reuters*, Oct. 24, 1996.

True, Philip. "Mexico's New Anti-Drug Czar Vows to Reorganize, Deepen Investigation." *Miami Herald* (International Satellite Edition), Mar. 23, 1997.

Tullis, Lamond. *Handbook of Research on the Illicit Drug Traffic: Socioeconomic and Political Consequences*. Westport, Conn.: Greenwood Press, 1991.

Twersky, David. "The Risks of Cozying Up to Syria." *New York Times*, July 28, 1992.

"Two Gentlemen of Verona." *Economist*, Nov. 11, 1989, p. 59.

"2½ Tons of Cocaine Seized." *Los Angeles Times*, Jan. 25, 1992.

"UN Conference in Naples Focuses on International Crime." National Public Radio, *Morning Edition*, Nov. 21, 1994. Transcript: NPR, Washington, DC.

U.S. Attorney General. *Drug Trafficking: A Report to the President of the United States*. Washington, D.C., U.S. Government Printing Office, 1989.

U.S. Department of Justice. *Drug Trafficking: A Report to the President of the United States*. Washington, D.C.: U.S. Government Printing Office, 1994.

———. *Oriental Organized Crime: A Report on Research Conducted by the Organized Crime Section*. Washington, D.C.: U.S. Government Printing Office, 1985.

_____. *Report on Asian Organized Crime.* Washington, D.C.: U.S. Government Printing Office, 1988.

U.S. Department of State. *Country Report on Human Rights: Colombia.* Bogotá, Colombia: U.S. Information Service, 1996.

_____. *Estudio Conciso de Medio Ambiente para la Erradicación de la Amapola y Marijuana en Guatemala.* Washington, D.C.: U.S. Dept. of State, 31 Mar. 1987.

"U.S. Drug Chief Stresses Reduction of Use." *New York Times,* Aug. 15, 1993.

U.S. General Accounting Office. "Coordination of Intelligence Activities: Briefing Report to the Chairman on Governmental Operations, House of Representatives" (Washington, D.C.: General Accounting Office, Apr. 1993.

_____. "Drug Control: Threats and Roles of Explosives and Narcotics Technology: Briefing Report to Congressional Requesters" (Washington, D.C.: General Accounting Office, Mar. 1996.

_____. *Drug Control: Counter Narcotics Efforts in Mexico.* Washington, D.C.: General Accounting Office, June 1996.

_____. *Drug Control: U.S. Heroin Program Encounters Many Obstacles in Southeast Asia.* Washington, D.C.: General Accounting Office, Mar. 1, 1996.

_____. *Drug Control: U.S. Interdiction Efforts in the Caribbean Decline.* Washington, D.C.: General Accounting Office, Apr. 1996.

_____. *Drug War: Observations on the U.S. International Drug Control Strategy: Statement of Joseph E. Kelly, Director in Charge, International Affairs Division.* Washington, D.C.: General Accounting Office, 27 June 1996.

_____. *Illicit Narcotics: Recent Efforts to Control Chemical Diversion and Money Laundering.* Washington, D.C.: U.S. Government Printing Office, 1993.

_____. *Money Laundering: Characteristics of Currency Transaction Reports in Calendar Year 1992.* Washington, D.C.: U.S. Government Printing Office, 1992.

_____. *Money Laundering: A Framework for Understanding U.S. Efforts Overseas.* Washington, D.C.: U.S. Government Printing Office, 1996.

_____. *Money Laundering: Progress Report: Treasury's Final Crimes Enforcement Network.* Washington, D.C.: U.S. Government Printing Office, 1993.

_____. *Money Laundering: Treasurer's Financial Crimes Enforcement Network.* Washington, D.C.: U.S. Government Printing Office, 1991.

_____. *Money Laundering: The U.S. Government Is Responding to the Problem.* Washington, D.C.: U.S. Government Printing Office, 1991.

_____. *War on Drugs: Arrests Burdening Local Criminal Justice System.* Washington, D.C.: U.S. Government Printing Office, 1994.

U.S. House Committee on Foreign Affairs, Subcommittee on International Security, International Organizations and Human Rights. *The Threat of International Organized Crime, Hearings of November 4, 1993.* Washington, D.C.: U.S. Superintendent of Documents, 1994.

U.S. House Committee on Foreign Affairs, Subcommittee on Western Hemisphere Affairs. *The Andean Initiative Hearings of June 6 and 20, 1990.* Washington, D.C.: U.S. Superintendent of Documents, 1990.

U.S. House Committee on Foreign Affairs, Task Force on International Narcotics Control. *Hearing of October 10, 1990.* Washington, D.C.: U.S. Superintendent of Documents, 1990.

U.S. House Committee on Government Operations, Justice and Agricultural Subcommittee. *Federal Strategies to Investigate and Prosecute Major Narcotics Traffickers, Hearings of April 4, 1989.* Washington, D.C.: U.S. Superintendent of Documents, 1989.

U.S. House Committee on the Judiciary. *International Drug Supply, Control and Interdiction, Hearing of July 15, 1993.* Washington, D.C.: U.S. Superintendent of Documents, 1994.

U.S. House Committee on the Judiciary, Subcommittee on Crime and Criminal Justice. *Heroin Trafficking.* Washington, D.C.: U.S. Government Printing Office, 1995.

U.S. House Select Committee on Narcotics Abuse and Control. *Colombian Drug Trafficking and Control Hearings before the Select Committee on Narcotics Abuse and Control.* Washington, D.C.: U.S. Government Printing Office, 1987.

U.S. Senate Committee on Commerce, Science, Transportation, Subcommittee on Foreign Commerce and Tourism. *U.S. Chemical Experts to Latin America, Hearing of February 6, 1990.* Washington, D.C.: U.S. Superintendent of Documents, 1990.

U.S. Senate Committee on Foreign Relations. *Treaty Between the U.S. and the Federal Republic of Nigeria on Mutual Legal Assistance in Criminal Matters* (Treaty Doc. 102–26) (Washington, D.C.: U.S. Superintendent of Documents, 20 May 1992), p. 7.

U.S. Senate Committee on Foreign Relations, Subcommittee on Terrorism, Narcotics and International Operations. *Recent Developments in Transnational Crime Affecting U.S. Law Enforcement and Foreign Policy.* Washington, D.C.: U.S. Superintendent of Documents, 20–21 Apr. 1994.

_____. *Report: Drugs, Law Enforcement and Foreign Policy.* Washington, D.C.: U.S. Government Printing Office, 1989.

U.S. Senate Committee on Governmental Affairs. *Asian Organized Crime.* Washington, D.C.: U.S. Government Printing Office, 1992.

U.S. Senate Committee on Governmental Affairs, Permanent Subcommittee on Investigations. *Arms Trafficking, Mercenaries and Drug Cartels, Hearings of February 27–28, 1991.* Washington, D.C.: U.S. Superintendent of Documents, 1991.

U.S. Senate Committee on the Judiciary. *U.S. Drug Control Policy: Recent Experience, Future Options: Seminar Proceedings, February 2, 1994.* Washington, D.C.: U.S. Superintendent of Documents, 1994.

U.S. Senate Committee on the Judiciary, Subcommittee on Improvements in the Federal Criminal Code. *Illicit Narcotics, Hearings of June 2–November 25, 1955.* Washington, D.C.: U.S. Government Printing Office, 1955.

"U.S. to Reveal Mafia Drug Link." *New York Times*, Dec. 16, 1994.

Unanue de Dio, Manuel. *Los Secretos de Cartel de Medellín.* Jackson Heights, N.Y.: Cobra Editorial, 1988.

"Uncertain Origins." *CO Researcher*, Mar. 27, 1992, p. 272–273, 283.

Valentine, Paul W. "Eight Nigerians Found Guilty in Heroin Smuggling Ring." *Washington Post*, July 21, 1992.

"Verdadero Poder de los Narcos Mexicanos." *El Espectador*, Feb. 23, 1997.

"Vietnamese Gangs Active in Florida." *New York Times*, Nov. 25, 1985.

Villamarin Pulido, and Luis Alberto. *El Cartel de las FARC.* Bogotá, Colombia: Ediciones El Faraon, 1996.

"Virginia ROHR System Covers Caribbean Drug Smuggling Routes." *Aviation and Space Technology*, Nov. 27, 1989, p. 76.

Viviano, Frank, and Holly Lloyd. "The New Mafia Order." *Mother Jones*, May–June 1995, pp. 44–55.

Von Raab, W. "How the U.S. Is Cracking Down on Drug Smugglers." *U.S. News and World Report*, June 7, 1982, pp. 45–46.

Vulliany, Ed. "Mafia Inc." *World Press Review*, Dec. 19092, p. 11.

"Wages of Prohibition, The." *Economist*, Dec. 24, 1994, pp. 21–24.

Wagner, Dennis. "Crackdown Shifted Drug Trafficking to Mexico." *Colombian Post*, Nov. 18–24, 1996.

Waint, J.A. "Narcotics in the Golden Triangle." *Washington Quarterly*, Fall 1985, pp. 125–40.

Wall, Tim. "Transnational Crime Busters Agree on New Action Plan." *UN Chronicle*, Mar. 1985, p. 89.

"Wall-to-Wall Drug Traffickers." *U.S. News and World Report*, June 19, 1989, p. 14.

Wardlaw, Grant. "Linkages Between Illegal Drug Traffic and Terrorism." *Conflict Quarterly*, Summer 1988, pp. 5–26.

Weiner, Tim. "Anti-Drug Unit of CIA Sends Tons of Cocaine to U.S." *New York Times*, Nov. 20, 1993.

Weir, William. *In the Shadow of the Dope Fiend*. North Haven, Conn.: Archon, 1995.

Weisberg, Jacob. "The Mafia and the Melting Pot." *New Republic*, Oct. 12, 1987, p. 33.

West, Stan. "Home of the Brave." *Hispanic*, Dec. 1991, p. 58.

"Why Do You Think They Call It Dope?" *Time*, Oct. 18, 1993, p. 25.

Williams, Daniel. "Revival of Terrorism in Italy Intensifies Aversion to Mafia, State." *Washington Post*, June 6, 1993.

Williams, William F. "Terrorism in the Nineties: The Skull and Crossbones Still Flies." *Police Chief*, Sept. 1990, pp. 47–50.

Wirpsa, Leslie. "U.S. Coalition Calls on Bush to Redirect Drug War Dollars." *National Catholic Reporter*, Sept. 15, 1991, p. 13.

_____. 'U.S. Militarization of Antidrug Campaign in Bolivia Fires More Peasant Opposition." *National Catholic Reporter*, Mar. 26, 1993, p. 15.

Witkin, Gordon. "The New Opium Wars: The Administration's Plan to Attack the Lords of Heroin." *U.S. News and World Report*, Oct. 10, 1994, p. 39+.

Wood, Christopher. "Limitless Discretion." *Economist*, June 24, 1989, p. S22.

Woolner, Ann. *Washed in Gold: The Story Behind the Biggest Money-Laundering Investigation*. New York: Simon and Schuster, 1994.

"World Conference on Organized Crime, Money Laundering to Be Hosted by Italy." *UN Chronicle*, Sept. 1993, p. 71.

World This Week, The. "Fighting International Organized Crime," Oct. 14, 1993. Transcript: Journal Graphics, Denver, Colo.

Wren, Christopher. "Colombians Taking Over Heroin Trade." *New York Times*, Feb. 11, 1996.

_____. "Two Democrats Says Mexico Is No U.S. Ally in Drug War." *Colombian Post*, Mar. 3–9, 1997.

Yelin, Lev. "Why the Golden Crescent Still Flourishes." *New Times*, Feb. 1985, pp. 28–30.

York, Byron. "Clinton's Phony Drug War." *American Spectator*, Feb. 1994, p. 40+.

York, Michael. "Security Tightens as Italian Trial Begins." *Washington Post*, July 17, 1992.

Index